Compositional Translation

THE KLUWER INTERNATIONAL SERIES
IN ENGINEERING AND COMPUTER SCIENCE

NATURAL LANGUAGE PROCESSING
AND MACHINE TRANSLATION
Consulting Editor
Jaime Carbonell

Other books in the series:

COMPOSITIONAL TRANSLATION

by

M. T. ROSETTA

KLUWER ACADEMIC PUBLISHERS
DORDRECHT / BOSTON / LONDON

Library of Congress Cataloging-in-Publication Data

Rosetta, M. T.
    Compositional translation / by M.T. Rosetta.
        p.   cm. -- (Kluwer international series in engineering and
    computer science ; v. 273)
    Includes index.

    1. Machine translating.   I. Title.   II. Series: Kluwer
international series in engineering and computer science ; SECS 275.
P308.R67 1994
418'.02'0285--dc20   94-20091

ISBN 978-90-481-5797-6

Published by Kluwer Academic Publishers,
P.O. Box 17, 3300 AA Dordrecht, The Netherlands.

Kluwer Academic Publishers incorporates
the publishing programmes of
D. Reidel, Martinus Nijhoff, Dr W. Junk and MTP Press.

Sold and distributed in the U.S.A. and Canada
by Kluwer Academic Publishers,
101 Philip Drive, Norwell, MA 02061, U.S.A.

In all other countries, sold and distributed
by Kluwer Academic Publishers Group,
P.O. Box 322, 3300 AH Dordrecht, The Netherlands.

Printed on acid-free paper

The authors of the chapters

Contents

PART II: ELABORATION OF THE METHOD

PART III: LINGUISTIC ASPECTS

xii

PART V: FORMAL ASPECTS

Preface

This book describes results of research on machine translation carried out in the Rosetta project at Philips Research Laboratories, Eindhoven, in the period 1985 – 1992. This project did not start from scratch, but was preceded by four years of small-scale basic research during which the basic idea of compositional translation was conceived and implemented in small experimental systems, named Rosetta1 and Rosetta2. In the period covered by the book, the research was continued on a larger scale, by a group averaging ten to twelve persons, and a large system, Rosetta3, was developed. In the sequel, this system will simply be referred to as the Rosetta system. The aim of the book is to provide the reader with the main insights developed in the project. For this, a number of aspects have to be discussed in detail, but it is not a goal in itself to give a meticulous description of the system. We do hope to convey our conviction that machine translation can be a good carrier for linguistic and computational research.

The intended audience for the book is the large group of people interested in language and translation, including theoretical and computational linguists, translators, computer scientists and logicians. No specialist advance knowledge is required, although a certain ability to deal with formal notations is desirable. Parts of the book have already been used successfully as course material for students in linguistics, computer science and philosophy.

To a large extent, the Rosetta project was a collective enterprise which also applies to the writing of the book, as the collective pen name indicates. One of the implications is that the authors are not always the only ones who developed the material presented in their chapters. In that regard we would like to give credit to the people who participated in the project for some time, but who could not contribute to the book: Carel Fellinger, Jeroen Medema, Agnes Mijnhout, Margreet Sanders, Jan Stevens, Frank Uittenbogaard and more than twenty students.

A variant of the compositionality principle, which plays such an important role in

xvii

the book, could read: the quality of a book is a function of the quality of its chapters and of the way they are combined. We as editors were responsible for the combination. We put a great deal of effort into seeing that the book would become a whole and not a mere collection of articles. We made a global plan first and then invited the authors to write the chapters. Most chapters had to be revised several times, partly because the global plan was adjusted in the course of time. The fact that there was overlap between editors and authors did not make this process easier. We are grateful to the authors for their patience and their flexibility.

One of the editors, Theo Janssen, occupied a special position. He did not participate in the Rosetta project, but he stimulated the project members to write this book and during its conception he played the role of a deeply interested outsider. He prevented the others from using too esoteric a jargon and had considerable influence on the way the work was presented, especially on the contents of the introductory chapters. Incidentally, especially for the linguistic chapters, Jan Odijk functioned as an additional editor. Finally, Jeanine Bader played the double role of 'language sieve' and technical editor. She improved the presentation of the text, the figures and the tables and checked the internal and external references.

We wish to thank all those that have contributed to the project and to the book, and also the institutes that made this possible: Philips Research Laboratories, the Institute for Perception Research, the Research Institute for Language and Speech and the Foundation for Language Technology. We also thank NEHEM (Nederlandse Herstructureringsmaatschappij) for financial support during the first phase of the project and Van Dale Lexicografie for making available its dictionary files. Finally, we would like to thank Kees van Deemter, Pierre Isabelle, John Nerbonne, Harold Somers and Louis des Tombe for their valuable comments on parts of the manuscript.

the editors:

Lisette Appelo
Theo Janssen
Franciska de Jong
Jan Landsbergen

Chapter 1

Introduction

The purpose of this book is to offer the reader an in-depth view on machine translation (MT) by discussing in detail a particular method, called compositional translation, and a particular system, Rosetta, which is meant to translate between English, Dutch and Spanish, and which has been developed according to this method. The aim of this introductory chapter is (i) to sketch some of the major questions that rise within the field of MT , and (ii) to indicate which of these questions have been guiding the Rosetta enterprise.

From the start, the Rosetta project approached machine translation by focusing primarily on the modelling of the linguistic knowledge that is involved in the translation of natural languages. Accordingly, for each of the languages the system deals with, Rosetta was supposed to offer a coherent description for a fragment of considerable size. Thanks to this limited focus and the scale on which linguistics was supposed to be mastered, the research has been very challenging. This book is written both to convey the importance of the linguistic perspective on machine translation, as well as to report the results achieved to date, which contribute both to the field of machine translation and to the field of computational linguistics in general.

Machine translation, i.e. the translation of texts by means of a computer, has been a research topic since the late 1940s. Remarkably enough, it was one of the very first non-numerical computer applications to be considered. As early as 1949, Warren Weaver sent a famous memorandum to 200 of his acquaintances in which he discussed the possibilities of MT. Since then there has been a lot of activity in the field. Its history has been described both extensively and excellently by Hutchins (1986, 1988).

Much progress has been made since 1949: insight into language has grown considerably and the power of computers has increased in a revolutionary way.

1

Many translation systems have been developed and some of them have reached the commercial stage, but there are as yet no systems which are able to produce a translation of an arbitrary text with a quality comparable to that of a human translator. In fact, in spite of all the effort and insights gained, the most pessimistic predictions uttered in the past decades have not been falsified, and optimistic estimations of what the next decades might bring tend to become more moderate every year.

One reason for the absence of an overall breakthrough is that human languages turn out to be more complex than early workers in the field expected. Another reason is that, for translation, knowledge other than linguistic knowledge is needed as well. In the sections that follow we will present our opinion on the state of the art for both kinds of knowledge and then indicate how Rosetta approaches the fundamental problems of the field.

1.1   Knowledge needed for translation

What is needed to let a machine translate natural language? For a start, let us discuss what requirements a translation - whether produced by a human translator or by a machine - must fulfill in order to count as adequate. Usually, this is expressed in terms like "preservation of the effect on the reader". Cf. Des Tombe (1992). The effect of a specific text in a specific language is the result of many things, the characteristics of the reader among them. We will abstract away from the latter aspects and concentrate on the quality of the translated text proper. In general, two aspects are considered of vital importance for the quality of a translation: *intelligibility* of the output and *fidelity*. An important requirement for intelligibility is that the output consists of sentences of the target language that are correct or, in other words, well formed. The most important condition for fidelity is that the meaning of the source language text be conveyed, but the translation should also stay close to the original in other respects. Meaning preservation is especially important for informative texts, the type of texts for which MT appears to be most appropriate.

So the primary task of a translation system is to map a source language text onto a correct target language text with the same meaning. In order to perform this mapping adequately, two kinds of knowledge are needed: linguistic knowledge (or: knowledge of language), and extra-linguistic knowledge (or: knowledge of the world).

1.1.1   Knowledge of language and world knowledge

1. Knowledge of language

It is obvious that translation requires knowledge about the languages involved and about their relation. In the first place, lexical information is needed for relating the words of the source language to words of the target language with the same meaning. This is not sufficient, however. Languages also differ in their linguistic structure: the word order may be different and also the way in which function words (e.g. articles, auxiliaries) and suffixes are used. Somehow, the system must perform the transition of one linguistic structure into another structure with the same meaning. In order to do so, in the first place, the linguistic structure of the input text has to be made explicit. For this, the specification of rules of grammar is needed, and, in addition, monolingual dictionaries are required. Linguistic knowledge of this kind is also needed in order to produce sensible output.

2. World knowledge

Even if all necessary linguistic knowledge is available, it cannot be guaranteed that only adequate translations are produced. The main problem is ambiguity. We can distinguish lexical and structural ambiguity.

- **Lexical ambiguity.** Many words have more than one meaning and different meanings may correspond to different words in the other language. Some types of lexical ambiguity can be solved by means of a good grammar. This is the case if the various readings of the word not only have different meanings, but exhibit different syntactic behaviour as well. In example (1) the meaning of the noun *coach* is not relevant as, according to the English syntax, a noun is not allowed in that position.

    (1)   Jane will coach our team

    However, if two readings of a word do not differ syntactically, the ambiguity cannot be solved by means of linguistic knowledge. Consider the example in (2).

    (2) a The two teams were trained by the same coach
        b The coach was heading for the station

    The word *coach* can denote a vehicle or a person. As argued by Bar-Hillel (1960), such ambiguities can only be solved by somehow using one's world knowledge (as in (2a)), or one's insight in what the context is about (as in (2b)).

- **Structural ambiguity.** We have already noticed that a grammar can solve part of the lexical ambiguities. But grammatical analysis may also reveal another type of ambiguity: when a sentence can be assigned more than one structure, different corresponding interpretations can often be distinguished.

(3)   The girl followed the man with the camera

In order to determine whether sentence (3) describes an event in which a camera is handled by a girl, or an event in which a camera is carried by a man, insight is needed into the context.

For fully automatic translation the two types of knowledge must be formalised in some way. What is the state of the art with respect to formalisation? The next section will go into this.

1.1.2   Formalisation

1. Knowledge of language

A good deal of progress has been made in recent decades in regard to the formalisation of linguistic knowledge. Under the influence of Chomsky, theoretical linguistics has developed into a more or less exact science. The work of Montague and other semanticists has increased our insight into the logical structure of language. A new field, computational linguistics, has emerged, in which grammar models have been developed that are suitable for automatic analysis. However, writing a formal grammar for a language is still a very ambitious enterprise. This holds for domain specific sublanguages, and a fortiori for the larger fragments that should be covered for any overall success of MT. Not only are there many different phenomena to describe, but their interaction is also often hard to unravel. As this book will demonstrate, results from theoretical linguistics are very useful, but cannot be absorbed without much extra effort. Theoretical linguists tend to study linguistic phenomena more or less in isolation and do not care much about descriptive completeness.

So, although there appear to be no fundamental barriers to the description of linguistic phenomena in such a way that a computer can deal with them, those who try to write grammars with a large coverage meet at least three problems for which no general coherent solution is available in the field: (i) how to organise a large grammar, (ii) how to do it in a computationally feasible way, and (iii) how to incorporate insights from different theories.

If translation is the task to be performed, descriptions of at least two languages are needed and, in addition, a formalisation of their translation relation. However, in theoretical linguistics no formal translation theory is available on which the account of this relation could be based.

2. World knowledge

The representation of world knowledge is an area in which there has been less progress from which we can profit. Certainly, some types of knowledge can be formalised, for example by means of a system of semantic features, or by theorems of some kind of logic. There have been isolated successes for extremely small and in fact more or less formalised subject domains. But so far it has not been possible to go from that to less restricted domains. For common-sense knowledge there is even less hope that this can be formalised than there was two decades ago, especially in Artificial Intelligence circles.

Formalisation of knowledge comes down to representing it by symbols and by symbol manipulation. This kind of representation seems to be feasible for linguistic knowledge, but not for some other kinds of knowledge. For a fundamental discussion about the limits of Artificial Intelligence we refer to Dreyfus and Dreyfus (1986). Cf. also Sag (1991:82).

1.1.3 The underestimation of linguistic problems

The resolution of ambiguities, as in the *coach* example above, would require a vast amount of encyclopaedic knowledge. As argued by Bar-Hillel (1960), meeting such a requirement seems 'utterly chimerical'. However, only if fully automatic, high-quality translation is the goal, the representation of large amounts of world knowledge is the most crucial problem of MT. Nowadays, most MT research projects have more modest goals (see Section 1.2). In that perspective, tackling the linguistic problems outlined above is the most important research task.

As the general public tends to associate MT with fully automatic high quality translation, the problem of MT has mostly been identified with the problem of ambiguity. Funny examples of incorrect translations have been circulating since the 1950s, most of them apocryphal. The most famous one is the sentence *The spirit is willing, but the flesh is weak*, which, when translated into Russian and back into English, would become: *The liquor is all right, but the meat is spoiled*. In fact, the most remarkable thing about this double translation is not that the words have been translated wrongly, but that the output is syntactically correct. That this was taken for granted illustrates the underestimation of the amount of linguistics required to solve the problems of MT.

1.1.4 The notion of possible translation

It is interesting to conceive of a system that would be perfect with respect to linguistic knowledge and have no world knowledge at all. Such a system would not be able to solve certain ambiguities, but would produce all *linguistically possible translations*. Given such a notion of possible translation the solution of the translation problem requires the performance of the following two tasks: (i) the determination of the set of possible translations, each translation expressing one of the meanings of the input sentence, and (ii) the selection of the correct translations (with the intended meaning) from the set of possible translations. We will see that this division is very important for the scope of our research and for the applications envisaged. But, admittedly, this view leaves several aspects of translation out of consideration.

- If we speak about linguistic knowledge, we automatically restrict our scope to sentences, because - with a few exceptions - theoretical linguistics is about isolated sentences. So, the 'possible translation relation' relates sentences to sentences. Because of stylistic differences between languages, a sentence in one language will sometimes correspond to two or more sentences in other languages. And there are also cases where it is extremely unnatural to restrict the notion of 'possible translation' to one sentence.

    Take, for example, the Dutch text (4a) which corresponds to the English sentences in (4b).

(4) a(D)   Jaco heeft de bruine enveloppen opgemaakt. Maria ge-
            bruikte de witte.
     b(E)   Jaco has finished the brown envelopes. Maria used the
            white ones.
     c(D)   Jaco heeft de bruine envelop opengemaakt. Maria nam de
            witte.
     d(E)   Jaco has opened the brown envelope. Maria took the white
            one.

For the pair (4a)-(4b) the Dutch elliptic NP *de witte* corresponds to the English *the white ones*. But in view of the pair (4c)-(4d), the singular NP *the white one* is also a possible translation for the Dutch *de witte*. An analysis dealing with sentences in isolation without accounting for elliptic continuations in the text would have to consider *de witte* as ambiguous.

- The division between possible and correct translation is meaningful only where semantically perfect translations are possible. This is not always the case. As is well known, there are many lexical differences between languages, apart from ambiguity. The most striking examples are 'lexical gaps', words in one language for which there is no translation in some other language, for example because the concepts they express are culture bound. Examples of this can be found in domains such as food and drink, weather, clothing, etc.

- Even if a semantically perfect translation is possible, a human translator will sometimes prefer a translation that is semantically imperfect, but that is better in other respects, e.g. stylistically. An example of this is the translation of *not above forty* into the Dutch *nog geen veertig*, (lit.'yet no forty', cf. Langeveld (1986), Des Tombe (1992)). So what a human translator considers a possible translation is not always a linguistically possible translation in our sense.

In fact, all operational MT systems ignore these aspects. Ignoring the latter two seem acceptable for translations of informative texts where the content of the message is more important than the style and where the concepts of the subject domain are common to both languages. Interesting research projects could be started for each of them, but such research presupposes that there is already a method available by which the set of linguistically possible translations can be derived, which is not the case.

1.2 Applications

From the previous section the conclusion can be drawn that, although in principle computers seem to be capable of processing natural language, *fully automatic*, *high-quality* translation of *arbitrary texts* is not possible. This does not imply that the whole enterprise is useless, but that one should look for applications where one or more of the abovementioned requirements (high quality, arbitrary text, fully automatic) can be dropped.

The following alternatives are relevant:

1. **Accept low quality of output**. In some situations a bad translation quality is acceptable. For example, a text retrieval system in combination with 'quick and dirty' translation can give access to text data bases in foreign languages. Usually, the translation will be good enough to judge what the retrieved documents are about and if necessary a human translation can be made.

2. **Translate texts in a sublanguage**. If the input texts are severely restricted with respect to the form of the sentences and the subject domain, good quality can be achieved. The best example of this is the Canadian system TAUM-METEO, which translates weather bulletins from English into French (cf. Chevalier *et al.* (1978) and Isabelle (1987)). This system is very successful, because the input texts are written in a very restricted sublanguage, in which most terms have very precise meanings. Unfortunately, there appear to be only few subject areas of a similarly restricted nature for which large numbers of texts must be translated.

3. **Do not translate fully automatic**. Some form of collaboration between man and machine may be the best solution. This can be achieved in several ways:

   • The first way is called **pre-editing**. The texts are adjusted before they are entered into the system by someone who knows its restrictions, or are immediately written in some kind of 'controlled language'. The difference between a sublanguage and a controlled language is that the former is restricted 'by nature', while in the latter case the text writers have to learn what the limits of the system are. A recent example of the controlled language approach is VLS (cf. Van der Steen and Dijenborgh (1992)).

- The second and most usual form of man-machine collaboration is **post-editing**. The system produces a rough translation, which is corrected afterwards by a human translator. Most systems that are commercially available today, operate in this way. Examples are Systran (cf. Hutchins and Somers (1992)), and METAL (Slocum (1984)). They are especially suited to the translation of technical texts with a specialised terminology. Post-edit systems may not only be cheaper and faster than a purely human translation, but they also have the advantage of a consistent use of terminology.

- There is a third type of man-machine collaboration, called **interactive** translation. In this case the system may consult the user during the translation process, if it encounters an ambiguity that it cannot solve. For example, in case of a lexical ambiguity it will list the various meanings of the word in the source language and ask the user to make a choice. Note that in this case the user need not (and should not) be a translator. An interactive system enables a monolingual user to produce a text in a foreign language.

For a better appreciation of the design of the Rosetta system and the emphasis that has been put on the solution of the linguistic problems, the interactive translation alternative will be given a closer inspection.

The idea of interactive translation is not new. In the form described here it was proposed for the first time by Martin Kay (Kay (1973)). Hutchins (1986:121) even refers to work done in the mid-1960's by the Cambridge Language Research Unit, which is based on similar ideas. Interactive translation is in conformity with the opinions expressed in the previous section about what computers are in principle capable and incapable of doing, and also with the simplifying assumptions mentioned above.

In the type of interactive system we envisage the two tasks mentioned in Section 1.1.4, i.e. (i) the determination of the set of possible translations and (ii) the selection of the correct translation, can be clearly separated, but they need not be performed by subsequent modules. Such a system must have all the linguistic knowledge needed for translation in order to define all possible interpretations and corresponding translations. During the analysis of an input sentence, the system will be assisted by the user in finding the intended interpretation. Then it will have to provide only one translation, for this selected interpretation, but it should be able to do so for any other selection. In order to reduce the number of interactions, the system should also contain some knowledge of the world. This can be restricted to types of knowledge that are easy to formalise, for example in the form of semantic features. The more sophisticated world knowledge and the necessary insight into the context can be left to the user.

The idea of a system that allows users to express themselves in a language they do not know, is extremely appealing (cf. Boitet (1990), Somers *et al.* (1990) and Somers (1990a)). At the moment there are no commercially available interactive systems for monolingual users. This is not surprising, because the linguistic quality of these systems has to be substantially higher than that of existing systems. Interactive systems must be very reliable, because the user is not able to revise the resulting translation.

1.3   A linguistic perspective on MT

From the previous sections it will have become clear that we approach the problem of MT from a linguistic angle. In this section we will consider more closely the consequences of this for the scope of the Rosetta project and for the scope of this book in particular.

1.3.1   Scope of the project

One of the goals of theoretical linguistics and computational linguistics is to develop formalisms and grammar models in which languages can be described in an elegant and compact way. As the development of a new formalism is less time consuming than the description of a substantial language fragment in a particular formalism, research pursuing this goal is often characterised by rapid succession of the following stages: designing a new formalism, writing a toy grammar in this formalism, discovering problems with the formalism, and then revising the formalism.

On the other hand, the results of descriptive work are often associated with lack of formalism and are therefore not highly esteemed in theoretical and computational linguistics. The field of MT is an exception to that, because systems, and especially those that are commercially available, often have a very long life. A typical example is Systran, which is a descendant of the Georgetown system developed in the 1950s. The problem is that these systems - though they should be respected as cases of virtuoso linguistic engineering - do not start from a clear method or vision of language, nor of translation. Therefore they do not meet the conditions for reusability: neither the underlying concepts nor their elaboration permit further exploitation by others.

Evidently, the presentation of the state of the art given above is biased by the implicit comparison with Rosetta. Rosetta differs from these early examples in that it is the result of applying a specific theory that on the one hand offers a formalisation of the translation relation, and on the other hand makes it possible to adequately account

for language-specific phenomena. In fact, Rosetta is primarily an investigation into
the question of how far the translation method based on this theory can be pursued.
Although the project does not aim at the development of an actual translation system
for a particular application, it does aim at carrying out the linguistic groundwork for
a class of applications. Therefore, the suitability of the method for the development
of very large grammars is one of the important research questions. Below, we will
first list the most salient decisions concerning organisation and design before we
sketch out the scope of the project in greater detail. Rosetta is unique because of
the following combination of properties.

- A formal theory of translation is developed, called 'compositional translation',
  which is taken as a theoretical foundation for the system to be implemented.

- Extra-linguistic knowledge and linguistic knowledge are clearly separated.
  Only the latter kind of information is implemented.

- The theory aims to specify the means to find all translations that are possible on
  the basis of linguistic analysis only. The notion of 'possible translation' should
  be distinguished from the notion of 'correct translation', which presumes the
  incorporation of knowledge about text, context, and stylistic preferences.

- In accordance with the previous characteristic, the system translates isolated
  sentences, not texts.

- The fragment to be covered by the system includes a sufficiently large number
  of constructions to be representative for the complexity of natural language
  syntax and natural language translation.

- Insights from different research frameworks are incorporated, such as Montague Grammar and various syntactic frameworks in the Chomskian tradition.

- The output meets both the requirements of intelligibility (wellformedness) and
  of fidelity (reliability, meaning preservation). In addition, the method chosen
  enables and in fact encourages the conveyance of other information, such as
  stylistic features, as well.

- The system is suited for interactive applications where in case of ambiguity
  the user is consulted about the intended meaning of the input.

As indicated, the Rosetta project is in fact a rare combination of fundamental research
and large-scale implementation. Because of its specific combination of characteristics
it does not only contribute to the MT research field. It also contributes to the field
of theoretical linguistics, due to the fact that it is the first large-coverage grammar

that pairs a Montagovian compositional analysis to the incorporation of the kind of linguistic generalisations that the Chomskian tradition is famous for.

Although the project did not aim at immediate application, the selection of the problems to tackle first was strongly influenced by the requirements of interactive translation, in the sense mentioned above. The focus on linguistic aspects, for example, is partly motivated by our conviction that an interactive system must be capable, in principle, of generating all the linguistically possible translations for a substantial fragment of the languages involved. The high degree of reliability that interactive translation requires was another reason for us to opt for an approach based on explicit linguistic rules and not for an approach based on statistics as has been proposed recently (cf. Brown *et al.* (1990)). However, statistical machine translation may be appropriate for post-edit systems.

The system was developed for Dutch, English and Spanish. The choice of the languages was determined by the knowledge available within the project, but also by the wish to investigate the feasibility of the method for languages from both the Germanic and the Romance families. We think that the results presented here are in principle generalisable to other members of these families, but make no claim about languages in other families. Three languages were studied instead of just two, because some applications of interactive translation are of a multilingual nature. Think, for example, of a system that translates from one language into several other languages, or - even more ambitious - of a multilingual communication network, where users enter and receive messages in their own language on their private work-stations, while the messages pass through the network in some interlingual form. See Witkam (1983) for a description of such an application.

1.3.2 Scope of the book

As indicated, the scope of the book is limited as compared to the total field of machine translation. It focuses on the linguistic aspects of translation, i.e. those translation problems that remain if we restrict ourselves to defining the 'possible translation' relation between isolated, syntactically correct sentences, for which a correct meaning-preserving translation is indeed possible. In the next few chapters we will show how this translation relation between languages can be defined in a systematic way and how translation processes can be derived from the way we approach this relation.

From the previous sections it is evident that this book discusses an approach to MT that is pre-eminently suited to interactive translation, but interactive translation proper is not within the scope of the following chapters, nor are several other features and applications that we paid attention to in the project, such as the use of semantic features for disambiguation, the use of statistical information, and robustness measures for dealing with ill-formed input. Applications outside the domain of translation have also been explored, such as computer-aided language learning, a topic which is of interest because of the reliability of the Rosetta grammars.

A second restriction concerns the temporal boundaries of the research reported. This book presents results of the Rosetta3 project. More precisely: it is about the work done in the period 1985 - 1992. Like most systems, Rosetta has gone through a number of development stages, and presumably more versions of the system will follow, but in this book we will not go into its history: whenever we use the term Rosetta, we refer to the Rosetta3 project and the experimental Rosetta3 system.

To readers unfamiliar with the field, it may appear that the book has a fairly narrow scope. Let us stress here that we would rather consider our work as an attempt to achieve mastery in a well chosen subset of problems, namely the huge domain of linguistic problems, that has not been mastered up to the same scale by any other research group working on machine translation. The solutions we will describe in the chapters to follow can be put to use in other systems as well. So we expect to convince our readers that our approach towards the tackling of the linguistic translation problems is a challenging alternative. For us, testing the method of compositional translation by searching for the ultimate degree to which linguistic knowledge could be accommodated by it has been a most exciting and stimulating way to do linguistics.

1.4   Organisation of the book

The book is organised into five parts, preceded by this introductory chapter and followed by a final chapter in which the results of the research are summarised and evaluated.

Part I *The Method* (Chapters 2 - 5). This part deals with the basic ideas underlying the method of compositional translation. It consists of an introductory cluster of three chapters concerned with the general method, the type of grammars used and the design of the Rosetta system, followed by a chapter in which the characteristics of Rosetta are recapitulated and discussed in relation to other approaches. This part has the additional goal of introducing the uninitiated reader to the field and it will therefore contain sections that specialists may prefer to skip.

Part II *Elaboration of the Method* (Chapters 6 - 9). This part is dedicated to a further refinement and a more detailed description of the grammars: the morphological component, the kind of dictionaries used, the form and function of the syntactic rules, the division of the grammar into subgrammars.

Part III *Linguistic Generalisations* (Chapters 10 - 11). This part discusses the integration of insights from various theoretical frameworks into the adopted formalism: compositional grammars with ample room for the expression of language-specific linguistic generalisations.

Part IV *Translation Problems* (Chapters 12 - 16). This part offers a detailed description of the treatment of phenomena that are notoriously problematic in MT. Special attention is paid to the problem of cross-linguistic and categorial divergences, temporal expressions, idiomatic expressions, scope and negation.

Part V *Formal Aspects and Implementation* (Chapters 17 - 20). This part discusses the system from a mathematical and computational point of view.

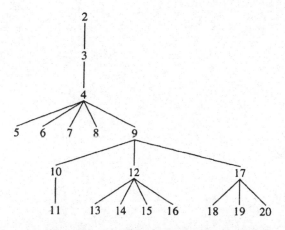

Figure 1.1: The relationships between the chapters of this book.

The structure in Figure 1.1 gives an overview of the relationships between chapters 2-20. Preferably, a chapter should not be read before the chapters dominating it in the tree have also been read.

Chapter 2

A compositional definition of the translation relation

2.1 The principle of compositionality of translation

In this book translation will be dealt with primarily as a *relation* between languages, from which a translation *process* can be derived. This chapter will introduce a particular way of defining the translation relation, which will be worked out in the remainder of this book. The step from relation to process will be described in Chapter 4.

The simplest way to define a translation relation would be to enumerate explicitly all pairs of sentences which are possible translations of each other. This is not feasible, however, because of the vast - in principle infinite - number of possible sentences. Mechanisms are needed to define the relation in a more compact way.

The most straightforward mechanism would be word-for-word translation, but this would lead to abominable results. We need a method that takes account of the structure of sentences. The method presented in this book is *compositional translation*. The purpose of this chapter is to introduce the general idea of this method without going into technical details. It therefore presents the compositional method in a highly simplified manner and only discusses rather trivial examples. Chapter 3 discusses the extensions that are needed to deal with more complicated cases.

Let us start with a simple example of compositional translation: the translation of English, Dutch and Spanish noun phrases consisting of an adjective and a plural noun, e.g. *intelligent girls*, *verstandige meisjes* and *muchachas inteligentes*. The word order and the use of suffixes in these noun phrases are different for the three

15

languages. For a compositional definition of their translation relation the following
ingredients are needed:

- For each language the word stems are enumerated in a dictionary, for example
  verstandig and *meisje* in the Dutch dictionary, *intelligent* and *girl* in the English
  dictionary, *muchacha* and *inteligente* in the Spanish dictionary. In translation
  dictionaries it is specified which word stems are considered translations of
  each other. For example:

  girl ⇔ *meisje* ⇔ *muchacha*
  intelligent ⇔ *verstandig* ⇔ *inteligente*

  In order to be considered translations, the words should have the same meaning. More precisely: they should have a meaning in common, in case they
  have more than one reading. Other aspects than meaning can be taken into
  account as well. For example, the distinction between formal, informal and
  slang words is also relevant for translation.

- For each language, a 'grammar rule' is formulated, which tells how to construct the plural noun phrase from the adjective and the noun in the dictionary.
  The English rule takes an adjective and a noun as input and returns the concatenation of the adjective and the plural noun form (the stem followed by an
  s), for example: *intelligent girls*. The Dutch rule is similar to the English one.
  The only difference is that the adjective is put into an inflected form, with
  the ending *e*, for example *verstandige meisjes*. The Spanish rule, on the other
  hand, places the adjective behind the noun and adjusts its form to the gender
  and number of the noun, for example *muchachas inteligentes*.

  These rules can be considered equivalent with respect to the effect they have
  on the meaning. Their common meaning can be described in mathematical
  terms, as follows. Assuming that both a noun and an adjective denote (refer
  to) a set of objects (e.g. the set of *girls* and the set of *intelligent* beings),
  the meaning of the rules that combine noun and adjective is the operation
  that constructs the intersection of the two sets (*intelligent girls*). The rules
  clearly differ with respect to the form, but apparently not in a way that would
  cause significantly different effects on the reader. Such rules will be called
  translation-equivalent.

Given this material, a translation relation between, e.g., English and Spanish noun
phrases can be defined as follows.

If the English rule is applied to an English noun and an English adjective, and
the translation-equivalent Spanish rule is applied to the corresponding Spanish noun
and adjective, then the noun phrases produced by the rules are considered translations of each other. So, *intelligent girls* and *muchachas inteligentes* are translations,

because they are built up from parts that are each other's translation (*girl - muchacha* and *intelligent - inteligente*) by means of translation-equivalent rules. Because the translation-equivalent rules of the two languages have the same meaning and they operate on words with the same meaning, it is obvious that the noun phrases derived in this way also have the same meaning.

This way of establishing the translation relation can be generalised as follows:

> **Principle of compositionality of translation**:
> Two expressions are each other's translation if they are built up from parts which are each other's translation, by means of translation-equivalent rules.

This is the basic principle underlying our approach.

The notion of a 'part' is used in the formulation of this principle. In the examples given the parts are simply the words, but in Section 2.3 'parts' will be defined in a more general and abstract way.

2.2 A formal notation

In this section we will introduce a precise notation for dealing with the translation example in the previous section, restricting ourselves from now on to English and Dutch.

For each language fragment a *grammar* is defined, consisting of a set of *basic expressions* (the lexicon) and a set of *rules*, which describe how larger expressions can be derived from the basic expressions. In order to organise the application of the rules we will assign syntactic categories to expressions, as follows: all expressions have the form $C(\alpha)$, where C is the category and α is an arbitrary string of symbols. The following categories will be used: N, an abbreviation for noun, ADJ, for adjective and NP for noun phrase.

First, we present a grammar for the small fragment of English noun phrases discussed in the previous section.

$G_{English}$1:
1. Basic expressions:
    N(*girl*), N(*boy*),
    ADJ(*intelligent*), ADJ(*brave*)
2. Rules:
    $R_{English}$1: $N(\alpha) + ADJ(\beta) \Rightarrow NP(\beta\ \alpha s)$

The grammar has only one grammar rule, $R_{English}1$. This rule has two arguments, indicated at the left hand side of the arrow: a noun $N(\alpha)$ and an adjective $ADJ(\beta)$, where α and β denote arbitrary symbol strings. This indicates that the rule is applicable to any noun and any adjective. During application of the rule the actual strings corresponding to the noun and the adjective are assigned to the variables α and β. The result of the application is the expression at the right hand side of the arrow, with the category NP and a string consisting of the string assigned to β and the string assigned to α followed by an *s*. Note that the order of the words in the result of the rule application need not correspond to the order of the arguments at the left hand side of the arrow.

Rule $R_{English}1$ is applicable to, for example, N(*girl*) and ADJ(*brave*). In that case β is instantiated as *brave* and α as *girl*. The result of the rule application then is NP(*brave girls*).

The grammar for the Dutch fragment reads:

$G_{Dutch}1$:
1. Basic expressions:
    N(*meisje*), N(*jongen*),
    ADJ(*verstandig*), ADJ(*dapper*)
2. Rules:
    $R_{Dutch}1$: $N(\alpha) + ADJ(\beta) \Rightarrow NP(\beta e\ \alpha s)$

The rule is similar to $R_{English}1$, apart from the fact that it attaches an *e* to the adjective. If it is applied to N(*meisje*) and ADJ(*dapper*), it constructs the noun phrase NP(*dappere meisjes*). Now the translation relation between the two language fragments can be defined by means of a relation between the two grammars:

Translation relation between $G_{English}1$ and $G_{Dutch}1$:
1. between basic expressions:

N(*girl*)	$\Leftrightarrow$	N(*meisje*)
N(*boy*)	$\Leftrightarrow$	N(*jongen*)
ADJ(*brave*)	$\Leftrightarrow$	ADJ(*dapper*)
ADJ(*intelligent*)	$\Leftrightarrow$	ADJ(*verstandig*)

2. between rules:
    $R_{English}1 \quad \Leftrightarrow \quad R_{Dutch}1$

So, according to the compositional definition of translation, which is completely symmetrical, *brave girls* and *dappere meisjes* are each other's translations, because these expressions can be *composed* (or *generated*, or *derived*) from parts, basic expressions in this case, which are each other's translations, by application of rules with the same meaning.

2.3 Isomorphic grammars

We will now extend the example grammars of Section 2.2 in such a way that a
few simple sentences can be derived. In addition to N, ADJ and NP, we will use
the following syntactic categories: IV for intransitive verb, VP for verb phrase and
S for sentence. We add two intransitive verbs and three rules to the English grammar.

$G_{English}2$:
1.   Basic expressions:
     N(*girl*), N(*boy*)
     ADJ(*intelligent*), ADJ(*brave*)
     IV(*cry*), IV(*laugh*)
2.   Rules:
     $R_{English}1$: N(α) + ADJ(β) $\Rightarrow$ NP(β αs)
     $R_{English}2$: IV(α) $\Rightarrow$ VP(α)
     $R_{English}3$: IV(α) $\Rightarrow$ VP(*do not* α)
     $R_{English}4$: VP(α) + NP(β) $\Rightarrow$ S(β α)

The sentences generated by this grammar are the symbol strings α such that S(α)
can be derived from basic expressions by application of one or more rules. The
set of sentences that can be generated in this way is called the language defined by
the grammar. Examples of generated sentences are *intelligent boys laugh* and *brave
girls do not cry*. We will show how the latter sentence is derived.

Step 1. The previous section showed that rule $R_{English}1$ can be applied to basic
expressions N(*girl*) and ADJ(*brave*), resulting in NP(*brave girls*).

Step 2. Rule $R_{English}3$ is applicable to an expression of the form IV(α), for example
to the basic expression IV(*cry*). The result is VP(*do not* α), in this case: VP(*do
not cry*).

Step 3. Rule $R_{English}4$ has two arguments. The first argument must have the form
VP(α), for example the expression VP(*do not cry*) generated in step 2. The second argument must have the form *NP(β)*, for example the expression NP(*brave
girls*) generated in step 1. The result is S(β α), i.e. S(*brave girls do not cry*).

This derivation process can be represented by a so-called *syntactic derivation tree*,
which is shown in Figure 2.1. The terminal nodes of the tree are labelled by the basic
expressions. The non-terminal nodes are labelled by rule names. The tree shows
that rule $R_{English}3$ is applied to IV(*cry*), that rule $R_{English}1$ is applied to N(*girl*) and
ADJ(*brave*), and that rule $R_{English}4$ is applied to the results of these rule applications.

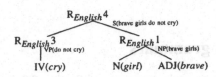

Figure 2.1: Syntactic derivation tree of *brave girls do not cry*. The derived expressions are also indicated, but they are not part of the tree as such.

The simple grammar formalism used in this chapter, which we will call *string grammar*, serves for expository purposes only and will not be elaborated in detail. String grammars are powerful from a purely formal point of view, but they are inadequate from a linguistic point of view, because the internal structure of the expressions is not represented in the strings. This will be pointed out in Chapter 3, where M-grammars will be introduced of which the rules operate on structured objects. However, string grammars share a number of properties with M-grammars which make them useful for introducing the most important concepts of compositional translation in a simple way.

One of these properties is the possibility to introduce words by means of rules, i.e. 'syncategorematically'. In $G_{English}2$ the words *do* and *not* are not introduced as basic expressions, but by rule $R_{English}3$. The auxiliary *do* cannot be treated as a basic expression, because a basic expression must have a 'meaning of its own' and a corresponding translation: *do* does not fulfill this requirement. On the other hand, the decision to treat the word *not* syncategorematically is fairly arbitrary; it could also be treated as a basic expression.

Another noteworthy property of string grammars is that the order of the basic expressions in a derivation tree is not related to the 'surface order' of the words in the actual sentence. The ordering in the derivation tree corresponds to the ordering of the arguments of the rules, which is to a certain extent arbitrary. The surface order results from the way the rules operate on their arguments. For example, the result of rule $R_{English}4$ is $S(\beta\ \alpha)$, which indicates that in the surface string the first argument of the rule α follows the second argument β.

The notion *part*, which we used in our formulation of the compositionality principle of translation, has now been formalised. The parts are the inputs for the rules. *VP(do not cry)* and *NP(brave girls)* are parts of the generated sentence; *N(girl)* and *ADJ(brave)* are parts of the NP and *V(cry)* is part of the VP. *Do* and *not* are not parts of the sentence *brave girls do not cry* in the sense of the principle.

A similar extension to the Dutch grammar is made by adding three intransitive verbs and three rules:

G_{*Dutch*}**2:**
  1. Basic expressions:
       N(*meisje*), N(*jongen*),
       ADJ(*verstandig*), ADJ(*dapper*)
       IV(*huilen*), IV(*schreeuwen*), IV(*lachen*)
  2. Rules:
       $R_{Dutch}1$: N(α) + ADJ(β) $\Rightarrow$ NP(βe αs)
       $R_{Dutch}2$: IV(α) $\Rightarrow$ VP(α)
       $R_{Dutch}3$: IV(α) $\Rightarrow$ VP(α niet)
       $R_{Dutch}4$: VP(α) + NP(β) $\Rightarrow$ S(β α)

One of the sentences generated by this grammar is *dappere meisjes huilen niet*. Its
syntactic derivation tree is shown in Figure 2.2. The translation relation between the

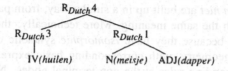

Figure 2.2: Syntactic derivation tree of *dappere meisjes huilen niet*.

language fragments generated by $G_{English}2$ and $G_{Dutch}2$ is specified by relating the
translation-equivalent rules and the translation-equivalent basic expressions of the
two grammars.

Translation relation between $G_{English}2$ **and** $G_{Dutch}2$**:**
  1. between translation-equivalent basic expressions:
       N(*girl*) $\Leftrightarrow$ N(*meisje*)
       N(*boy*) $\Leftrightarrow$ N(*jongen*)
       ADJ(*brave*) $\Leftrightarrow$ ADJ(*dapper*)
       ADJ(*intelligent*) $\Leftrightarrow$ ADJ(*verstandig*)
       IV(*cry*) $\Leftrightarrow$ IV(*huilen*)
       IV(*cry*) $\Leftrightarrow$ IV(*schreeuwen*)
       IV(*laugh*) $\Leftrightarrow$ IV(*lachen*)
  2. between translation-equivalent rules:
       $R_{English}1$ $\Leftrightarrow$ $R_{Dutch}1$
       $R_{English}2$ $\Leftrightarrow$ $R_{Dutch}2$
       $R_{English}3$ $\Leftrightarrow$ $R_{Dutch}3$
       $R_{English}4$ $\Leftrightarrow$ $R_{Dutch}4$

The translation relation between $G_{English}2$ and $G_{Dutch}2$ shows that the correspondences between basic expressions need not be one-to-one: IV(*cry*) corresponds to IV(*huilen*) (meaning: to weep) and IV(*schreeuwen*) (meaning: to shout). A basic expression of one grammar will often have more than one meaning and, for each meaning, there may be more than one basic expression of the other grammar. A rule usually has a unique meaning, but each rule may correspond to a set of rules with the same meaning in the other grammar.

From now on, the term *translation-equivalent* will be used not only for the translation relation between the rules, but also for the postulated translation relation between basic expressions and for the derived translation relation between derived expressions. In all these cases the term must be interpreted as 'having a common meaning' and 'as closely related as possible with respect to other translation-relevant information'.[1]

The syntactic derivation trees of Figures 2.1 and 2.2 visualise the idea of compositional translation. The trees show that the sentences *brave girls do not cry* and *dappere meisjes huilen niet* are built up in a similar way, from parts having the same meaning by rules with the same meaning. More technically: the two sentences are translation-equivalent because they have *isomorphic* syntactic derivation trees, i.e. trees with the same geometry, with corresponding basic expressions at the terminal nodes and corresponding rules at the non-terminal nodes. Note that a syntactic derivation tree may correspond to more than one syntactic derivation tree in the other language. Figure 2.1 not only corresponds to Figure 2.2, but also to a tree similar to figure 2.2, in which IV(*huilen*) is replaced by IV(*schreeuwen*). This indicates that *brave girls do not cry* has two possible translations: *dappere meisjes huilen niet* en *dappere meisjes schreeuwen niet*.

In order to define the translation relation along these lines, we have to write grammars in such a way that sentences that are translations of each other indeed get isomorphic derivation trees. The grammars must be attuned to each other. In other words, the choice of rules and basic expressions of the two grammars cannot be made fully independently, but has to take into account the translation relation as well. For example, the syncategorematic treatment of *not* in $G_{English}2$ implies a similar treatment of *niet* in $G_{Dutch}2$. Grammars that are attuned in this way are called *isomorphic grammars*.

Two grammars are called isomorphic if and only if:

1. for each basic expression in one grammar there is at least one translation-equivalent basic expression in the other grammar;

---

[1]Note that translation equivalence is not an equivalence relation in the mathematical sense. The relation is not transitive, due to the fact that expressions may have more than one meaning. If sentences s1 and s2 have a meaning in common and sentences s2 and s3 have a meaning in common, this does not imply that s1 and s3 have a meaning in common.

2. for each rule in one grammar there is at least one translation-equivalent rule in the other grammar.

The property of being isomorphic will be referred to as *isomorphy*. Isomorphy of grammars implies that for every syntactic derivation tree of one grammar there is at least one isomorphic syntactic derivation tree of the other grammar. However, this does not imply that for every sentence generated by one grammar there is a corresponding sentence generated by the other grammar. The point is that a syntactic derivation tree, i.e. a tree labelled with rules and basic expressions, does not necessarily define a sentence, because the rules in the tree are not necessarily applicable to their arguments. We can illustrate this point by modifying $G_{English}2$ in the following way.

We replace the adjective ADJ*(brave)* by the noun N*(hero)*, and in the translation relation we connect N*(hero)* with the Dutch ADJ*(dapper)*. From a purely semantic point of view this may be allowed, because, with some simplification, we may consider the set of heroes identical to the set of brave persons. After this modification the grammars are still perfectly isomorphic according to the definition and the derivation tree of Figure 2.3 is isomorphic to the tree of Figure 2.2. Nevertheless,

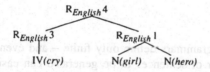

Figure 2.3: Syntactic derivation tree with inapplicable rule.

rule $R_{English}1$ is not applicable to N*(girl)* and N*(hero)*, so no English translation of *dappere meisjes huilen niet* would be defined.

This example is very artificial, but that is due to the fact that in the simple grammars used here the applicability of the rules is only determined by the syntactic categories of the arguments. In the actual grammars used in the Rosetta system, the applicability of rules may depend on rather subtle properties of the arguments and then it is much more difficult to guarantee that rules are applicable. Moreover, translation of a word into a word of a different category is sometimes inevitable; for example the verb *like* corresponds to the Dutch adverb *graag*.

Let us define a well-formed syntactic derivation tree as one in which all rules are applicable, so that a sentence is generated. The derivation tree of Figure 2.2 is well-formed, the one of Figure 2.3 is not. Ideally, for each well-formed tree of one language, there would be at least one well-formed tree of the other language. The grammars would then define a translation for all sentences of the language.

Grammars that are perfectly attuned to each other in this sense are called *strictly isomorphic*. Strict isomorphy is desirable because it guarantees that a translation is defined for each correct sentence.

The grammars $G_{English}2$ and $G_{Dutch}2$ are clearly strictly isomorphic, but for grammars that are more complicated and cover larger language fragments, it is hard to guarantee strict isomorphy. The current grammars of the Rosetta system are isomorphic and, although it is the intention of the grammar writers that they are strictly isomorphic, this has not been proved formally (see Chapter 17 for the relevant formal definitions).

Two important results have been achieved in this section. First, we have formalised the notion of compositional translation which was informally introduced in Section 2.1. This has led us to the 'isomorphic grammar method' as a mechanism to define a symmetric translation relation. Typical of this method is that the relation between languages is defined by means of a relation between grammars. Second, if the translation relation between the grammars is defined correctly, i.e. if corresponding rules have the same meaning and if corresponding basic expressions have the same meaning, then the translation relation between the sentences of the languages is guaranteed to be meaning-preserving.

2.4   Recursion

Up till now the example grammars define only finite – and even very small – sets of sentences. The number of sentences to be generated can easily be enlarged by extending the dictionaries, but then the language remains finite. We can define infinite languages, with sentences of arbitrary length, by introducing recursive rules, i.e. rules that can be applied an unlimited number of times in a derivation. We will show this by extending $G_{English}2$ and $G_{Dutch}2$.

Grammar $G_{English}2$ is extended to $G_{English}3$, as follows. Some basic expressions with the new category TV (for verbs that can have a '*that* sentence' as a complement) are added: TV(*believe*), TV(*hope*) and TV(*expect*), and one new rule: $R_{English}5$: TV(α) + S(β) $\Rightarrow$ VP(α *that* β). This rule combines a verb like *hope* with a sentence like *brave girls do not cry* into the verb phrase *hope that brave girls do not cry*. The verb phrase can be combined with the noun phrase *intelligent boys* by rule $R_{English}4$ into the sentence *intelligent boys hope that brave girls do not cry*. Rule $R_{English}5$ can combine this sentence with a TV verb again, and then rule $R_{English}4$ can be applied again, yielding for example *intelligent girls believe that intelligent boys hope that brave girls do not cry*. This process can be repeated an unlimited number of times.

Notice that it is the combination of $R_{English}4$ and $R_{English}5$, which causes the recursion.

$G_{English}3$:
1. Basic expressions:
   N(*girl*), N(*boy*)
   ADJ(*intelligent*), ADJ(*brave*)
   IV(*cry*), IV(*laugh*)
   TV(*believe*), TV(*hope*), TV(*expect*)
2. Rules:
   $R_{English}1$: N(α) + ADJ(β) $\Rightarrow$ NP(β αs)
   $R_{English}2$: IV(α) $\Rightarrow$ VP(α)
   $R_{English}3$: IV(α) $\Rightarrow$ VP(*do not* α)
   $R_{English}4$: VP(α) + NP(β) $\Rightarrow$ S(β α)
   $R_{English}5$: TV(α) + S(β) $\Rightarrow$ VP(α *that* β)

$G_{Dutch}3$ is an extension of $G_{Dutch}2$. New basic expressions are TV(*geloven*), TV(*hopen*) and TV(*verwachten*) and there is one new rule:
$R_{Dutch}5$: TV(α) + S(β) $\Rightarrow$ VP(α *dat* β).

$G_{Dutch}3$:
1. Basic expressions:
   N(*meisje*), N(*jongen*),
   ADJ(*verstandig*), ADJ(*dapper*)
   IV(*huilen*), IV(*schreeuwen*), IV(*lachen*)
   TV(*geloven*), TV(*hopen*), TV(*verwachten*)
2. Rules:
   $R_{Dutch}1$: N(α) + ADJ(β) $\Rightarrow$ NP(βe αs)
   $R_{Dutch}2$: IV(α) $\Rightarrow$ VP(α)
   $R_{Dutch}3$: IV(α) $\Rightarrow$ VP(α *niet*)
   $R_{Dutch}4$: VP(α) + NP(β) $\Rightarrow$ S(β α)
   $R_{Dutch}5$: TV(α) + S(β) $\Rightarrow$ VP(α *dat* β)

The translation relation is extended accordingly:

Translation relation between $G_{English}3$ and $G_{Dutch}3$:
1. between basic expressions:
   TV(*believe*) $\Leftrightarrow$ TV(*geloven*)
   TV(*hope*) $\Leftrightarrow$ TV(*hopen*)
   TV(*expect*) $\Leftrightarrow$ TV(*verwachten*)
2. between rules:
   $R_{English}5$ $\Leftrightarrow$ $R_{Dutch}5$

With these extensions, the grammars relate the English sentence *intelligent girls hope that brave boys laugh* to the Dutch sentence *verstandige meisjes hopen dat dappere jongens lachen* and the sentence *brave boys believe that intelligent girls hope that brave boys cry* to its Dutch counterpart *dappere jongens geloven dat verstandige meisjes hopen dat dappere jongens huilen.*

Note that the Dutch grammar also generates sentences like **verstandige jongens hopen dat dappere meisjes huilen niet* as the translation of *intelligent boys hope that brave girls do not cry*, but the Dutch sentence is incorrect.[2] Namely, in Dutch complement sentences the word order differs from the word order in main clauses: the finite verb has to be in 'final position': *...dat dappere meisjes niet huilen.* For the small language fragment discussed here, the grammar could easily be adjusted by making a distinction between main sentences and complement sentences and defining them by different rules. However, this would be an unattractive solution for larger language fragments, because both grammars would have to contain large duplicate parts. Problems like this are signals that we need a more sophisticated syntactic framework. This point will be discussed further in Chapter 3.

After the introduction of recursion, the results of Section 2.3 are even more valuable. First, the isomorphic grammar method enables us to define the *infinite* relation between languages by means of a *finite* relation between grammars. Second, given a finite set of assumptions about meaning relations between basic expressions and between rules, we can prove preservation of meaning for an infinite set of sentences.

2.5   Translation and grammars

In the previous sections the term 'grammar' has been used for the compositional formalisms that establish the translation relation. The question is, whether these formalisms are indeed grammars in the usual linguistic sense, i.e. formalisms that define exactly the correct sentences of a language.

An obvious consequence of the described method is that no translation relation is defined for sentences outside the scope of the grammar. So the set of sentences defined by the grammar must at least include all correct sentences of the language fragment that we want to cover. But why couldn't it contain incorrect sentences as well? After all, our goal is to define translations and not to define languages. If the translation relation could be defined in a more efficient way by allowing a certain degree of over-generation by the grammars, there would be no reason to avoid this.

It turns out, however, that such an approach would cause great problems. We have already met one problem caused by a tolerant grammar. If we accept that grammars define incorrect sentences, it is hard to avoid correct sentences of one language (*...that intelligent girls do not cry*) being related to incorrect ones of the other language (**...dat intelligente meisjes huilen niet*).

---

[2] Following a linguistic convention, incorrectness is indicated by prefixing the sentence with an asterisk.

Another, more subtle, problem is the following. Because of the recursive properties of languages, allowing incorrect sentences will imply allowing incorrect parts of sentences. If incorrect parts are put together, this will not always result in an incorrect sentence, but sometimes in a correct sentence with a deviant derivation and therefore presumably with a misleading translation. E.g., if an English grammar accepts phrases like *is knowing* and *are knowing* (assigning them the same interpretation as *knows*), it will not only be tolerant, in the sense of accepting the incorrect sentence *he is knowing English*, but it will also assign an incorrect interpretation to the correct sentence *they are knowing readers* (cf. Isabelle (1989)). Under this interpretation it would be translated incorrectly.

The latter example shows that tolerant grammars would lead to a sloppy definition of the translation relation, relating sentences which are syntactically correct, but which have different meanings. This would obliterate an essential advantage of compositional translation: correct translation at the 'global' level is achieved by 'local' definitions of translation relations, in terms of basic expressions and rules. Only if the rules are part of a precise grammar, is there a guarantee that the totality of the locally defined translation relations will constitute an adequate translation relation for full sentences.

2.6 Compositionality of meaning

In the previous sections we have come to the conclusion that, for compositional translation, we need grammars of the languages involved. Implicitly we have also made a decision about the kind of grammars: we use compositional grammars, i.e. grammars that obey the following principle.

Principle of compositionality of meaning:

The meaning of an expression is a function of the meaning of its parts and of the way they are combined.

In the grammar formalism presented in this chapter, the basic expressions are the ultimate parts and the rules indicate the way they are combined. The compositionality principle requires that the basic expressions and the rules have well-defined meanings.

The principle - often called Frege's Principle - has a long history in the philosophy of language. It underlies the semantics-based approach to language which is known as Montague Grammar (cf. Thomason (1974), Janssen (1986a), Janssen (1986b), Gamut (1991)).

In a Montague grammar the syntactic component specifies a set of basic expressions and a set of syntactic rules, in the way described in the previous sections. The semantic component assigns an interpretation to the language as follows. First, a semantic domain is defined, consisting of individual entities, truth values, special indices called 'possible worlds' and sets and functions defined in terms of these objects. Each basic expression is associated with an element of the domain. Then, an operation on objects in the domain (for example function application) is associated with each rule. In parallel with the application of the syntactic rules, the semantic operations associated with these rules are applied to the semantic values of their arguments, starting with the values of the basic expressions. The final result is the semantic value of the complete expression.

We illustrate the compositional way of defining semantics by adding a simple semantic component to example grammar $G_{English}2$. It assigns semantic values to the basic expressions (called basic meanings) and semantic operations (meaning rules) to the syntactic rules.

Semantic component of $G_{English}2$

1. Assignment of basic meanings to basic expressions:
   The basic meanings are sets of individual objects, indicated as $brave'$, $girl'$, etc. A difference from traditional Montague Grammar is that basic expressions can have more than one meaning, e.g. IV(cry) has two meanings: cry_1' and cry_2'.

basic expressions	basic meanings
N($girl$)	$girl'$
N(boy)	boy'
ADJ($intelligent$)	$intelligent'$
ADJ($brave$)	$brave'$
IV(cry)	cry_1', cry_2'
IV($laugh$)	$laugh'$

2. Assignment of meaning rules to syntactic rules:
   In principle, it is possible that a syntactic rule corresponds to more than one meaning rule, but we will not make use of that possibility here.
   $R_{English}1$:   N(α) + ADJ(β) $\Rightarrow$ NP(β αs)
   S1: $\phi + \psi \Rightarrow \phi \cap \psi$
   Here ϕ and ψ indicate the semantic values of the two arguments of the rule. They are the sets of individuals denoted by the noun and the adjective respectively; the result is the intersection of these sets.
   $R_{English}2$:   IV(α) $\Rightarrow$ VP(α)
   S2: $\phi \Rightarrow \phi$
   S2 is the identity operation: the VP has the same denotation as the IV.

$R_{English}3$:   IV(α) $\Rightarrow$ VP(*do not* α)

   S3: $\phi \Rightarrow$ Complement(ϕ)

S3 takes the complement of the set denoted by the IV.

$R_{English}4$:   VP(α) + NP(β) $\Rightarrow$ S(β α)

   S4: $\phi + \psi \Rightarrow \psi \subseteq \phi$

A truth value is assigned to an expression of category S: the value is *true* if the set denoted by the NP is included in the set denoted by the VP, else *false*. Summarised in tabular form:

syntactic rule	meaning rule
$R_{English}1$	S1
$R_{English}2$	S2
$R_{English}3$	S3
$R_{English}4$	S4

So the process of derivation of the semantic value runs parallel with the syntactic derivation process and can be represented in a tree with the same geometry as the syntactic derivation tree, but labelled by meaning rules and basic meanings. This tree is called a *semantic derivation tree*. The semantic derivation tree of *brave girls do not cry*, according to $G_{English}2$, is given in Figure 2.4.

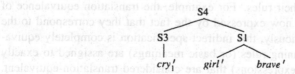

Figure 2.4: Semantic derivation tree of *brave girls do not cry* (for one of the two interpretations of *cry*). It denotes the value *true* if no individuals that belong to the sets *brave'* and *girl'* belong to the set cry'_1.

2.7 Definition of translation equivalence with semantic derivation trees

Section 2.3 introduced isomorphic grammars as a way of defining a translation relation. Isomorphy of grammars, e.g. $G_{English}2$ and $G_{Dutch}2$, can be established by stating a translation-equivalence relation between their rules and their basic expressions. If grammars have an explicit semantic component, there is an alternative, indirect, way of defining isomorphy of grammars: by assigning the same basic meanings to basic expressions that are considered translation-equivalent and the same meaning rules to translation-equivalent syntax rules. For example, the isomorphy of grammars $G_{English}2$ and $G_{Dutch}2$ can be established by assigning the following semantic component to $G_{Dutch}2$.

basic expressions	basic meanings
N(*meisje*)	*girl'*
N(*jongen*)	*boy'*
ADJ(*verstandig*)	*intelligent'*
ADJ(*dapper*)	*brave'*
IV(*huilen*)	cry'_1
IV(*schreeuwen*)	cry'_2
IV(*lachen*)	*laugh'*

syntactic rule	meaning rule
$R_{Dutch}1$	S1
$R_{Dutch}2$	S2
$R_{Dutch}3$	S3
$R_{Dutch}4$	S4

$G_{English}2$, specified in the previous section, and $G_{Dutch}2$ are isomorphic grammars, because their semantic components establish a translation-equivalence relation between their basic expressions and their rules. For example, the translation equivalence of rules $R_{English}1$ and $R_{Dutch}1$ is now expressed by the fact that they correspond to the same meaning rule, S1. Obviously, this indirect specification is completely equivalent to the direct one, if meaning rules (or basic meanings) are assigned to exactly those syntax rules (or basic expressions) that are considered translation-equivalent. Syntax rules are translation-equivalent if and only if they have a meaning rule in common. Basic expressions are translation-equivalent if and only if they have a basic meaning in common.

There is now also an alternative way to define the translation equivalence of two sentences: they not only have isomorphic syntactic derivation trees, they also have the same semantic derivation tree. More precisely, taking possible ambiguities into account: translation-equivalent sentences have at least one semantic derivation tree in common. For example, the sentences *brave girls do not cry* and *dappere meisjes huilen niet* are translation-equivalent, because they have the semantic derivation tree of Figure 2.4 in common.

In the previous section it was shown how the basic meanings and the meaning rules can be spelled out in set-theoretical terms. This simple way of defining the semantics would cause problems for more interesting language fragments. Montague and other semanticists working in the model-theoretical tradition have formulated more powerful and more subtle ways of defining the semantics of natural language sentences. But even for the most sophisticated logical formalisms there are language constructs that cause problems. Belief-sentences are an example of this. A semantic component of grammar $G_{English}2$ was specified in the previous section. It would have been impossible to do the same for $G_{English}3$, because no adequate formalisation of the meaning of the verb *believe* and of the construction rule for belief-sentences, $R_{English}5$, is available.

Fortunately, it is not necessary for compositional translation to elaborate the meaning of the rules and the basic expressions. It is sufficient to establish equivalence of meaning between rules and between basic expressions of different grammars and to decide on translation equivalence on the basis of this and other considerations. For this purpose, an extremely simple semantic component is sufficient, in which only *names* of meaning rules and basic meanings are assigned to syntax rules and basic expressions. With respect to belief-sentences, for example, it is intuitively clear that the English verb *believe* has the same meaning as the Dutch *geloven* and although we cannot formalise the meaning of the rules $R_{Dutch}5$ and $R_{English}5$, we can still state their translation equivalence by relating them to the same meaning rule, S5, without specifying this rule in any detail.

On the one hand, a detailed specification of the semantics is not needed for translation. On the other hand, such a specification would not be sufficient for defining translation equivalence. In a model-theoretical semantic framework sentences like *grass is green or it isn't* and *snow is white or it isn't* are semantically equivalent because they are both true 'in all possible worlds' (cf. Lewis (1972)). Obviously, these sentences should not be considered translation-equivalent and therefore the translation relation cannot be based on this type of semantic equivalence alone. More subtle kinds of model-theoretical semantics may solve this problem, but even then we would have to face a requirement that may be typical of translation: we not only want to preserve the meaning, we also want to preserve other, less tangible, information, related to the style, for example, and therefore usually want to stay close to the original form.[3] For example, the verb *to die* and the idiomatic expression *to kick the bucket* have the same semantics, but they certainly cannot be arbitrarily interchanged in a text. There is a similar distinction between the Dutch verb *sterven* and the idiom *de pijp uitgaan*. The compositional approach allows us to define the translation relation only between *to die* and *sterven* on the one hand, and between *to kick the bucket* and *de pijp uitgaan* on the other hand. They are assigned different basic meanings in the semantic components. In an analogous way a distinction can be made between syntactic rules that have the same logical meaning, by assigning different names of meaning rules to them in the semantic component.

---

[3]In fact, this requirement may be not so typical of translation as is suggested here. Cf. Van Deemter (1991) for a discussion of syntactic structure as a parameter of meaning.

So, semantic derivation trees will be used as carrier of all translation-relevant information. The term *semantic* reflects the opinion that meaning preservation is the most important aspect of translation, but at the same time it is slightly misleading, because the tree represents more information than what is usually included in semantic representations.

2.8 Challenges

This chapter has outlined the basic idea of compositional translation: two sentences are translation-equivalent if they are built up from parts which are translation-equivalent by means of translation-equivalent rules. We have seen that the elaboration of this idea leads us to the use of grammars for the languages involved and that these grammars have to be attuned to each other, i.e. they have to be isomorphic. Because we use grammars that obey the compositionality principle of meaning, on the one hand meaning preservation during translation can be guaranteed, while on the other hand the approach makes it possible to convey other translation-relevant information as well. Another advantage of the compositional approach is that it enables us to describe translation relations locally and yet be confident that the effects on a global level are correct.

The compositional method may appear to be very restrictive at first sight. It is indeed restrictive in the organisation of the translation, but it is very powerful in the sense that it is able to define translation relations between sentences that differ considerably at the surface level. One of the main challenges of this book is to show that the method works for linguistic phenomena that at first sight appear to require a non-compositional treatment. Some of these phenomena are:

- Temporal expressions, i.e. tensed verbs and temporal adverbials. It seems difficult to establish their translation relation by means of local compositional rules, because there is an interplay between the tenses and the adverbials.

- Idiomatic expressions, like *to pull one's leg*. Their meaning and, consequently, their translation cannot be derived from the meaning of their parts. There is a discrepancy between what one would want to consider basic expressions from a syntactic point of view and from a semantic point of view.

- Categorial divergences. In some cases a word has to be translated into a word of a different category, for instance the Dutch adverb *graag* and the English verb *like*. This is a challenge for the definition of the translation relation by means of isomorphic grammars.

It turned out that compositionality was a useful guideline for finding a systematic and elegant solution for these and other problems, which are notoriously difficult for any translation system. However, before these solutions can be discussed, the compositional method has to be elaborated further. A precondition for the treatment of interesting linguistic phenomena, is an extension of the rather primitive grammar formalism presented in this chapter. Chapter 3 will go into this. In order to show that the compositional approach is not only theoretically interesting and elegant, but also practically useful, we have to make the step from the rather abstract, generative way of defining the translation relation to the design of a translation system, which can perform the actual translation process. This step will be taken in Chapter 4.

Chapter 3
M-grammars

3.1 Introduction

The grammars presented in Chapter 2 were extremely simple because it was the main purpose of that chapter to clarify the concept of isomorphy. In this chapter we will consider some of the essential concepts that are required in order to be able to use more realistic grammars. The type of grammar actually used is called *M-grammar*, a computationally viable variant of *Montague Grammar* (the prefix *M* in *M-grammar* derives from *Montague*). It will soon become clear that more realistic grammars require much more than just operations on strings. Most of the concepts to be introduced are fairly standard, though they have certain specific properties in M-grammars.

This chapter will first discuss some problems with the grammar from the preceding chapter, which will be called a *string grammar* since it operates with strings; structure will be introduced to solve these problems (Section 3.2), and an abstract object to represent this structure (Section 3.3). The new kind of rules that must be adopted to operate on these structures (M-rules) and the grammar formalism (M-grammars) are described in Section 3.4. An example derivation to illustrate M-grammars is given. Then the relation between morphology and syntax is discussed (Section 3.5). Finally, an indication is given of how several kinds of ambiguities can be dealt with in the M-grammar framework (Section 3.6).

3.2 Structure

As the preceding chapter showed, the string grammar presented there ran into trouble, because it could derive the ill-formed string *verstandige jongens hopen dat dappere *meisjes huilen niet* and it was not able to derive the well-formed string *verstandige jongens hopen dat dappere meisjes niet huilen.* We might try to solve this problem by formulating different rules for main and subordinate clauses, but this is undesirable, because it would imply that the common properties of main and subordinate clause must be stated twice, which leads to more complex and hence descriptively inadequate grammars. We might also try to ameliorate the grammar by formulating a rule which puts a verb in a subordinate position into a different position. This approach, however, faces at least the following problems: (1) how can such a rule identify the verb in an arbitrary string; (2) how can the rule determine when to put the verb in a different position; and (3) how can it determine where to put the verb. Recall that this rule has only the information contained in the string at its disposal. All these problems can be solved by assuming that the objects manipulated by the grammar are structured objects, and by making the rules of the grammar sensitive to this structure. This point has been made by many grammarians (e.g. Chomsky (1972)) and the relevant detailed argumentation for it can be found in virtually every introductory textbook on linguistics. This chapter will sketch what kind of additional information must be contained in such structures, and how they are represented.

3.2.1 Constituents

A first step to take, in order to solve the problems mentioned above, is to assume that certain groups of words form a unit while other groups of words do not. Such units are usually called *constituents* (or *phrases*). By assuming that certain sequences of words form constituents and others do not, a structure is assigned to sentences. Since a substring that is a constituent can contain another substring that itself is also a constituent, this syntactic structure is a hierarchical one. Because of its hierarchical nature, the structure can be represented by using trees.

Of course, which structure must be assigned to a string is a complex issue. There is no simple operational method for determining the syntactic structure of a sentence. It must also be emphasised that there is is no simple correlation between semantics and the syntactic structure of a string. In particular, the structure of derivation trees cannot be used as constituent structures.

The syntactic structure assigned to a sentence must be chosen in such a way that it makes it possible to account for the properties of the sentence in the simplest and most adequate way. There are, of course, many tests that can be used to determine the syntactic structure of a sentence, but these do not in general determine the constituent structure uniquely. Which structure must be assigned to a sentence is, of course, also to a great extent dependent on the grammar assumed. A small number of tests that can be used to determine the constituent structure of a sentence are the following, although the provisos made above have to be borne in mind. It should also be emphasised that these tests are not part of the grammar, but serve as tools for linguists to determine which groups of words form a constituent and which ones don't.

1. *substitution*: if a sequence of words can be replaced by a single word (e.g. a pronoun), then this is an indication of the constituency of this sequence of words.

2. *movement*: if a sequence of words can be put into another position in the sentence, then this is an indication of the constituency of this sequence of words.

3. *impenetrability*: if a sequence of words cannot be separated by certain other words (e.g. adverbs of time, or modal adverbs), then this is an indication of the constituency of this sequence of words.

4. *subject in passive sentences*: if a sequence of words can become the subject of a sentence under passivisation, then it is a constituent.

5. *Vorfeld test*: a test specific to Dutch (and German) is the following: if a sequence of words can precede the finite verb in a main clause, then this sequence is a constituent.[1]

These tests will be used below to determine the constituency of certain sequences of words (see Section 3.6.2).

Notice that in most cases no conclusions can be drawn with respect to constituency if the test fails. This is a typical situation. The conclusion that a certain sequence does not form a constituent if some test fails can only be drawn if all alternative explanations for this failure can be excluded.

3.2.2 Syntactic categories

The preceding section has shown that a constituent structure must be assigned to each sentence in order to account adequately for its syntactic properties. It is, however, not only necessary to assume such a structure, but also to classify constituents into a number of distinct groups. This classification is usually done by assigning to each constituent a label called a *syntactic category*. Syntactic categories have already been used in the previous chapters, but there only a full string was assigned a syntactic category. We now extend this, so that a substring can also be assigned a syntactic category, provided this substring is a constituent. The notion of *syntactic category* is an extension of the notion *part of speech*: just as words are classified into several classes (*parts of speech*), constituents are classified according to *syntactic categories*. We will use the term *syntactic category* from now on as a term that

---

[1]This formulation is not fully accurate, but it will do for present purposes.

includes *part of speech*. Some of the syntactic categories for words are *nouns* (abbreviated N), *adjectives* (ADJ), *adverbs* (ADV), *verbs* (V), *articles* (ART), *quantifiers* (Q), *adpositions*, i.e. *prepositions and postpositions* (P), etc. A distinction is made between categories of the words listed in the dictionary (these have the prefix *B-* (from *basic*): BN, BADJ, BADV, etc.) and categories for inflected words (N, ADJ, ADV, V, etc.). It is usual to partition syntactic categories of words into two classes: the class of *open* syntactic categories and the class of *closed* syntactic categories. *Open* syntactic categories allow new words (newly formed, or borrowed) into its class, *closed* syntactic categories do not. *Adjectives, adverbs, nouns* and *verbs* are *open* syntactic categories, though *articles, quantifiers, prepositions, determiners, etc.* are *closed* categories in all languages.

A classification of constituents is necessary because certain constituents share properties with some constituents but not with others. For example, in the context *he saw* _ certain constituents can replace _, but others cannot. Constituents that can are, for example, *the man, the pretty girls, all ships*, etc.; constituents that cannot replace _ here are, for instance, *in the garden, right before the match, very nice*, etc. Apart from this, rules must also be given to describe what elements can occur in a constituent and in which order they can or must occur. Thus *the big man* is a constituent of English, but *the man big* is not, *the man in the garden* is a possible constituent of English, but *in the garden the man* is not, etc. In order to account for such phenomena, a classification of constituents is made.

It is generally assumed that one of the elements of a constituent has a special status. This element is called the (syntactic) *head* of the constituent. The syntactic category of the head determines the syntactic category of the whole constituent, and the syntactic category of the constituent determines the distribution of the constituent, i.e. the set of positions where it can occur, and the internal structure of the constituent. In this way, the *head* relates the distribution of the constituent to its internal structure.

A constituent with a *noun* as its head is called a *Noun Phrase* (NP), a constituent with a *preposition* or *postposition* as its head is called a *Prepositional Phrase* (PP), constituents headed by *adjectives* are called *Adjectival Phrases* (ADJPs), constituents headed by *adverbs* are called *Adverbial Phrases* (ADVPs), constituents headed by *verbs* are called *Verb Phrases* (VPs), etc.

The notion *head* is illustrated with the example *beautiful money*. This is a constituent of English. Which word is the head in this constituent? It can be either the adjective *beautiful*, or the noun *money*. If the noun is the head, the whole phrase is an NP, hence it should be able to occur in positions where NPs typically can occur. Some of these positions are: the context _ *is ADJ* (for example *beautiful money is rare*), the context *he saw* _, the context *he looked at* _, the context *NP and* _, etc. The phrase *beautiful money* can indeed occur in all of these positions. On the other hand, it should not be able to occur in positions where NPs typically cannot occur, e.g. in the contexts *I wonder* _, *the man* _, *ADJP and* _, etc., and it cannot. If the whole phrase is an NP, it should behave like an NP with respect to its internal structure. NPs can consist of an ADJP and a noun. NPs can be introduced by articles and other determiners, and the constituent *beautiful money* can, too (e.g. *the/this/all beautiful money*). The head noun of NP can be followed by PPs and relative clauses: this holds for *beautiful money* as well: *beautiful money from Holland, beautiful money from Holland that has been stolen*, etc. It is generally assumed that non-head parts of a constituent are phrases. Therefore, if the noun is the head, the other word must form an adjectival phrase. Hence, instead of *beautiful*, other ADJPs that can occur prenominally should be able to occur, and indeed they can: *very beautiful money, too beautiful money, more beautiful money*, etc. Suppose now, that the adjective is the head. Then the whole phrase is an ADJP, and it should be able to occur in positions where ADJPs can typically occur: in the context *it sounds _, it appears _, _* and ADJP. But it cannot occur in any of these contexts. Conversely, it should not be able to occur in contexts where ADJPs cannot occur (e.g. *he saw _, he looked at _*, etc.), but it can occur here. If the adjective is the head, then the noun (as a non-head part) must form an NP. But adjectives normally do not allow NPs as complements in English. Similarly, if the noun *money* is an NP, it should be possible to replace it by other NPs. However, this is not possible: **beautiful the money, *beautiful all money, *beautiful no money*, etc. So for the constituent *beautiful money* we can safely conclude that the noun *money* is the head. Simple operational tests to determine the syntactic category or the head of a constituent do not exist. One assigns to a constituent the syntactic category that accounts for its properties in the simplest and most adequate way, for example, in which contexts it can occur and how it is structured internally.

3.2.3   Attribute-value pairs

Words and constituents not only have a syntactic category, they must be further subclassified. For words this can be illustrated by the following example. The words *goes, went, gone, going* and *go* are all verbs, and they are all forms of the same stem *go*. In order to express this, attribute-value pairs (attributes are often called *features* in other frameworks) are used to subclassify verbs. For the examples mentioned, for instance, assume the attributes *number, form, tense, key* with the following possible values:[2]

---

[2]The number of attributes is limited for expository convenience. The attributes are insufficient to classify all English verb forms.

attribute	possible values
number	singular, plural, unspecified
form	finite, participle, infinitive, ingform
tense	present, past, unspecified
key	GO, BUY, WALK,....

The attribute *key* takes unique names of stems as its possible values (these unique names are called *keys*, because they function as unique keys in the lexical data base). These are represented here in small capitals to distinguish them from the strings 'go', 'buy', 'walk', etc. The forms mentioned can be characterised as indicated in the following table:

word	attributes			
	key	**number**	**form**	**tense**
goes	GO	singular	finite	present
went	GO	unspecified	finite	past
gone	GO	unspecified	participle	unspecified
going	GO	unspecified	ingform	unspecified
go	GO	plural	finite	present
go	GO	unspecified	infinitive	unspecified

Such a further subclassification of words correctly expresses the fact that all these words are forms of one stem and indicates precisely which grammatical properties these forms share and in which they differ. This subclassification also simplifies the formulation of grammatical rules. The representation of word forms as sets of attribute-value pairs introduces a certain degree of abstraction. In particular, it is now possible to write a very general rule, e.g. for the formation of past tense sentences. The only thing that has to be done is resetting the value for the attribute *tense* from *unspecified* to *past*. At this level of abstraction no attention has to be paid to the fact that the past tense of the verb *go* is formed irregularly in a particular way (*went*), that the past tense of the verb *see* is also formed irregularly (but in another way than the past tense of *go*: *saw*), etc. The abstraction introduced by means of these attribute-value pairs considerably simplifies the syntactic rules. It is, of course, also necessary to relate the abstract representations of the words in the form of attribute-value pairs to their string representations. This is the task of the morphological component, which is described in Chapter 6.

Not only words, but also constituents must be subclassified. Some very simple examples show this. In the following sentences all sequences of words in italics are constituents of category NP:

(1) a   *The boy* is in the garden
    b   **The boys* is in the garden
    c   **The boy* are in the garden
    d   *The boys* are in the garden

However, only the NP *the boy* can precede *is*, and only the NP *the boys* can precede *are* in these examples. This can be accounted for very simply if it is assumed that constituents of category NP are subclassified for an attribute **number** with as possible values *singular, plural, unspecified* and if there is a grammatical rule that states that an NP and a V must have the same value for the attribute *number* in sentences of this type.

As a second example, consider the following facts. In the sentences in (2) the parts in italics are all constituents of category NP. However, only the NPs *a boy* and *boys* can occur in this syntactic context. The NPs *the boy* and *the boys* are excluded here.

(2) a   There is *a boy* in the garden
    b   There are *boys* in the garden
    c   *There is *the boy* in the garden
    d   *There are *the boys* in the garden

So, apparently there is a class of NPs that can occur in the syntactic context *There is/are...*, and a class of NPs that cannot appear here. The two classes of NPs can be distinguished by some attribute. It is usually assumed that the *definiteness* of NPs plays a role here. A distinction is made between *definite* and *indefinite* NPs. This distinction, which plays a role elsewhere in the grammar as well, makes it possible to account for the examples given.

It might be suggested that, in the cases mentioned, the phrases themselves need not be marked with attribute-value pairs, since this can be determined from the parts of the phrase. For instance, it might be said that in the first example it is sufficient that the head N is distinguished with respect to number. Though this is true, it should be pointed out that the computation of the properties of a phrase is a rather complex operation, which in addition does not always yield unique results. One simple example where the computation of number is more complicated is formed by an NP such as *John and Peter*, in which none of the words is plural while the constituent as a whole is (cf. *John and Peter *is/are in the garden*). Similarly, the computation of the definiteness of an NP involves a very complex computation (cf. *a boy, milk, boys* are indefinite, while *the boy, exercise 3, John* are definite). Furthermore, an NP such as *time* in English can be either definite or indefinite. If the computed properties were not stored in the form of attribute-value pairs in the phrasal node, this complex computation would have to be repeated each time these properties are referred to. This would clearly lead to a more complex grammar, and there would be no guarantee that a consistent choice is made throughout the derivation.

In the Rosetta grammars a very detailed system of attribute-value pairs has been worked out for each syntactic category, both for syntactic categories corresponding to single words and for syntactic categories for constituents. It would take too much space to discuss this in detail here. Wherever relevant, the attributes and their possible values will be specified explicitly. See Section 7.2 for some detailed examples of some of the attributes and their possible values for some syntactic categories.

It must be emphasised, however, that the role of attribute-value pairs in M-grammars is much more limited than in many other frameworks. In other frameworks attributes allow complex values which are formed recursively. This is not allowed in M-grammars: possible values for attributes are either atomic or finite sets of atomic values. Recursion in linguistic structures is expressed by trees, not by attribute-value structures.

3.2.4   Grammatical relations

Constituents bear a certain *grammatical relation* when used in a larger constituent. Some well-known grammatical relations (the abbreviations used in Rosetta are given between brackets) are *subject (subj), direct object (obj), indirect object (indobj), predicate (pred), prepositional object (prepobj), modifier (mod), head, determiner (det)*, etc.

It is necessary to distinguish grammatical relations because many rules apply to constituents only if they bear a specific grammatical relation. Thus, agreement between the verb and some NP occurs only if this NP bears the grammatical relation *subject*. In passive constructions direct objects can, but indirect objects cannot become subjects in Dutch and Spanish. Consider, for instance, the following two sentences: *Hij gaf mij het boek* ('He gave me the book') and *Hij vond mij een idioot* ('He considered me a fool'). The constituent structures of these two sentences are identical (both are sequences of the form NP V NP NP). In the first sentence, the first NP to the right of the verb, *mij*, cannot become the subject under passivisation (**Ik werd het boek gegeven*, lit. *I was given the book*), though the second one can (*Het boek werd mij gegeven*, 'The book was given me'). In the second sentence, however, the first NP to the right of the verb can become the subject of the sentence under passivisation (*Ik werd een idioot gevonden* ('I was considered a fool')), though the second one cannot (**Een idioot werd mij gevonden*, lit. *A fool was considered me*). This difference can easily be accounted for by distinguishing between *direct objects* and other complements of verbs.

In Rosetta, grammatical relations are not really used in the same way as in traditional grammar. Apart from its grammatical function, the position of the phrase also plays a role in determining the grammatical relation. Thus, traditional grammar would call the boldface phrases *subjects* in both following examples from Dutch: *leest* **de man** *een krant?* (lit. *reads the man a newspaper*) 'Is the man reading a newspaper', **de man** *leest een krant* (lit. the man reads a newspaper) 'The man is reading a newspaper'. In Rosetta, however, these phrases do not bear the same grammatical relation: In the first example the phrase is a *subject*, but in the second a topic (called *shiftrel*, because it always contains elements which have been shifted into this position, such as topicalised phrases and sentence-initial interrogative pronouns). We will not motivate this analysis here; we only want to point out that the relative position of a phrase co-determines which grammatical relation it bears in syntax.

3.3   S-trees

In order to represent all the different kinds of information that are required in a real grammar as discussed above, a special type of object is defined. This object is called an *S-tree* (the *S* in S-tree is from *syntactic*). An S-tree is a structured object (a *tree*) in which *constituency*, *grammatical relations*, *syntactic categories*, further classifications of syntactic categories in the form of *attribute-value pairs*, and *linear order* can (and must) be represented.

S-trees are labelled ordered trees. The following notation is used to represent them:

$$N \ [\ r_1/t_1,...,r_n/t_n \ ]$$

The notation states that node N dominates a sequence of pairs consisting of a grammatical relation (r_i) and an S-tree (t_i). If the sequence of pairs (relation, S-tree) has length 0, i.e. if it is empty, we write $N[\ ]$ or simply N.

A node consisting of a syntactic category C and a set of attributes a_i with values v_i is represented as follows:

$$C\{ \ a_1{:}v_1,...,a_n{:}v_n \ \}$$

An S-tree for a completed utterance is called a *surface tree*. The tree in (3) might be the surface tree for the sentence *a car passed quickly*:

(3)   S   {voice:active, mood:declarative, type:main}
        [subj / NP   {def:false, number:singular}
                            [det/ART{ key:A },
                                head/N{number:singular}
                                [head/BN{key:CAR}]
                            ],
             head / V   {form:finite, tense:past, number:singular}
                          [head/BV{key:PASS}]
             mod / ADV
                          [
                                mod/BADJ{key:QUICK}
                                head/BADVSF{key:LY}
                          ]
        ]

S-trees will also often be represented by means of a graphical tree representation.
Many details will usually be left out and only the crucial properties are represented.
If the exact details of a part of the structure are not relevant, triangles will be used
to represent this structure. In the example below we have left out the attribute-value
pairs, except for the key attributes.

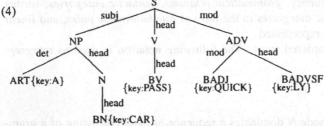

A property of a surface tree is that its 'leaves' correspond to the words of the
actual sentence. These leaves are small S-trees, called *lexical S-trees*, which are
characterised by special syntactic categories, so-called *lexical categories*. In this
example these lexical categories are ART, N, V and ADV, and the lexical S-trees
in this example are the trees with these categories as their top categories.

Representation (3) expresses that the top node of the S-tree consists of a category
S (sentence) and a number of attribute-value pairs which subclassify this S as an active main declarative clause. This top node dominates three S-trees, one of category
NP, one of category V, and one of category ADV, in that order. The first S-tree
bears the grammatical relation *subj*, the second one bears the grammatical relation
head, and the third one bears the grammatical relation *mod*. The node with NP as
category has an attribute to indicate the indefiniteness of the NP and an attribute
number to indicate whether the NP is *singular* or *plural*. The node with category V

has attributes to express that it is a singular past finite form; it dominates a node of category BV (relation: *head*) with PASS as its unique name. The node with category ADV has no attributes. The node of category NP, dominates two S-trees, the first one with category ART and relation *det*, the second one with category N and relation *head*. The node of the first S-tree has an attribute to specify its unique name (A) and the top node of the second one has attributes to represent number; it dominates a node of category BN (relation: *head*) with a unique name (CAR). The node of category ADV dominates two S-trees, one of category BADJ with grammatical relation *mod*, and one of category BADVSF with grammatical relation *head*. The first S-tree represents the stem with unique name QUICK, the second one the suffix with unique name LY.

3.4   M-grammars

3.4.1   The components of M-grammar

In the preceding sections the objects that the grammar manipulates have been changed from strings to S-trees. This change requires that we reconsider the global design of the grammar and the contents of each of its components, too. The type of grammar described here and which is actually used is called *M-grammar*. An M-grammar consists of three components: (1) the syntactic component, (2) the semantic component, and (3) the morphological component.

The syntactic component of an M-grammar defines a set of surface trees. As in the string grammar, it consists of basic expressions and rules. The basic expressions in an M-grammar are not strings, but S-trees, so-called *basic S-trees*. The rules of the syntactic component are compositional rules that take S-trees as their arguments and produce an S-tree as their result; they are called M-rules and will be discussed in more detail in Section 3.4.2 and in Chapter 8. Essentially, derivations proceed in the same way as in the string grammar discussed above: rules (M-rules) are applied to basic expressions (basic S-trees) creating larger S-trees, to which M-rules can again be applied, etc. The derivation of an expression is represented in a syntactic derivation tree (from now on we will also use *D-tree* as an abbreviation for *derivation tree*), basically in the same way as in the string grammar.

The semantic component of an M-grammar is essentially identical to the semantic component of a string grammar. It relates semantic derivation trees to syntactic derivation trees, by relating basic expressions to basic meanings, and syntactic rules to meaning operations.

The morphological component relates lexical S-trees occurring in surface trees to strings. The morphological component will be described in more detail in Chapter 6.

If one compares M-grammars to the string grammars used earlier, a number of differences can be observed, but also a number of similarities: the differences are that there is one additional component (the morphological component) in M-grammars and that the syntactic component defines S-trees instead of strings.

One of the similarities with the string grammar is the fact that M-grammars are also compositional grammars, and that the role of isomorphy remains the same. Isomorphy is defined, as with string grammars, via the semantic component. The compositional translation method described in the preceding chapter can therefore remain the same. Note that isomorphy holds for the derivation process, and is defined in terms of D-trees, not in terms of S-trees. The reader should realise that a sharp distinction between D-trees and S-trees is essential: an *S-tree* is a representation of the syntactic structure, and consists of constituents, syntactic categories, grammatical relations, linear order (which corresponds to the surface linear order in a surface tree) and attributes and their values. A *D-tree* is a representation that indicates how an S-tree can be derived, and consists of names of rules and of names of basic expressions. Isomorphy is defined in terms of D-trees, so two translation-equivalent sentences must have isomorphic D-trees; their S-trees, however, can differ quite drastically.

We will now first introduce some more details about M-rules, and then illustrate how a sentence can be derived in an M-grammar.

3.4.2   M-rules

As has been pointed out above, the syntactic component of an M-grammar consists of basic expressions (basic S-trees) and rules which operate on S-trees (M-rules). Chapter 8 will describe these rules in more detail, but here we will introduce some aspects which are necessary to illustrate an example derivation and to show how certain kinds of ambiguity are dealt with in this grammar formalism.

A special type of element in S-trees, called a *syntactic variable*, plays an important role throughout the syntax. A syntactic variable is an S-tree consisting of one node, having some category and associated attribute-value pairs, and a special attribute called the *index*. The *index* attribute takes integers as values.

Indices are put to use in a set of special M-rules, called *substitution rules*. These are parametrised rules, taking an *index parameter* that can assume integer values, and two arguments, i.e. two S-trees. A substitution rule with index parameter i applies to an S-tree containing a variable with index equal to i, and some other S-tree (the so-called *substituent*), and substitutes this latter S-tree for the variable with index i occurring in the former S-tree. So the index parameter determines the variable for which the substituent must be substituted. In derivation trees the notation RSUBST,i is used to indicate that the substitution rule RSUBST replaces the syntactic variable with index i.

A derivation usually begins with a so-called *start rule*, i.e. a rule that combines some argument-taking basic expression with a number (zero or more) of variables. These variables function as place-holders for the phrases that will be substituted for them later in the derivation. Substitution rules play a crucial role in representing scope relations (see Section 3.6 and Chapter 16). Variables also play a crucial role in accounting for the syntactic properties of expletives and idioms (see Chapter 15). Finally, variables play a role in several anaphoric rules, i.e. rules that determine whether two phrases have the same reference. Some examples of such rules are Control rules (dealing with the interpretation of nonovert subjects of infinitival constructions), Pronominalisation rules (dealing with the interpretations and generation of the correct personal pronouns) and Reflexivisation rules (dealing with the correct distribution and interpretation of reflexive pronouns).

3.4.3 Example derivation

In order to clarify how a sentence can be derived by an M-grammar, we will derive the example sentence *a car passed quickly*. The major steps in this derivation can be described in the following manner. The syntactic component derives a surface tree for this sentence. By recording how the S-tree has been derived, a D-tree is created, which can be mapped onto one or more semantic derivation trees in the semantic component. The morphological component turns the sequence of lexical S-trees occurring in the surface tree into a string.

We will now illustrate this derivation in more detail. We start by applying M rules. A start rule (RSTART1) is applied to the basic expression BV{key:PASS} and a variable VAR{index:1} to form an active sentence. This yields the following S-tree:

(5)

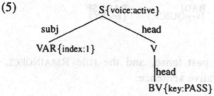

In addition, an adverb is created from the basic expression QUICK (of category BADJ) and the suffix LY (of category BADVSF) by the M-rule RADV. This yields:

(6)

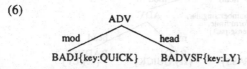

This latter S-tree is combined with the former S-tree by the rule RMOD (modification). Applying this rule yields the following S-tree:

(7)

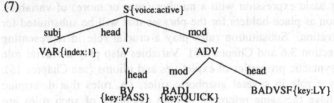

The M-rule RNP forms an S-tree of category NP from the basic expression CAR (of category BN), putting the noun in singular and syncategorematically introducing the article A:

(8)

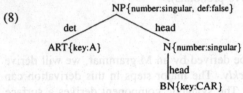

A substitution rule substitutes this NP for the variable with index 1, and makes the verb and the subject agree:

(9)

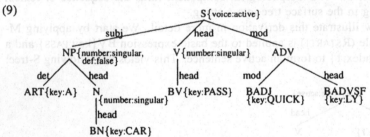

The M-rule RPAST puts the head verb into past tense, and the rule RMAINDECL determines that the sentence is a main declarative sentence:

(10)

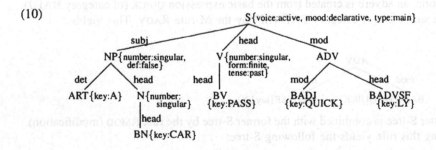

At this point surface tree (3) has been derived. The corresponding D-tree is given in (11):

(11)

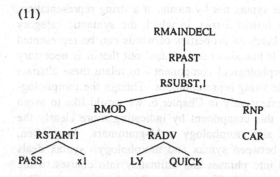

Note that the terminal nodes of D-tree (11) are not labelled by basic expressions (as in Chapter 2), but by their unique names (as indicated by the small capitals). This also holds for the indexed variables. From now on we will stick to this convention. The morphological component must now turn each lexical S-tree from surface tree (3) into a string, while retaining the relative order of the S-trees. The lexical S-trees of the surface tree (3) are:

(12)   ART{key:A}
      N{number:singular}[head/BN{key:CAR}]
      V{form:finite, number:singular, tense:past}[head/BV{key:PASS}]
      ADV[mod/BADJ{key:QUICK}, head/BADVSF{key:LY}]

The first lexical S-tree is turned into the string *a*. The second one is turned into the string *car*. The third one is changed into the string *passed* by applying morphological rules to form the past tense of a verb. The last lexical S-tree has internal structure. First, the parts of this lexical S-tree are turned into the strings *quick* and *ly* respectively, and then a rule combines these strings to form the string *quickly*. The sentence *a car passed quickly* has now been derived.

The example illustrated is very simple. In reality it is possible that the M-rules yield more than one S-tree (in the case of paraphrases). Furthermore, the morphological component can also yield several variants (e.g. if there are spelling variants, or if a word can be conjugated in more than one way). The next chapter will make clear how these aspects are dealt with.

3.5   The relation between syntax and morphology

In the preceding sections, abstract representations were introduced to represent
words. Words are represented in the syntax not by means of a string representation,
but by a special kind of S-tree, a *lexical S-tree*, in which the syntactic category
of the word is represented and all kinds of properties of words can be represented
by means of attribute-value pairs. It has also been pointed out that it is necessary
to have some component - the morphological component - to relate these abstract
representations to the more concrete string representations. Though the morphological component will be described extensively in Chapter 6, we would like to avoid
misunderstandings with respect to this component by indicating more clearly the
division of labour between syntax and morphology in M-grammars. Very often,
the following distinction is made between syntax and morphology: syntax deals
with the way words are combined into phrases and ultimately into clauses, while
morphology deals with the way stems and affixes are combined into words. This
bifurcation does not exist in M-grammars. All structure-creating operations, whether
internal or external to the word, apply in M-grammars in *syntax*. There is no component dealing with morphology in the sense described above. Of course, there is a
morphological component, but this component has as its task to define the relation
between abstract representations of words as structured objects (lexical S-trees) and
their representations as strings.

There are several reasons for not having the bifurcation indicated above. First of
all, it entails a theoretical claim (i.e. that word-internal structure and word-external
structure are independent of one another), which is very controversial. There are all
sorts of phenomena that at least cast doubt on this hypothesis. A well-known example
is the case of verbs with particles in Dutch: the particle sometimes behaves as a word-
internal affix (e.g. in a word such *onafleidbaar* (lit. *un-off-lead-able* 'underivable'))
and sometimes it behaves as a separate word (e.g. in *hij* **leidt** *de zin* **af**, 'he derives the
sentence'). Furthermore, it has been argued that it must be possible for *phrases* to be
input to rules of derivation or composition (see Cinque (1993:274) for references).
Of course, when there are strong reasons for making such a bifurcation, the linguist
can subdivide the syntax into two parts, one dealing with intra-word syntax and the
other with inter-word syntax, but nothing in the M-grammar formalism forces him
to such a partitioning.

Apart from these monolingual reasons there are also translational arguments
for not having the bifurcation between word-internal and word-external structure:
a phenomenon which is word-internal in one language need not correspond to a
word-internal phenomenon in another language. A very trivial example of this is
compounding: in Dutch, compounds are written as one word, but most English
compounds are written as two (or more) words. In Spanish, the translation of
compounds often involves two (or more) separate words combined by means of a

preposition. A more interesting example is the fact that Dutch has a productive process of diminutive formation, though the relevant translations in English must be circumscribed by means of phrases consisting of a noun modified by the adjective *little* or *small*.

So it is important to bear in mind that what is usually called 'morphology' is just one part of syntax in M-grammars, and that what is called the 'morphological component' in M-grammars deals only with defining the relation between abstract representations of words (in the form of lexical S-trees) and their corresponding strings.[3] The morphological component in M-grammars is a purely 'interpretive' component, i.e. it turns certain abstract objects into other abstract objects, but it does not 'create' new structure.

3.6 Ambiguity

This section describes how the M-grammar formalism makes it possible to adequately describe different kinds of ambiguity. We speak of *ambiguity* if more than one semantic D-tree is related to one utterance. Ambiguity can arise in several components. A basic distinction can be made between *semantic ambiguity* and *morphosyntactic ambiguity*. *Semantic ambiguity* is created in the semantic component: (1) a basic expression has more than one meaning (homonymy), or (2) a rule has more than one meaning (rule ambiguity). *Morphosyntactic ambiguity* is created in the syntactic or morphological component. The following subcases of morphosyntactic ambiguity can be distinguished: (1) more than one lexical S-tree is related to a word (homophony); (2) more than one surface tree is related to a sequence of lexical S-trees (surface structural ambiguity); (3) more than one syntactic D-tree is related to a surface tree (derivational ambiguity). This section will discuss each of these types of ambiguity in more detail.

3.6.1 Semantic ambiguity

Homonymy

If several basic meanings correspond to one basic expression, we speak of *homonymy*. Examples of *homonymy* can be found in almost every entry in each dictionary. A typical example is the English word *bank* which can designate an object to sit on or a financial corporation. A second example is the Dutch verb *innemen* which can mean *take up* (of cloths), *occupy* (of a city), *swallow* (of pills), etc.

---

[3]The morphological component of M-grammars corresponds most closely to the so-called PF-component in models of modern generative grammar (see Chomsky and Lasnik (1977)).

The amount of homonymy is somewhat larger than in traditional dictionaries. This is due to the fact that M-grammars are used in a translation system: distinctions made in some language L1 must be taken into account in semantic derivation trees, and these may lead to ambiguities in some other language L2 even if this language does not make the relevant distinction. An example of this phenomenon is e.g. English *wall* which is ambiguous because Dutch makes a distinction between *wand* and *muur* (as in German *Wand* v. *Mauer*)

Homonymy is accounted for in the semantic component.

Rule ambiguity

If several meaning operations correspond to one *syntactic rule*, we speak of *rule ambiguity*. One possible example of such a rule might be a rule to form finite relative clauses in Dutch. In Spanish, relative clauses can be formed either in indicative mood, or in subjunctive mood, and there are subtle semantic differences between indicative and subjunctive relative clauses. In the grammar of Spanish two rules are required for this, and these different rules correspond to different meanings. In Dutch, however, the subtle distinction made in Spanish is not formally represented in any way. So in the grammar of Dutch it would be most natural to have only one rule to form finite relative clauses, and to map this rule onto two different meaning operations, so that the rule is ambiguous. Rule ambiguity, like homonymy, is dealt with in the semantic component. Rule ambiguity does not occur very often.

3.6.2 Morphosyntactic ambiguity

Homophony

When several lexical S-trees correspond to one word, we speak of *homophony*.[4] An example is the verb *hang* in English which is either conjugated as *hang-hanged-hanged* or as *hang-hung-hung*. This difference in conjugation corresponds to a syntactic difference (transitive v. intransitive) and to a semantic difference ('to kill someone in a specific manner' v. 'being located in a specific manner').

The amount of homophony in M-grammars is somewhat larger than in traditional dictionaries. This is due to the fact that different lexical S-trees must be associated to a word when there is a difference in *any* of the morphosyntactic properties of the words. In traditional dictionaries usually only a difference in syntactic category leads to homophony. One example of such a property which leads to additional homophony is the argument structure of words: this is indicated explicitly in M-grammars, but usually ignored in traditional dictionaries. Homophony is accounted for in the morphological component.

---

[4] Note that we make an explicit distinction between *homonymy* and *homophony*, which is not standard.

Surface structural ambiguity

When several surface trees correspond to one sequence of lexical S-trees, we speak of *(Surface) Structural Ambiguity*. We will illustrate structural ambiguity with the example *Zij bevalen de man bij Philips aan*. This Dutch sentence is ambiguous. The translation of this sentence into English differs depending on the interpretation:

1. They recommended the man to Philips
2. They recommended the man at Philips

These two interpretations correlate with the following syntactic structures: Under the first interpretation, syntactic structure (13) must be assigned to the sentence (the triangles indicate that the internal structure of certain trees has been abstracted from):

(13)

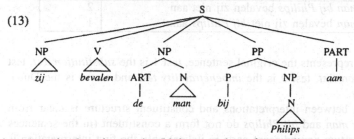

i.e., the substring *de man bij Philips* consists of *two* adjacent constituents.

Under the second interpretation structure (14) must be assigned to this substring:

(14)

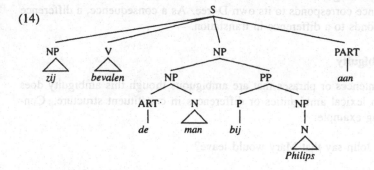

i.e, the substring *de man bij Philips* forms *one* constituent.

The correlation between the interpretations and these constituent structures can be shown by applying the constituent tests mentioned earlier and considering which interpretations remain and which disappear.

The following table summarises these tests. The first column contains a number referring to a specific constituent test, the second contains the relevant sentence and the third contains the interpretation(s) available for the test sentence.

Test	Sentence	Interpre-tation
0	Zij bevalen *de man bij Philips* aan	1,2
1	Zij bevalen *hem* aan	2
	Zij bevalen *hem bij Philips* aan	1
4	*De man bij Philips* werd door hen aanbevolen	2
	De man werd door hen *bij Philips* aanbevolen	1
3	Zij hebben *de man bij Philips* gisteren aanbevolen	2
	Zij hebben *de man* gisteren *bij Philips* aanbevolen	1
2/5	*De man bij Philips* bevalen zij niet aan	2
	De man bevalen zij niet *bij Philips* aan	1

In this table, test 0 represents the original sentence, test 1 is the *substitution test*, test 2 is the *passivisation test*, test 3 is the *impenetrability test* and test 4 is the Dutch specific *Vorfeld test*.

The correlation between interpretations and constituent structure is clear from this table: when *de man* and *bij Philips* do not form a constituent (in the sentences where they occur as two non-adjacent parts in italics) only the first interpretation is available; when they do form a constituent only the second interpretation is available.

The sentence is assigned two different S-trees. Each S-tree is derived in a different manner, hence corresponds to its own D-tree. As a consequence, a difference in S-trees corresponds to a difference in translation.

Derivational ambiguity

There are also sentences or phrases that are ambiguous though this ambiguity does not correlate with lexical ambiguities or differences in constituent structure. Consider the following example:

(15) When did John say that Mary would leave?

This sentence is ambiguous: it can either asks for the moment when John made a particular utterance, or it can ask for the moment of Mary's departure. The ambiguity of the sentence is not due to a lexical ambiguity, nor does it correlate with a difference in the syntactic surface structure. Under both interpretations its surface structure is as indicated in (16):

(16)

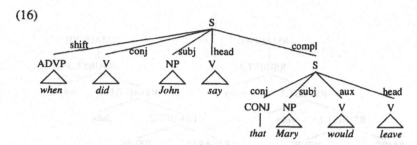

The ambiguity, however, does correspond to a difference in the derivation trees. In one interpretation, the adverbial phrase *when* is introduced as a modifier of the subordinate clause. In the other interpretation it is introduced as a modifier of the main clause. There is a different syntactic derivation tree (D-tree) for each interpretation. For this reason this kind of ambiguity (i.e. ambiguity where the S-trees for the two interpretations are identical but the D-trees are not) is called *derivational ambiguity*.

We will work out this example in more detail, and show how the difference in interpretation corresponds to a difference in syntactic D-trees.

Under both interpretations, first the part *Mary would leave* of the subordinate clause is formed. Let us assume that the last rule to form this part is called RCL. Under interpretation (2), a variable (x_3) for the adverbial phrase *when* is added to this phrase by a rule of modification (RMOD). Under the other interpretation (1), this modification rule does not apply here. Next, the subordinate clause is formed in both cases by a rule (RSUB), which adds the conjunction *that*.

The verb *say* is combined with two variables (x_1 and x_2) by a start rule (RSTART2). Under interpretation (1) the rule of modification (RMOD) is now applied, and it introduces a variable (x_3) for the adverbial phrase *when*. Next, the arguments are substituted for the variables by a substitution rule (RSUBST): the subordinate clause derived earlier is substituted for x_2, and the NP *John* is substituted for x_1. Finally, the variable for the adverbial phrase is preposed to a clause-initial position: under interpretation (1) the variable is moved from a position in the main clause, and under interpretation (2) it is moved out of the subordinate clause. Then the adverbial phrase is substituted for this variable, and finally a rule (RMAINWH) is applied which determines that this sentence is a main WH-interrogative sentence. The derivation trees which correspond with both interpretations are given in (17).

(17)

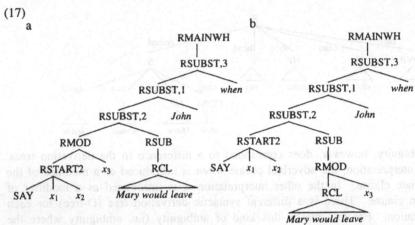

In these derivation trees the expressions *when, John* and *Mary would leave* are used
as abbreviations for the derivation trees which derive them.

D-tree (17a) corresponds to interpretation (1), in which the question relates to the
moment of John making a certain utterance. The rule RMOD is part of the formation
of the main clause (headed by *say*). D-tree (17b) corresponds to interpretation (2),
in which the question relates to the moment of Mary's departure. The rule RMOD
is part of the formation of the subordinate clause (headed by *leave*). Mapping these
different syntactic D-trees onto semantic D-trees will automatically lead to a different
interpretation, and may lead to different translations into other languages.

There are many other examples of derivational ambiguities, for instance scope
ambiguities (see Chapter 16); also certain ambiguities in nominalisations can in
principle be dealt with in this way.

3.7 Concluding remarks

This chapter has introduced the notion of M-grammar. This is a unique combination
of elements that are not unique in themselves: (1) a Montague-type framework
with compositional rules, and (2) the notion of constituents, which plays a role
in almost all grammatical frameworks. The consequence of the combination is
that the grammar consists of powerful rules (M-rules) which operate on constituent
trees (S-trees). We have shown that the formalism makes it possible to adequately
represent different kinds of ambiguities, viz. (1) homonymy, (2) rule ambiguities,
(3) homophony, (4) surface structural ambiguities and (5) derivational ambiguities,
and their correlations with syntactic structure. The grammatical framework in the
literature to which the M-grammar framework comes closest is the extension of
Montague grammar proposed by Partee (1973).

Chapter 4

The translation process

4.1 From translation relation to translation system

In Chapter 2 the translation relation between two languages was defined by means of isomorphic string grammars. Chapter 3 introduced the M-grammar formalism, which is used in the actual Rosetta system. M-grammars have a more sophisticated syntactic component than string grammars, but the semantic component and the way in which the translation relation is defined are essentially the same. For both types of grammars, two sentences s_1 and s_2 of languages L_1 and L_2 are considered translation-equivalent if they can be derived by isomorphic syntactic derivation trees, which implies that they share a semantic derivation tree.

This chapter will show how the relational definition of translation equivalence introduced in Chapter 2 can be used for designing a translation *system* that executes a translation *process*. One of the languages L_1 and L_2 is considered the source language (SL) and the other language is the target language (TL). The system gets a sentence of the source language as its input and yields sentences of the target language as output. The resulting sentences of the target language should be the possible translations of the input sentences according to the isomorphic grammars, i.e. they should have a common semantic derivation tree.

First, in Section 4.2 the global architecture of a translation system based on isomorphic grammars will be discussed. In Section 4.3 this will be elaborated for the example string grammars of Chapter 3. Special attention will be paid to the process of *syntactic analysis*. Section 4.4 describes the transition from relation to process for M-grammars. This results in the global design of the Rosetta system. In Section 4.5 it is shown how an example sentence is dealt with by the eight modules of this system.

57

4.2   Global architecture of translation systems

There are two well-known ways of structuring a translation system: the *interlingual* architecture and the *transfer* architecture. In an interlingual system, translation proceeds in two stages, called *analysis* and *generation*. In the analysis stage, sentences of the source language are mapped onto expressions of an intermediate language (IL), in the generation stage the IL expressions are mapped onto target language sentences. In a transfer system there are three stages: *analysis*, *transfer* and *generation*. In the analysis stage, SL sentences are mapped onto some syntactic or semantic representation, in the transfer stage this representation is mapped onto a corresponding TL representation, and in the generation stage this is mapped onto a TL sentence.

For a system based on isomorphic grammars, where sentences bear a translation relation if they have a common semantic derivation tree, an interlingual architecture as presented in Figure 4.1 is the most natural. Semantic derivation trees can function as expressions of the intermediate language. There is a systematic relation between the components of the grammars and the four modules of the system. (Note that we use the term *modules* for the parts of the translation system, in order to distinguish them clearly from the corresponding parts of the grammars, called *components*.)

 (i) a module, called PARSER$_{SL}$, which assigns to the input sentence the set of syntactic derivation trees that would generate that sentence according to the syntactic component of the SL grammar,

 (ii) a module A-TRANSFER$_{SL}$ (analytical transfer), which maps each syntactic derivation tree of the source language onto a set of semantic derivation trees, according to the semantic component of the SL grammar,

 (iii) a module G-TRANSFER$_{TL}$ (generative transfer), which maps each semantic derivation tree onto a set of syntactic derivation trees of the target language, according to the semantic component of the TL grammar,

 (iv) a generation module, called GENERATOR$_{TL}$, which receives syntactic derivation trees of the target language as input and executes the derivation process as pr in the trees, according to the syntactic component of the TL grammar, yielding sentences of the target language as output.

The interlingual design of Figure 4.1 is the one that has been selected for the Rosetta system which will be discussed in Section 4.4, where it will be shown that the modules PARSER and GENERATOR have to be further subdivided. First, Section 4.3 will introduce the basic notions for the example string grammars of Chapter 2.

It is good to notice that isomorphic grammars could also be the basis for a transfer system, as outlined in Figure 4.2, with a transfer component that maps syntactic

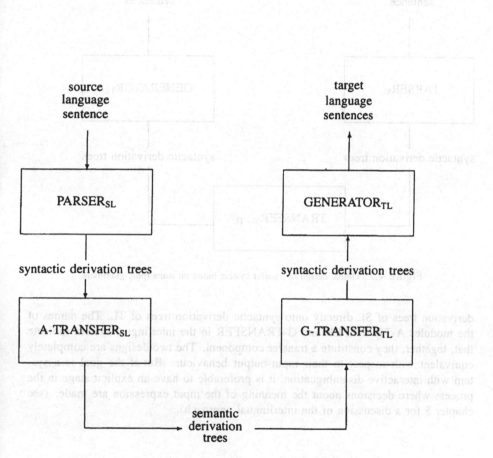

Figure 4.1: Global design of interlingual system based on isomorphic grammars.

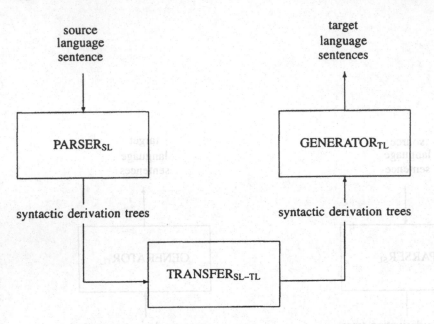

Figure 4.2: Global design of transfer system based on isomorphic grammars.

derivation trees of SL directly onto syntactic derivation trees of TL. The names of the modules A-TRANSFER and G-TRANSFER in the interlingual system indicate that, together, they constitute a transfer component. The two designs are completely equivalent with respect to their input-output behaviour. But if the goal is a system with interactive disambiguation, it is preferable to have an explicit stage in the process where decisions about the meaning of the input expression are made. (see chapter 5 for a discussion of the interlingual approach).

4.3   A translation system based on string grammars

In this section, an interlingual translation system will be designed on the basis of the isomorphic string grammars $G_{English}2$ and $G_{Dutch}2$, introduced in Chapter 2. It should be noted once again that string grammars are used in this book for expository purposes only. In Chapter 2 they enabled us to introduce the notion of a compositional translation relation without having to bother about the complexities of more realistic grammars. Here they will serve a similar purpose with respect to the translation *process*, in particular the process of syntactic analysis.

4.3.1   The four modules

First, the two example grammars, $G_{English}2$ and $G_{Dutch}2$, are recapitulated in tabular form. For each grammar the tables show the basic expressions and syntactic rules as specified by the syntactic component and their meanings as specified by the semantic component.

$G_{English}2$:

1.	basic expressions	basic meanings
	N(*girl*)	girl′
	N(*boy*)	boy′
	ADJ(*intelligent*)	intelligent′
	ADJ(*brave*)	brave′
	IV(*cry*)	$cry_1′$, $cry_2′$
	IV(*laugh*)	laugh′
2.	syntactic rules	meaning rules
	$R_{English}1$: N(α) + ADJ(β) $\Rightarrow$ NP(β αs)	S1
	$R_{English}2$: IV(α) $\Rightarrow$ VP(α)	S2
	$R_{English}3$: IV(α) $\Rightarrow$ VP(*do not* α)	S3
	$R_{English}4$: VP(α) + NP(β) $\Rightarrow$ S(β α)	S4

$G_{Dutch}2$:

1.	basic expressions	basic meanings
	N(*meisje*)	girl′
	N(*jongen*)	boy′
	ADJ(*verstandig*)	intelligent′
	ADJ(*dapper*)	brave′
	IV(*huilen*)	$cry_1′$
	IV(*schreeuwen*)	$cry_2′$
	IV(*lachen*)	laugh′
2.	syntactic rules	meaning rules
	$R_{Dutch}1$: N(α) + ADJ(β) $\Rightarrow$ NP(βe αs)	S1
	$R_{Dutch}2$: IV(α) $\Rightarrow$ VP(α)	S2
	$R_{Dutch}3$: IV(α) $\Rightarrow$ VP(α *niet*)	S3
	$R_{Dutch}4$: VP(α) + NP(β) $\Rightarrow$ S(β α)	S4

We will show how the four modules of the interlingual English - Dutch translation system, based on these grammars, operate for an example input: the sentence *brave girls do not cry*. Since the sentences defined by the grammars have the form S(α), it will be assumed that the input and the output sentences are presented in that format.

(i) The module PARSER$_E$ assigns to the input sentence S(*brave girls do not cry*) the syntactic D-tree for that sentence, according to the syntactic component of G$_{English}$2. In principle, there might be more than one syntactic D-tree, in case of syntactically ambiguous sentences, but in this case there is exactly one tree. Because both *do* and *not* are introduced syncategorematically, no corresponding basic expressions occur in the D-tree:

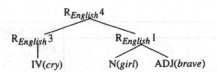

The process of syntactic analysis will be discussed in detail in Section 4.3.4 .

(ii) The module A-TRANSFER$_E$ maps the syntactic D-tree onto a set of semantic D-trees, by replacing each syntactic rule with the corresponding meaning rule and each basic expression with the corresponding basic meanings, according to the semantic component of G$_{English}$2. Because the example sentence of the source language contains a lexical ambiguity (for *cry*), the resulting set will consist of two semantic derivation trees:

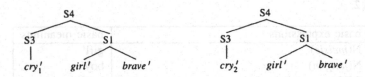

(iii) The module G-TRANSFER$_D$ maps each semantic D-tree onto a set of syntactic D-trees of the target language Dutch, by replacing each meaning rule with the corresponding syntactic rules and each basic meaning with the corresponding basic expressions, according to the semantic component of G$_{Dutch}$2. For this grammar the mapping happens to be one-to-one, but this is very atypical. In a realistic grammar, a basic meaning may correspond to more than one basic expression of the target language (in case of synonyms). Also, and very important for the power of this translation method, a meaning rule may correspond to more than one syntactic rule of the target language. For example, in a more elaborate grammar, S1 would not only be the meaning rule for the combination of an adjective and a noun, but also for the combination of a relative clause and a noun. That is necessary because an adjective may have to be translated into a relative clause (cf. Chapter 13 for a discussion of these categorial divergences). Whether this will actually happen is not known during the local transfer of semantic rule S1 into syntactic rules. So both possibilities must be taken into account. Returning to the example, the output of G-TRANSFER$_D$ is a set of two Dutch syntactic D-trees:

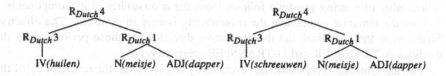

(iv) The module GENERATOR$_D$ executes the rules of the syntactic D-trees in a bottom-up way. First, rule R$_{Dutch}$1 may be applied, then R$_{Dutch}$3, and finally R$_{Dutch}$4 to the output of these rules. The final result is a set of two sentences: S(*dappere meisjes huilen niet*) and S(*dappere meisjes schreeuwen niet*), the possible translations of the input sentence.

4.3.2 Reversibility

We outlined the translation system for English-to-Dutch, but a Dutch-to-English system can be designed in a completely analogous way. These two systems are each other's *reverse*, i.e.: if the Dutch-to-English system translates a sentence *s* into a set of sentences including *s'*, then the English-to-Dutch system translates *s'* into a set of sentences including *s*, and vice versa. This is a consequence of the fact that translation equivalence as defined in Chapter 2 is a symmetric relation and that the Dutch-to-English and the English-to-Dutch systems both implement this relation, but in different directions. The implicit assumption is that the same grammars can indeed be used in both directions, i.e. for generation and for analysis. Grammars that have this property are called *reversible*. This notion will now be defined in terms of the more general notion of an effectively reversible relation.

A *relation*, i.e. a set *R* of pairs (*a, b*), is called *effectively reversible*, if there exist two effective functions: one that for each input *a* produces all elements *b* such that (*a, b*) in *R*, and one that for each input *b* produces all elements *a* such that (*a, b*) in *R*. These two functions are each other's reverse.

A *function* is called *effective* if it can be performed by a finite procedure, which produces the output set in finite time, for any input. Thus, a precondition for effectiveness is that the output set is always finite.

A *grammar*, or a grammar component, is called *reversible* if it defines an effectively reversible relation between representations. In the case of a string grammar this relation is between semantic derivation trees and sentences.

A string grammar consists of a syntactic component which defines a relation between syntactic derivation trees and sentences, and a semantic component which defines a relation between semantic derivation trees and syntactic derivation trees. The reversibility of a string grammar follows from the reversibility of its components.

For the semantic component the reversibility is easy to establish. The effective functions in the analytical and the generative direction are those performed by the modules A-TRANSFER and G-TRANSFER, respectively.

For the syntactic component the reversibility follows from the reversibility of the individual syntactic rules, which will be discussed in Subsection 4.3.3. The modules PARSER and GENERATOR perform the two functions. GENERATOR applies the rules in a syntactic derivation tree and its effectiveness is easy to establish. The way in which PARSER produces the syntactic derivation trees for an input sentence will be discussed in Subsection 4.3.4, its effectiveness in Subsection 4.3.5.

The fact that the Dutch-to-English system and the English-to-Dutch system are each other's reverse follows from the reversibility of their modules.

- PARSER$_D$ is the reverse of GENERATOR$_D$, because they are both based on the same syntactic component of the Dutch grammar. Analogously, PARSER$_E$ is the reverse of GENERATOR$_E$.

- A-TRANSFER$_D$ is the reverse of G-TRANSFER$_D$, because they both implement the same relation defined by the semantic component of the Dutch grammar. Analogously, A-TRANSFER$_E$ is the reverse of G-TRANSFER$_E$.

- From this, it follows immediately that the combinations of the modules in the Dutch to English system and the English to Dutch system, respectively, are each other's reverse. The combination of PARSER$_D$, A-TRANSFER$_D$, G-TRANSFER$_E$ and GENERATOR$_E$ is the reverse of the combination of GENERATOR$_D$, G-TRANSFER$_D$, A-TRANSFER$_E$ and PARSER$_E$.

4.3.3 Reversible rules

In Subsection 4.3.2 it was stipulated that the module PARSER is the reverse of GENERATOR. This is the case because PARSER and GENERATOR make use of the same - reversible - rules, as will be shown in this subsection. The syntactic rules of the string grammars may be simplistic from a linguistic point of view, but from a purely formal point of view they are powerful. They can perform various operations on strings; not only concatenation[1], but they may change the order and may introduce syncategorematic elements. However, in order to make syntactic analysis possible, they must obey one important condition: they must be reversible. The notion of reversibility of rules will now be illustrated by means of the rule from example grammar $G_{English}2$ which constructs a plural noun phrase from a noun and an adjective.

$R_{English}$ 1: $N(\alpha) + ADJ(\beta) \Rightarrow NP(\beta \; \alpha s)$

In Chapter 2 this rule was assigned a generative interpretation: it is applicable to a pair of input expressions if they match the two expressions at the left hand side of the rule. Then α and β get a value and the output can be constructed in the way prescribed by the right hand side of the rule.

But the rule can be interpreted in a more general way: as the definition of a *relation* between pairs of expressions of the form $(N(\alpha), ADJ(\beta))$ and expressions of the form $NP(\beta \; \alpha s)$. This relation is effectively reversible in the sense of Subsection 4.3.2. There is an effective function in the left-to-right direction, corresponding to the generative interpretation described above. There is also an analytical interpretation for the rule, by reading it from right to left. Then it is applicable to an expression of the form $NP(\beta \; \alpha s)$ and produces pairs of expressions of the form $(N(\alpha), ADJ(\beta))$. The expressions to which the rule is applicable must have category NP and the string part must be divided into two parts (where each part is a word or a sequence of words separated by spaces), such that the second part ends with *s*. Thus, it is applicable to expressions like NP(*brave boys*), but also to NP(*Porgy worries about Bess*), and not to NP(*brave boy*) or to NP(*Bess worries about Porgy*).

An important property of rule $R_{English}$ 1, which illustrates its relational nature, is that - under the analytical interpretation - it may be applicable in more than one way. If it is applied to NP(*Porgy worries about Bess*), there are three ways to split the string into the parts β and αs: *Porgy* + *worries about Bess*, *Porgy worries* + *about Bess*, *Porgy worries about* + *Bess*. Each possible application of the analytical rule yields a pair of results:

$N(\alpha) + ADJ(\beta)$

In this case the output consists of three pairs:

N(*worries about Bes*) + ADJ(*Porgy*),
N(*about Bes*) + ADJ(*Porgy worries*),

---

[1] If the only operation on the strings is concatenation, the rules of string grammars are equivalent to context-free rules. In that case the reversibility of the rules is obvious.

N(*Bes*) + ADJ(*Porgy worries about*).

Intuitively, none of these output expressions is correct, but that cannot be decided by this rule. It has only a limited responsibility. It is up to the remainder of the grammar to decide whether its output is correct. Note that the same holds, mutatis mutandis, for the generative rule. It would also be applicable to N(*about Bes*) and ADJ(*Porgy worries*). The only difference is that, during generation, the rule will never get such input expressions, because these must have been constructed by other syntactic rules (or must be basic expressions), and thus will be correct expressions according to the grammar. On the other hand, application of an analytical rule always has a tentative nature: according to analytical rule $R_{English}1$, expression NP(*Porgy worries about Bess*) is correct if the output expressions, N(*about Bes*) and ADJ(*Porgy worries*), are correct. The analysis algorithm will be discussed further in the next section.

In the example grammars the possibility that a rule is multiply applicable only occurs under the analytical interpretation, but in principle this can also be the case in the generative direction. For example, we can imagine a rule which is intended to construct the negated form of a sentence as follows:

$$S(\alpha \ \beta) \Rightarrow S(\alpha \ do \ not \ \beta)$$

The intended use of the rule could be to apply to expressions like S(*brave boys laugh*) and to turn it into S(*brave boys do not laugh*), but the rule would also have an unintended interpretation, yielding S(*brave do not boys laugh*).

Although multiply applicable rules are allowed, they must obey the requirement that they can only be applied in a finite number of ways, because otherwise the rule application will never terminate for certain inputs. An example of a rule which has an infinite number of results under the analytical interpretation, would be:

$$S(Mary \ knows \ \alpha) \Rightarrow S(Mary \ knows)$$

From left to right there is no problem: for each input there is only a finite number of matches and for each of them the α part is simply deleted, but from right to left the rule has an infinite set of results, for all imaginable strings α.

Summarising, a syntactic rule must be reversible, i.e. it must define a relation which obeys the conditions on effectively reversible relations formulated in Subsection 4.3.2. Then the rule has both a generative and an analytical interpretation, and the set of results in each direction is finite, for any possible input. The rules of grammars $G_{English}2$ and $G_{Dutch}2$, presented in Subsection 4.3.1, are all reversible.

4.3.4 Parsing with a reversible string grammar

The way in which the module PARSER applies the reversible rules will now be discussed in some detail. Although string rules are not used in the actual Rosetta system, the top-down way in which they are applied by the parser is quite similar to the way M-rules are applied in the parser of the Rosetta system.

The task of PARSER is, for a given grammar and a given input sentence, to construct the set of syntactic D-trees that would generate this sentence. This is done by applying the reversible syntactic rules in the analytical direction. The analysis process will be illustrated by following step by step the actions needed for analysing the familiar sentence *brave girls do not cry*, offered to the parser in the form: S(*brave girls do not cry*). So it is hypothesised that the input is an S, and the parser will try to confirm this hypothesis for a given grammar, in this case $G_{English}2$.

There are two possible ways in which an expression can be parsed successfully:

  (i) it is a basic expression,

 (ii) an analytical rule is applicable and the outputs of the rule can be successfully parsed.

S(*brave girls do not cry*) is not a basic expression. So a rule must be found of which the right hand side matches the input. There are four candidate rules:

$R_{English}1$: $N(\alpha) + ADJ(\beta) \Rightarrow NP(\beta \; \alpha s)$
$R_{English}2$: $IV(\alpha) \Rightarrow VP(\alpha)$
$R_{English}3$: $IV(\alpha) \Rightarrow VP(\; do \; not \; \alpha)$
$R_{English}4$: $VP(\alpha) + NP(\beta) \Rightarrow S(\beta \; \alpha)$

Only analytical rule $R_{English}4$ is applicable to an expression with category S. The rule prescribes that the input string has to be split up in two parts. There are four ways to do this:

(i)	VP(*girls do not cry*)	+	NP(*brave*)
(ii)	VP(*do not cry*)	+	NP(*brave girls*)
(iii)	VP(*not cry*)	+	NP(*brave girls do*)
(iv)	VP(*cry*)	+	NP(*brave girls do not*)

Which of these alternative decompositions will turn out to be the first step of a successful parse, has to be determined by further application of the parser. That is, by trying to confirm each of the hypotheses introduced.

In the case of alternative (i) the outputs are VP(*girls do not cry*) and NP(*brave*). The VP is not a basic expression, but there is an applicable rule: $R_{English}2$, which is applicable to any VP and turns it into a IV. However, the result, IV(*girls do not cry*), is not a basic expression and there is no rule applicable to it. So this is a dead end path. In fact, this makes it unnecessary to inspect whether NP(*brave*) could be parsed. But if this is tried anyway, the result is another dead end path, because the NP is not a basic expression and the only analytical rule for NP, rule $R_{English}1$ fails to match, because *brave* lacks the required suffix -*s*. For similar reasons, alternative (iii) fails. Alternative (iv) fails too: VP(*cry*) can be parsed, but the analysis of the NP fails.

Alternative (ii) turns out to be the only correct path:

- To VP(*do not cry*) rule $R_{English}2$ and $R_{English}3$ are both applicable. Application of $R_{English}2$ yields IV(*do not cry*). This is again a dead end. Application of $R_{English}3$ yields IV(*cry*), which is a basic expression. So this is a successful path.

- To NP(*brave girls*) $R_{English}1$ is applicable. It produces N(*girl*) and ADJ(*brave*), which are both basic expressions. So this is a successful path too and therefore it can be decided that rule $R_{English}4$, alternative (ii), was the start of a successful analysis and indeed the only one.

The successful analysis can be resumed as follows:

$R_{English}4$: S(*brave girls do not cry*) $\Rightarrow$
                VP(*do not cry*) + NP(*brave girls*)
$R_{English}3$: VP(*do not cry*) $\Rightarrow$ IV(*cry*)
$R_{English}1$: NP(*brave girls*) $\Rightarrow$ N(*girl*) + ADJ(*brave*)

This can be depicted in the following D-tree, which is indeed the syntactic derivation tree of the sentence.

So PARSER fulfills its task: to find for an input sentence the D-trees that would derive it.

The crucial advantage of reversible rules is: although conceived and written in a generative way, they can be used for analysis as well. Given a grammar for a specific language, the modules PARSER and GENERATOR implement the same relation between expressions and derivation trees, but in reverse directions. This has been illustrated for an example sentence. For an actual proof, more precise definitions of the rules and the modules would be needed. Such definitions will be provided for M-grammars in Chapter 17.

4.3.5   Measure condition

One aspect of PARSER still has to be discussed: it must terminate in finite time. Without further conditions on the syntactic rules this cannot be guaranteed. E.g., if a rule

$R_{English}6: \text{VP}(\alpha) \Rightarrow \text{IV}(\alpha)$

were to be added to the grammar, which already contains rule

$R_{English}2: \text{IV}(\alpha) \Rightarrow \text{VP}(\alpha)$

the parser might run into an eternal loop, constantly applying $R_{English}2$, then $R_{English}6$, then $R_{English}2$ again, etc., without making any progress.

A way to guarantee that PARSER terminates after a finite number of steps - for any possible input - is a so-called *measure condition*. First a measure function must be defined, which assigns to each expression a positive integer, its measure. Then it is required that an analytical rule produces output expressions smaller than its input expression, according to this measure. This guarantees that, after a finite number of rule applications, the measure of the produced S-trees must be 0 and the analysis process must stop. For example grammar $G_{English}2$ an adequate measure could be defined as follows: all expressions with lexical categories (i.e. N, IV, ADJ) get measure 0, for all other expressions the measure is the length of the string. Of course, for a simple grammar like $G_{English}2$ a measure is not really needed, because it is immediately clear that the analysis process will terminate. But this is not so easy to decide for more complicated grammars with various types of recursion.

4.4   A translation system based on M-grammars: Rosetta

In the previous sections, the design of a translation system based on isomorphic string grammars was discussed. This section will discuss the design of the actual Rosetta system, which is based on isomorphic M-grammars, as defined in Chapter 3. It will be shown how the modules of the Rosetta system are derived from the three components of an M-grammar. First the definitions of these components are recapitulated.

1. The **syntactic component** defines a relation between syntactic derivation trees and S-trees. It is analogous to the syntactic component of a string grammar

in that it specifies basic expressions and compositional syntactic rules. The important difference is that the syntactic rules (the M-rules) operate on S-trees rather than strings: the basic expressions of an M-grammar are simple S-trees, called basic S-trees, and the final result of a derivation is a surface tree, an S-tree that represents the surface structure of a sentence. Syntactic derivation trees (D-trees) play a similar role as in string grammars: they are explicit representations of the way in which a surface tree is derived from basic S-trees by application of M-rules.

The 'leaves' of a surface tree correspond to words. Because words may have internal structure, these leaves need not be terminal nodes, but are so-called lexical S-trees, which may consist of more than one node. A separate function is needed that collects the sequence of lexical S-trees from the hierarchical surface tree. This function is called LEAVES. It can recognise the lexical S-trees by their specific lexical categories (N, V, ADJ, etc.). If an arbitrary path is followed from the top of a surface tree to the terminal nodes, a node labelled by a lexical category will always be met and then the subtree under this node is a lexical S-tree.

The M-rules have a more complicated notation than the string grammar rules, but they are similar to them in two respects: (i) their applicability depends on a kind of pattern match and therefore they may be multiply applicable, (ii) they are reversible, i.e. each rule can be applied in the generative direction and in the analytical direction.

2. The **morphological component** defines the relation between the lexical S-trees which occur as leaves in a surface tree and actual spelled-out words. This relation is defined by means of morphological rules and by a dictionary that relates word stems to the corresponding S-trees. In most cases these are basic S-trees, but the dictionary also includes lexical S-trees for words that do not correspond to basic expressions, because they are introduced syncategorematically by M-rules.

3. The **semantic component** defines a relation between syntactic derivation trees and semantic derivation trees. It is completely analogous to the semantic component of the string grammars. For each syntactic rule there is a meaning rule and for each basic expression there is a set of basic meanings. What is considered a meaning rule or a basic meaning is decided not on purely semantic grounds, but more generally by deciding what is translation-relevant information. Only the unique names of these meaning rules and basic meanings are specified.

Summarising, an M-grammar defines a relation between semantic derivation trees and sentences. The semantic component relates semantic derivation trees to syntactic derivation trees; the syntactic component relates syntactic derivation trees to sequences of lexical S-trees, via surface trees; the morphological component relates sequences of lexical S-trees to sequences of word forms that constitute sentences.

Isomorphy of M-grammars is defined in the same way as for string grammars: the semantic components should establish a translation-equivalence relation between the basic S-trees and between M-rules of the grammars. Two sentences are considered translation-equivalent if they correspond to the same semantic derivation tree.

4.4.1 Reversibility of M-grammars

An important property of an M-grammar is that the relation it defines between semantic derivation trees and sentences, is reversible, i.e. that it defines two effective functions: a generation function from semantic derivation trees to sentences and an analysis function from sentences to semantic derivation trees. The reversibility of an M-grammar follows from the reversibility of its three components. We will discuss this for each grammar component separately.

Reversibility of the grammar components and the corresponding system modules

1. Reversibility of the syntactic component.

    At first sight, establishing the reversibility of this component is not problematic. A generative module, called M-GENERATOR, can be defined which applies the generative M-rules in the D-tree to the basic S-trees, in a 'bottom-up' way. If all rules are applicable, the result is a surface tree. Because M-rules may be applicable in more than one way, it is in fact a set of surface trees. An analytical module, called M-PARSER, can be defined which applies the analytical M-rules to the surface tree, in a top-down fashion. During this analysis process a syntactic D-tree is constructed, which is an explicit representation of the rules that have been applied and of the resulting basic expressions.

    The modules M-GENERATOR and M-PARSER operate in a similar way as the modules GENERATOR and PARSER for string grammars, described in Section 4.3. That M-PARSER is the reverse of M-GENERATOR follows from the reversibility of the M-rules. In order to guarantee termination of M-PARSER we impose a measure condition, in the same way as for string grammars. In this case an example of a measure could be the number of nodes in an S-tree. [2]

---

[2] In large grammars, the definition of an adequate measure becomes a problem. In Chapter 9 a modular version of M-grammars will be introduced, for which this problem is much easier to solve, as will be explained in Chapter 17.

So, with respect to the reversibility of M-GENERATOR and M-PARSER there is perfect analogy with the reversibility of GENERATOR and PARSER for string grammars. However, the syntactic component also includes the function LEAVES, which maps a surface tree onto its sequence of lexical S-trees. So, during generation, the module M-GENERATOR has to be followed by a module LEAVES. Then one would expect that during analysis the module M-PARSER would be preceded by the reverse of LEAVES, which would produce the surface trees that M-PARSER expects as input. The strict reverse of LEAVES would map a sequence of lexical S-trees onto the set of all possible S-trees with these lexical S-trees as leaves. The problem is that this is an infinite set. We will return to this problem after discussing the reversibility of the other components.

2. Reversibility of the morphological component.

This component is discussed in Chapter 6. The morphological rules are reversible and due to this, the morphological component defines two modules: G-MORPH and A-MORPH, which are each other's reverse. In generation, G-MORPH maps a sequence of lexical S-trees onto a set of sentences. In analysis, A-MORPH maps the input sentence onto a set of sequences of lexical S-trees.

3. Reversibility of the semantic component.

The modules G-TRANSFER and A-TRANSFER can be derived from the semantic component in the same way as described in Section 4.3 for string grammars. G-TRANSFER maps a semantic D-tree onto a set of syntactic D-trees and A-TRANSFER performs the reverse function.

The 'reverse' of LEAVES

It has already been stated that there can be no reverse module for LEAVES in analysis, because the reverse of LEAVES would yield an infinite number of S-trees. LEAVES is applied to the surface trees yielded by M-GENERATOR and therefore it need not check the well-formedness of these surface trees. It simply follows the paths from the top of the surface tree to the lexical S-trees (the subtrees with a lexical category: N, V, ADJ, etc.), deleting all other information in the surface tree. So LEAVES is applicable to any S-tree of which the 'leaves' are lexical S-trees. As a consequence the reverse of LEAVES would have to map a sequence of lexical S-trees to the set of all S-trees that could be constructed on top of these, without any further restriction. This is obviously an infinite set, including incorrect and even completely nonsensical S-trees.

For example, LEAVES is applicable to (1), a somewhat simplified surface tree for the sentence *John smokes cigars*, but also to the nonsense tree (2). In both cases the result of applying LEAVES would be the sequence of lexical S-trees (3).

(1)   S   [subj / NP [head / N(*John*)],
             head / V(*smokes*),
             obj / NP [head / N(*cigars*)]
      ]

(2)   S   [obj / S   [subj / N(*John*),
                              subj / V(*smokes*)],
             head / N(*cigars*)
      ]

(3) N(*John*), V(*smokes*), N(*cigars*)

If the reverse function for LEAVES were to be applied to (3), the result would be an infinite set, including not only (1), but also trees like (2). Obviously, this would not be an effective function. Fortunately, for an adequate analysis a module that performs this function is not needed. It is sufficient to have an analysis module that, in combination with M-PARSER, performs a function that is the reverse of the combination of M-GENERATOR and LEAVES. This module, which is called S-PARSER (Surface Parser) should assign a finite set of tentative surface trees to any sequence of lexical S-trees. It should assign all correct surface trees to its input, but in addition it may assign incorrect surface trees, too, and it may also accept incorrect sentences. M-PARSER is applied subsequently; by applying the analytical M-rules it will reject the incorrect S-trees and it will only yield syntactic derivation trees for the correct S-trees.

S-PARSER can make use of syntax rules, called *surface rules*, which are much simpler than the M-rules of M-PARSER, because S-PARSER can be less selective than M-PARSER.

The surface rules in the Rosetta system are equivalent to context-free rules with additional conditions and operations on the attribute values. They are described in Chapter 8. S-PARSER can use standard context-free parsing algorithms, such as the Earley parser. Within the conditions formulated above, the exact choice of surface rules is to some extent arbitrary. There is a trade-off between making them very simple and tolerant, which may result in many outputs of S-PARSER (and therefore many inputs for M-PARSER), and making them as precise as possible, which comes down to a duplication of effort.

A simple example of this trade-off is provided by the rules for agreement between the subject and the finite verb in English. The M-rules will have to adjust the number of the verb to the number of the subject. The surface rule writer has the choice between being tolerant and allowing any combination of subject and verb with respect to number, or being more precise and taking the agreement into account. The more tolerant version of S-PARSER will assign a surface tree to the sequence of lexical S-trees (3), but also to (4).

(4)   N(*John*), V(*smoke*), N(*cigars*)

The surface tree for (4) will be rejected by M-PARSER. Other examples of over-acceptance of S-PARSER will be given in Chapter 8.

Surface rules are indispensable for analysis, but for the definition of the correct sentences of the language they are redundant. Although S-PARSER is not the reverse of LEAVES, the combination of S-PARSER and M-PARSER is the reverse of the combination of M-GENERATOR and LEAVES.

The reversibility of an M-grammar can now be established as follows.

- The morphological component defines the analysis module A-MORPH and the generation module G-MORPH, which are each other's reverse.

- The syntactic component defines the analysis modules S-PARSER and M-PARSER and the generation modules M-GENERATOR and LEAVES. The combination of these two analysis modules is the reverse of the combination of the two generation modules.

- The semantic component defines the analysis module A-TRANSFER and the generation module G-TRANSFER, which are each other's reverse.

- The analysis function is performed by subsequent application of the modules A-MORPH, S-PARSER, M-PARSER and A-TRANSFER. The generation function is performed by subsequent application of the modules G-TRANSFER, M-GENERATOR, LEAVES and G-MORPH. It follows that the analysis function and the generation function defined by an M-grammar are each other's reverse.

4.4.2 Global design of the Rosetta system

The previous subsections explained how the functionality of the modules for analysis and generation can be derived from the definition of an M-grammar (For more formal definitions we refer to Chapter 17, for information about the actual implementation to Chapter 20). Given isomorphic M-grammars for a source language, SL, and a target language, TL, a translation system can be designed, which combines the analysis function for SL and the generation function for TL. The analysis function is performed by the modules A-MORPH$_{SL}$, S-PARSER$_{SL}$, M-PARSER$_{SL}$

and A-TRANSFER$_{SL}$; the generation function is performed by the modules G-TRANSFER$_{TL}$, M-GENERATOR$_{TL}$, LEAVES$_{TL}$ and G-MORPH$_{TL}$. These eight modules constitute the Rosetta system, as presented in Figure 4.3.

Obviously, the same two M-grammars can also be the basis of the reverse system, from TL to SL.

In the remainder of this section the task of each of the modules will be outlined. It should be noticed that we describe the modules here from a purely functional point of view, abstracting away from implementation details. For example, the output of a module is simply considered a set of expressions and each expression is processed separately by the next module. In the actual implementation these sets are usually represented and processed more efficiently by making use of 'shared storage', but such aspects are ignored here.

The tasks of the eight modules, in order of application, are:

- **A-MORPH.** This module converts the words of the input sentence into lexical S-trees, by means of a dictionary for stems and morphological rules for inflection and derivation. So A-MORPH produces a set of lexical S-trees for each word and, as a consequence, a set of sequences of lexical S-trees for each sentence. Note that lexical semantic ambiguities are dealt with by A-MORPH only if they correspond to morphosyntactic differences. In principle, purely semantic ambiguities could be spelled out here as well (in that case basic expressions would always have exactly one meaning), but in the actual system this step is postponed until A-TRANSFER, which has the advantage of alleviating the task of S-PARSER and M-PARSER.

- **S-PARSER.** Each sequence of lexical S-trees that is output of A-MORPH is parsed by this module, by means of surface rules. For each input sequence that is accepted by S-PARSER the result is a non-empty set of S-trees, possible surface trees for the input.

- **M-PARSER.** This module analyses each surface tree by applying analytical M-rules. Each successful parse produces a syntactic derivation tree, the leaves of which are names of basic expressions and the other nodes of which are labelled with the names of the M-rules that have been applied. M-PARSER may produce more than one syntactic derivation tree for an input S-tree, if it discovers an ambiguity that was not visible at the surface level. On the other hand, it will filter out incorrect input S-trees. The result of M-PARSER, for each input S-tree, is a set of syntactic derivation trees.

- **A-TRANSFER.** This module converts each syntactic derivation tree into a set of semantic derivation trees of the interlingua. Each M-rule name in the syntactic derivation tree is replaced by a semantic rule name and each basic expression name is replaced by one or more names of basic meanings.

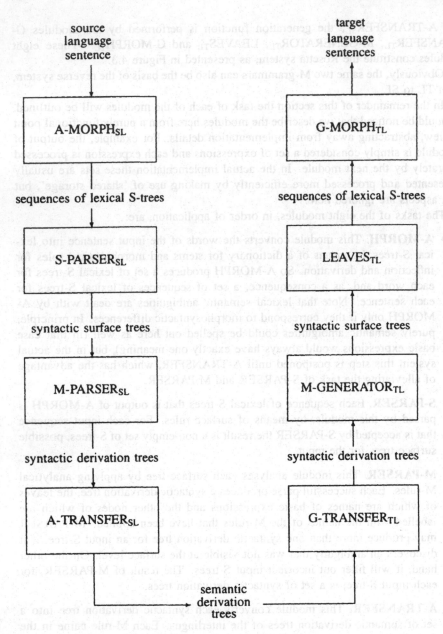

Figure 4.3: Global design of the Rosetta system.

- **G-TRANSFER**. This module converts each semantic derivation tree into a set of syntactic derivation trees. A meaning rule name in the semantic derivation tree is replaced by one or more M-rule names of the target language and the names of basic meanings are replaced by names of basic expressions of the target language.

- **M-GENERATOR**. The input of M-GENERATOR is a set of syntactic derivation trees. For each derivation tree, M-GENERATOR replaces the names of basic expressions by the actual basic S-trees and then tries to apply the rules in the tree. A successful application of M-GENERATOR to a syntactic derivation tree yields one or more surface trees (S-trees).

- **LEAVES**. This module extracts the leaves of each surface tree, i.e. the subtrees with specific lexical categories at the top. The result is a sequence of lexical S-trees for each input surface tree.

- **G-MORPH**. The lexical S-trees are converted into words (strings) by applying morphological rules. The result is a sentence of the target language.

In this book the Rosetta system is usually considered a translator of *sentences*. In fact, it is also capable of translating other expressions, for example noun phrases. Henceforth we will also use *utterance* as a term that generalises over the various types of input that are allowed.

4.5 The Rosetta modules at work

In the preceding sections the modules have been introduced that together perform
the analytical and generative functions in the process of translation. This section
describes the interface expressions of each of the modules on the basis of the translation of the Dutch sentence (5a) into its English counterpart (5b).

(5) a Er   kwam een auto voorbij
     There came a   car   past

   b A car passed

The operations that will be mentioned in the explanation below exemplify the actual
M-grammars in a highly simplified way.

1. First, for each word of the input expression (5a) the syntactic category and
   other syntactic properties must be determined on the basis of lexical information and a morphological analysis. This task is performed by the morphological
   module A-MORPH which takes word forms as input and, for each word form,
   yields one or more **lexical S-trees** as output. In case of an inflected word,
   e.g. a noun or a verb, the corresponding lexical S-tree consists of a basic
   expression dominated by a node containing the information expressed by the
   inflectional affixes. In the case of compounds and/or derivational affixes a
   lexical S-tree consists of more than one basic expression.

   In (5a) there are two word forms that are mapped onto more than one lexical S-tree, namely *kwam* and *voorbij*. The word form *kwam* is mapped onto
   the lexical S-tree for the verb *komen*, but also to the lexical S-tree for the verb
   voorbijkomen. The latter analysis only makes sense if the particle *voorbij* occurs elsewhere in the sentence. The word form *voorbij* does indeed occur, but
   it may belong to three different syntactic categories. Checking which of the
   six combinations is correct is not the task of A-MORPH, but of the modules
   for syntactic analysis.[3]

   The dictionary consulted by A-MORPH assigns lexical S-trees to all word
   stems, including those that do not correspond to basic S-trees, because they
   are introduced syncategorematically. The adverb *er* and the article *een* are
   examples of this. We will see that their lexical S-trees occur as leaves in the
   surface tree constructed by S-PARSER, but not as basic expressions in the
   D-tree constructed by M-PARSER.

---

[3] In fact *kwam* is much more ambiguous than described here, because *voorbij* is only one of the many
particles that may occur with *komen*. In the actual implementation this ambiguity is immediately reduced
by checking which of these particles are actually present in the sentence.

A-MORPH	
input	output
er	ADV [head/BADV{key:ER, subclass:existential, ... }]
kwam	1. V{tense:pasttense, ...}
	[head/BV{key:VOORBIJKOMEN,
	particle:VOORBIJ, ...}]
	2. V{number:singular, tense:pasttense,...}
	[head/BV{key:KOMEN,
	particle: noparticle, ...}]
een	ART{key:EEN, possnumber:singular, definite:indef, ...}
auto	N{number:singular, ...}
	[head/BN{key:AUTO, temporal:false, ...}],
voorbij	1. PART{key:VOORBIJ }
	2. PREP{key:VOORBIJ, subclass:locative, ...},
	3. ADJ [head/BADJ{key:VOORBIJ,
	subclass:predicative, ...}]

2. The output of A-MORPH is input for the second module, S-PARSER, the
surface parser, which yields one or more S-trees. These are candidate surface
trees: constituent structures that accommodate the syntactic categories found
for each word form. S-PARSER may disambiguate part of the output of A-
MORPH. In this example, only the combination of *kwam* interpreted as part of
the verb *voorbijkomen* and the particle interpretation of *voorbij* is compatible
with the rest of the sentence, so the six-fold path resulting from A-MORPH
will be reduced to one after S-PARSER has been applied. S-tree 6 presents
the output of S-PARSER in a somewhat reduced form, in which the attribute-
value pairs have been omitted.

S-PARSER	
input	output
ADV(*er*)	S-tree (6)
V(*komen/voorbij*), V(*komen*)	
ART(*een*)	
N(*auto*)	
PART(*voorbij*), PREP(*voorbij*), ADJ(*voorbij*)	

(6)

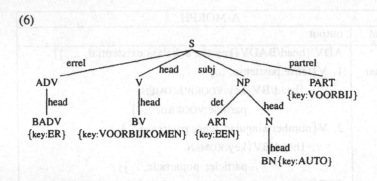

3. The S-trees that are output of S-PARSER are input for the third module,
M-PARSER, the analytical function of M-grammar. As indicated above, M-
PARSER yields a set of D-trees, one for every possible analysis of the input
S-tree. For this example we will assume that the analysis of (6) results in only
one D-tree: (7).

M-PARSER	
input	output
S-tree (6)	syntactic D-tree (7)

(7)

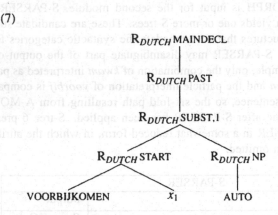

D-tree (7) indicates what analytical M-rules have been applied successfully.
First, the rules R_{DUTCH} MAINDECL and R_{DUTCH} PAST have detected that (6) is
an S-tree of a declarative sentence in the past tense and have turned the values
of the attributes mood and tense into 'undefined' values. Rule R_{DUTCH} SUBST.1
has decomposed the S-tree for *er komen een auto voorbij* into S-trees for

voorbijkomen x_1 and *een auto*. These have been further analysed by rules R_{DUTCH} START and R_{DUTCH} NP, respectively, resulting in basic expressions for the words *voorbijkomen* and *auto*, the keys of which, VOORBIJKOMEN and AUTO, occur in the D-tree. As indicated by their absence as leaves of D-tree (7), *er* and *een* have not been treated as basic expressions, but have been dealt with syncategorematically.

4. Next, the analytical module A-TRANSFER replaces the syntactic rules in syntactic D-tree (7) with meaning rules and the keys of the basic expressions with the keys of basic meanings. The result is a set of semantic D-trees. Usually, this set contains more than one tree, which is mainly due to lexical ambiguities. As has already been mentioned, the ambiguities dealt with in A-TRANSFER are purely semantic ambiguities, which do not correspond to morphosyntactic differences. The basic expressions in this example are assumed to have only one meaning.

A-TRANSFER	
input	output
syntactic D-tree (7)	semantic D-tree (8)

(8)

MDECLMOOD
|
MPASTTENSE
|
MSUBST,1

MSTART   MNP

3_0892   X 1   2_3827

The leaves of semantic D-trees are either semantic variables or keys representing the basic meanings. In (8) 3_0892 is the meaning key for *voorbijkomen* and its translations, while 2_3827 is the meaning key for *auto* and its translations.

5. G-TRANSFER transforms the semantic D-tree that is the output of A-TRANSFER, into a set of syntactic D-trees specifying: (i) which keys of basic expressions

of the English grammar correspond to the keys of basic meanings in the semantic D-tree, and (ii) which rules of the English grammar correspond to the meaning rules. Usually, this is a one-to-many mapping, but here this complication is ignored and only one syntactic D-tree is displayed.

G-TRANSFER	
input	output
semantic D-tree (8)	syntactic D-tree (9)

(9)

$$R_{ENGLISH}\text{MAINDECL}$$

$$R_{ENGLISH}\text{PAST}$$

$$R_{ENGLISH}\text{SUBST,1}$$

$$R_{ENGLISH}\text{START} \qquad R_{ENGLISH}\text{NP}$$

PASS x 1   CAR

The fact that D-tree (7) is not directly mapped onto D-tree (9), but via the semantic derivation tree (8) is in accordance with the interlingual approach that we adopted. This was explained in Section 4.2 and will be further discussed in Chapter 5.

6. The syntactic derivation tree (9), which is yielded by G-TRANSFER, is the input for the module M-GENERATOR. Here the generative versions of the M-rules are applied. This module yields surface trees.

M-GENERATOR	
input	output
syntactic D-tree (9)	S-tree (10)

(10)

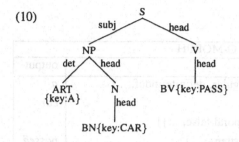

First, the keys in the D-tree are replaced by the actual basic expressions. Then the rules are applied in a bottom-up order. Rule $R_{ENGLISH}$ START combines basic expressions PASS and x_1 into an S-tree for x_1 *pass*. Rule $R_{ENGLISH}$ NP forms the NP *a car* by introducing the indefinite article syncategorematically. Then this NP is substituted for the variable by rule $R_{ENGLISH}$ SUBST,1. Rule $R_{ENGLISH}$ PAST assigns the past tense to the sentence: the tense attribute of the V is assigned the value *pasttense*. Finally, rule $R_{ENGLISH}$ MAINDECL assigns the declarative mood.

7. Next, the output of M-GENERATOR, surface tree (10), is mapped onto its sequence of lexical S-trees. This task is performed by the module LEAVES. Mark again the difference between S-PARSER and LEAVES. In analysis, a sequence of lexical S-trees may be analysed in several ways by S-PARSER, resulting in a set of surface trees. In generation, LEAVES simply produces the sequence of lexical S-trees contained in the surface tree.

LEAVES	
input	output
S-tree (10)	ART{key:A, possnumber:singular, definite:indef,...}
	N{number:singular, ...}
	[head/BN{key:CAR, temporal:false, ...}]
	V{number:singular, tense:pasttense,...}
	[head/BV{key:PASS, ...}]

8. Finally, the lexical S-trees, consisting of the basic expressions plus the information on the proper word form, are converted into the lexical strings of the resulting translation. This task is performed by the module G-MORPH, which maps the basic expressions to the corresponding symbol strings, e.g. *pass*, and applies the relevant morphological rules, e.g. for the formation of the past

tense of *pass*: *passed*.

G-MORPH	
input	output
ART{key:A, possnumber:singular, definite:indef, ...}	*a*
N{number:singular, ...}	*car*
[head/BN{key:CAR, temporal:false, ...}]	
V{number:singular, tense:pasttense,...}	*passed*
[head/BV{key:PASS, ...}]	

In the translation example discussed above several divergencies between Dutch and English had to be coped with. This has been achieved by tuning the M-grammars of the two languages. For these simple grammars the chosen way of tuning is to a certain extent arbitrary. In larger grammars the decisions about the way of tuning are made more systematically, trying to yield the simplest account of the relevant facts. Numerous examples of tuning will be discussed extensively in Chapters 12 – 16 .

4.6 Concluding remarks

This chapter has shown that the design of an interlingual translation system can be derived in a straightforward way from the compositional definition of translation equivalence, through isomorphic grammars. This design was outlined and the interfaces between the modules of the system were illustrated by means of an example.

The transition from translation relation to translation process has been discussed first for simple string grammars and then for M-grammars. In both cases the system yields a set of possible translations for each input sentence, in accordance with the way the translation relation is defined by the isomorphic grammars. Therefore, the main virtue of the way the translation relation was defined pertains to the translation system: for sentences within the scope of the grammar it is guaranteed that the meaning is preserved during translation.

Chapter 5

The Rosetta characteristics

5.1 Introduction

This chapter will summarise and discuss the characteristics of the method of compositional translation that has been presented in the previous chapters. This method has been used for the development of the Rosetta machine translation systems since 1981 and will be referred to often as the 'Rosetta approach or method'. The Rosetta characteristics will be compared with characteristics and notions of other important machine translation approaches or theories. The comparison will be made at a theoretical level and will not involve the actual performance of particular systems and only aspects within the limited goals formulated in Chapter 1 will be discussed. Sometimes, specific machine translation systems will be mentioned as examples, but this chapter does not offer a review of existing machine translation systems. For such a review, the reader is referred to, for example, Hutchins (1986) and Hutchins and Somers (1992).

The Rosetta approach, as presented in previous chapters, can be considered as a combination of five characteristics:

1. Explicit grammars for both source and target language.
   Chapter 2 explained that, for an adequate definition of the translation relation, explicit grammars are needed.

2. Compositional grammars with powerful syntactic rules.
   In Chapter 2 *compositional* grammars have been chosen, adopting the principle of compositionality of meaning, and Chapter 3 has argued for *powerful syntactic* rules.

85

3. Reversible grammars or one grammar for each language in both directions.
   Chapter 4 showed that the grammar rules can be used for analysis as well as
   generation. Then, only one reversible grammar for each language is needed.

4. Attuned or isomorphic grammars.
   The tuning of grammars is the most remarkable characteristic of the Rosetta
   approach. It is the realisation of the principle of compositional translation
   presented in Chapter 2.

5. Translation is done via an interlingua.
   Sentences that are translation-equivalent share a semantic derivation tree. Such
   semantic derivation trees may play the role of interlingua in an MT system,
   as was explained in Chapter 4.

Together they form the basic 'working principles' that served as guidelines for the
development of the Rosetta systems. They have been presented in various papers
(for example, cf. Appelo and Landsbergen (1986); Appelo *et al.* (1987); De Jong
and Appelo (1987); and Odijk (1992))

This chapter will discuss each of these characteristics in some more detail, paying
most attention to the tuning of grammars, which is the most distinctive aspect of
this approach. But it will start by comparing the Rosetta notion of *compositionality
of translation* with other opinions on this notion.

5.2   Other views on compositionality of translation

The observation that different languages are more alike in their derivational histories
than in their surface appearance has also been made by others. Dowty *et al.* (1981)
discuss the similarity of the derivational histories in English, Breton, Japanese and
Latin. Curry, in a paper about mathematical foundations of language (cf. Curry
(1963)), was one of the first to point to the relationship between natural languages
in this respect. The notion *isomorphy* has already been discussed in Carnap (1947)
in the context of a discussion on *synonymy* of complex expressions which are required to be *equivalent* and *intensionally isomorphic*. Translation-equivalence can
be considered a special kind of synonymy, in the sense that expressions belonging
to different languages share a meaning. The Rosetta approach is in accordance with
Carnap's definitions. However, Carnap used a very simple arithmetical example to
illustrate his ideas for which it was almost trivial to decide on the presence or absence
of synonymy. In natural language, the notions synonymy and isomorphy are less
straightforward to define because, on the level of surface syntax, there are numerous
sources of mismatches between languages. See De Jong and Appelo(1987) for more
details on the comparison between the Rosetta approach and Carnap's definitions.

The formulation 'principle of compositionality of translation' can also be found in Nagao (1989), where it was defined very loosely, and in publications on the Eurotra project, such as, for example, Arnold *et al.* (1985, 1986).

Nagao (1989) argues for compositionality of translation as follows: as it is impossible for a translation system to store all possible combinations and their translations as separate entities, compound expressions have to be broken down into more fundamental units, and a one-to-one translation is made at that level. It will be obvious that most current translation systems are built on the principle of compositionality of translation in this very global sense.

In the English-to-Japanese system presented in Nagao (1989), an English sentence is analysed, resulting in some kind of abstract, syntactic structure. After that, an 'interlingual transformation rule' is applied which changes the English sentence structure into a Japanese sentence structure. Such a rule may change the order of elements, as well as remove or introduce them. If a phrase cannot be treated in terms of the global principle of compositionality, it is treated as an idiom. This view of compositionality of translation shows three main differences with the method of compositional translation presented in this book. In the first place, a transfer system is described and not an interlingual approach. So, comparing the two approaches, one should consider for the Rosetta approach the transfer system as described in Chapter 4 with transfer between derivational trees. The next difference is that in Nagao's system transfer is performed at the level of some kind of syntactic structure and not at the level of semantically motivated derivational histories. Furthermore, his transfer may perform structural changes, which is not allowed in the Rosetta approach with transfer between derivational trees.

In the Eurotra project, a system is developed that translates between all nine EC languages. Since the start of the project in 1978, several approaches for the design of that system have been proposed by several research groups. One of those proposals was the CAT framework (cf. Arnold *et al.* (1985, 1986); Arnold and des Tombe (1987); and Des Tombe (1985)) which is based upon 'compositionality of translation'.[1] In that framework, the translation from source language to target language was done via a number of translation between several representations. The designers of the framework had more or less the same interpretation of compositionality of translation as presented here (in fact, it had been influenced strongly by the Rosetta approach: Arnold *et al.* (1986); Arnold and des Tombe (1987)) and derivational histories play a similar role. However, compositionality of translation as presented in this book is realised as 'tuning of grammars' and is related to com-

---

[1]Note that the CAT framework was rejected in 1987 and replaced by a new framework, the 'E-formalism', which has similarities with the CAT framework, but also differences (cf. Bech and Nygaard (1988)).

positional grammars in the Montagovian sense and therefore, to semantics. This is not the case for all levels in the CAT framework. A second difference between this framework and the framework presented in this book, is that the translation process is seen as a *homomorphism*, whereas the Rosetta approach presents it as an *isomorphism*. This topic will be elaborated in Chapter 19.

The following sections will deal with the five characteristics of the Rosetta approach. The strongest effect of the 'principle of compositionality of translation' as put forward in this book can be found in the characteristics *Compositional grammars* and *Attuned (or Isomorphic) grammars*.

5.3 Explicit grammars

5.3.1 Definition

A first characteristic of the Rosetta method is the fact that an explicit grammar is defined for both source and target language :

Characteristic 1: Explicit grammars
Both the source language and the target language are defined by explicit grammars.

This is the basis for the generative, constructive definition of the translation relation discussed in Chapter 2. What is particularly interesting is the fact that the output sentences are formed according to a grammar of the target language. This increases the confidence that the output of the translation process is a correct sentence of the target language.

5.3.2 Other MT approaches

Some translation systems are not based on grammars at all. Among them are the systems which are based on the oldest programs for MT, which work by means of word-to-word translation, extended with some kind of bilingual 'syntactic pattern matching' rules to solve the problems with the different word order, ambiguities, idiomatic expressions, etc. An example of such a rule is

V *niet* $\longrightarrow$ *do not* V

Chapter 2 already showed that such a rule is not applicable in all situations and therefore can result in wrong translations.

An example of this kind of system is the GAT system (cf. MacDonald (1963)). The same holds for the early versions of Systran, which is a further development of this program (cf. Hutchins (1986)). Later systems seem to incorporate more syntactic information.

Most translation systems do not have an explicit grammar for the target language, but only for the source language. Usually, the target language is defined by means of contrastive transfer rules that specify the differences with the source language, for instance in terms of some kind of syntactic-semantic structures. Examples are older versions of the bilingual direct systems Metal (cf. Bennett and Slocum (1985)) or ENGSPAN (cf. Vasconcelles and Leon (1985)), the bilingual transfer-based systems GETA (cf. Vauquois and Boitet (1985)) or the Japanese Government Project for MT (cf. Nagao *et al.* (1985)). The transfer module is followed by a rather straightforward generation module, to which not much attention is paid (see also Hutchins and Somers (1992)).

The main disadvantage of these approaches is the fact that it is difficult to guarantee the *correctness* of the target-language sentences. But note that the comparison made here should be viewed in the context of the limited goals formulated in Chapter 1. For post-edit systems, for example, correctness of the output may be less important than robustness.

With the development of multilingual systems, a need is felt for a generation module that is less dependent on the source language analysis module. This is the case, for example, for Eurotra (cf. Arnold *et al.* (1985)) or the more recent versions of Metal (cf. Thurmair (1990)).

It should be noted, in addition, that attempts have recently been made to translate by means of statistical information derived from some corpus of translated sentences in which grammar and translation rules remain implicit. These systems do not use grammar rules or transfer rules at all or use them in an entirely different way. See, for instance, Nagao (1984), Brown *et al.* (1988) or Sumita *et al.* (1990).

5.4   Compositional grammars

5.4.1   Definition

The second characteristic is the use of *compositional grammars*. It has been formulated as:

> **Characteristic 2: Compositionality of Meaning**
> The grammars are organised in such a way that the meaning of an expression is a function of the meaning of its parts and the way they are combined.

As preservation of meaning is one of the most important targets of translation, some way of expressing meaning is essential. The Rosetta approach is an example of the elaboration of the so-called principle of *compositionality of meaning* (see Chapter 2) which characterises Montagovian approaches.

5.4.2   The use of Montague Grammar in machine translation

The topic of the use of Montague Grammar in machine translation is discussed in Landsbergen (1987b). He enumerates the main objections that have been raised against the use of pure Montague Grammar (cf. Thomason (1974)) in machine translation systems:

1. the simplicity of its syntactic formalism;

2. the fact that intensional logic is too complicated for practical use in a large system;

3. the fact that it is an exclusively generative framework and not designed for analysis.

M-grammars overcome these objections because:

1. The rules do not operate on strings as in Montague's example grammars, e.g. PTQ (cf. Montague (1973)), but on *structured objects* (S-trees) as has been discussed in Chapter 3.

2. The translation into intensional logic is not carried out. The semantic representation consists of a *semantic derivation tree*. See also Section 5.7.

3. The grammars are reversible and can also be used for the *analysis* of natural language, as has been discussed in Chapter 4.

The Rosetta approach includes grammars with *powerful syntactic* rules to deal with the syntactic complexity in all natural languages. It has been claimed that by allowing powerful syntactic operations (and even purely syntactic transformations, cf. Chapter 9) the Montague framework has been corrupted and that as a consequence the whole enterprise has become theoretically uninteresting. But, firstly, although mainly categorial, in Montague's own grammar, PTQ, and other Montagovian approaches syntactically powerful rules occur, for instance the quantification rules. And, secondly, it is not our primary goal to search for the most restricted formalism in which translation relations can be defined. Montague Grammar is interesting for the Rosetta approach because it provides a reliable semantic basis, and this basis is not corrupted by the power of the rules nor by the introduction of syntactic transformations (see Chapter 9). The grammars of the Rosetta system are based on a combination of Montague grammar and Transformational Grammar (see also Chapter 11), but for the latter other choices would have been theoretically possible as well, although every other choice brings its own limitations. See, for example, Rupp (1986) for an attempt to use isomorphic grammars with Generalized Phrase Structure Grammar for a machine translation system.

Only a few other MT systems have been based on (Montagovian) compositional grammars. Two of them are:

1. The system of Godden (cf. Godden (1981)) from Thai to English which has a transfer at the level of intensional logic. The transfer rules have the status of meaning postulates. It has only been worked out for the small fragment of PTQ.

2. The system described by Nishida and Doshita (1982) that translates from English into Japanese. In this system, the transfer module converts the logical expression yielded by the analysis module into a function argument structure. Application of the functions yields target language expressions. There is no separate target language grammar.

Nagao (1984:9) states that "research on machine translation using Montague Grammar has ended in failure," without explicit references. But it can be assumed that this statement relates to systems that stay close to the PTQ-type of grammar and therefore suffer from at least the first two objections to the use of Montague Grammar in MT explained above.

5.5 Reversible grammars

5.5.1 Definition

The third characteristic of the Rosetta method is the reversibility of the grammars:

> **Characteristic 3: Reversible grammars**
> The analysis and the generation module for a particular language are
> based upon the same, *reversible* grammar.

In theoretical contexts, having just one grammar to characterise a language is nothing special. No theoretical linguist would think of having two grammars, one for generation and one for parsing, because they are interested in neither parsing nor generation. But in natural language processing, parsing and generation are often seen as two distinct disciplines, carried out by different people and each with its own problems and solutions. For example, analysis usually is a less deterministic process than generation.

Besides the theoretical elegance, the use of reversible grammars is economical, because an analysis module and a generation module can be derived while doing the design work only once. Besides, it turned out that linguists in the Rosetta project found it convenient to write grammars in a generative, compositional way.

5.5.2   Other machine translation approaches

Most operational systems for machine translation perform translations in one direction for a specific language pair. If they use grammars, they do not need reversibility. Examples are Metal, TAUM, GETA, SPANAM, ENGSPAN and the Japanese Government Project for MT.

But reversible grammars or systems have recently become more popular in natural language processing under the influence of declarative unification-based grammars. Several of the more modern MT systems or approaches claim to be reversible: for example, MiMo2, an experimental transfer system with unification grammars for Dutch, English and Spanish, developed at the University of Utrecht (cf. Van Noord *et al.* (1990), Arnold and Sadler (1990)), the CRITTER system (cf. Isabelle *et al.* (1988)), Symmetric Slot Grammar, to be used in an IBM MT system (cf. Newman (1990)) and the relational approach used in the POLYGLOSS project (cf. Zajac (1990)).

5.5.3   Deviations

In practice, slight deviations from reversibility occur for practical reasons. In some cases the 'analysis' part of the grammar has a larger coverage than the 'generation' part. For example, in English the paraphrases *She broke off the negotiations* and *She broke the negotiations off* exist. The 'analysis part' of the grammar accepts both sentences, but the 'generation part' only generates *She broke off the negotiations*. As a consequence, in an English-English system *She broke the negotiations off* would be translated only into *She broke off the negotiations*. The motivation for this kind of deviation is to reduce the number of possible translations generated.

Another deviation is illustrated in Chapter 13, where one of the options for solving difficult translation problems is allowing for non-reversible 'generative robustness rules'.

5.6 Attuned grammars

5.6.1 Definition

The most important characteristic of the Rosetta approach is the requirement that grammars have to be attuned. This has been called the isomorphy property of the grammars:

> **Characteristic 4: Attuned grammars**
> Grammars are organised in such a way that
> (i) for each basic expression in one grammar, there is at least one translation-equivalent basic expression in the other grammar, and
> (ii) for each rule in one grammar, there is at least one translation-equivalent rule in the other grammar.

> (Basic expressions, or rules, are considered translation-equivalent if they have at least one meaning in common and are also related in other translation-relevant aspects.)

The characteristic of attuned or isomorphic grammars expresses how closely related the grammars of source language and target language should be. It can be considered as a formalisation of compositionality of translation. During the design of the Rosetta grammars, attention is paid to this correspondence of grammars permanently. Decisions concerning the grammar of one language can have consequences for the grammar of another language. This aspect of the development process is called 'tuning of grammars'. The next two sections will discuss arguments in favour of tuning of grammars in comparison to other machine translation systems and the objections raised to tuning of grammars, respectively.

5.6.2 Arguments pro tuning of grammars

There are two main advantages of tuning of grammars:

1. It is a solution to the 'subset problem' of interface structures that all systems using a kind of abstract interface representation have and that guarantees meaning preservation.

2. Only simple transfer modules are needed; the contrastive research is done during the development of the isomorphic grammars.

Solution to the subset problem of interface structures

The most important problem of interlingual approaches is that the structures that are yielded by the analysis module must be accepted by the generation module. This problem can be illustrated by assuming two Montague grammars that map natural language into a subset of intensional logic that is supposed to be the interface structure for a machine translation system. This does not guarantee that the two Montague grammars for the two languages map them onto the same subset. The situation is sketched in Figure 5.1. The grammar of SL maps onto a subset IL_1 of IL.

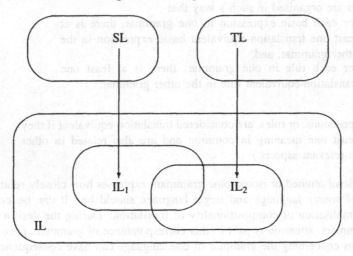

Figure 5.1: The subset problem of IL.

The grammar of TL maps onto a subset IL_2 and consequently, the generation module based on this grammar is only applicable to expressions of IL_2. So translation is only possible for the sentences that are mapped onto the intersection of IL_1 and IL_2.

Notice that there is no independent definition of IL_1 and IL_2. They are only defined indirectly by the mappings that follow from the grammars of SL and TL. Therefore, it is very difficult to come to grips with this problem. In order to solve it, it is not sufficient that the terms of IL_1 and IL_2 are the same, but in addition sentences that are to be translated into each other should get exactly the same logical structure and not just equivalent logical structures.

This 'subset problem' occurs in some guise in all systems — both interlingual and transfer systems — which translate via deep structures of some kind or distinguish more levels within the system. In general, it is not possible to define translation for all 'possible' (deep) structures (many of them will not correspond to any sentence at all), but on the other hand it is not possible to characterise what the subset of relevant (deep) structures is and to guarantee their translation. The only fundamental way to solve this problem appears to be that the grammars of SL and TL are not developed independently, but in close cooperation. In the Rosetta approach, this has been worked out in a specific way: by designing isomorphic grammars.

Most transfer systems do not have a solution for this problem. In Krauwer and des Tombe (1984), the notion *isoduidy*, meaning 'equivalent with respect to the essence of translation', is introduced as a guideline for Eurotra. It prescribes that the structures delivered by the analysis module for some language be accepted by the generation module of that same language. This notion gives some direction to the transfer design, but it still does not account for translation between *different* languages.

'Tuning of grammars' is only possible by a group of people working rather closely together. In the Eurotra project, for example, this would have been very difficult because of the decentralised organisation of the project. In every EC country a group of people was working on the project for analysing (and generating) their own language. The final analysis of one language group did not necessarily correspond with the kind of structures needed to generate the translation in another language. This problem had to be solved in some other way. In the Rosetta approach, the structures for source and target language are alike: the discrepancy problem is solved in the 'tuning stage'. The question is, however, whether a transfer approach can do without some 'tuning' of its interface structures.

Simple transfer

Most MT systems that adopted some kind of transfer approach try to minimise the transfer steps as much as possible, because so many steps are needed in a multilingual system (in a system with n languages, $n(n-1)$ transfer modules are needed). In the Rosetta approach the transfer steps are very simple. Isomorphic derivation trees are mapped 'node-by-node'. The pursuit of simple transfer has been less successful in other MT projects. Two of these projects will be discussed:

1. **Eurotra**
   The principle of 'simple transfer' was adopted for the Eurotra system (cf. Arnold *et al.* (1985); or Allegranza *et al.* (1991)). Ideally, a transfer step consists only of simple lexical substitution. It is recognised that this is unrealistic in case analysis and generation are developed independently and the possibility of adding languages exists. For those reasons, the possibility of some 'complex transfer' is accepted, although it should be minimised. To fulfill that desire, the Interface Structures (IS), which form the result of an analysis module and which a generation module must cope with, have to be made 'specific'

to each language group. Establishing this 'specific' representation theory did cost a lot of effort and was presumably one of the most time-consuming tasks of the project, because this representation theory should be so general and so 'specific' that "every language group must be able to produce a device that characterizes the right set of pairs [T,R]" (Arnold *et al.* (1985:161); T is a text and R is a representation). That goal probably involved a lot of 'tuning' on an abstract level, i.e. specifying a set of guidelines or legislation for the IS representation and discussing them in multilingual groups. In those cases where the languages diverge too much (or the abstract tuning had failed), the 'complex transfer' option comes in. In the Rosetta approach, probably, comparable situations may lead to an 'unnatural' grammar rule in one of the grammars. However, Chapter 13 will present an elegant general solution to a lot of syntactic category mismatches between languages - one of the most frequent causes of divergences - which keeps the number of 'unnatural' rules very small.

2. Metal

In Thurmair (1990), it is stated that both 'complex lexical transfer' and 'structural transfer' are needed in the Metal approach, which is likewise transfer-based. The difference between these two kinds of transfer is that 'structural transfer' is defined on certain tree properties, whereas in complex lexical transfer severe structural changes are caused by the translation of particular lexical items, because they differ, for example, in syntactic category. It is argued that both functional and categorial information, represented in MIR (Metal Interface Representation), are needed for proper transfer testing and it is doubted whether it is possible in multi-layered systems "where 'deeper' level information might not be available anymore at transfer time" (Thurmair (1990:96-97)).

In the Rosetta approach such information is coded in derivation trees, consisting of the names of rules that deal with, for example, functional structure that is relevant for translation, or in the lexicon of basic expressions, that are both attuned to the ones in other languages. In Chapter 9, the Rosetta view on 'translational relevance', will be discussed and, in Chapters 13 and 15, the solutions for problems with syntactic category mismatches and 'multiwords' (or translation idioms), respectively, will be presented.

For the Metal approach also holds that the degree of abstraction or attuning of the MIR is decisive for the complexity of the transfer modules.

Although no quantitative data are available, it is suspected that the trouble of developing interface structures with the objective to reach simple transfer, but often still having to write complex transfer rules, is at least comparable to the extra effort needed to make compositional grammars isomorphic.

5.6.3 Arguments contra tuning of grammars

The two main objections that have been raised to tuning of grammars are:

1. the mutual dependency of the grammars;
2. extending the system with new languages can have consequences for already existing grammars.

They will both be discussed below, and for the most part rejected.

The mutual dependency of the grammars

Objections to the mutual dependency of the grammars concern the essence of the approach, which requires tuning of grammars. Against this tuning two - related - arguments have been stated:

1. a practical argument: writing a grammar for a single language is a very difficult task in itself and tuning will make it even harder;
2. a theoretical - or even aesthetic - argument: the grammars become 'polluted' by 'relics' of other grammars.

Both arguments are based on the assumption that tuning requires a large extra effort and will lead to unnatural grammars from a monolingual point of view. Experience, however, shows proof to the contrary, although this experience relates to the extended framework introduced in Chapter 9, where a distinction is introduced between translation-relevant rules, which are subject to the isomorphy condition, and purely syntactic transformations, which can be written separately for each language. This technical solution solves most of the potential tuning problems (cf. Chapter 10 for the consequences for the view on compositionality).

Notwithstanding, incidentally, 'relics' of one grammar do occur in another grammar. For example, in English, a meaningful distinction is made between simple tense and progressive tense, as illustrated in (1a) and (1b):

(1) a She *draws* circles
    b She *is drawing* circles

There is no corresponding tense distinction in Dutch, but in the Dutch grammar the distinction has been made anyway.[2] However, in our experience the frequency of these phenomena is low for Romance and Germanic languages. In the actual grammars of Dutch, English and Spanish, only about 1% of the rules have a clear 'relic' nature. So the extra effort needed for tuning is relatively small and should be

---

[2]The distinction was needed for other reasons too, see Chapter 14 for more details.

compared with the cost of developing a transfer module in a system with structural transfer.

Because the extra rule can be clearly separated from the other rules, the theoretical argument against 'pollution' of the monolingual grammars is not valid either. The endeavour of attuning grammars is in fact very challenging from a theoretical point of view. On the one hand, it stimulates the grammar writers to look for properties that languages have in common and to develop a common view on grammars and, on the other hand, it offers a framework for contrastive linguistics.

Extensibility

It cannot be denied that adding a new language to the system can cause changes in the already existing grammars. If a distinction must be made in the new grammar that is translation-relevant and that was not made in the existing grammars, then that distinction has to be added to the already existing grammars. In fact, in that case the interlingua has to be extended. This is a disadvantage, but it is expected that in case of adding Romance and Germanic languages to the Rosetta system (already accounting for Dutch, English and Spanish) this will mean only a few additions on the structural level. But if this turns out to be wrong, the alternative as presented in Landsbergen (1989) is possible: isomorphic grammars with transfer parts, in which a clear distinction is made for each grammar between the general aspects and the parts that are inserted because of translation into or from a particular language. Singling out aspects that are specific for one language pair is, of course, the philosophy behind transfer systems, but there it is linked with a specific design, where the system consists of an analysis module, a transfer module and a generation module, in that order. In the Rosetta variant the specific 'transfer' part may contain both rules and lexical entries, interleaved with general rules and lexical entries, so it is not a separate module that is applied before or after the general part.

Note that the extensibility disadvantage should be compared with the effort that has to be invested in the development of new transfer modules between existing analysis and generation modules and those of the new language in systems with a transfer approach. In most transfer system designs, some kind of general *interface structure* is defined between analysis and transfer on the one hand and transfer and generation on the other. For example, in Eurotra it is called IS (cf. Allegranza *et al.* (1991)) and in Metal MIR (cf. Thurmair op. cit.). Adding a language to these systems, which pursue simple transfer, can also involve a change of these interface structures and then, changes in existing analysis and generation modules.

The extensibility problem is more serious at the lexical level. However, even when ignoring the extensibility problems, designing an interlingua on the lexical level is very problematic. See Section 5.7 for a discussion of this issue.

Finally, it should be stressed that the Rosetta grammars are developed according to a general plan that was designed before and refined during the development of the actual Rosetta grammars. This gives grammar writers a head start when a language is added. In fact, the Rosetta approach probably has an advantage over other MT approaches in this respect in the case of extending the system with a new language.

5.7 Interlingua

5.7.1 Definition

A consequence of compositional translation with isomorphic reversible grammars is that the semantic derivation trees play the role of an interlingua:

Characteristic 5: Translation via an Interlingua
Analysis modules and generation modules of various languages map into
and from the same intermediate language.

This characteristic is not and has never been a very principled one. It is the consequence of the idea of compositional translation as was already introduced in Chapter 2. If isomorphic grammars are developed for a given set of languages, semantic derivation trees are the common meaning representation of translation-equivalent sentences. So they constitute an interlingua in the sense of this characteristic.

5.7.2 Form of the interlingual expressions

Why does a system based on Montague grammar not use a version of Intensional Logic as its interlingua? This question has already been answered implicitly in Chapter 2. The two main arguments are repeated here.

1. There are language constructions which we do not yet know how to express their meaning in a logical language, while on the other hand, their translation equivalence with constructions of other languages is intuitively clear. The latter is sufficient if semantic derivation trees are used.

2. During translation, more information has to be conveyed than can be expressed in intensional logic.

An additional argument against the use of a 'real' interlingua results from the subset problem, already discussed in Section 5.6.2.

5.7.3 Problems with interlinguas

Given isomorphic grammars for a set of languages, semantic derivation trees form a perfect intermediate language. However, it is important to realise that the definition of isomorphic grammars includes certain assumptions about languages, which are correct within the scope of this book, as formulated in Chapter 1, but which do not necessarily hold outside that scope. The idealising assumption that is made is that 'perfect' meaning-preserving translation of sentences is indeed possible. In isomorphic grammars this implies that:

(i) corresponding basic expressions with the same meaning must be found; and

(ii) corresponding syntactic rules with the same meaning must be formulated.

In practice, the first assumption is problematic. Due to well-known differences in vocabularies, it is not always possible to find basic expressions in two languages with a common meaning. Note that the problem here is not ambiguity, but concerns other aspects, for example the fact that the meaning of a word may be somewhat more precise than its translation or that words may have only overlapping meanings. So, at the lexical level compromises have to be made and these may disturb the equivalence properties of the translation relation: the reversibility and transitivity. The best compromise, if we translate from language A into language B, need not be the best compromise in the opposite direction. The best compromise translation from A to B combined with the best compromise translation from B to C does not imply that the resulting translation from A to C is the most preferable. These problems are well known and common to all interlingual approaches. See, for example, the negative observations made on the 'pivot' language of the CETA system (Vauquois and Boitet (1985)). On the other hand, it is useful to notice that these lexical differences hold especially for 'everyday language' and to a much lesser extent for technical texts on which most MT systems are focused. In these texts, meanings tend to be more universal. In the Rosetta project we decided to concentrate first on the structural aspects of translation. An alternative approach was chosen in the KBMT project (cf. Nirenburg and Goodman (1990)) where the research is focused on the lexical semantic aspects in the interlingual MT and on the role played by knowledge of the world.

The consequence of all this is that semantic derivation trees are in practice only a real interlingua from a structural point of view and not necessarily at the lexical level. The basic meanings in the semantic derivation trees represent lexical meanings of the source language, which may not always match perfectly with the lexical meanings of the target language. The elaboration of this approach in a practical system may lead to a mixture of a structural interlingua and bilingual transfer. This mixture is also pursued in the Eurotra project and is the goal of the Transfer Interface Structure (TIS) proposed by Alonso (1990) (but see Section 5.6.2 for objections to these approaches). Chapter 4 already indicated that the choice between an interlingual and a transfer system (with transfer between syntactic derivation trees) is fairly arbitrary. The main reason for an interlingual architecture is to have a level of semantic representation. In the envisaged interactive system this is the level where the interaction with the user takes place, in the terms of the source language. This level can also be the point of departure for further semantic analysis in later versions of the system.

So, to sum up, the crucial advantage of semantic derivation trees as intermediate representations is not that they are ideal interlingua expressions, but that they are adequate semantic representations. This idea is also supported by Nirenburg and Goodman (1990) who state that a *meaning*-based approach should be the most important feature of a system and that the methodological debate between advocates of an interlingua and advocates of a transfer approach is misplaced.

5.8 Concluding remarks

This chapter has discussed the characteristics of the Rosetta approach and compared them with other MT theories and approaches. They have formed the guidelines for the development of Rosetta systems.

Summarising, the following points have been put forward:

- The notion of *Compositionality of Translation* is interpreted in a strict sense which has been worked out in compositional, isomorphic (or attuned) grammars.

- Semantics-based grammars for source and target language are required, but with a semantics that is needed for MT.

- The isomorphic grammar approach pays attention to the 'subset problem' of interface structures and the guarantee of *correct, meaning-preserving* translation in contrast to other approaches of MT.

- The mutual dependency of the grammars is necessary and should be compared with the prescription of certain interface structures in other approaches.

- Extension with new languages may affect existing modules, but the extra effort will presumably be less than for other systems. The general 'grammar scheme' already developed can be used for the new language.

- The effort of developing a multilingual system with isomorphic grammars is at least comparable with the effort of developing it with a transfer approach. The same problems have to be solved and the question is whether there is a great difference between 'tuning interface structures' and 'tuning grammars'.

- The *interlingua* versus *transfer* issue is not an important issue in MT. It should be replaced by the issue *semantics-based* versus *form-based* MT.

- A transfer approach need not be coupled with a transfer design.

- Reversible grammars are elegant, economical and convenient.

- The characteristics of the Rosetta approach should be taken as guidelines for the implementation of real systems and should not be seen as dogmas. Practical reasons can imply deviations.

In the following chapters some parts of the Rosetta framework will be discussed in more detail (Chapters 6, 8, 7) or refined (Chapter 9). Chapter 10 discusses the relation between compositionality and syntactic generalisations. The influence of Transformational Grammar will be elaborated in Chapter 11. Chapter 12 discusses divergences between languages and solutions that can be dealt with easily in the Rosetta framework. The solutions of some more difficult translation problems will then be discussed (Chapters 13, 14, 15 and 16). Chapters 17 — 20 are dedicated to formal, mathematical and software aspects. Finally, Chapter 21 deals with some evaluations of the method over the last ten years of experience.

Chapter 6

Morphology

6.1 Introduction

As has been explained in Chapter 3, in Rosetta the phenomena that are often called *morphological* are dealt with in two separate components of M-grammars: first, the description of the word-internal structure and its relation to semantics is dealt with in the syntactic component, which specifies the set of well-formed lexical S-trees; and second, the relation between abstract representations of words in the form of lexical S-trees and their representations in the form of strings is dealt with in the morphological component. This chapter will mainly deal with the morphological component, though in certain cases considerations relevant to the rules from the syntactic component dealing with word-internal structure will play a role.

As was pointed out in Chapter 4, two morphological modules, A-MORPH and G-MORPH, can be derived from the abstract relational characterisation of the morphological component. These modules establish the relation between syntactic structures (S-trees) and word forms. In each S-tree that is defined by an M-grammar, a *lexical level* can be distinguished, as is illustrated in Figure 6.1. Below the lexical level an S-tree specifies the internal structure of word forms. The exact place of the lexical level is determined by specific syntactic categories.

It is the task of the morphological modules to relate all S-trees that can emerge at the lexical level, that is, all *lexical S-trees*, to word forms and, vice versa, to relate all correct word forms of a language to lexical S-trees. The linguistic rules inside the morphological modules have to be written in such a way that they relate each lexical S-tree to a word form. So, G-MORPH maps each lexical S-tree onto the corresponding word form, and A-MORPH performs the reverse mapping.

The relation between lexical S-trees and word forms is a composition of two relations. The first relation associates lexical S-trees with morpheme sequences.

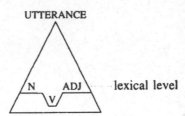

Figure 6.1: Schematic representation of an S-tree with its lexical level.

This relation is established by means of a reversible grammar which exactly defines how morphemes can be combined to ultimately form a lexical S-tree. The grammar used for this purpose is called a W-grammar[1] and the phase in which the grammar is used is called the W-grammar phase. Secondly, a set of reversible orthographic rules defines a relation between morpheme sequences and word forms. The orthographic rules define how word forms can be constructed out of morphemes. The relation composition is depicted in Figure 6.2.

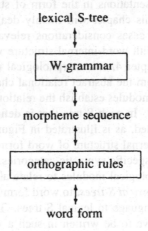

Figure 6.2: The relation between lexical S-trees and word forms

The generative morphological module starts off with a lexical S-tree which is

---

[1]The term W-grammar stands for Word-grammar and should not be confused with the well-known Van Wijngaarden grammars for which the same abbreviation is sometimes used.

decomposed into a sequence of morphemes. Next, this sequence of morphemes is used to compose a word form. During analysis the reverse process takes place. A word form is decomposed into a sequence of morphemes, which is subsequently used to compose a lexical S-tree.

In the actual system the generative morphological module is followed by a module (G-Layout) which formats the sequence of word forms according to the notational conventions of the language in question, e.g. word forms are concatenated, separated by a space, unless the second word form is a punctuation mark. The G-Layout module has also an analytical counterpart, A-Layout, which first transforms the input sentence into a standard format and then extracts the word forms.

The rest of this chapter is organised into five sections. Section 6.2 gives an overview of the phenomena that occur at the morphological level, of the structures that are used and of the linguistic coverage of the Rosetta morphology. The generative morphological module is elaborated in Section 6.3. The analytical counterpart is described in Section 6.4. For ease of exposition, Sections 6.3 and 6.4 do not describe the full Rosetta morphology. Although the 'kernel' presented in these sections can only deal with two of the phenoma discussed in Section 6.2, they are meant to give the reader a clear insight into the strategy that is followed. Section 6.5 extends the formalism further and presents the treatment of another morphological phenomenon of Section 6.2. Finally, some concluding remarks are made in Section 6.6 .

6.2   Phenomena and representations

6.2.1   Morphological phenomena

The Rosetta morphological modules are able to deal with the following phenomena:

inflection
> Conjugation and declination of words, e.g. *ship→ships*,
> *walk→walked, take→took, take→taken*.

derivation
> Creation of new word forms by combining words with affixes, e.g. the diminutive form of Dutch *huis 'house'* is *huisje 'little house'*, *read+able→readable*.

clitics and, more generally, cases where two or more words are written as one word.
> Examples are:

> **- prepositions and articles**
>> In Spanish a combination of *a* followed by *el* must be changed into *al*.

- **Spanish personal pronouns**
  In Spanish instead of *da me lo*, which means 'give it to me', *dámelo* has to be written.

- **particles and prepositions**
  In Dutch verbs and particles have to be combined in some contexts, e.g. *oppakken* ('pick up') v. *op pakken*, adverbials, e.g. *hierbij* ('hereby/at this') v. *hier bij* and verbs and prepositions, e.g. *overgezwommen* ('swum across') v. *over gezwommen*.

- **subject-verb contraction**
  Combining parts of two word forms, e.g. *we'll* v. *we will*, *I've* v. *I have*.

context dependencies
Sometimes the spelling of a word depends on the word form that follows, e.g. *an object* but *a man*. In general, it does not depend on the form of the word but on its pronunciation, e.g. it is *an hour* but *a house*.

compounding
Word creation by combining two or more words, e.g. *cab+driver→ cabdriver, door+bell→doorbell*.

The morphological formalism is capable of handling all inflectional phenomena in Dutch, English and Spanish, and complete implementations of the inflectional phenomena in these languages have actually been made, so that in principle **all** forms of **all** words in all three languages can be handled.

In theory, the morphological formalism is also able to deal with all derivational and compounding phenomena[2].

At this point, however, some remarks are in order concerning the nature of derivational and compounding rules in the syntactic component. Many derivational and compounding rules are very unproductive, so that the words that can be formed by them must be listed in the lexicon anyway. In addition, many words that can be derived by productive rules have also been lexicalised (i.e. they acquired a specific meaning that cannot be derived compositionally), so that they must be listed in the lexicon as well. The internal structure of such words will be described only if there is a need to, e.g. if ellipsis rules are added which can apply across word boundaries, or if describing this structure would yield simplified lexicons. Such phenomena considerably reduce the number of cases of derivation and compounding that can be described by compositional rules in the M-grammar formalism.

---

[2] Including cases where compounding and derivation apparently must apply in one rule, e.g. *driewieler* lit. *three-wheel-er* ('tricycle'), which cannot be derived by derivation from *driewiel, nor by compounding *drie* and *wieler*.

Even for rules which are fully productive and semantically transparent, additional problems arise when looking at translation. In many cases the semantics of a certain affix or of a compounding rule is extremely vague. A correct translation into other languages requires a more specific formulation, but it is difficult to find systematically corresponding constructions in the other languages.

An example of this in Dutch is -*er* affixed to abbreviations, as in *A.O.W.'er*, *P.T.T.'er* and *P.v.d.A.'er*. This affix is very productive but it has a very vague semantics and we know of no systematically corresponding construction which can serve as a translation in English. This affix does not have a counterpart in English and the only way to translate a combination of an abbreviation A and this affix is by means of a paraphrase such as *person, who is somehow related to A*. But this does not yield acceptable translations, because the nature of the relation in many cases is very specific: an *A.O.W.'er* is a person who receives old-age pension under the A.O.W.-law, a *P.T.T.'er* is an employee of the Post Office, and a *P.v.d.A.'er* is a member (or supporter) of the political party named P.v.d.A. In the English translation this relation has to be expressed more explicitly, which makes it problematic to translate such words. One might perhaps consider these examples as lexicalised cases and list them in the dictionary, but this will not help for newly formed words, which also have a very specific meaning in specific situations, which can be determined only by world knowledge and by knowledge of the situation. And the meanings of the examples mentioned are perhaps their most common meanings, but in different situations these words can be used in different ways. It is, for instance, not difficult to imagine a situation in which the word *A.O.W.'er* could appropriately be used to refer to an official who implements the A.O.W. law.

Similar remarks can be made with respect to compounds. Very often the relation between the two elements of a compound is highly dependent on world knowledge and on knowledge of the situation, cf. *autodief* (lit. *car thief*), which refers to a thief of cars, v. *winkeldief* (lit. *shop thief*), a thief stealing **in** shops. The relation between the word *dief* and the other word, its modifier, cannot remain vague in many other languages, like Spanish; in these languages a preposition that explains the relation between *dief* and its modifier must be used, but it is very difficult to determine the best preposition for most of the compound constructions.

Examples like these can perhaps be dealt with if the number of possible relations is finite, or if a small number of often-occurring relations and a translation to fall back on can be specified. These can be offered to the user, so that the user can supply the world knowledge and the knowledge of the situation required. This, however, requires the development of a very extensive system of interaction with the user.

The problems sketched here, concerning the limited productivity and restricted semantic transparency of derivational and compounding rules, are general problems for translation systems which have been encountered by other frameworks as well.

For the reasons sketched out above, only a few derivation rules have actually been implemented. One of them is the construction of diminutives out of nouns in Dutch (*kindje* ('little child', from *kind*), *weggetje* ('small road', from *weg*)). This is a very productive and frequently used construction in Dutch.

Rules to form adverbs from adjectives (which is considered as derivation) have also been implemented: in English the suffix *-ly* is added to an adjective (for example *loud* then becomes *loudly*) and in Spanish the suffix *-mente*. In Dutch there is no overt suffix: corresponding adjectives and adverbs have the same string, but Dutch has a corresponding abstract affix.

Some compounding rules have been implemented as well, but only for a limited number of cases in which the head is a noun and only for Dutch and English.

6.2.2 Representations

The morphological structure of a word can be represented by means of a lexical S-tree; lexical S-trees are built from a word (or, in case of compounds, several words) and some derivational and/or inflectional affixes; there are categories at three levels:

- the base- or B-level: categories for (stems of) words: BV, BN, BADJ, BADV, etc.; categories for suffixes: BVSUFF, BNSUFF, BADJSUFF, BADVSUFF and BSUFFIX; and a category for prefixes: BPREFIX. Elements of these categories are all listed in the dictionary.

- the SUB-level: SUBV, SUBN, etc. A default rule generates a SUB-level from a B-level;[3] then, other SUB-levels can be made from an already existing SUB-level by recursively combining the word with one or more derivational affixes or, in case of compounding, with another word.

- the word level (V, N, etc.), which is made from the SUB-level, for example by combining it with an inflectional affix.

Figure 6.3 is a typical example of a lexical S-tree. This S-tree could, for example, correspond with the string *ex-husbands*, with *ex-* as BPREFIX and *husband* as BN. Inflectional affixes are not represented as nodes in the S-tree: the information about

---

[3] This rule is motivated by the following consideration: derivation and compounding can apply to words without any word-internal structure (B-level categories, e.g. *loud* → *loudly*) or to words which have been derived by earlier applications of derivation and/or compounding rules (SUB-level categories, e.g. *vertaal-systeem* 'translating system' → *vertaal-systeem-pje* 'little translating system') themselves. If the default rule did not exist, it would be necessary to formulate *two* rules for each case of derivation or compounding: one which applies to B-level categories, and one which applies to SUB-level categories (alternatively, to complicate each rule so that it applies in both cases). The existence of the default rule makes it possible to formulate all rules in a much simpler way so that they apply to SUB-level categories only.

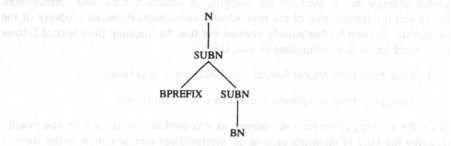

Figure 6.3: A lexical S-tree, which represents the morphological structure of a word.

inflection is contained in attribute-value pairs. So, if the tree in the example above were to represent the word *ex-husbands*, the attribute *number* at the N level would have the value *plural*; if the tree were to represent *ex-husband*, *number* would have the value *singular*.

Derivational affixes are represented as terminal nodes. Several levels with 'SUB'-categories are possible when there are more derivational affixes. The affixes are listed in the dictionary and — just like words — have inherent attributes. A number of attributes will be passed on to each newly created SUB-level, some from the affix and some from the original SUB-level. For example, for Dutch diminutives (which are treated as derivation in Rosetta), the affix determines the plural form: this will always be formed with an *-s*, regardless of how the plural form of the original word was made (example: the plural form of the word *boek* ('book') is *boeken*, the plural form of the diminutive *boekje* is *boekjes*). In the same way, the diminutive affix also determines the value of the attribute *gender* of diminutives, which is always *neuter*. Other attributes however, like the attribute *animate* will get their values from the SUBN: thus *boekje* will inherit the value *inanimate* for the attribute *animate* from *boek*.

S-trees produced by rules for compounds are similar to the S-tree of this example except for the fact that a word (V or N) is added instead of a BPREFIX.

6.3 The generative morphological module

6.3.1 Introduction

For expository convenience, a simplified version of the Rosetta formalism is presented in this section. It is only able to deal with inflection and derivation, which, however, does not hamper the primary goal of this section: the description of the global strategy that is used for the mapping of lexical S-trees onto correct word forms and the introduction of the reversibility and compositionality property of the formalism. Section 6.1 has already pointed out that the mapping from lexical S-trees onto word forms is accomplished in two steps:

1. a mapping from lexical S-trees onto morpheme sequences;

2. a mapping from morpheme sequences onto word forms.

Since the meaning of the term *morpheme*, as it is used in linguistics, does not exactly describe the kind of elements used as an intermediate representation in the Rosetta morphology, we will henceforth use the word *segment* for these elements.[4] The conceptual difference between the two steps can be elucidated as follows:

- Lexical S-trees contain information concerning morphosyntactic properties. It is the purpose of the first phase to translate this morphosyntactic information into a representation that is more orthographically oriented. This representation should contain sufficient information for the orthographic phase to generate word forms using general spelling rules of the language exclusively. It is, for example, not sufficient to map the lexical S-tree for the past tense of *hang* onto a representation of the form *hang + Past*. From this information only, the correct word form can never be generated, because the past tense of *hang* can be *hanged* or *hung*, dependent on the meaning of the verb. Therefore, it is necessary to be more specific. First, two lexical entries must be distinguished, say *hang1* and *hang2*. Next, these entries have to be classified into morphological classes, in the case of verbs so-called conjugation classes. These classes have to be chosen in such a way that all words belonging to it behave morphologically in a similar way. For example, *hang1* is put into the class RegConj (regular conjugation), and *hang2* into IrregConj (irregular conjugation). The rules mapping lexical S-trees onto segment sequences should now specify that a past tense verb from class RegConj is mapped into *stem + RegPast*, and that a past tense verb from class IrregConj is mapped into *stem + IrregPast*.

- The result of step 1 is a representation which can be interpreted as an application prescription of orthographic rules. The orthographic rules used in this second step will apply the general spelling rules of a language wherever possible.

    - The past tense of *walk* is represented as *walk + RegPast*, which is turned into *walked* by the orthographic rules, using the general spelling rule for

---

[4] As will be explained in the next sections, segments are (1) unique names of morphemes or (2) names of orthographic rules.

past tense formation in English. In case of *hang* + *IrregPast*, however, a special rule has to be applied which yields *hung*.

- The third person singular of the verb *fly* is *fly* + *RegS*, which yields *flies* instead of *flys*. The general rule here is that *y* turns into an *ie* if followed by an *s*.

- The second person singular of the Dutch verb *loop* ('walk') is *loop* + *RegT*, which becomes *loopt*. However, the second person singular of the verb *eet* ('eat') is *eet* + *RegT*, which yields *eet*. Here, the general rule is applicable which says that the ending *t* is omitted if the word already ends in a *t*.

Steps 1 and 2 are called the *W-grammar* phase and the *orthographic* phase, respectively. The next two sections will describe them.

6.3.2 The W-grammar phase in more detail

In this phase, well-formed lexical S-trees are related to segmented word structures. As pointed out before, a so-called W-grammar is used to establish this relation. A W-grammar comprises the following components:

- a set B of *terminal S-trees*.[5] Each element of B has a unique name, which is called the *key* of the element;

- a set R of W-rules. Each rule $r \in R$ operates on an S-tree and breaks it down into a sequence of S-trees.

This definition is similar to the definition of the syntactic component of an M-grammar.

In the generative W-grammar phase, lexical S-trees are broken down into terminal S-trees and, subsequently, into the keys of these terminal S-trees, in a recursive process in which decompositional W-rules are applied to results of former W-rule applications. Below, a small example shows how the lexical S-tree for the third person singular of *walk* is broken down into a sequence of terminal S-trees, consisting of an S-tree for *walk* and an S-tree for the suffix *s*. Next, each of these S-trees is replaced by its key. An example of this is the following:

---

[5]The set of basic S-trees (cf. Chapter 3) is a subset of the set of terminal S-trees. The set of terminal S-trees also includes S-trees with which no meaning is associated, e.g. S-trees which are introduced syncategorematically in the M-grammar (some determiners, punctuation elements, etc.) and S-trees corresponding with suffixes and prefixes in the morphology.

(a)   V {person: 3, number: singular}
       |
       SUBV {..........}
       |
       BV {conjclass:regular, key: walk_BV}

(b)   BV {conjclass: regular, key: walk_BV}   +   SFCAT {key: SFs}

(c)   walk_BV   +   SFs

This example shows that if a W-rule should be able to map S-tree (a) onto the S-trees of (b) it needs to have transformational power. Here too, there is a link with the syntactic component of an M-grammar. The notation used to specify W-rules is a subset of the notation that is used for M-rule specification (cf. Chapter 8).

6.3.3   The orthographic phase in more detail

In the orthographic phase *affix rules* are used to build word forms. We distinguish two types of rules:

- *prefix* rules that put strings like *ge-* (the Dutch prefix for past participles), *super-* and *hyper-* in front of other strings, using the spelling rules of the language in question;

- *suffix* rules for adding suffixes like *-ed, -able* to the end of strings. Also, suffix rules are used to treat morphological phenomena that have no direct relation with a concrete prefix or suffix, like vowel changes in irregular verbs, as in *sink → sank, sunk.*

A segment sequence which is the result of the W-grammar phase is in fact a sequence of keys (unique names of terminal S-trees) and names of affix rules. It can be mapped onto one or more word forms through the application of affix rules, the names of which are recorded in the segment row itself. For that purpose the segment sequence is interpreted in a special way. For instance, a sequence of the form

(1)   pf1 + pf2 + k + sf1 + sf2 + sf3

(two prefix rule names pf1, pf2 followed by a key k followed by three suffix rule names sf1, sf2 and sf3) is interpreted as the following rule application prescription:

(2) `pf1(pf2(sf3(sf2(sf1(stem(k))))))`

The interpretation shows an ordering between suffixes and prefixes. First, the function `stem` is applied to the key `k`. The result of this function application is a set of stems (in string representation) that correspond with `k`. The result of the function `stem` can be ambiguous because morphological variants that are syntactically and semantically equivalent are associated with the same terminal S-tree and, consequently, with the same key, e.g. *realise* ↔ *realize*. Next, the suffix rules and, finally, the prefix rules are applied. There is no profound meaning behind this ordering. The motivation for a fixed ordering is based on efficiency aspects. In fact, the current formalism allows for a more sophisticated ordering in which a regular expression specifies the exact order in which prefix and suffix rules may be applied. Because all affix rules are set-valued, a more precise formulation of the interpretation of (1) is (3).

(3) $\{r \mid \exists r_1, r_2, r_3, r_4, r_5 : r \in \text{pf1}(r_1) \wedge r_1 \in \text{pf2}(r_2) \wedge$
$\quad r_2 \in \text{sf3}(r_3) \wedge r_3 \in \text{sf2}(r_4) \wedge r_4 \in \text{sf1}(r_5) \wedge r_5 \in \text{stem}(k)\}$

For example, for Dutch, an orthographic rule `SFen` exists that deals with the word ending *-en*. It implements the general spelling rule that says that long vowels written as *aa*, *ee*, *oo* and *uu* followed by a single consonant, are written with a single letter if the word is suffixed by *-en*. The rule yields the following result if it is applied to the string *loop* ('walk'), *slaap* ('sleep'), *steek* ('stab'), respectively:

(4) `SFen(`*loop*`)` → {*lopen*}
     `SFen(`*slaap*`)` → {*slapen*}
     `SFen(`*steek*`)` → {*steken*}

Using the Rosetta notation, we can specify the rule `SFen` as:

```
VAR:    V  =  [a,e,o,u]
        C  =  [d,g,k,l,m,n,p,r,t]
RULE:   *(V)(V)(C)  +  SFen  ::  *(V)(C)en
```

In the variable declaration part the variables V and C are defined, together with the character values they can have. The interpretation of the rule that is specified in the rule definition part is rather straightforward. In generation the input string (e.g. *loop*), is matched with the expression `*(V)(V)(C)` of the left-hand side of the rule. During this match the variables of the expression are instantiated. In the case of *loop* the variable V gets value o and to variable C value p is assigned. The `*` symbol matches the rest of the input string. For the construction of the output string the expression `*(V)(C)en` is used, in which the variables are replaced by their values. Notice that the rule specification is symmetric: it can just as well be read from right to left for analytical purposes.

6.4   The opposite direction: the analytical morphological module

The analytical morphological module A-MORPH generates for a word form the associated set of lexical S-trees. In order to achieve that, the phases that we distinguished in the generative morphological module are completed in reverse order. This is possible because each W-grammar and orthographic rule also has a *reverse*, decompositional interpretation, in accordance with the 'One Grammar Principle'.

1. The orthographic phase, in which a word is reduced to its stem by means of application of (decompositional) affix rules. The result of this phase is the derivational history of the way in which this was achieved, represented as segment sequences.

2. The W-grammar phase, which yields a set of lexical S-trees by repeated application of (compositional) W-rules.

ad 1. Whereas in the generative morphology this phase is deterministic, in the opposite direction it is not. All affix rules have to be applied in order to find out which stems and affixes make up the input word. If a word stem is the result of repeated application of these rules, a possibly correct word segmentation has been found. Because the only information that is present on this level is the character string itself, it is inevitable that wrong paths will be taken in the course of this process. The two main causes of possible erroneous paths are:

(i) Affix rules can be applied to strings other than those for which they are intended.

For example, the English suffix rule SFing yields the string *think* if it is applied to the string *thinking*. However, the rule is also applicable to a string like *lightning* resulting in **lightn*. Eventually, this path will be a dead end because **lightn* is not a correct word stem. Another English suffix rule, SFcding, (cd for consonant doubling) yields *refer* if it is applied to *referring*. However, if we apply the same rule to *herring* we get *her*, which is a correct English word. If such an incorrect segmentation is found, it will not be rejected during the orthographic phase. The information necessary to detect that the segmentation is wrong is typically available in the next phase, the W-grammar phase.

(ii) It is possible that multiple paths, some of which are not appropriate, are created while translating stems into keys.

For example, the word form *panning* can be segmented into: *pan* + SFcding. Looking up the stem *pan* in the lexicon yields both the noun *pan* and the verb *pan*. In the orthographic phase, in which only character string information plays a role, we cannot distinguish these alternatives. When the stems are translated into keys, an ambiguity is created, which is resolved in the W-grammar phase.

The result of applying the orthographic phase to a word form is a set of sequences of keys and names of affix rules, some of which may not result into a lexical S-tree in the next phase.

ad 2. In this phase the W-grammar is used to build lexical S-trees and, at the same time, to find out which of the segment sequences are correct. The compositional version of the W-rules is used for a parse of the segment sequence. Repeated bottom-up application of the W-rules will eventually yield a set of S-trees. If the set is not empty and if it contains at least one S-tree with a lexical top category, the segment sequence is considered to be correct. In the course of this parse, segmentations like *her* + SFcding are rejected. Also the segmentation of *panning* in which *pan* has been interpreted as a noun is filtered out. Apart from the rejection of some ambiguities it is also possible that new ambiguities are introduced as, for instance, in the following example. Several lexical S-trees are associated with a segmentation of the word form *walk*, because it is the infinitive, the first and second person singular and the first, second and third person plural form of the stem *walk*.

Ultimately, the analytical morphological module associates with each input word form a set of lexical S-trees. Some of the S-trees in these sets will be filtered out in subsequent modules of the system.

6.5   Extensions

The morphological system that has been described in the previous sections is very well suited for the treatment of inflection and derivation. It deals with cases in which a lexical S-tree corresponds to a word form. Sometimes, however, it is necessary to relate a *sequence* of lexical S-trees to a word form. An example of a phenomenon which requires such a treatment is cliticisation. In Rosetta, the decision that two or more adjoining elements in an S-tree have to be cliticised is made in the syntactic component. The morphological component of Rosetta decides *how* the word forms associated with the adjoining lexical S-trees should be combined. Whether two adjoining lexical S-trees have to be cliticised or contracted is specified in the syntax by placing a special lexical S-tree with top category GLUE in between the two lexical S-trees. The W-grammar phase will generate a segment sequence for each of these lexical S-trees. For example, the M-grammar syntax generates three lexical S-trees corresponding with *do not*:

```
     V          GLUE        NEG
    △                      △
    do                     not
```

Next, the W-grammar phase associates the following three unary segment sequences with these S-trees:

    do-key,   glue-key,   not-key

Recall that a segment sequence is interpreted in the orthographic phase as a pre-scription of how the orthographic rules have to be applied. In this case the presence of a glue-key triggers the orthographic component to interpret the three adjoining unary sequences as:

    glue(stem(do-key),stem(not-key))

Applying the function stem to do-key and not-key yields the strings *do* and *not*, respectively. The function glue combines these two strings to the string *don't* by applying a third set of orthographic rules called the *glue rules*. These glue rules specify how the concatenation of adjoining word forms ordered by the syntactic component has to be realised on the string level.

In English there are rules that specify how auxiliary and subject have to be cliti-cised and subsequently contracted and how a contracted negative form of auxiliaries is created. The following example gives an impression of the notation of the glue rules used for contraction in English.

```
VAR:     M1  = [ I, we, they, you ]
         M2  = [ I, you, he, she, it, we, you, they]
RULE:    (M1)    + have  ::   (M1)'ve
         (M2)    + will  ::   (M2)'ll
         shall   + not   ::   shan't
         should  + not   ::   shouldn't
         do      + not   ::   don't
```

In Spanish the cliticisation phenomenon is dealt with by means of glue rules. Gen-eratively, the rules concatenate a verb and the pronouns that follow. This process is complicated by the fact that an accent has to be placed on the verb. Here, a fragment of the Spanish cliticisation rules dealing with the regular imperative forms ending on *-a* (e.g. *coma + lo → cómalo* ('eat it')):

```
VAR:     CL   = [se,te,me,le,lo,la,os,nos,les,los,las]
         C    = [b,c,d,f,g,j,l,m,n,ñ,p,q,r,s,t,v,x,y,z]
         DIF  = [ai<>ái,oi<>ói,ei<>éi,iu<>íu,au<>áu,
                 ou<>óu,eu<>éu]
         V    = [a<>á,e<>é,i<>í,o<>ó,u<>ú]
RULE:    *(V)a      + (CL)  ::   *(V)a(CL)
         *(V)(C)a   + (CL)  ::   *(V)(C)a(CL)
         *(DIF)(C)a + (CL)  ::   *(DIF)(C)a(CL)
```

(The o<>ó notation means that if a variable in the right-hand part of a rule is
instantiated as an ó, e.g. during a match with *cómalo*, it will occur with the value o
at the left-hand side of the rule.) In fact the accent placing in Spanish is an example
of a discontinuous dependency. This example shows that the notation is not very
well suited for dealing with discontinuous dependencies. Correct accent placing
can only be achieved by enumerating all possible character strings that can occur
between the clitic and the stressed vowel or diphthong. In the example only the case
is described in which the stressed vowel is followed by one consonant. Extra rules
have to be added to deal with the cases in which the vowel is followed by two or
three consonants.

In generation, the set of glue rules is the last set of rules to be applied in the
orthographic phase. Consequently, the glue rules are the first orthographic rules to
be applied in the analysis module. Notice that the rule notation used in the examples
is neutral with respect to analysis or generation. For analytical purposes the rules
have to be read in the reverse direction, i.e. from right to left.

6.6   Conclusion

The Rosetta morphological module is capable of handling all kinds of morphological
constructions, like inflection, derivation, compounds, clitics, contraction and context
dependencies. For derivation and compounding, however, only a few rules have been
written since it only makes sense to write rules for such phenomena in a machine
translation system if the morphological phenomenon is productive, has compositional
semantics and if there are systematically corresponding constructions in the other
languages. The other phenomena can be dealt with **completely** for Dutch, English
and Spanish by the morphological module.

The most important properties of the Rosetta approach to morphology are compositionality, reversibility and the clear distinction between algorithms and linguistic
information. Although the Rosetta approach differs very much from the approach
chosen in the KIMMO system (Koskenniemi (1983), Karttunen (1983)), the two
approaches share the reversibility property and the fact that linguistic information is

separated from the algorithms that use the information. We think, however, that it is desirable to have an explicit grammar that describes the syntax of word forms. In the original KIMMO system the word internal syntax has to be specified by means of continuation classes, the drawbacks of which have been explained in Karttunen (1983). The Rosetta formalism, on the other hand, provides the possiblity to express the word internal syntax by means of powerful rules. The desirability of having syntax rules for word forms in a morphology model was also expressed by several authors (Bear (1986), Alistar (1986) Russel *et al.* (1986)). In Russel *et al.* (1986) a system is described that is structured in the same way as the Rosetta morphological formalism. It also comprises the components, 'Word Grammar', 'Lexicon' and 'Spelling Rules'. However, unlike Rosetta, the system was developed only for use in the analysis phase of natural language processing systems.

Chapter 7

Dictionaries

This chapter describes some aspects of the dictionaries used in the Rosetta system. Section 7.1 discusses the general organisation of the dictionaries, Section 7.2 gives some examples of the detailed information that the dictionaries contain and shows how this information is used in the grammars, and Section 7.3 describes our attempts to derive the relevant information automatically from the existing Van Dale dictionaries.

7.1 The general organisation of the dictionaries

Chapter 2 indicated that a compositional grammar as used in the Rosetta system must specify (apart from a set of rules) a set of *basic expressions*. This set of basic expressions must be specified in dictionaries. In Chapter 3 the grammatical formalism has been extended: a separate morphological component is distinguished, and the syntax has been enriched considerably. This affects the representation of basic expressions in dictionaries. There are several representations for a basic expression, in particular a *string representation* and a representation as an object with morphosyntactic properties. For this reason the basic expressions are represented in a set of interrelated dictionaries, each of which plays its own role in certain modules of the Rosetta system and each of which describes certain properties of the lexical items. Below we will describe the dictionaries, indicate very globally which information they contain, and specify in which modules of the system they are used.

Above, we spoke only of *dictionaries*, but in fact a distinction is made between two types of dictionaries, *dictionaries* (indicated by the postfix *DICT*), and *lexicons* (indicated by the postfix *LEX*). *Lexicons* describe the properties of an object, and *dictionaries* specify relations between objects from two different *lexicons*. Each

119

object in a lexicon is given a unique name, called a *key*. We distinguish *syntactic keys* and *semantic keys*. The dictionaries relate objects from lexicons by specifying relations between keys. These binary relations are in general many-to-many. We will see examples of these relations below. From the relations specified in *dictionaries* two functions can be derived, one for analysis and one for generation. In this way the lexicons and dictionaries can be used in both generation and analysis.

The Rosetta system uses the following dictionaries and lexicons:

MORPH-DICT relates a stem, i.e. a canonical string representation for an inflectional paradigm, to a syntactic key, which is the unique name for a set of morphosyntactic properties. It is possible that one string is mapped onto several syntactic keys (e.g. the string *attempt* is mapped onto a key for the noun *attempt* and onto a key for the verb *attempt*), and it is possible that several strings are mapped onto one syntactic key (i.e. spelling variants, e.g. the Dutch strings *contract* and *kontrakt* 'contract' are both mapped onto the same syntactic key). Also, there may be syntactic keys for which no associated string exists (see below), but strings for which no syntactic key exists are not allowed. Context conditions may influence the relation. Several examples of such context conditions are the following: in English, the syntactic key for the indefinite article corresponds to *an* if the next word begins with a vowel sound, otherwise it corresponds to *a*; the syntactic key for the Spanish conjunction meaning *'and'* corresponds to *y* only if the next word does not begin with the sound *[i]* and to *e* otherwise; the syntactic key for the Spanish conjunction meaning *'or'* corresponds to *o* only if the next word does not begin with the sound *[o]* and to *u* otherwise; the syntactic key for the Spanish definite feminine article corresponds to *la* only if the next word is not a noun beginning with an accented *a* and *el* otherwise. These context conditions often involve the pronunciation of words, so some phonetic information (for instance, whether a word begins with a vowel sound) is represented here, as well.

MORPH-DICT is used in the morphological modules (A-MORPH and G-MORPH).

S-LEX specifies for each syntactic key the corresponding morphosyntactic properties.[1] The main attribute is the syntactic category. Other morphological prop-

---

[1] There is no separate dictionary to represent morphological properties as opposed to syntactic properties. This is connected with the fact that the morphological modules in Rosetta have only an interpretive function, i.e. they relate lexical S-trees to strings. This relation must specify a string for each well-formed lexical S-tree, so morphology has neither a 'creative' function nor a 'filtering' function. This approach has certain drawbacks. In particular the treatment of particled verbs in morphology in Dutch is unsatisfactory from a linguistic point of view and from a computational point of view (because of inefficiency in analysis). Some of these drawbacks have partially been solved in the implementation of

erties are specified by means of a fixed set of attribute-value pairs - dependent on the value of the category attribute. Examples of these morphological properties are, for instance, how the stem is inflected, whether productive derivational suffixes can be attached (e.g. diminutive suffixes, suffixes to form adverbs from adjectives, etc.), whether words amalgamate with other words (e.g. in Spanish *de+el* becomes *del*), etc. Syntactic properties are also specified by means of a fixed number of attribute-value pairs dependent on the syntactic category, for instance for entries of category *verb* there is an attribute to specify the number of arguments and their nature, there is an attribute that specifies how complements must be realised syntactically, there is an attribute to specify the control properties, etc. See Section 7.2 for more detailed information.

S-LEX is used in A-MORPH and M-GENERATOR.[2].

IL-DICT relates syntactic keys to semantic keys of the intermediate language. A syntactic key can be related to several meaning keys (in the case of ambiguous words), and several syntactic keys can be related to one meaning key (in the case of synonyms). A semantic key identifies the meaning of a word or idiomatic expression. This dictionary contains for each pair <syntactic key, semantic key> a short meaning description, which is used to ask the user which meaning is intended if the system itself cannot resolve an ambiguity.

IL-DICT is used in the semantic modules (A-TRANSFER and G-TRANSFER).

IL-LEX is intended for specifying the semantic properties for each semantic key, e.g. the semantic type of the meaning and the semantic types of arguments of the meaning.

IL-LEX will be used in the semantic component. At the time of writing, we still are investigating which semantic properties have to be specified and how they can be represented most adequately. However, a description of these properties is beyond the scope of this book.

In addition to the dictionaries described above, there are dictionaries to describe the exact form and properties of idiomatic expressions and complex predicates (See also Chapter 15 for more detail about the treatment of idiomatic and semi-idiomatic expressions):

ID-DICT for idiomatic expressions (e.g. *to kick the bucket*, *to pull someone's leg*). Idiomatic expressions are represented as syntactic D-trees in the Rosetta system, but in the dictionaries they are entered by specifying

---

the morphological modules.

[2]In analysis this lexicon is not used in the syntactic modules because the relevant lexicon is accessed in the morphological modules, and the information obtained from it is passed on to the syntactic modules without additional accesses to the lexicons. For similar reasons, in generation, S-LEX need not be accessed in G-MORPH.

- the idiom class;
- the syntactic keys of the content words in the idiom, in a specific order;
- the syntactic key of the idiom as a whole.

The idiom class defines the internal syntactic structure of the idiom, including the positions of the free arguments. The idiom class and the ordered keys of the content words together provide the system with all the information needed for constructing the S-tree of the idiom. See Chapter 15 for more detail.

ID-DICT is used in the syntactic modules (M-PARSER and M-GENERATOR). The syntactic key of the idiom is mapped onto a semantic key in the normal manner in IL-DICT.

CP-DICT for complex predicates. These are, among others things, expressions such as *to have a bath* or *to make a decision*, consisting of a light verb (cf. Chapter 15) and an object which determines the meaning of the verb. This dictionary specifies which pairs of words are semi-idioms. More precisely, it defines a relation between three syntactic keys, *s1*, *s2* and *s3*. This relation can be used by rules that replace a basic expression with syntactic key *s1* by an (abstract) basic expression with syntactic key *s2* if a basic expression with syntactic key *s3* is present in the context in a way indicated in the rule. The syntactic key *s2* is mapped onto a meaning key that represents the meaning of *s1* when occurring in the context of *s3*.

CP-DICT is used in the syntactic modules (M-PARSER and M-GENERATOR).

Finally, it is possible to specify all sorts of constraints that hold in the lexicons. In this way all kinds of interdependencies, for instance between the values of two different attributes, can be expressed. Whenever the dictionary is updated, these constraints are checked, and when they are violated an error occurs or a warning is issued. In this way the integrity of the data can be guaranteed.

An object in S-LEX is a *basic expression* if it has a corresponding object in IL-LEX. The subset of S-LEX which contains all and only the basic expressions is called B-LEX. A *basic expression* is either *simple* or *complex* (e.g. idioms). It does not necessarily have an associated string. Expressions without associated strings are called *abstract basic expressions*; also, in idiomatic and semi-idiomatic expressions there is no string corresponding to the syntactic object. For certain objects from S-LEX no corresponding object in IL-LEX exists. This must be allowed for words that do not have a meaning at all, e.g. the Dutch word *brui* and the English word *lurch*, which occur in idiomatic expressions only, and for words which have a purely grammatical function (e.g. the passive auxiliary *be*) and for other words which are introduced *syncategorematically*, for instance the articles *the, a(n)* in the current grammar.

Though, in principle, the Rosetta system is an interlingual system, we expect that in a system with very large dictionaries,[3]Rosetta will not use an interlingua in the strict sense of the word as far as lexical information is concerned. The terms of the intermediate language will simply be the meanings of the words of the source language. In such a system the intermediate language will not be the same for the Dutch-to-English version as for the English-to-Dutch version. Only if an application is chosen in which a real interlingua is desirable, will we invest in the construction of this interlingua. See Chapter 4 for a discussion of the status of the interlingua in Rosetta and Chapter 21 for a discussion of a mixed interlingual/transfer system.

7.2   Some example entries

The grammar uses syntactic specifications of lexical items, represented in S-LEX, in the formulation of M-rules and transformations. In this section we will illustrate by means of some example lemmas how dictionary and grammar interact to allow for elegant descriptions of various syntactic phenomena.

7.2.1   Lexical entry structure

As pointed out in Section 7.1, basic expresssions are represented in a set of in-terrelated dictionaries, each relating to different types of properties of the basic expression. In the interface to a lexicographer, the information contained in these dictionaries is combined, yielding for each syntactic category a specific set of attributes (morphological, syntactic and semantic) and possible values. For each category (and each phrasal constituent) a template is defined which specifies which attributes belong to this category and which values are possible values for these attributes. An example of such a template is the set of attributes and values of an English basic verb (forming a BVrecord), which is defined as in Table 7.1. The BVrecord consists of a list of attributes (e.g. ingform) on the left-hand side and a type specification followed by a default value on the right-hand side (e.g. ingformtype:reging (i.e. regular)). In contrast with other systems, notably unification systems, every verb needs to be specified for all these attributes. Also the assignment of types, which is becoming increasingly popular, is not common to all systems. The types are either sets of enumerated types (these contain the substring *SET* in their names), or are defined by enumeration. Some example definitions of enumerated types are:

---

[3]See Section 7.3.3 for a description of the dictionary that was actually used in the project.

```
BVrecord = <
    conjclasses:        conjclassSETtype:[regular]
    ingform:            ingformtype:reging
    sform:              sformtype:regS
    particle:           keytype:0
    possvoices:         VoiceSETtype:[active, passive]
    reflexivity:        reflexivetype:notreflexive
    synvps:             SynpatternSETtype:[ ]
    thetavp:            Thetavptype:vp100
    adjuncts:           adjunctSETtype
    CaseAssigner:       CaseAssignertype:true
    subc:               Verbsubctype:mainverb
    oblcontrol:         oblcontroltype:omegaOblcontrol
    prepkey1:           keytype:0
    prepkey2:           keytype:0
    controller:         controllertype:none
    classes:            classSETtype:[durativeclass]
    thatdel:            thatdeltype:omegadel
    req:                polarityEFFSETtype:[pospol, negpol,
                        omegapol]
    env:                polarityEFFSETtype:[pospol, negpol,
                        omegapol]
    KEY
>
```

Table 7.1: A definition of BVrecord.

```
adjuncttype     =   (ResAP, ResPP, SubjComit, ObjComit, BenfactNP,
                    BenfactPP, LocAdjunct, DirAdjunct, ResNP)
oblcontroltype  =   (yesOblcontrol, noOblcontrol, omegaOblcontrol)
Thetavptype     =   (omegathetavp, vp000, vp100, vp010, vp120,
                    vp012, vp123, vp132, thetavpaux )
```

where all possible values for a specific attribute are given on the right-hand side. The use of default values is intricate. In the lexicon, the default values correspond to the most frequent value of a specific attribute. Since most verbs are not control verbs, the default value for oblcontrol is omegaOblcontrol, which means that it is unspecified for this attribute. In the grammar, the use of default values guarantees that each time a record is created uniform values are assigned to all attributes.

7.2.2   Role of the lexicon

The lexicons contain highly detailed syntactic information to allow the grammar to make the detailed syntactic analysis which is required for translation. It is not possible, however, to account for all syntactic behaviour in the lexicon. The complexity of the syntactic behaviour which needs to be dealt with would lead to an explosion of the number of attributes and lemmas in the dictionary and makes it difficult to produce consistent dictionaries. Moreover, some syntactic properties follow from general principles for which a grammar is essential. In these cases only the interaction of lexicon and grammar yields the proper results.

In the following section we will illustrate the subtle balance between grammar and lexicon by means of some example entries. We will focus on a number of syntactic attributes and explain their functions. Moreover, we will discuss constructions illustrating the necessity for a grammar to make correct analyses.

7.2.3 Example of a lexical specification

As mentioned in Section 7.2.1, the attributes of a basic expression are represented in one lemma in the dictionary. The lexical specification of the verb *promise* is given in Table 7.2. The top part of the lemma consists of the string promise, the syntactic

```
promise
  : PROMISE1
  : PROMISE1"to give an assurance of"
  : BV (
conjclasses:    [10],
ingform:        reging,
sform:          regS,
particle:       0,
possvoices:     [active, passive],
reflexivity:    notreflexive,
synvps:         [ synEMPTY_OPENTOSENT, synEMPTY_THATSENT, synIONP_DONP,
                synDONP_PREPNP, synDONP_EMPTY, synIONP_OPENTOSENT,
                synIONP_THATSENT, synIONP_PROSENT, synEMPTY_PROSENT ],
thetavp:        vp123,
adjuncts:       [ ],
CaseAssigner:   true,
subc:           mainverb,
oblcontrol:     yesoblcontrol,
prepkey1:       $toPREPkey,
prepkey2:       0,
controller:     subject,
classes:        [momentaryclass],
thatdel:        yesdel
req:            [pospol, negpol, omegapol],
env:            [pospol, negpol, omegapol],
  );
```

Table 7.2: Lexical specification of the verb *promise*.

key PROMISE1, a meaning key PROMISE1 and a category label BV. The rest of the lemma consists of attributes on the left-hand side and their specific values on the right-hand side. The morphological properties of the verb are accounted for by the following attributes:

conjclasses   indicates the conjugation class or classes of the verb.

ingform   indicates how the ing-form of a verb is formed.

sform   indicates how the third person singular of the verb must
                 be spelled.

The other attributes are mainly of a syntactic nature and we will discuss some of
them in more detail below.

Attributes for argument structure

An important part of the grammatical information represented in the lexicon regards
the argument structure of a verb. The attribute thetavp specifies for each verb the
number of semantic arguments, as well as whether they are internal or external
arguments.[4] The external argument of a verb is that argument that receives the subject role when combined with the verb. All other arguments are internal. Promise is
assigned the value vp123 for thetavp, indicating that it allows three arguments (somebody *promises* somebody something). These arguments are ordered according to
their grammatical function (see Odijk (1993)), though one can deviate from this
when required for a proper translation. Both the order and the number of arguments
need to be preserved in translation as an immediate consequence of the isomorphic
approach.

A second attribute, synvps, specifies how these arguments are realised syntactically. *Promise* can, for instance, be followed by two noun phrases bearing the
relation indirect object and direct object, respectively (the value of synvps then is
synIONP_DONP), but also by a noun phrase and a subordinate clause (the value of
synvps is synIONP_THATSENT):

(1) a I never promised you a rose garden
     b I promise you that all will go well

The indirect object of the verb *promise* is optionally present in the syntactic structure
(see (2)). To account for this, it is assumed that this argument position is occupied
by a special, abstract basic expression, called *EMPTY*, which has no surface realiza-
tion. A separate verb pattern is assigned to the verb *promise* to indicate that it has
this option.

(2) a I never promised a rose garden
     b I promise that all will go well

---

[4] Notice that expletives like *it* and *there* are not considered arguments.

A third attribute, adjuncts, specifies the bound adjuncts a verb can take and their syntactic realisation.[5] Typical bound adjuncts are resultatives (as in *He painted the door* **green**) and beneficiaries (as in *He bought* **me** *a house*). Unlike arguments, bound adjuncts are always optional.

Attributes for control

The attribute oblcontrol indicates the nature of the relation between the subject of an embedded infinite clause and a noun phrase higher up in the sentence. Consider the two sentences in (3):

(3) a The musicians try to leave at six
     b The committee decided to leave at six

where in (3a) the subject of *to leave at six* has to be co-referential with the subject *the musicians* (controller), whereas in (3b) this need not be the case. This is indicated by giving *try* the value yesoblcontrol. It is not always the subject that acts as the controller, however. Although on the surface both structures in (4) seem to be identical, the subjects of the embedded clauses need to be interpreted differently:

(4) a The general promised the soldiers *to leave*
     b The general told the soldiers *to leave*

In (4a) the subject of *to leave* is *the general*, in (4b) it is *the soldiers*. This difference is accounted for by the attribute controller, which indicates which argument is the controller. In the grammar this information is used to rule out the incorrect sentences in (5) as well as to spell out the proper subject and modal when this is needed in translation (6):

(5)   *The general promised the soldiers to perjure themselves

(6) (E) The general told the soldiers how to cope with emotions
     (D) De generaal vertelde de soldaten hoe zij met emoties
          The general   told   the soldiers   how they with emotions
          om moeten gaan
          have to   cope

The recognition of a Theory of Control (see, among others, Jackendoff (1972), Chomsky (1980)) also explains the fact that *promise* in sentence (7a) can be passivised (7b), whereas for sentence (8a) this is not possible, cf. (8b).[6]

---

[5] In the Rosetta grammars a distinction is made between arguments, bound adjuncts and free adjuncts. Free adjuncts correspond to what is usually called *adjuncts*. For a justification of these distinctions, see Odijk (1993).

[6] These facts are instances of Visser's Generalisation, discussed in Bresnan (1982)

(7) a I promised him that I would write an article
     b He was promised that I would write an article

(8) a   I promised him to write an article
     b   *He was promised to write an article

An option is to account for the ungrammaticality of (8b) in the lexicon by assigning the value active to the attribute possvoices, indicating that the verb can only occur in the active voice. This, however, also incorrectly rules out sentence (7b). The option of creating two entries must clearly be rejected as well, since the meaning of *promise* in both sentences is the same. Moreover, the inability of *promise* to passivise in sentences like (8b) is not an idiosyncrasy of the verb *promise*, but a general property of all subject-control verbs.[7] The difference in grammaticality therefore must be explained in the grammar. In sentence (8b) the process of passivisation blocks the identification of the controller of the infinitival clause, hence the sentence is ruled out. Since no control relation needs to be established in sentence (7b), this sentence is grammatical.

7.2.4 Other categories

Of course, it is not only verbs that need such detailed specification. Other categories, such as nouns and adjectives, have a set of specific attributes and values, some of these attributes being particularly relevant for one category. Nouns, for instance, have the attribute posscomas which distinguishes mass and count nouns. Mass nouns typically select the determiner *much* instead of *many* and may occur without a determiner in singular:

(9) a He drank much water/*much drinks
     b There is bread/*rose on the table

Adjectives specify, among others things, whether they form a morphological (by adding *-er*, cf. (10a)) or periphrastic (by adding *more*, as in (10b)) comparative:

(10) a big - bigg*er* - bigg*est*
      b careful - *more* careful - *most* careful

As with verbs, the morphological, syntactic and semantic attributes in combination with the grammar allow the system to make the proper analyses required for translation.

---

[7]Notice that a sentence like *He was promised to be elected in June* is grammatical because in this case the indirect object serves as the controller.

7.3 Rosetta dictionaries and Van Dale dictionaries

7.3.1 Introduction

As we have seen in the previous sections, the dictionaries contain highly detailed information. For testing the system itself, small dictionaries would be sufficient. For experimenting with texts or for a product, on the other hand, large dictionaries are essential. Obviously, the development of such dictionaries (containing, for instance, fifty thousand words) is a time-consuming activity. We hoped that much time could be saved by converting existing machine-readable dictionaries and therefore we investigated the possibility of developing dictionaries for Rosetta by using tapes (1986 version) of the Van Dale Dutch-Dutch (monolingual, abbreviated to 'N-N') dictionary, and the bilingual Dutch-English ('N-E') and English-Dutch ('E-N') dictionaries. These tapes form the basis of the prestigious printed dictionaries and they are the best material available for the Dutch-English language pair. It should be pointed out, however, that they were *not* developed specifically for application in the field of computational linguistics. This section discusses our experiences in converting these files to Rosetta dictionaries.

The conversion deals only with words from the *open* categories (nouns, verbs, adjectives and adverbs); dictionaries for the other categories, such as prepositions, conjunctions, pronouns, etc., were created completely by hand.

7.3.2 The Van Dale tapes

Three different Van Dale dictionaries were available on tape: the N-N, the N-E and the E-N; each dictionary had been divided into a number of linear text files that contain entries.

Each entry is organised systematically: every part of the information is preceded by a code indicating the type of the information that follows. So the entry word is always preceded by the entry word code, meanings are preceded by the meaning code, synonyms by the synonym code, etc. The text files with the codes had to be transformed into structured files. By using the codes, we had to locate the positions of the lexical entries in the text file, find the grammatical information, the given translations etc., and then store all this information. Of course, we preferred to do this fully automatically. In order to do so, a syntax of the dictionary and its entries was required, which was not available. For this reason, we derived this syntax ourselves from the dictionary, in the form of regular expressions, which can be recognised by the computer using standard techniques. By doing so we found several errors in the structure of the entries, such as typing errors in the codes, missing brackets, missing grammatical information, errors in enumerations inside the lemma, etc. In a paper dictionary such errors are irrelevant, but they had to be corrected manually before automatic conversion of the entries was possible.

7.3.3 The use of Van Dale dictionaries

Information offered by N-N, N-E and E-N

Section 7.2 described in detail the kind of information that is necessary for the Rosetta dictionaries. Obviously, the information for many attributes cannot be found in 'paper' dictionaries like the Van Dale dictionaries. The Van Dale dictionaries do not give explicit information about, for instance, the number of arguments of a verb or the type of the arguments, or about the structure of idioms. They often give examples of how a word or an idiom is used, but in general such examples cannot be interpreted automatically, they do not specify *all* ways in which a word can be used, and they tend to illustrate special rather than normal uses of a word. This is fully understandable, since the Van Dale dictionaries were intended for Dutch-speaking human users, for which these are no defects.

The information that the monolingual dictionary for Dutch (N-N) does contain which is structured enough to be processed (partially) automatically is: an entry word, the category of the entry word (noun, verb, etc.), some grammatical information, like gender and the way the plural is formed for nouns, and type (intransitive, transitive, reflexive, etc.) and the way they are conjugated for verbs (together with some other information like: which auxiliary verb of perfect tense should be used (*hebben* or *zijn*)), and a meaning description.

The N-E and E-N offer entry words with their categories and a translation, or — when a word has two or more senses — a number of (brief) meaning descriptions, with the appropriate translation.[8] Both N-E and E-N contain little grammatical information: N-E only contains gender of nouns and the type ((in)transitive, reflexive, etc.) of verbs and E-N contains only information for irregular nouns, verbs and adjectives.

It will be clear that the grammatical information for the entry word in the Van Dale files is too poor to assign values to all the attributes in the Rosetta dictionaries, but it is useful for determining the values of the main morphological attributes.

How to create dictionaries for Rosetta based on the Van Dale files

Our goal was to develop large dictionaries for Rosetta for the Dutch-English and English-Dutch language pairs. This section describes several approaches, as well as the reasons why most of them did not work.

---

[8] The translation string could not always be interpreted automatically without problems; the Dutch word *jeugdafdeling* for instance has the translation: *youth/young people's/young persons' section*. The 'scope' of the slashes is not defined for such strings and they can only be reduced correctly by human beings.

The N-N, of course, contains a vocabulary that covers Dutch. The N-E is mainly based on the same vocabulary; both files share the majority of their entry words. The E-N is based on an English vocabulary. This means that the E-N is *not* the reverse of the N-E. Many of the translations in the E-N **cannot** be found in the N-E.

The ideal situation would be to *merge* both files, but this is extremely difficult for several reasons. Ideally, one would like to map the meanings from one dictionary onto the meanings of the other. But the translations from the E-N are just strings of Dutch *without* any morphological, syntactic or semantic information. Thus, these strings cannot be associated automatically to entries in the N-E, and not at all to meanings in the N-E.[9]

Another possibility is to use *two separate* dictionaries: the N-E for translating Dutch into English and the E-N for translating English into Dutch (which implies that there is no real IL at the dictionary level). Then there is no merging problem, but it is still difficult to assign values to all attributes of the translations. For Dutch, it is impossible to do this (semi-)automatically: some Dutch attributes have *several* frequent values. The attribute *plurforms* for nouns for instance has two frequent values: *en-plural* (like: *boek<u>en</u>*, *appel<u>en</u>*) and *s-plural* (like: *telefoon<u>s</u>*, *appel<u>s</u>*), which do not correspond to certain stem-endings and thus cannot be filled in automatically. This has as a consequence that *every* Dutch noun that is given as translation in the E-N should be evaluated in order to get the proper values assigned to its attributes.

A *weaker* solution would be to take only *one* of the bilingual dictionaries. In that case we do not have the problem of merging the original 90,000 words with the translations (although there might be some overlap among the translations themselves), but we still have to assign the right values to the attributes of the translation words in one of the two languages.

Fortunately, compared to Dutch, English is very regular in morphology (formation of plurals, conjugation of verbs). Therefore it is possible to use the N-E as a base for the Rosetta dictionaries: the English translations will constitute the English dictionary and the morphological attributes can be filled in (semi-)[10]automatically, which means that the 'new' English vocabulary will have at least the same grammatical (mainly morphological) information as it would have if it would be based on the E-N. The N-N contains useful (mainly) morphological information like: *genders*, *plurforms*, etc. of nouns, and *conjclasses*, *particle*, *reflexivity* etc. of verbs,

---

[9]Assume the word *bank* is in the Dutch vocabulary — from the intersection of N-N and N-E —, and the same string in the E-N as its translation. How do we know whether or not this word is a 'new' sense, i.e. a sense which is not distinguished in the E-N? And if it is not, which of the senses of *bank* that we had already distinguished does it belong to? Of course, this would require evaluating several hundreds of thousands of translations.

[10]Irregular words — which form quite small groups — can be done separately (by hand). Most of these words are listed in literature on English grammar.

etc. Because the N-N and N-E share most of their entry words, this information can be transferred to the N-E (in fact, not the N-E itself but the intersection of N-E and N-N will therefore be the base for the Rosetta dictionary).

The intersection of N-E and N-N yields the relations between keys that are needed for a Rosetta dictionary: MORPH-DICT and IL-DICT can be generated from it. As we have seen before, most of the morphological information in S-LEX can also be extracted from this intersection.

The problem of filling the other attributes in S-LEX still remains. Because this is a time-consuming task, the dictionary had to be made smaller: a selection of approximately 5000 frequent Dutch words was made (with all their senses and English translations). The attributes in the Dutch and English dictionaries that resulted from this selection were filled in by hand.[11]

A Rosetta dictionary based on the *complete* intersection was also made: this was useful for testing the morphology and for the translation of single inflected words; the information in the Van Dale files was sufficient for this kind of use.

7.4   Concluding remarks

This chapter has described the organisation of the Rosetta dictionaries. As we have seen, the Rosetta dictionaries are highly structured objects that contain very detailed morphological and syntactic information needed for the numerous phenomena that have to be accounted for in the Rosetta grammars.

In the Rosetta project we also investigated the reusability of the tape version of the Van Dale N-N, N-E and E-N dictionaries in order to create large dictionaries for Rosetta. It turned out to be impossible to generate complete Rosetta dictionaries *automatically*: the syntactic information in the Van Dale dictionaries is not sufficiently detailed for the Rosetta grammar. A lot of work had to be done *manually*; therefore the size of the Rosetta dictionaries had to be limited.

---

[11]Similar problems were encountered in other research projects on reusability of machine-readable dictionaries (cf. Akkerman *et al.* (1985) and Boguraev and Briscoe (1989)). A more detailed discussion of the problems we encountered can be found in Smit (1990).

Chapter 8

Syntactic rules

8.1 Introduction

This chapter will describe the form and functioning of the rules used in the syntactic component, i.e. M-rules and surface rules. Examples of rules will be supplied as illustrations. The characteristics of the rules will be compared with some of the characteristics of other computationally oriented frameworks. The role of the surface rules will be discussed in some detail, since the other chapters will not go into this. Though many notational details are supplied, these are not essential for a correct understanding of the rest of this book; the main purpose of the sections dealing with these notations is to give an impression of the form of the syntactic rules actually used in the system.

8.2 M-Rules

8.2.1 General characterisation

M-rules were introduced in Chapter 3, and they were characterised as rules operating on S-trees. From a formal point of view M-rules are relations between tuples of S-trees and S-trees. This relation can be used to derive two functions, one for generation and one for analysis (see Chapter 4). In generation there is a function from a tuple of S-trees to a set of S-trees, and in analysis a function from an S-tree to a set of tuples of S-trees. Notice that in both analysis and generation the result of applying an M-rule is a finite *set* of objects. If this set is empty, we say that the rule is not applicable. The set can also contain more than one element: M-rules can create more than one result.

133

M-rules describe the S-trees to which they are applicable, and what the resulting S-trees look like. M-rules consist of a *structural part* and an *attribute-value* part. The structural part describes which structural conditions an S-tree must satisfy for the M-rule to be applicable, and it describes the structural changes to be performed. The attribute-value part describes conditions on the values of attributes, and changes in the values of attributes.

M-rules are very powerful rules, in other words, they can perform complex operations on S-trees. We supply a few examples of the complex operations that M-rules can perform. M-rules can combine two (or more) S-trees into one new S-tree, they can permute elements in an S-tree, delete parts of an S-tree, and introduce new elements into an S-tree (*syncategorematic introduction*, see Chapter 2). M-rules can build additional structure in an S-tree, they can move one part of an S-tree to some other position and they can substitute an S-tree for a variable with a specific index. In addition, M-rules can combine these operations in arbitrary ways.

M-rules can also operate on *abstract basic expressions*, i.e. basic expressions that never appear on the surface, because they are always deleted or replaced by some other element during the derivation.

It is useful to have powerful rules when a large, concrete system is to be built. Though it may be interesting from a theoretical point of view to try to build systems with restricted rules, it is unwise to build these restrictions directly into the formalism when a concrete system is to be developed. Doing so would prevent escapes from the restrictions in cases where these turn out to complicate the description or even to make it impossible. When developing a concrete system it makes more sense to adopt certain restrictions (if these appear desirable) but to allow for escapes from them in a simple manner (see also Shieber (1987)).

There are also theoretical reasons which make it necessary to have powerful rules, at least to have rules which go beyond the weak generative power of context-free rules. It has been shown that natural language cannot be described by context-free rules, and certain phenomena from Dutch figured prominently in the relevant proof. (see Huybregts (1984), Shieber (1985) and Pullum (1986, 1987,1991) for an overview of the relevant literature).

Apart from monolingual reasons for having powerful M-rules, there are also reasons having to do with translation: M-rules must relate the possibly completely different surface trees for sentences from different languages to isomorphic D-trees if these sentences are translation-equivalent. This entails that M-rules must at least go beyond the power of context-free rules, since if M-rules were context-free rules this would imply that also the surface trees for these sentences should be isomorphic.

Comparison with other frameworks

M-rules can perform powerful operations in turning an S-tree into another S-tree. Such operations are very often not allowed in other frameworks, e.g. those of Lexical Functional Grammar (LFG, Kaplan and Bresnan (1982)), Generalized Phrase Structure Grammar (GPSG, Gazdar et al. (1985)), Head-driven Phrase Structure Grammar (HPSG, Pollard and Sag (1987)) and in extensions of Categorial Grammar (CG, Ades and Steedman (1982)). In Tree Adjoining Grammars (TAG, Kroch and Joshi (1985)) only a limited number of operations on trees are allowed (i.e. only substitution and adjunction).

Many phenomena which are described by making use of the power of M-rules are described in other (computationally oriented) frameworks by techniques to pass features from one node to another (e.g. gap-threading techniques, Pereira and Shieber (1987)). In our opinion, however, using powerful operations on trees generally yields simpler, more elegant and descriptively more adequate analyses. Consider, for example, simple movement rules (e.g. WH-movement). Using M-rules makes it possible to really describe this as a movement rule so that movement can be factored out of all other rules. One can simply write one (set of) rule(s) dealing with this phenomenon, and let it interact with all the other rules. Furthermore, given such a (set of) rule(s), the formulation of certain other rules can be kept simple as well. Using feature-passing techniques, however, will require the addition of features to virtually each node occurring in a rule, and each node in the syntactic objects (trees or directed acyclic graphs, etc.) will - so to speak - be 'contaminated' by the presence of features only required to pass on information concerning other parts of the structure. Thus, many other rules are actually made more complex. In addition, there are certain differences between analyses using movement and analyses using feature-passing techniques concerning descriptive adequacy (and these differences are clearly related to the different techniques used). Comparing these analyses, movement analysis is, in our judgement, superior to analyses using feature passing techniques. These differences relate to the behaviour of parts of idioms and inversion of verbs in Spanish. These phenomena will be discussed in more detail in Chapter 11.

In contrast to many other (computationally oriented) frameworks such as GPSG, Functional Unification Grammar (FUG, Kay (1983)), HPSG and certain frameworks in which Categorial Grammar is combined with unification (Categorial Unification Grammar, Uszkoreit (1986), or Unification Categorial Grammar, Zeevat et al. (1987)), the operation of *unification* plays no role in M-rules. This is related to the fact that M-rules can make changes in trees, hence perform non-monotonic operations, while unification is typically a monotonic operation. Monotonic operations only add information and never destroy information, but complete reorganisations of trees and explicit changes of the values of attributes can be described in M-rules. Such operations are necessary to obtain adequate descriptions. See Chapter 11.

8.2.2   M-rule notation

A special notation has been developed for M-rules. We will illustrate this notation by means of an example.

In a rule, a number of *models* are first specified. A *model* is a description of a class of S-trees. The structural conditions that S-trees must satisfy if the rule is to be applicable and the structural changes that are to be performed by the rule are specified by means of these models. Since M-rules relate a tuple of S-trees $< t'_1, ..., t_n >$ to an S-tree t, a model is specified for each S-tree t_i from the tuple, preceded by a label mi, and a model (preceded by a label m) is specified to describe the S-tree t. In addition, a number of conditions and actions on attribute-value pairs are specified.

An example M-rule is given in in figure 8.1. A description of the entities occurring in this M-rule is given in Table 8.1. For expository convenience, this example is a simple rule. Nevertheless, it is a representative example: the rule is not context-free, it takes two arguments, and the rule can (and must) be associated with a meaning operation.

$X\{Xreci\}$	a node of category X with a variable $Xreci$ for its attribute-value pairs
Ni	a node
mui	a (possibly empty) arbitrary list of relation-S-tree pairs
$Xreci.a$	attribute a of $Xreci$
GEN	the condition-action pairs for generation
AN	the condition-action pairs for analysis
Ci	conditions
Ai	actions
@	the null action
&	end-of-rule
% RULE	beginning of rule
mi	the model for the ith S-tree of a tuple of S-trees
m	the output model for generation and the input model for analysis
SUBST	indicates the substituent
A = COPYT_xxx(B)	A and B have the same values for common attributes
A := COPYT_xxx(B)	A gets the same values as B for common attributes

Table 8.1: Entities of the M-rule notation.

We will explain the notation by first considering the example rule from a generative point of view, and then look at it from an analytical point of view.

The example rule has the name *RScompl*. Informally, this rule takes two clauses and substitutes the second clause for a variable in the first clause. This is illustrated graphically in figure 8.2.

In this example the partially derived sentence *he said x_2* is combined with the sentence *that he was ill* and turned into the sentence *he said that he was ill*. Note that

```
% RULE RScompl
< m1:N1    [    mu1,
                predrel/VP{VPrec1}
                [      mu2,
                       complrel/SVAR{SVARrec1},
                       mu3
                ],
                mu5
           ]

SUBST:
   m2:S{Srec1}[  mu4  ]
>

< m :N1    [    mu1,
                predrel/VP{VPrec1}
                [      mu2,
                       complrel/S{Srec1}[  mu4  ],
                       mu3
                ],
                mu5
           ]
>
PARAMETERS
   <
   index
   >
GEN
           <
           C1:    SVARrec1.index = index AND
                  SVARrec1 = COPYT_StoVAR(Srec1)
           A1:    @
           >
AN
           <
           C1:    true
           A1:    SVARrec1 := COPYT_StoVAR(Srec1);
                  SVARrec1.index := index
           >
&
```

Figure 8.1: M-rule *RScompl*. It is a substitution rule which substitutes the S-tree indicated by m2 for the syntactic variable in occurring in m1.

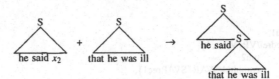

Figure 8.2: Informal graphical representation of the function of *RScompl*.

the rule is a substitution rule, i.e. it substitutes some phrase for a syntactic variable (x_2 in this example). In the remainder we will use the term *variable* in two senses: as an element occurring in S-trees, and as an element occurring in models as the name of an unspecified part of an S-tree, e.g. *N1* for a node, *mu1* for a sequence of relation-S-tree pairs, etc. In order not to confuse these two senses, we will use the term *syntactic variable* in this section for variables occurring in S-trees, and the term *model variable* for variables occurring in models.

Formally, there is a separate rule to substitute phrases for syntactic variables for each index. This is implemented, however, by one rule which is parametrised for an index value. For this reason, substitution rules have a parameter to indicate the index of the syntactic variable which is substituted for. The rule *RScompl* takes two arguments (described by *m1* and *m2*) and substitutes the substituent (described by *SUBST: m2*) for a syntactic variable (described by the model variable SVAR) with its index equal to the parameter *index*. The first argument must be an S-tree with some node (*N1*) and containing a VP with relation *predrel* which contains an SVAR with relation *complrel*. The fact that arbitrary material can precede and follow VP and SVAR is indicated by the model variables *mu1*, *mu2*, *mu3* and *mu5* surrounding these categories. The second argument consists of an S-tree of category S dominating some unspecified (possibly empty) sequence of relation-S-tree pairs (*mu4*). In addition, the conditions and actions on attribute-value pairs under GEN specify that the index of SVAR must be equal to the parameter *index* and that the values common to S and SVAR must be equal (indicated by the function COPYT_StoVAR). The model *m* states that the resulting structure takes the same form as the S-tree described by model *m1*, though with the S-tree described by SVAR replaced by the S-tree described in *m2*. No additional actions are to be performed (indicated by @).

In analysis the model *m* describes the S-trees that can serve as input. It states that the top node of an incoming S-tree (of any category) must dominate a VP which bears the grammatical relation *predrel*, and which dominates an S bearing the grammatical relation *complrel*. The conditions on attribute-value pairs under AN specify that no specific conditions hold, which is indicated by *true*. Two new

S-trees must be created, as specified in the models *m1* and *m2*. According to *m2* an S-tree is created which looks the same as the S-tree headed by S in *m*. According to *m1* an S-tree is formed which has the same form as the input S-tree, with the S-tree headed by S removed, and replaced by an S-tree as described by SVAR. The actions in the attribute-value part specify that all attributes of the new node SVAR get the values of the corresponding attributes of the node S (indicated by the function COPYT_StoVAR), and that the *index* attribute gets a unique index.

Note that the structural part of the notation is really reversible: the models are identical in generation and analysis. The condition-action pairs differ for generation and analysis. The reversibility of the condition-action pairs must be guaranteed by the rule writer. Recently, a new notation for M-rules (the language 4_2) has been developed which is fully reversible: both models and the attribute-value part have to be written only once, and automatically two functions are generated, one for generation, and one for analysis (see Jansen (1992) and Rous and Jansen (in prep)).

8.3 Surface rules

8.3.1 General characterisation

S-PARSER is a complex function, which takes as input a sequence of lexical S-trees and has as its task to form surface trees with the elements occurring in the input sequence of lexical S-trees as their leaves. These surface trees are formed by applying rules which are called *surface rules*.

Surface rules are, in essence, context-free rewriting rules, with the following extensions:

- The right-hand side of a rule is a regular expression over syntactic categories. Alternatives, optionality, iterativity and linear order can be expressed by means of this regular expression. The right-hand side of a surface rule is a regular expression for two reasons. First, indefinitely many branches are allowed under a node in an S-tree. Such structures cannot be described by normal context-free grammars. Second, it appears to be very convenient to have regular expressions at the right-hand side: many similar parts of rules can be collapsed into one rule. This extension increases the strong generative power, but not the weak generative power of surface rules.

- Conditions and actions on attribute-value pairs can be specified for each element in the regular expression.

- Interconnections between different elements from the regular expression can be accounted for by means of variables, called *parameters*. Parameters are also used to assign values to the attributes of the new top node.

As explained in Chapter 4, the grammar of S-PARSER is derivative. It has no independent status, it is fully dependent on the grammar underlying M-GENERATOR and M-PARSER, and it is usually written after the M-rules have been written. The main function of S-PARSER is to quickly create a set of candidate structures that are subjected to M-PARSER. Because of the derivative status of S-PARSER, and its function of parsing efficiently, there is no need for this grammar to describe the language correctly. It is sufficient that S-PARSER yields a superset of all S-trees that are accepted by M-PARSER. M-PARSER analytically uses the grammar that describes the language correctly, so incorrect candidate S-trees will be rejected by M-PARSER. Though S-parser may create S-trees which are not accepted by M-PARSER, it is not allowed that S-parser does not create an S-tree which would be accepted by M-PARSER: S-PARSER must be able to create at least all trees which are accepted by M-PARSER, and possibly more, but certainly not fewer.

In comparison with M-rules, surface rules have limited power. They can only combine a number of nodes, build a new top node on top of them, assign grammatical relations to the newly created daughters, and pass values of attributes to the top node. They cannot delete or add nodes. What a surface rule can do has been represented graphically in figure 8.3: it can put a new node with category C on top of a sequence of S-trees headed by categories $C_1,...,C_n$ and assign grammatical relations $r_1,...,r_n$ to them. Surface rules resemble the rules from attribute grammars with synthesised

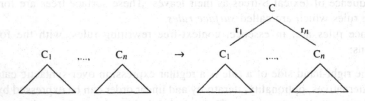

Figure 8.3: A surface rule can combine a number of S-trees into one by creating a new node above them and assigning grammatical relations to each S-tree.

attributes only. The fact that surface rules can perform only a very limited kind of operation makes it possible to use efficient parsing algorithms (see Chapter 18 and Leermakers (1993)). On the other hand, the very same fact makes it very difficult (if not impossible) to write a grammar which correctly describes the language with such rules. Though many interdependencies can be dealt with in principle by passing attribute-value pairs through nodes, in practice this is rather limited, because the attribute-value pairs are taken care of in M-GENERATOR and M-PARSER as well, so necessarily they must be there independently, and also because the possible values of attributes are either atomic or finite sets of atomic elements. So the possible values of attributes cannot be structured objects without restrictions on their size.

For these reasons, the surface parser will overaccept; in other words, it will accept certain sentences which are not part of the language. This is not a problem, either from a theoretical or from a practical point of view, given the derivative status of S-PARSER. However, it has an additional consequence: the parser will have a correct parse for each correct sentence, but it will also have a number of incorrect parses for certain correct sentences. From a theoretical point of view, this is again no problem, because M-PARSER will reject the incorrect parses. From a more practical point of view, however, it might lead to rather severe inefficiency if too many incorrect parses are accepted. So it remains desirable to write a surface parser which is as good as possible within the limitations imposed. This will be illustrated in more detail in the following sections.

8.3.2   Surface rule notation

This section will introduce the notation for surface rules and illustrate the notation with an example surface rule. The example given makes it possible to illustrate in some detail the trade-off between making surface rules simple and tolerant and making them as precise as possible, as pointed out in Chapter 4, and to illustrate some cases of over-acceptance by S-PARSER. This will be done in the next section.

A surface rule consists of two parts: one part describes the possible sequences of the syntactic categories of the top nodes of S-trees by means of a regular expression, and the other part describes conditions on attribute-value pairs, and actions that must be applied to them. In addition, conditions and actions can be formulated in terms of so-called *parameters*. These parameters have two functions: first, they make it possible to check conditions which hold between the top nodes of more than one input S-tree, and, second, they serve as local variables to pass information to the newly created top node.

Consider the following example surface rule for English[1] the regular expression of which is:

$$S = [NP/1 \mid PP/9] . [V/2] . NP/3 . [V/4] . V/5 .$$
$$[NP/6] . [NP/7] . \{PP/8\}$$

This regular expression specifies that an S consists optionally of an NP (optionality is indicated by the square brackets '[' and ']') or (alternatives indicated by ' | ') a PP, followed by (indicated by the dot '.') an optional verb, followed by an NP, followed by an optional verb, followed by a verb, followed by an optional NP, followed by an optional NP, followed by any number (zero or more, indicated by braces '{'

---

[1]This example rule is of course a simple rule for illustrative purposes; the rules actually used in the system are in general much more complex than the one given here.

and '}') of PPs. Each occurrence of a category occurring in the regular expression has been assigned a unique number (following the slash). This makes it possible to uniquely specify a grammatical relation for each occurrence of a category, and — as we shall see below — also to specify additional conditions and actions. Let us assume that the following grammatical relations are assigned to each occurrence: *shift* (NP/1,PP/9), *conj* (V/2), *subj* (NP/3), *aux* (V/4), *head* (V/5), *indobj* (NP/6), *obj* (NP/7) and *adjunct* (PP/8). Assuming that interrogative pronouns such as *who, what, whom* and personal pronouns (*I, you, he, him, she, her,* etc.) are NPs, this regular expression correctly accepts sentences such as

(1) a Who did he kill
     b He killed her
     c Did I kiss her
     d What will she give us

In addition, it characterises these strings as being of category S and correctly describes that *he* in (1a,b) is a subject, that *kill(ed)* in (1a,b) is the head, etc. We can illustrate this in more detail with the first example. According to the regular expression each S must consist at least of an NP and a verb, in that order. This means, that for the string *who did he kill,* which is a sequence of the form *NP V NP V,* either *did* or *kill* can be associated with V/5 from the regular expression, and that either *Who* or *he* can be associated with NP/3. It is easy to see that only a correct parse can be found if *who* is associated with NP/1 (it gets relation *shift*), *did* with V/2 (relation: *conj*), *he* with NP/3 (relation: *subj*), and *kill* with V/5 (relation: *head*). Since a match with the regular expression has been found, a new node (S) is created, dominating the whole sequence, and the grammatical relations are represented in the tree in (2).

(2)   NP(*who*) +   V(*did*) +   NP(*he*)+   V(*kill*)   ⇒
                                  S

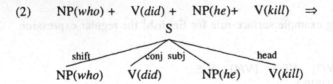

The regular expression, however, also incorrectly accepts sentences like

(3) a *Who did him kill
     b *What will him did kissed I
     c *He did he walk
     d *Who bought he did
     e *He sell can it

REGULAR EXPRESSION

S = [NP/1 | PP/9] . [V/2] . NP/3 . [V/4] . V/5 . [NP/6] . [NP/7] . {PP/8}

DECL		auxfound	=	BOOLEAN;
		whshiftfound	=	BOOLEAN;
		shiftfound	=	BOOLEAN;
		conjfound	=	BOOLEAN;
INIT		auxfound	:=	false;
		whshiftfound	:=	false;
		shiftfound	:=	false;
		conjfound	:=	false;
1	**REL:** *shift*			
	C:	NP.cases	≠	nominative
	A:	shiftfound	:=	true;
	C:	NP.wh	=	true
	A:	whshiftfound	:=	true;
2	**REL:** *conj*			
	C:	V.subc	=	auxverb
	A:	auxfound	:=	true;
		conjfound	:=	true
3	**REL:** *subj*			
	C:	NP.cases	=	nominative
4	**REL:** *aux*			
	C:	V.subc		auxverb AND
		(NOT auxfound)		
	A:	auxfound	:=	true
5	**REL:** *head*			
	C:	V.subc		mainverb AND
		auxfound	⇒	(V.form = infinitive) AND
		(NOT auxfound)	⇒	(V.form = finite)
6	**REL:** *indobj*			
7	**REL:** *obj*			
8	**REL:** *adjunct*			
9	**REL:** *shift*			
FINAL	C:	(whshiftfound	⇒	conjfound) AND
		(shiftfound	AND	(NOT whshiftfound)) ⇒
		(NOT conjfound)		
	C:	whshiftfound		
	A:	S.type	:=	whq;
	C:	(NOT shiftfound) AND		
		conjfound		
	A:	S.type	:=	ynq;
	C:	(NOT conjfound)		
	A:	S.type	:=	decl;
	A:	–		

Table 8.2: Example surface rule.

Many incorrect sentences can be excluded by adding conditions to the categories. Since each category has been assigned a unique number, we can uniquely specify a number of conditions for each. For example, we might specify that NP/3 must have *case=nominative*. This will exclude examples (3a,b) and it will correctly allow *Who did he kill*. We might further specify for NP/1 that it cannot have *case=nominative*, to exclude a sentence such as (3c). We might specify for V/2 and V/4 that the verbs must be auxiliary verbs, but for V/5 that the verb must be a main verb. This will exclude sentences such as (3d,e).

The conditions proposed impose restrictions on the attribute-value pairs of a single node. But other conditions are also possible, which relate the values of attributes of different nodes, or relate the presence of different nodes. In addition, *actions* can be specified which change the values of parameters or of the attributes of the new top node. For example, in a correct English sentence, V/2 and V/4 cannot both be present at the same time. They can both be absent (e.g. *he bought it*), or one of them can be present (*he will buy it, will he buy it*), but if both are present the sentence is ill-formed (cf. *will he can buy it*). This interdependency can be accounted for by reformulating the regular expression or by so-called parameters. A parameter is a variable which can pass information from one occurrence of a node to another in the same regular expression. We could, for example, adopt the parameter *auxfound*, and initially assign the value *false* to it. If V/2 is encountered, this parameter is reset to *true*. Initialisation and resetting of this parameter is performed by *actions*. A condition on V/4 states that it can only be found if the parameter *auxfound* is *false*. In this manner we correctly exclude all sentences with two auxiliary verbs, one to the left, and one to the right of the subject. Another restriction is that, if an auxiliary is found, the main verb (V/5) must be in its infinitival form, and if no auxiliary is found, the verb must be in its finite form. This restriction excludes sentences such as *He will kissed her*, *I can buys it*, *Must I working*, etc. and *he kiss her*, *We buying it*, *We hidden*, etc. This condition can be captured by adding a condition to V/5, stating that if *auxfound=true*, then *form=infinitive*, and if *auxfound =false*, then *form=finite*.

All conditions and actions proposed above, and some others, are specified explicitly in Table 8.2. If no condition or action is explicitly specified for a certain node in the example surface rule, the condition is to be interpreted as *true*, and the action as the null action. In addition, all parameters used and their types have been declared, an *initial* action (to set the initial values of parameters), *final* conditions (conditions which can be evaluated only after all elements have been encountered) and *final* actions to create the new top node (of category S in the example given here) and assign values to its attributes have been added. In the example rule conditions are preceded by the notation **C:**, actions follow **A:**, and relations are preceded by **REL:**. Note that conditions and actions can be nested, as in the *final* conditions and actions. The rule given correctly accepts sentences such as in (4), and it characterises them correctly as declarative (a,b), as a yes-no question (c) and as a wh-question (d), respectively.

(4) a He can see her
   b Her he can see
   c Can he see her
   d Who can he see

8.3.3 Over-acceptance

Though the regular expression given originally has been extended with a number of conditions to reduce the number of incorrect sentences it accepts, the example rule still accepts many incorrect sentences. The ill-formed examples in (5a,b,d) are still incorrectly accepted, as are many, many other examples. Of course, it is possible to add more conditions to exclude these examples, though for the phenomena illustrated in (5) this is not so simple. Example (5a) could be excluded by adding a condition that *saw* is member of a class of verbs which allow a direct object but no indirect object. One might try to exclude example (5b) in a similar manner, by stating that *kiss* is a verb which requires a direct object to its right. However, this will incorrectly exclude (5c), so a more subtle treatment is required here. The fact that the absence of the direct object to its right is allowed here is clearly related to the fact that the initial position in the sentence is occupied by *who*, and one could formulate conditions to take this fact into account. In a realistic grammar, however, one should also take into account that such phrases can be at an indefinite distance from the relevant verb. Though standard techniques to deal with such phenomena exist (e.g. gap-threading, Pereira and Shieber (1987)), it is not easy to use these in S-parser, since these techniques require that the surface parser is able to parse gaps (i.e. non-lexical nodes dominating nothing) and it requires structured objects as possible values for attributes. In the actual surface grammar, a different technique is used, which, however, does not make all relevant connections, and overaccepts, i.e. it accepts certain strings which are not well-formed strings of the relevant language.

(5) a *I saw him her
   b *He kiss
   c Who did he kiss
   d *Who did he kiss her
   e He gave it
   f What did he give
   g *Who did he give it
   h What did he give him

Example (5e) illustrates a different but related kind of phenomenon: the sentence is well-formed, and it is accepted by the example rule, but it is assigned two different analyses: the pronoun *it* can be either a direct object, or an indirect object. This problem can perhaps be circumvented if it is specified that *give* requires the presence of a direct object, but (5f) indicates that we have to solve the same problems as mentioned above. And a double analysis cannot be avoided for the examples (5g,h), which illustrates the overaccepting nature of the surface rules.

Since it is difficult to convincingly illustrate the overaccepting character of the surface rules in simple examples (it appears that these can always be ameliorated) we will simply indicate some examples of over-acceptance that actually occur in the current S-PARSER. First, we allow that singular count nouns form NPs on their own. This is necessary because such NPs occur rather frequently in idiomatic expressions (e.g. *rekening houden met* lit. *account hold with*, 'to take into account') and when the NP is used predicatively (e.g. *hij is dokter*, lit. *he is doctor*). When such NPs are used neither predicatively nor as a part of an idiomatic expression, they are ill-formed. S-PARSER, however, is not capable of recognising whether the relevant NP occurs in an idiomatic expression, and in the current version the internal form of the NP is not related to the grammatical relation of the whole NP. For these reasons, S-PARSER accepts sentences such as **man gave book*. As a further consequence, a sentence such as *he gave this book* receives two different parses, a correct one in which *this book* is the direct object, and an incorrect one, in which *this* is the indirect object and *book* the direct object. For similar reasons, the Dutch sentence *leest het kind* (lit. *reads the/it child*, 'does the child read') gets several analyses, a correct one in which *het kind* is the subject, and an incorrect one in which *het* is analysed as the subject[2] and *kind* as the direct object. In Dutch, certain NPs can occur without an overt head noun. For example, NPs can consist of an adjective, or a determiner and an adjective only, cf. *hij zag (een) mooie* (lit. *he saw (a) beautiful*, 'he saw a beautiful one/beautiful ones'). Accepting such NPs leads to three parses for a sentence such as *hij gaf het mooie boek* (lit. *he gave the/it beautiful book*): *het* as indirect object, and *mooie boek* as a direct object; *het mooie* as indirect object, and *boek* as direct object; or *het mooie boek* as direct object. Such examples can be multiplied at will. In the actual surface grammar, the examples illustrating the interaction between verbal complementation and extraction phenomena given above (cf. (5b,c,e,f)) actually occur. Agreement between noun and attributive adjective is not taken into account in S-PARSER, leading to wrong parses for *hij kocht enthou-siast boeken* (lit. *he bought enthusiastic books*, 'he bought books enthusiastically'): *enthousiast* is correctly analysed as an adverb, but also incorrectly as an adjectival modifier of *boeken*. Subject-verb agreement is dealt with in S-PARSER, though not perfectly, but well enough to avoid spurious parses due to it. The relation between arguments and verbs in so-called cross-serial dependencies in Dutch (see Chapter 11)

---

[2] The word *het* is ambiguous: it can be a determiner (English: *the*), or a personal pronoun (English: *it*).

are not dealt with adequately in S-PARSER, leading to over-acceptance and spurious parses. This construction is an example which actually cannot be dealt with adequately in S-PARSER: the formalism used is weakly equivalent to a context-free grammar, so that it cannot distinguish the well-formed sentences from the ill-formed ones. In these constructions the current S-PARSER imposes no constraints on the number of NP arguments of the verb *leren* in a verbal sequence such as *wilde leren zwemmen* (*wanted to teach to swim*) so that any sentence of the form *..dat* $\{NP\}^3$ *wilde leren zwemmen* is accepted. This leads to spurious parses for a sentence such as *..dat dit meisje dat jongetje wilde leren zwemmen* (*..that this girl wanted to teach that boy how to swim*), in which the sequence *dit meisje dat jongetje* can be analysed in four ways, indicated in (6), only one of which (6d) is correct.

(6) a NP[dit] NP[meisje] NP[dat] NP[jongetje]
    b NP[dit] NP [meisje] NP[dat jongetje]
    c NP[dit meisje] NP[dat] NP[jongetje]
    d NP[dit meisje] NP[dat jongetje]

However, we want to emphasise again, that these defects of S-PARSER pose no problems, because of the derivative status of S-PARSER: all incorrect parses of S-PARSER will be rejected and all correct parses accepted by M-PARSER, which uses the analytical version of the grammar that correctly describes the relevant language.

8.4 Concluding remarks

This chapter has characterised and illustrated the syntactic rules of the Rosetta system. Two kinds of rules have been described: (1) M-rules, which are powerful rules operating on S-trees, and which form the rules of the grammar that characterises the relevant languages and explicitly describes the relation of syntactic structures to their semantics; and (2) surface rules, which are rules which can perform only a very limited number of operations and which constitute the rules for S-PARSER, which is a module for obtaining candidate S-trees in a very efficient manner. The notation for both kinds of rules have been introduced and illustrated. A brief comparison between M-rules and rules from other frameworks has been made, in which we stressed that the power of the M-rules is useful:

(1) to be able to describe natural language at all,

(2) not to be obstructed by limitations inherent to the formalism when constructing a realistic system, and

---

[3]The braces, as in regular expressions, are used here to indicate that the elements inside can occur zero or more times.

(3) for reasons of isomorphy between grammars of different languages.

In addition, we have given some detailed examples illustrating the trade-off between making surface rules simple and tolerant on the one hand and as precise as possible on the other.

Chapter 9

Modular and controlled M-grammars

9.1 Introduction

The framework described in the previous chapters is elegant and has proved its value in practice, but it also has a number of deficiencies, the most salient of which is the impossibility of assigning an explicit structure to the grammars. This may cause problems, especially in situations in which large grammars have to be written by a group of people. In the extended framework presented in this chapter, a grammar is divided into subgrammars in a linguistically motivated way and the application of rules in a subgrammar is explicitly controlled. Two kinds of rules are distinguished only one of which is involved in the isomorphy requirement. Next to that, these two kinds of grammar rules are grouped together into rule classes. The use of these divisions naturally leads to a highly modular structure for the system, which helps in controlling its complexity.[1]

9.2 Problems with free M-grammars

The framework outlined above has been worked out in a simple and mathematically elegant way. However, the *free M-grammars* described there have some shortcomings which may cause problems in the case of large grammars. Three kinds of problems can be distinguished.

---

[1]The ideas presented in this chapter have been discussed first in Appelo *et al.* (1987) and have also been presented in Appelo (1993).

1. Lack of structure in M-grammars

Grammars for natural languages are very large and therefore very complex. To give an idea of the size and complexity of the grammars it should be mentioned that before rule-writing for the Rosetta system began, about 300 linguistic phenomena to be accounted for per grammar were listed. The actual implementation, in 1991, covers about 200 phenomena which resulted in about 1000 M-rules per grammar. Some of these rules are very extensive and cover several pages, mostly because they consist of subrules. Some of the phenomena are simple, while others are very complex or require extensive description. For example, the description of the set of possible 'verb patterns' of a language is rather extensive. In English, we distinguish about 125 verb patterns and we need a (sub)rule for each verb pattern.

Besides, the interaction of phenomena has to be taken into account. A good example of such interaction is the example concerning negation and word order in main and subordinate clauses in Dutch, described in Chapter 2.

In a *free M-grammar*, as described in previous chapters, the syntactic component specifies a set of rules without any internal structure. Although the mathematical elegance of free production systems is appealing, they are less suited to large grammars. As the number of rules grows, it becomes more and more desirable that the syntax be subdivided into parts with well-defined tasks and well-defined interfaces with other parts.

This particularly is the case if the grammars are being developed by a group of people. It is necessary to have an explicit division of tasks and to coordinate the work of the individuals flexibly so that the system will be easy to maintain, modify and extend.

In computer science it is common practice to divide a large task into subtasks with well-defined interfaces. This is known as the **modular approach**. This approach has gained recognition in the field of natural language processing, too (see for some of the first in MT Vauquois and Boitet (1985); Isabelle and Macklovitch (1986)).

Note that the grammars have already been subdivided into a morphological, syntactic and semantic *component* and the translation process into *modules* (cf. Chapter 2). In this chapter, however, we will discuss subdivisions of the syntactic component of M-grammar, the basis for the modules M-GENERATOR and M-PARSER, and corresponding subdivisions of the semantic component, the basis for the modules G-TRANSFER and A-TRANSFER. The main question is how a modular approach can be applied in a compositional grammar, in an insightful and linguistically motivated way.

2. Lack of control on M-rule applications

In many cases grammar writers have a certain ordering of rules in mind, e.g.

they may want to indicate that the rules for inserting determiners during NP-formation should be applied after the rules for inserting adjectives. In the free M-grammar formalism explicit ordering is impossible, but the rules could be ordered implicitly by characterising the S-trees in a specific way, e.g. by splitting up a syntactic category into several categories, and by giving the rules applicability conditions which guarantee that the ordering aimed at is actually achieved. For example, if it is desired to order two rules that both operate on an NP, this can be achieved by creating categories NP1, NP2 and NP3 and letting one rule transform an NP1 into an NP2 and another rule an NP2 into an NP3. One of the disadvantages of this treatment is that it leads to a proliferation of rather unnatural categories.

In large grammars some means of expressing the order of application of rules is necessary in order to give the grammar writers something to go by. However, it is hard to find an elegant and transparent way of specifying rule order in a compositional grammar; the situation is more complicated than in transformational systems like ROBRA (cf. Vauquois and Boitet (1985)), because rules may have more than one argument.

In addition to linear ordering, other means of controlling the application of rules are desirable, e.g. a distinction between obligatory, optional and iterative rules.

Examples of such rules are the following:

obligatory: the rule that accounts for subject-verb agreement in a finite clause is obligatory. That rule *must* apply and only *once* for that clause.

optional: the rule that puts *om* in a Dutch infinitival complement sentence is optional. It should apply *once* or should *not* apply.

iterative: the rule that inserts an adjective into an S-tree during the composition of a noun phrase is iterative. It can apply *several* times but *need not* apply.

In free M-grammars all rules are optional and potentially iterative. It is not clear how to add obligatory rules to such a free production system; in fact it is hard to understand what that would mean.

3. **Lack of structure in the translation relation**

As explained in Chapter 2, the translation relation between languages is defined by attuning the grammars to each other. One of the complications in the isomorphic grammar framework is that *each* syntactic rule of one grammar *must* correspond to at least one rule of every other grammar. For rules that contribute to the meaning or express other information that is considered relevant to translation, this is exactly what is needed, because it is not only the meaning that has to be conveyed during translation, but also the way in which the meaning is derived. However, rules that are only relevant to the form of the sentence and that do not carry translation-relevant information are problematic, especially if they are language-specific. A purely syntactic transformation as the insertion of *om* in Dutch does not correspond naturally to a syntax rule of English. In the free M-grammar framework this problem could be solved in one of the following two ways: 1) by adding a corresponding rule to the English syntax which does nothing more than change the syntactic category and which is superfluous from an English point of view, or 2) by merging the Dutch transformation rule with a meaningful rule, which can result in a complex rule. These solutions are not very elegant and complicate the grammars unnecessarily. It would be better if the correspondence between rules must hold for meaningful rules only and such superfluous or complex rules can be avoided. It is necessary to distinguish between meaningful rules and purely syntactic language-specific rules.

In subsequent sections the modular approach chosen will be described, which helps to solve the above problems. Section 9.3 discusses a syntax-oriented division into *subgrammars* and Section 9.4 describes translation-oriented divisions into *rule* and *transformation classes*. In Section 9.5 it will be argued that a combination of these divisions is needed. Finally, in Section 9.6 it will be shown that the way in which subgrammars are defined enables us to define the control of rule applications in a transparent way.

9.3   Subgrammars, a syntax-oriented division

In this section, a syntax-oriented division into subgrammars will be described. First, two concepts which inspired this division, namely *module* from the programming language Modula-2 (Section 9.3.1) and *projection* from $\overline{X}$-theory (Section 9.3.2), will be explained. An informal subgrammar definition will then be given (Section 9.3.3), followed by an example (Section 9.3.4). A more formal definition of subgrammars will not be given until a division into classes of rules has been introduced (Section 9.4), that division has been combined with the division proposed in this section (Section 9.5) and the notion of control expression has been introduced (Section 9.6).

9.3.1   A modular approach

The computer language Modula-2 (cf. Wirth (1985)) is a well-known example of applying a modular approach. It requires that one

1. divide the total into smaller parts (**modules**), each with a well-defined task;

2. define explicitly what is used from other parts (**import**) and what may be used by other parts (**export**);

3. separate the definition from the implementation.[2]

The explicit definition of import and export and the strict separation of implementation and definition make it possible to prove the correctness of a module in terms of its imports, without having to look at the implementation of the imported modules. In this way, the above mentioned complexity problem and the coordination problem caused by the lack of structure in the M-grammars can be tackled. Applying this modular approach to grammars can come down to the following requirements:

1. dividing the grammar into **subgrammars** with a well-defined linguistic task;

2. defining explicitly what is visible to other subgrammars (**export**) and what is used from other subgrammars (**import**);

3. ensuring that the actual implementation (i.e. the rules) is of local significance only.

9.3.2 Projection

$\overline{X}$-theory

The actual subdivision chosen was inspired by the notion of **projection** from the $\overline{X}$-theory (or X-bar theory) of Transformational Generative Grammar (cf. e.g., Chomsky (1970)). This theory states that every phrasal category has a lexical head X. This is expressed by composing the phrasal categories as X + a 'bar level': $\overline{X}, \overline{\overline{X}}$. They are projections of X. The lexical categories are: N (noun), V (verb), P (preposition) or A (adjective or adverb), although in the Rosetta approach we use for A: ADJ and ADV. For $\overline{\overline{X}}$, the maximal projection, we will use XP as a variable for the conventional symbols NP, AP, VP and PP. So, a noun phrase (NP) has a head N etc. An NP as, for example, *the smart girl*, is projected from an expression (*girl*) with category N. These projections correspond to constituents in language and appear to be a useful choice for modular units in a natural language system.

---

[2]The definition part contains the interface description of the exported objects, while the implementation part contains the actual implementation. An importer of a module needs to have available the definition part only, the implementation part remains the property of the designer of the module.

Projection path
Applying the essentials of this idea to the compositional grammars of the Rosetta
approach implies that for the basic expressions which are of lexical category type BX,
with B for *basic* and X a variable for a lexical category (e.g. N, V, ADJ, etc.)[3], there
are syntactic rules that will ultimately compose S-trees of category type XP. For each
maximal projection a subgrammar can now be defined that expresses how S-trees of
category type XP can be derived from basic expressions of category type BX and
other imported categories. A possible derivation process of the projection from BX
to XP is called a **projection path**. The BX-categories are called **head categories**.
The names of top categories of intermediate S-trees during the projection consist of
some prefix α + X. For example, SUB + N (SUBN) or C(ommon) + N(OUN) (CN).
The projection path can be shown in a derivation tree, as the path $BX - R_1 - R_2 -
R_{3,1}$, drawn in thick lines, in the schematic Figure 9.1. We follow the convention
that the head category and its projections are the leftmost arguments in the tree. All
imported categories are in their turn maximal projections (with top category type
XP), too. They are also represented with a thick projection path in the derivation
tree. In Figure 9.1, BX –......– R_4 represents a projection path for an imported
category.

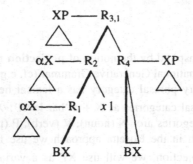

Figure 9.1: $BX - R_1 - R_2 - R_{3,1}$ is a simplified, partial projection path from an S-tree of the head
category BX to an S-tree of the top category XP. αX is the top category of an intermediate S-tree and $x1$
is a variable. Rule $R_{3,1}$ substitutes the result of another projection, represented by the projection path BX
- .....- R_4, resulting in an S-tree with top category XP, for $x1$.

Note that although the notion *projection* was borrowed from $\overline{X}$-theory, no correspondence is claimed between $\overline{X}$-categories and top categories (αX) of intermediate
S-trees that are yielded during the projection from our head category to its maximal

---

[3]In practice, we use the 'major' categories N, V, P, ADJ and ADV next to some 'minor' categories
such as D(eterminer) and Q(uantifier). The specification of such categories is left to the grammar writers.

projection. $\overline{X}$-theory states that all maximal projections have similar syntactic structures, but although S-trees resemble these syntactic structures vaguely, this aspect is less relevant for the Rosetta grammars. It is of more interest whether they are the result of similar derivations. We will come back to this point in Section 9.4 and will use the fact that the derivations are alike in solving categorial divergence problems in Chapter 13. More details about the differences from $\overline{X}$-theory can be found in Appelo (1993).

Small clauses or XPPROP

A sentence is usually seen as a subject-predicate relation, i.e. a combination of an NP and a VP. But other XP categories than VP, together with an NP, can express a subject-predicate relationship as well (cf. Stowell (1981)). Such subject-predicate relations are called **small clauses**. For example, the NP *him* and the ADJP *funny* in *I think* [*him funny*], or the two NPs *him* and *a fool* in *I consider* [*him a fool*] form a small clause. Such a tenseless subject-predicate expression will be called **XPPROP** in which X stands for the X of the predicate and PROP for proposition. For example, in [*him funny*] we have ADJPPROP (with X = ADJ) and in [*him a fool*] we have NPPROP (with X = N). We consider XPPROP a further projection of the predicate XP.

Clauses

A tensed subject-predicate expression will be called **CLAUSE** and considered another further projection of the predicate XP. For example, in the sentences *I think that he is sleeping* and *I think that he is funny* we have the embedded CLAUSEs [*that he is sleeping*] and [*that he is funny*], respectively.

Different top categories

Starting from a basic expression of category type BX, in principle three S-trees with different top category types can be derived: XP (the 'normal' projection), XPPROP and CLAUSE (the subject-predicate expressions).

Figure 9.2 shows some of the resulting derivation trees and S-trees of the examples above.

Subgrammars

The concepts of $\overline{X}$-theory are applied in the modular approach to M-grammars in the following way:

- there is a subgrammar for every maximal projection.

Figure 9.2: The (simplified) derivation trees with the resulting S-trees of the projection of BV to CLAUSE, BADJ to ADJPPROP and BN to NPPROP.

- exports or results from subgrammars are maximal projections, i.e. S-trees with top categories of category type XP or CLAUSE, or small clauses, i.e. S-trees with top category XPPROP.

- imports of subgrammars are:

  - obligatory: a basic expression, i.e. an S-tree with a basic category type BX. This S-tree is an element of the lexicon. The most important BX-categories are: BV, BN, BADJ, BADV, BP, BD and BQ (basic verb, noun, adjective, adverb, preposition, determiner and quantifier, respectively).

  - optional: exports from other subgrammars, i.e. S-trees with top category of category type XP, (embedded) CLAUSE and XPPROP (small clauses). They are the specifiers, modifiers and complements and are imported by substitution and modification rules in the M-grammar framework.

- linguistic tasks of subgrammars are specifications of how to project a certain basic expression of category type BX to certain S-trees of category type XP, CLAUSE or XPPROP.

Defining subgrammars of M-grammars in accordance with 'projection paths' provides a natural way of expressing the application order of the M-rules: they are defined with respect to the projection path only. Additionally, it is possible to indicate whether they are obligatory, optional or iterative.

9.3.3 An informal subgrammar definition

In this section, a more systematic, but still informal, definition of 'projection' subgrammars will be given. A 'projection' subgrammar can be characterised as follows:

1. **name**: a name constructed in accordance with convention 1 (to be defined below).

2. **export**: a specification of a set of S-trees with a top category of category type XP, XPPROP or CLAUSE. This category is called the **export category**.

3. **import**: a specification of the set of S-trees that can be imported, subdivided into three classes:

   (a) S-trees with a specific category of the category type BX, also called the **head category**.

   (b) S-trees that are exported by other subgrammars and that can be taken as an argument by rules that take more than one argument. So these S-trees have a top category from the set of export categories, i.e. they are of the category type XP, XPPROP or CLAUSE.

   (c) Variables for which S-trees of category type XP, XPPROP or CLAUSE can be substituted.

   The import set of a subgrammar always contains at least a head category. For every import S-tree in the import set, there must be at least one rule that takes it as an argument.

4. **rules**:   a set of M-rules that take care of the projection from S-trees of the head category to S-trees of the export category. Every rule has one argument, which is called the **head argument**, i.e. the S-tree with the head category or one of the intermediate results during its projection (an S-tree of category αX). The other arguments of a rule are called the **non-head arguments**. These non-head arguments are part of the set of import S-trees and must be specified in the import of the subgrammar.

5. **control**: a definition of the possible application sequences of the M-rules, ordered with respect to their head arguments, indicating the kind of application (obligatory, optional or iterative).

With respect to this subgrammar characterisation there are a few conventions that should be mentioned here:

convention 1 : (preliminary version) a subgrammar is referred to by a name that follows the following schema: '**head category name**'to'**export category name**'.

convention 2 : the head argument of a rule is always the *first* argument of that rule.

As we follow convention 2, viz. that the head argument of a rule is always the first argument, the ordering of the rules is defined with respect to the first argument only.

In the ideal case, neither the rules nor the intermediate results have to be known to the writers of other subgrammars. In that case they are considered local to the subgrammar. So items 2 and 3 of the above characterisation specify the relation with other subgrammars, whereas 4 and 5 are only of local significance, thus meeting the requirements of the modular approach. The advantages of this division into projection subgrammars are, firstly, that the structure of the grammar has become more transparent, and, secondly, that the grammar consists of well-defined parts which can be tested separately. This makes it possible to divide the work between several people.

9.3.4 An example subgrammar

An example of a subgrammar is the NP-projection subgrammar with a BN as head and exporting an NP. Other categories imported by this subgrammar are OPENADJPPROP[4], DP, etc. The set of rules contains formation, substitution and modification rules. The control expression indicates that, for example, the modification rules can be applied iteratively and that they precede the NP-formation rules.

To give some idea, an example for the English NP projection subgrammar is shown. It serves as an illustration of the method and is, of course, simplified, but it is also rather realistic in its essential aspects. It is not claimed that the rules described here are the best rules for the phenomena they take into account.

Example of an English subgrammar for the projection from BN to NP

1. **name**: BNtoNP

2. **export**: S-tree of category **NP**

3. **import**:

    - S-tree of head category: **BN**.
    - S-trees with categories that are exported by other subgrammars with export category: **OPENADJPPROP, DP, NP, CLAUSE**.
    - variables for S-trees of category **NP**.

---

[4]One way to encode the property of an S-tree of category **XPPROP** that it still contains a subject variable is to give it the category **OPENXPPROP**. If the subject variable has been substituted for, the category will be **CLOSEDXPPROP**. In fact, all **XPPROP** categories have been duplicated in this way.

4. **rules**:
The rule notation that is actually used in the Rosetta grammars is fairly complicated. For this illustration the following informal notation will be used:

name of rule   a: number of arguments of the rule
                b: applicability conditions
                c: informal characterisation of the result
                d: optional: additional explanation

The value *omega* indicates 'unspecified'.

RBNtoSUBN: a: 1 argument
               b: S-tree of category BN
               c: S-tree with top node SUBN dominating the S-tree of category BN

RSUBNtoN1:   a: 1 argument
               b: S-tree of category SUBN
               c: S-tree of category N, with *number = singular*;
                   N dominates the S-tree of category SUBN
               d: accounts for singular count nouns

RSUBNtoN2:   a: 1 argument
               b: S-tree of category SUBN
               c: S-tree of category N, with *number = plural*;
                   N dominates the S-tree of category SUBN
               d: accounts for plural count nouns

RCNformation: a: 1 argument
                b: S-tree of category N
                c: S-tree of category CN (Common Noun);
                    CN dominates the S-tree of category N

RNPformation1:   a: 1 argument
                 b: S-tree of category CN
                 c: S-tree with top node NP, dominating an S-tree for the
                     definite article *the* and the S-tree of category CN
                 d: syncategorematic introduction of *the*

RNPformation2:   a: 1 argument
                 b: S-tree of category CN
                 c: S-tree with top node NP, dominating an S-tree for the
                     indefinite article *a* and the S-tree of category CN
                 d: syncategorematic introduction of *a*

RNPformation3:   a: two arguments
                 b: 1) S-tree of category CN and 2) S-tree of category DP
                 c: S-tree with top node NP, dominating the S-tree
                     of category DP and the S-tree of category CN
                 d: categorematic introduction of a determiner phrase

RCNsuperdeixis1:   a: 1 argument
                    b: S-tree of category CN, *superdeixis = omega*
                    c: S-tree of category CN, *superdeixis = present*
                    d: accounts for the temporal value *present*
                       that can play a role if the CN is modified by a
                       relative sentence (see Chapter 14),

RCNsuperdeixis2:   a: 1 argument
                    b: S-tree of category CN, *superdeixis = omega*
                    c: S-tree of category CN, *superdeixis = past*
                    d: accounts for the temporal value *past*
                       that can play a role if the CN is modified by a
                       relative sentence (see Chapter 14),

RNargmod: a: two arguments
                    b: 1) S-tree of category CN and 2) a variable x_i
                    c: S-tree of category CN with the variable inserted to the right of N
                    d: The variable represents an argument of an N.
                       It also inserts the required preposition.
                       e.g. *to x_i* in *answer to x_i*

RCNmodADJP: a: two arguments
                    b: 1) S-tree with top node CN, dominating an S-tree of
                       category N and 2) S-tree with top node OPENADJPPROP,
                       dominating a variable and an S-tree with category ADJP
                    c: S-tree of category CN with S-tree of category ADJP
                       inserted to the left of N,
                       (the variable is substituted for by the CN)
                    d: rule to introduce an ADJP modifier

RCNmodRELSENT: a: two arguments
                    b: 1) S-tree with top node CN, dominating an S-tree of
                       category N and 2) S-tree with top node CLAUSE,
                       containing a free variable
                    c: S-tree of category CN with S-tree of category CLAUSE
                       inserted to the right of N,
                       (the variable is substituted for by the CN)
                       A relative pronoun is inserted syncategorematically
                    d: modification rule for a relative clause

RNPargmodsubst,i: a: two arguments
                    b: 1) S-tree of category NP, containing a variable x_i
                       2) S-tree of category NP (the substituent)
                    c: S-tree of category NP with the variable substituted
                       by the substituent S-tree
                    d: substitution rule for an argument variable x_i of an N

5. **control:**
   The possible rule application sequences are expressed: the projection path
   starts *obligatorily* with RBNtoSUBN, followed by RSUBNtoN1 or RSUB-
   NtoN2, and then RCNformation, followed by RCNsuperdeixis1 or RCNsu-
   perdeixis2. The *optional* rule RNargmod may then be applied or not. After
   that, RCNmodADJP and RCNmodRELSENT can be applied zero or more
   times. They are *iterative* rules. Then RNPformation1, RNPformation2 or
   RNPformation3 is *obligatorily* applied, which *optionally* can be followed by
   RNPargmodsubst,i.

It will be clear that the example subgrammar above is not complete. The real subgrammar also contains rules to account for possessive constructions, other kind of
modifiers, NPs with an empty head, numerals, partitive constructions, extraposition
of modifiers, compounds etc.

Some examples of derivations
Given the BNs *girl, answer, question* and the CLAUSE *x was ill*, the following NPs
can be derived with the example subgrammar:

a girl

	applied rules	*informal characterisation of result*
head: BN		BN: *girl*
	RBNtoSUBN	SUBN: *girl*
	RSUBNtoN1	N: *girl*
	RCNformation	CN: *girl*
	RCNsuperdeixis1	CN: *girl* with superdeixis = *present*
	RNPformation2	NP: *a girl*
export: NP		NP: *a girl*

the girl who was ill

	applied rules	*informal characterisation of result*
head: BN		BN: *girl*
	BNtoSUBN	SUBN: *girl*
	RSUBNtoN1	N: *girl*
	RCNformation	CN: *girl*
	RCNsuperdeixis2	CN: *girl* with superdeixis = *past*
import: CLAUSE	RCNmodRELSENT	+ CLAUSE: *x was ill*
		→ CN: *girl who was ill*
	RNPformation1	NP: *the girl who was ill*
export: NP		NP: *the girl who was ill*

the answer to the question

head: BN	applied rules	informal characterisation of result
head: BN		BN: *question*
	RBNtoSUBN	SUBN: *question*
	RSUBNtoN1	N: *question*
	RCNformation	CN: *question*
	RCNsuperdeixis1	CN: *question* with superdeixis = *present*
	RNPformation1	NP: *the question*
export: NP		NP: *the question*
head: BN		BN: *answer*
	RBNtoSUBN	SUBN: *answer*
	RSUBNtoN1	N: *answer*
	RCNformation	CN: *answer*
	RCNsuperdeixis1	CN: *answer* with superdeixis = *present*
import: x_1	RNargmod	CN: *answer to* x_1
	RNPformation1	NP: *the answer to* x_1
import: NP	RNPargmodsubst,1	**substituent**: NP: *the question* →
		NP:*the answer to the question*
export: NP		NP: *the answer to the question*

Note that subgrammar BNtoNP has been applied twice.

9.4   Classification of M-rules, a translation-oriented division

In the previous chapters the translation relation has been defined at the level of M-rules and basic expressions. If there is an M-rule or basic expression in one grammar, there must be at least one M-rule or basic expression in the other grammar with the same meaning (the isomorphy requirement). It is hard to grasp the translation relation as a whole in terms of these primitives alone. More structure is therefore needed. This can be achieved by subdividing the set of M-rules as follows:

1. A distinction is made between meaningful **'translation-relevant rules'** and meaningless (in the sense of *not* adding to the meaning, i.e. expressing meaning identity) **'transformation' rules**.

2. Both sets of rules are further subdivided on the basis of linguistic criteria.

We will discuss these divisions in the above order.

9.4.1 Transformations versus translation-relevant rules

Some M-rules in the grammars do not carry 'meaning', but only serve a syntactic, transformational purpose. Examples are *subject-verb agreement* and *spelling out reflexive pronouns*. These translation-irrelevant M-rules, which are often of a highly language-specific character, sometimes require corresponding M-rules in other languages that are of no use there. From now on, such M-rules are no longer considered to be part of the translation relation that is expressed by the isomorphy relation between the grammars. Therefore, they can be added freely to a grammar. In this way a better distinction can be made between purely syntactic (and hence language-specific) information and **translation-relevant** information. We refer to the different kinds of rules as **transformations** and **rules** respectively. Note that both are instances of M-rules. The translation relation can now be freed from improper elements, which is highly desirable.

The translation relation is now defined in terms of a reduced derivation tree, which is labelled with meaningful rules. The generation component (M-GENERATOR) operates on such a reduced tree and will have to decide which syntactic transformations are applicable at which point of the derivation. This requires some way of controlling the applicability of the transformation rules and this is provided by the subgrammar definition in Section 9.3 (see also Section 9.6).

As a consequence, the grammars are less dependent on each other. Next to that, transformations make it easier to apply insights from theoretical linguistics, as will be explained in Chapter 11.

9.4.2 Linguistic classification

The set of M-rules of the grammars is subdivided further into groups called **classes**, each of which handles some semantic-syntactic construction type in the case of rules or just a syntactic construction in the case of transformations. So such a class deals with an aspect that is either translation-relevant or not. These classes are therefore subdivided into translation-relevant **rule classes** and non-translation-relevant **transformation classes** according to the classification above.

Rule classes
Translation-relevant construction types that are handled by meaningful or translation-relevant rules are, for instance, derivational morphology, valency/semantic relations (i.e. how many and what kind of arguments a basic expression has), modification (degree, temporal, locative, diminutive, etc.), scope and negation, deictic relations, non-lexical aspect, substitution (function application), voice, mood, determination and number. They are found in almost every subgrammar, and in subsequent chapters

we will present an elaboration of some of these construction types. In the example
subgrammar BNtoNP, we can distinguish, for example:

name	meanings	rules
number	singular, plural	RSUBNtoN1, RSUBNtoN2
deixis	present, past	RCNsuperdeixis1, RCNsuperdeixis2
valency	unary function application	RNargmod
modification	function application	RCNMODADJP, RCNMODRELSENT
determination	definiteness	RNPformation1
	indefiniteness	RNPformation2
	function application	RNPformation3
substitution	function application	RNPargmodsubst,i

Several constructions, each with a different translation-relevant meaning, can belong
to one construction type, but only one rule of a particular class is applied in a specific
derivation. This means that rules in a rule class are usually disjunct with respect
to each other. For instance, assuming that the rule class *voice rules* consists of the
rules *active voice rule* and *passive voice rule*, these rules are said to have a distinct
meaning (i.e. they correspond to distinct IL-rules, i.e. meaning operations) and either
the active rule or the passive rule is applied in the derivation of a sentence. It is
possible that two or more rules in a rule class have the same meaning (i.e. correspond
to the same IL-rule). This can occur if they apply to syntactic structures (S-trees)
with different syntactic properties for which the M-rule notation was unsuited to
generalising about or for which it was convenient to write separate M-rules. In fact,
the corresponding part of a rule class in the semantic component contains exactly
the possible translation-relevant aspects of which a certain construction type consists.

If we abstract away from syntactic properties of the S-trees to which the rules apply,
a translation-relevant rule class need not be restricted to one subgrammar. For example, substitution rules for arguments of an N (RNPargmodsubst), a V (RVPargsubst)
or a P (RPPargsubst) are all substitution rules with the same meaning, although
they belong to different subgrammars. As will be discussed in Chapter 13, we take
advantage of that fact in the case of categorial divergence problems.

Obviously, a rule class is not restricted to one M-grammar either. It contains rules
of all M-grammars for a particular translation-relevant construction type. In fact,
only rules of different grammars that belong to the same translation-relevant rule
class may correspond to each other or, to put it in other words, rules that do not
belong to the same translation-relevant rule class can never be translation equivalents
(see Figure 9.3). The set of translation-relevant rule classes represents the kind of

information that has to be preserved during translation. This information is expressed by the corresponding set of IL-rule classes. The meaning operations (IL-rules) that correspond to these M-rules together with the basic meanings constitute the semantic derivation trees.

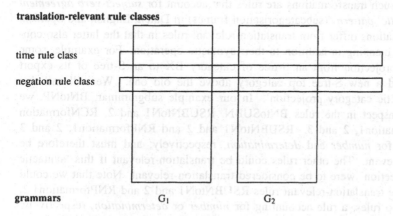

Figure 9.3: Translation-relevant rule classes organise the translation relation between the grammars of the languages involved.

Rule classes also play a role in the definition of the control of rule applications, but first we will discuss the transformation classes.

Transformation classes

Transformation classes group together rules that only contribute to the form of sentences. Each class deals with a syntactic construction that is not or need not be considered translation-relevant. Such a construction may be expressed by several rules, because the S-trees to which the rules are applied can differ in such a way that the M-rule notation is not suited to expressing the generalisation over these S-trees or because it is convenient to write separate transformations. The transformations within a class are usually disjunct with respect to each other in a specific derivation. We distinguish the following cases:

1. constructions that are language-specific.
   Examples are: *verb-second* in Dutch, *subject-adjective agreement* in Spanish or *do-insertion* in English;

2. constructions that account for a syntactic aspect of some translation-relevant construction which can better be handled by a separate rule.
   For example, the *shift rules*, accounting for the movement of wh-phrase variables and variables of relative clauses in the BXtoCLAUSE subgrammars.

Monolingual criteria for this latter case are syntactic generalisations, as will be discussed in Chapter 10. This case can also result in 'corresponding' transformation classes in the grammars for different languages, because the same syntactic generalisations can be applied, although the application of these classes need not correspond. Examples of such transformations are rules that account for *subject-verb agreement* or for *'syntactic' patterns* (subcategorisation frames) in Dutch, English and Spanish.

Transformations differ from translation-relevant rules in that the latter also contribute to the meaning in addition to their syntactic operation. For example, some steps in the projection from an S-tree of category BX to an S-tree of its export category build a new S-tree top category above the old one. We will call this aspect 'syntactic category projection'. In our example subgrammar, BNtoNP, we can see this aspect in the rules BNtoSUBN, RSUBNtoN1 and 2, RCNformation and RNPformation1, 2 and 3. RSUBNtoN1 and 2 and RNPformation1, 2 and 3 also account for *number* and *determination*, respectively, and must therefore be translation-relevant. The other rules could be translation-relevant if this 'syntactic category projection' were to be considered translation-relevant. Note that we could split up all the translation-relevant rules RSUBNtoN1 and 2 and RNPformation1,2, and 3 into two rules, a rule accounting for *number* or *determination*, respectively, and a transformation for a particular 'syntactic category projection'. Such decisions have to be made collectively by the grammar writers. The only requirement is that there are corresponding rules for *number* and *determination* in all grammars. The decision as to how many transformations are used (zero, one or more) is left to the writer of a particular grammar.

Note that transformation classes are restricted to one M-grammar or even to a particular subgrammar in contrast to rule classes, because of their language-specific or 'dependent' character.

9.5 Combination of subgrammars and classification of M-rules

This section will combine the conclusions of Sections 9.3 and 9.4. In Section 9.3 it was shown that subgrammars help to structure the grammar in a more modular manner. In Section 9.4 it was explained that translation-relevant rule classes group together semantically related rules, yielding insight into what has to be preserved during translation. However, M-rule classes, which are not restricted to subgrammars or grammars, are not the right units to make a modular structure in the way we did with subgrammars, because it is hard to define an adequate interface (i.e. import and export) between M-rule classes. For example, the rule for negating sentences is determined by the M-rules that form sentences rather than the other negation rules (e.g. in an adjective phrase) with which it forms the negation rule class.

Both subgrammars and M-rule classes allow for a division of the labour among people. That this is the case with subgrammars is trivial, as they form a modular structure. The reason why M-rule classes are also useful units by which to divide the work, is that knowledge of a specific linguistic topic is needed for every M-rule class; knowledge that can typically be handled by one person.

In order to have the benefits from both divisions, subgrammars and M-rule classes have been combined as follows:

1. An M-rule class is divided into **subclasses**, an abbreviation of 'subgrammar M-rule classes', in which each subclass is a set of rules belonging to one subgrammar of a particular M-grammar. It deals with one particular linguistic construction type in one particular subgrammar. For example, the substitution rules in the example subgrammar - containing in this case only one rule - form a subclass of the large rule class that accounts for the substitution of arguments in all subgrammars of all M-grammars and that, for example, also contains the M-rules for the substitution of arguments of verbs. These rules have the same meaning.

2. The application sequences of rules are defined in terms of subclasses instead of individual M-rules. In fact, we have already seen this in our example subgrammar: we start obligatorily with the projection from BN to SUBN, and then go on to the projection from SUBN to N including an account of number, etc.

This combination results in a modular structure of each grammar and helps to reduce the complexity of the translation relation. Chapter 13 will discuss how we can take advantage of this modular structure in the case of notorious translation problems.

9.6   Controlled M-grammars

As already stated in Section 9.1, some means of ordering is necessary in the case of large M-grammars. Additionally, a distinction between obligatory, optional and iterative M-rules is desirable. Also, the introduction of transformations requires some kind of control on their application. The key problem was how to do that in a compositional framework where rules can have more than one argument.

Subgrammars and classes of M-rules having been introduced, a solution can be found for this problem. M-grammars consist of subgrammars, and subgrammars must express control of the application of M-rules (cf. Section 9.3). M-grammars consisting of such subgrammars are called *controlled M-grammars*. The key solution is provided by the notion of 'projection path' and the convention that the rules of a subgrammar are ordered with respect to their *first* argument. Together with the notion of subclasses of M-rules, rule and transformation classes within subgrammars, it is now possible to define the possible sequences of M-rule applications in a transparent way. We will do that formally with a control expression (Section 9.6.1). After that, it is possible to give a formal definition of subgrammars (Section 9.6.2). Finally, we will discuss what control expressions mean for the isomorphy characteristic of M-grammars (Section 9.6.3).

A side effect of this explicit ordering of M-rule application is that it makes a more efficient parsing algorithm (M-PARSER) possible.

9.6.1   Control expression

The **control expression** indicates what the subclasses are, how they are ordered, what M-rules they consist of, and whether they are iterative, optional or obligatory. As a control expression is always restricted to a subgrammar, we will often refer to the subclasses simply as classes within this context.

A control expression *ce* has the following form:

$$ce = A_0 . A_1 . \ldots . A_n,$$

where each A_i is an M-rule class, either a translation-relevant rule class or a transformation class.

A class A_i, containing M-rules R_i, where R_i are either translation-relevant rules or transformations and not a combination of both, may be

- obligatory: written as (R_1 | ... | R_k)
- iterative: written as { R_1 | ... | R_k }
- optional: written as [R_1 | ... | R_k].

An example:

$$(R_1) . [R_2 | R_3] . \{ R_4 | R_5 \} . (R_6 | R_7)$$

This control expression defines all sequences beginning with R_1, then R_2 or R_3 or neither, then an arbitrarily long sequence (possibly empty) of R_4 or R_5, then either R_6 or R_7.

Actually, a control expression is a restricted kind of regular expression over the alphabet of M-rule names. It is not restricted in its constructions but in the possible combinations of these constructions. (For an explanation of terms such as *regular expression, alphabet* etc., see for instance, Hopcroft and Ullman (1979)) Each regular expression denotes a set of instances: sequences of M-rule names. Each such M-rule sequence is a possible **projection path** in the subgrammar (cf. Section 9.3). In fact, each sequence of rules (i.e. with the transformations left out!) defines a possible sequence of left branches in a derivation tree. Note that the rules in a sequence need not be applicable; this depends on the applicability conditions of the rules themselves.

9.6.2 A formal definition of subgrammar

Having defined a control expression in Section 9.6.1, we can now give a more formal definition of a subgrammar.

A **subgrammar**$_i$ is defined by

1. **name**$_i$: a name constructed in accordance with convention 1 (to be defined below).

2. **export**$_i$: a specification of a set of S-trees whose top nodes have specific categories, the **export categories**, which are all elements of the category set EXPORTCATS$_i$.

3. **import**$_i$: a specification of the set of S-trees that can be imported, represented by a tuple $< a, b, c >$.

   a: a specification of a set of S-trees with specific categories, the **head categories**, which are elements of the category set HEADCATS$_i$;

   b: a specification of a set of S-trees that are exported by other subgrammars and that can be taken as an argument by rules that take more than one argument. The top categories are elements of the category set IMPORTCATS$_i$;

   c: variables for which S-trees with a top category which is an element of the category set IMPORTCATS$_i$ can be substituted.

4. **rules**$_i$: a set of M-rules that take care of the projection from S-trees of a head category specified in import$_i$ to S-trees of an export category specified in export$_i$.
   The S-tree with a head category (an element of HEADCATS$_i$) or one of the intermediate results during its projection is called the **head argument** of a rule. The other arguments, S-trees with categories that are an element of IMPORTCATS$_i$ or variables, are called **non-head arguments**.
   An M-rule is classified as either **rule** or **transformation** and both types are grouped together into **rule classes** and **transformation classes**.

5. **control expression**$_i$: a restricted kind of regular expression over the alphabet of the names of the M-rules specified in rules$_i$.
   A control expression ce_i has the following form:

$$ce_i = A_0 \cdot A_1 \cdot \ldots \cdot A_n,$$

where each A_j is an M-rule class, either a class of translation-relevant rules or a class of transformations.

A class A_j, containing M-rules R_j, where R_j are either all rules or all transformations, may be

- **obligatory**: written as ($R_1 \mid \ldots \mid R_k$),

- **iterative**: written as { $R_1 \mid \ldots \mid R_k$ },

- **optional**: written as [$R_1 \mid \ldots \mid R_k$].

The rules are ordered with respect to their first arguments, which are specified in accordance with convention 2.

Conventions
The following conventions exist:

convention 1 : (final version) The name of a subgrammar$_i$ follows the scheme 'AtoB', where A is the name of HEADCATS$_i$ and B the name of EXPORT-CATS$_i$.

convention 2 : The **head argument** of each rule is the first argument of that rule.

Conditions
Given the following sets:

TOPCATS : the set of all possible top categories of S-trees that can be in the export set of full projection subgrammars (category type XP, XPPROP and CLAUSE).

BASICCATS : the set of all possible categories of basic expressions (category type BX).

the following conditions hold for subgrammars:[5]

- HEADCATS$_i$ $\cap$ TOPCATS $= \varnothing$

- EXPORTCATS$_i$ $\cap$ BASICCATS $= \varnothing$

- IMPORTCATS$_i$ $\subseteq$ TOPCATS

- EXPORTCATS$_i$ $\subseteq$ TOPCATS

- HEADCATS$_i$ $\subseteq$ BASICCATS

---

[5]In Chapter 13 some conditions will have to be revised.

- HEADCATS$_i$ $\neq$ $\emptyset$

- For every import S-tree in the import$_i$ of subgrammar$_i$, there must be at least one rule in rules$_i$ that is applicable to it.

- The non-head import S-trees that are taken as an argument by a rule that takes more than one argument, specified in rules$_i$ of subgrammar$_i$, must be specified in the import$_i$ of that subgrammar$_i$.

For subgrammars$_i$ as introduced in this chapter, a typical feature is that HEADCATS$_i$ and EXPORTCATS$_i$ consist of one element. In Chapter 13, however, it will become clear that this is not always the case for each subgrammar. It will turn out there the subgrammars introduced here are a special kind of subgrammars which we will call 'projection subgrammars'.

9.6.3   Isomorphy and control expressions

Isomorphy of grammars in free M-grammars is expressed by means of relations between rules and between basic expressions. In controlled M-grammars, there has to be a relation between subgrammars as well, i.e. a relation between their control expressions. We have already seen that corresponding rules of corresponding subgrammars must belong to the same translation-relevant rule class, but also the order and the 'application kind' (obligatory, optional, iterative) of the classes of rules of those subgrammars must be the same because, for each translation-relevant rule sequence (projection path) in one grammar, there should be a corresponding sequence in the other grammar. Note that this requirement does not hold for transformations. They can be added freely to each subgrammar without affecting the isomorphy with other subgrammars. An example:

Assume a control expression for subgrammar G_i of grammar G of the following form (we indicate *rules* with R and *transformations* with T):

$$(R_1) \cdot [R_2 \mid R_3] \cdot \{ R_4 \mid R_5 \} \cdot (T_1 \mid T_2) \cdot (R_6)$$

A subgrammar G_j of grammar G' with the following control expression is isomorphic with G_i if, for example,

R_1 corresponds to R_1'
R_2 corresponds to R_2'
R_3 corresponds to R_3' and R_4'
R_4 and R_5 correspond to R_5' and R_6' respectively

R_6 corresponds to R_7'

and the control expression is:

$$(R_1') \cdot [R_2' \mid R_3' \mid R_4'] \cdot \{ R_5' \mid R_6' \} \cdot (R_7') \cdot (T_1')$$

An example of a transformation that is needed in a particular subgrammar but not in a corresponding subgrammar is the transformation that accounts for the correct assignment of *-e* to adjectives in a Dutch BNtoNP subgrammar, corresponding to the English example subgrammar BNtoNP specified in Section 9.3.4. In Dutch, we have, for instance, a transformation that accounts for *-e* in *mooie* as in (1a).

(1) (*D*) a een mooi*e* vrouw
        a   beautiful woman

    (*D*) b een mooi   huis
        a   beautiful house

The English subgrammar for BN to NP does not need such rules. The Dutch rule is language-specific. The subgrammars referred to are nevertheless isomorphic since the definition of the translation relation now takes only translation-relevant rules into account.

Chapter 18 will present M-grammars from the attribute grammar point of view, in which control is made the central issue: control expressions are transformed into regular grammars. This view is based on Rous (1991) which also shows that the notion of isomorphy can be formalised very elegantly in the attribute grammar framework.

9.7 Concluding remarks

Section 9.2 has listed three problems with the free M-grammar formalism presented in the previous chapters.

The first problem was the lack of structure in free M-grammars. This was solved in Section 9.3 by introducing a modular approach, whereby M-grammars are divided into projection subgrammars in a way that was inspired by the programming language Modula-2 on the one hand, and by the notion projection from $\overline{X}$-theory on the other.

The second problem was that there is no way to control the application of rules in free M-grammars explicitly and that it is not obvious how this kind of control could be introduced in a compositional grammar, where rules may have more than one argument. The insight that was important for the solution of this problem was that application of a projection subgrammar comes down to following a projection path, from the imported head to the exported projection. This implies that defining control in a subgrammar comes down to specifying a set of possible sequences of

M-rule applications, which can be done by means of a control expression, a restricted regular expression over M-rule names.

The third problem concerned the consequences of defining the translation relation by means of isomorphic grammars. The introduction of an explicit distinction between translation-relevant rules and syntactic transformations in Section 9.4 avoids unnecessary complications of the grammars without affecting the isomorphy characteristic. Transformations are not contained in the derivation trees, which are therefore still isomorphic. Because the applicability of syntactic transformations is constrained by the control expressions, they do not cause any problems of effectivity or efficiency.[6]

As a consequence, the grammars of the different languages have become less dependent on each other. Also, the introduction of M-rule classes gave further insight into complex translation relations, since the various aspects involved are distinguished and grouped.

Note that syntactic transformations and meaningful M-rules can be used alternately. In this respect this grammatical framework differs from the *Aspects* framework (Chomsky (1965)) when looking at the relation between form and meaning. One might consider the rules forming deep structures in the *Aspects* framework as meaningful rules and the transformations as meaningless rules. Under this view all meaningless rules follow the meaningful rules. The controlled M-grammar framework is superior to the *Aspects* framework in this respect, since it is well known that certain aspects of meaning are most properly accounted for under abstraction of certain surface order phenomena (e.g. predicate-argument relations) while surface order (e.g. scope relations) is crucial for other semantic aspects (see Chomsky (1972)).

The controlled M-grammar formalism adopts the rule-to-rule approach in its strictest form. Though rules with the identity operation as their meaning are allowed, the grammar is still a compositional grammar. The meaning of an expression is derived from the meanings of the parts of this expression and their mode of combination. Syntactic structures are built up in a bottom-up manner (starting with basic expressions, applying rules to them to form larger structures, etc.), and their corresponding meanings are derived in parallel. This clearly differs from non-compositional grammars in which meaning aspects are not dealt with at all, or in which the meaning is determined on the basis of an abstract representation generated by syntactic rules in complete isolation from semantic rules.

A compositional system in which rules are allowed that have the identity operation as their meaning, is more restricted than a non-compositional system in which rules need not have a meaning at all. It follows from the compositional nature of

---

[6]Note that iterative transformations have to meet the measure condition.

the grammar that rules with the identity operation as their meaning take exactly one argument (cf. Janssen (1986b)). In a non-compositional grammar meaningless rules might take more than one argument, for example, the generalised transformations in Chomsky (1957, 1992).

The extension of the framework with syntactic transformations has been called 'a complete mockery of the claim that the grammars are isomorphic' (Somers (1990b) quoting Carroll (1989)). This judgement must be based on a misunderstanding about our objectives as we do not claim that grammars *are* isomorphic, but that a translation method is used which involves isomorphic grammars. Formally, there is no difference between free and controlled M-grammars, but the method has been improved. The isomorphy characteristic is only relevant for meaningful rules and that still holds. The extension to syntactic transformations has only been carried out to make the grammars and the correspondences more transparent. The grammars can always be rewritten into the original framework by including the syntactic operations of transformations in meaningful rules or by adding corresponding 'dummy' rules to the other grammars, but this is not very attractive in practice.

9.8   Another example subgrammar

To conclude this chapter, a simplified example is given of a BVtoCLAUSE projection subgrammar and it is illustrated how - in combination with the example projection subgrammar BNtoNP - a sentence such as *a boy hopes that a girl does not cry* can be derived. Only rules and transformations that are relevant to the example sentence are described. It is not claimed that the rules described here are the best rules for the phenomena they take into account.

Example of an English subgrammar for the projection from BV to CLAUSE

1. **name**: BVtoCLAUSE

2. **export**: S-tree of category **CLAUSE**

3. **import**:

   - head category: **BV**
   - S-trees with categories that are exported by other subgrammars with top category: **NP, CLAUSE**
   - variables

4. **rules**:

Again, the following informal notation will be used for this illustration:

name of rule   a: number of arguments of the rule
                b: applicability conditions
                c: informal characterisation of the result
                d: optional: additional explanation

The value *omega* indicates 'unspecified'.

rule class: derivational morphology
BVtoSUBV: a: 1 argument
             b: S-tree of category BV
             c: S-tree with top node SUBV, dominating that of BV

rule class: inflectional morphology
RSUBVtoV: a: 1 argument
             b: S-tree of category SUBV
             c: S-tree with top node V, dominating that of SUBV

rule class: valency or start rules
RVPPROPformation1:   a: 2 arguments
                      b: 1) S-tree of category V 2) a variable
                      c: S-tree with topnode VPPROP, dominating a
                         category VP above V; the variable is
                         adjacent to the VP and has relation *argrel*.
                      d: This rule accounts for valency/semantic
                         relations of a 1-place verb.

RVPPROPformation2:   a: 3 arguments
                      b: 1) S-tree of category V, 2) a variable, 3) a variable
                      c: S-tree with top node VPPROP, dominating a
                         category VP above V; the first variable is
                         adjacent to the VP and the second is dominated
                         by VP; both have relation *argrel*
                      d: This rule accounts for valency/semantic relations
                         in the case of a 2-place verb.

rule class: voice rules
RVPPROPvoice1:   a: 1 argument
                  b: S-tree of category VPPROP, *voice = omega*
                  c: S-tree of category VPPROP, *voice = active*
                  d: This rule accounts for the *active voice*

rule class: negation rules[7]

RCLAUSEnegation: a: 1 argument
                      b: S-tree of category CLAUSE, not containing *do* or *not*
                      c: S-tree of category CLAUSE, containing the auxiliary V
                         do and the negative adverb *not* in this order under
                         the CLAUSE node, to the left of the VP
                      d: This rule accounts for sentence negation

rule class: deixis rules

RCLAUSEdeixis1:   a: 1 argument
                      b: S-tree of category CLAUSE, *deixis = omega*
                      c: S-tree of category CLAUSE, *deixis = present*,
                         the leftmost V in VP has *tense = present*
                      d: This rule accounts for the temporal value *present*
                         (see Chapter 14).

RCLAUSEsuperdeixis1: a: 1 argument
                      b: S-tree of category CLAUSE, *superdeixis = omega*
                      c: S-tree of category CLAUSE, *superdeixis = present*,
                         the leftmost V in VP has *tense = present*
                      d: This rule accounts for the temporal value *present*
                         (see Chapter 14), which can play a role if the CLAUSE is
                         substituted for a variable in another CLAUSE.

rule class: argument substitution rules

RCLAUSEargsubst1,i: a: 2 arguments and a parameter
                      b: 1) S-tree of category CLAUSE, containing a
                         variable x_i, 2) S-tree of category NP
                      c: S-tree of category CLAUSE with the substituent
                         S-tree substituted for the variable x_i
                      d: substitution rule for an argument variable x_i of a V.
                         The deixis or superdeixis value of the head argument
                         must be the same as the superdeixis value of the substituent.

RCLAUSEargsubst2,i: a: 2 arguments and a parameter
                      b: 1) S-tree of category CLAUSE, containing a
                         variable x_i, 2) S-tree of category CLAUSE, with
                         kind = complsent.
                      c: S-tree of category CLAUSE with the substituent
                         S-tree substituted for the variable x_i
                      d: substitution rule for an argument variable x_i of a V.
                         The deixis or superdeixis value of the head argument
                         must be the same as the superdeixis value of the substituent.

rule class: mood rules

RCLAUSEmood1:   a: 1 argument
                      b: S-tree of category CLAUSE, *mood = omega, kind = omega*
                      c: S-tree of category CLAUSE, *mood = declarative*,
                         kind = mainsent
                      d: This rule accounts for the *declarative mood* of main sentences.

---

[7]In the Rosetta grammars the insertion of *do* is a separate transformation. For simplicity reasons, it is incorporated in the negation rule here.

RCLAUSEmood2:   a: 1 argument
                b: S-tree of category CLAUSE, *mood = omega, kind = omega*
                c: S-tree of category CLAUSE, *mood = declarative*,
                   kind = complsent. It contains the conjunction *that*
                   in the leftmost position in the S-tree under the CLAUSE.
                d: This rule accounts for the *declarative mood* of
                   complement sentences.

RCLAUSEmood3:   1 argument
                b: S-tree of category CLAUSE, *mood = omega, kind = omega*
                c: S-tree of category CLAUSE, *mood = declarative*,
                   kind = relsent
                d: This rule accounts for the *mood* of relative sentences.

transformation class: verb pattern transformations

TVPPROPvp1:   a: 1 argument
              b: S-tree with top node VPPROP dominating a variable
                 with relation *argrel* and a VP containing a one-place V
              c: S-tree with top node VPPROP dominating a variable
                 with relation *subjrel* and a VP containing a one-place V
              d: This rule accounts for the verb pattern of
                 one-place verbs with a subject NP.

TVPPROPvp2:   a: 1 argument
              b: S-tree with top node VPPROP dominating a variable
                 with relation *argrel* and a VP containing a one-place V
                 and another variable with relation *argrel*
              c: S-tree with top node VPPROP dominating a variable
                 with relation *subjrel* and a VP containing a one-place V
                 and a variable with relation *complrel*.
              d: This rule accounts for the verb pattern of two-place verbs
                 with a subject NP and a complement sentence.

transformation class: clause formation transformations

TVPPROPtoCLAUSE1:   a: 1 argument
                    b: S-tree of category VPPROP, *voice = active*
                    c: S-tree of category CLAUSE, *voice = active*

transformation class: subject-verb agreement transformations

TCLAUSEsv-agreement: a: 1 argument
                       b: S-tree with top node CLAUSE, dominating a subject
                          NP and a VP containing at least one V
                       c: S-tree with top node CLAUSE, dominating a subject
                          NP and a VP of which the leftmost V has *person =*
                          person value of NP and *number = number* value of NP
                       d: This rule accounts for subject-verb agreement.

5. **control expression:**

    (RBVtoSUBV)
   . (RSUBVtoV)
   . (RVPPROPformation1 | RVPPROPformation2)
   . (TVPPROPvp1 | TVPPROPvp2)
   . (RVPPROPvoice1)
   . (TVPPROPtoCLAUSE1)
   . [RCLAUSEnegation]
   . (RCLAUSEdeixis1 | RCLAUSEsuperdeixis1)
   . { RCLAUSEargsubst1,i | RCLAUSEargsubst2,i }
   . (TCLAUSEsv-agreement)
   . (RCLAUSEmood1 | RCLAUSEmood2 | RCLAUSEmood3)

As already noted, this is a simplified subgrammar for the projection from BV to CLAUSE. For example, the rules for zero-place and three-place verbs are missing, we have not accounted for ergative verbs, there are many more verb patterns than the two mentioned here, there is no rule for passive voice, accounting for time involves more than two deixis rules, the rules for interrogative, subjunctive or imperative mood are missing, no modifiers are allowed, etc. This subgrammar is only meant to give an indication of what such a subgrammar looks like and to give an example of how this subgrammar and the one for BNtoNP work together.

The translation-relevant classes which are distinguished and should be taken into account for the correspondence to a subgrammar of, e.g., Dutch are:

application	class	rules
obligatory	derivational morphology	RBVtoSUBV
obligatory	inflectional morphology	RSUBVtoV
obligatory	valency	RVPPROPformation1, RVPPROPformation2
obligatory	voice	RVPPROPvoice1
optional	negation	RCLAUSEnegation
obligatory	deixis	RCLAUSEdeixis1, RCLAUSEsuperdeixis1
iterative	argument substitution	RCLAUSEargsubst1,i, RCLAUSEargsubst2,i
obligatory	mood	RCLAUSEmood1, RCLAUSEmood2, RCLAUSEmood3

Example derivation of

a boy hopes that a girl does not cry

a boy

	applied rules	informal characterisation of result
head: BN		BN: *boy*
	RBNtoSUBN	SUBN: *boy*
	RSUBNtoN1	N: *boy*
	RCNformation	CN: *boy*
	RCNsuperdeixis1	CN: *boy* with superdeixis = *present*
	RNPformation3	NP: *a boy*
export: NP		NP: *a boy*

a girl

	applied rules	informal characterisation of result
head: BN		BN: *girl*
	RBNtoSUBN	SUBN: *girl*
	RSUBNtoN1	N: *girl*
	RCNformation	CN: *girl*
	RCNsuperdeixis1	CN: *girl* with superdeixis = *present*
	RNPformation3	NP: *a girl*
export: NP		NP: *a girl*

that a girl does not cry

	applied rules	informal characterisation of result
head: BV		BV: *cry*
	RBVtoSUBV	SUBV: *cry*
	RSUBVtoV	V: *cry*
import: $x3$	RVPPROPformation1	VPPROP: *x3 cry*
	TVPPROPvp1	VPPROP: *x3 cry* with *subjrel/x3*
	RVPPROPvoice1	VPPROP: *x3 cry* with voice = *active*
	TVPPROPtoCLAUSE1	CLAUSE: *x3 cry*
	RCLAUSEnegation	CLAUSE: *x3 do not cry*
	RCLAUSEsuperdeixis1	CLAUSE: *x3 do not cry*
		superdeixis = *present*
import: NP	RCLAUSEargsubst1 *x3*	**substituent**:
		NP(superdeixis=*present*): *a girl* →
		CLAUSE: *a girl do not cry*
	TCLAUSEsv-agreement	CLAUSE: *a girl does not cry*
	RCLAUSEmood2	CLAUSE: *that a girl does not cry*
		kind = *complsent* and mood = *declarative*
export: CLAUSE		CLAUSE: *that a girl does not cry*

a boy hopes that a girl does not cry

	applied rules	informal characterisation of result
head: BV		BV: *hope*
	RBVtoSUBV	SUBV: *hope*
	RSUBVtoV	V: *hope*
import: *x1, x2*	RVPPROPformation2	VPPROP: *x1* hope *x2*
	TVPPROPvp2	VPPROP: *x1* hope *x2*
		with *subjrel/x1* and *complrel/x2*
	RVPPROPvoice1	VPPROP: *x1* hope *x2*, voice = *active*
	TVPPROPtoCLAUSE1	CLAUSE: *x1* hope *x2*
	RCLAUSEdeixis1	CLAUSE: *x1* hope *x2*, deixis = *present*
import: CLAUSE	RCLAUSEargsubst2,*x2*	**substituent:**
		CLAUSE(superdeixis=*present*):
		that a girl does not cry →
		x1 hope *that a girl does not cry*
import: NP	RCLAUSEargsubst1,*x1*	**substituent:**
		NP(superdeixis=*present*):
		a boy →
		CLAUSE:
		a boy hope that a girl does not cry
	TCLAUSEsv-agreement	CLAUSE:
		a boy hopes that a girl does not cry
	RCLAUSEmood1	CLAUSE:
		a boy hopes that a girl does not cry
		kind = *mainsent* and
		mood = *declarative*
export: CLAUSE		CLAUSE:
		a boy hopes that a girl does not cry

Figures 9.4 and 9.5 contain the D-tree (with an indication of the subgrammars) and the resulting S-tree for this example, respectively. In the S-tree in Figure 9.5 the attribute-value pairs are only indicated at the first place of introduction in the S-tree. Usually, they percolate to the higher nodes in the S-tree.

In practice, the last rule of M-grammar is always a so-called *UTTERANCE rule* which puts category UTTERANCE on top of the S-tree that is built. In the case of a clause this is rule RUTTERANCE1:

RUTTERANCE1: a: 1 argument
              b: S-tree of category CLAUSE
                 attribute *kind* has value *mainsent*.
              c: S-tree with top node UTTERANCE dominating CLAUSE

Chapter 13 will go into this subject further.

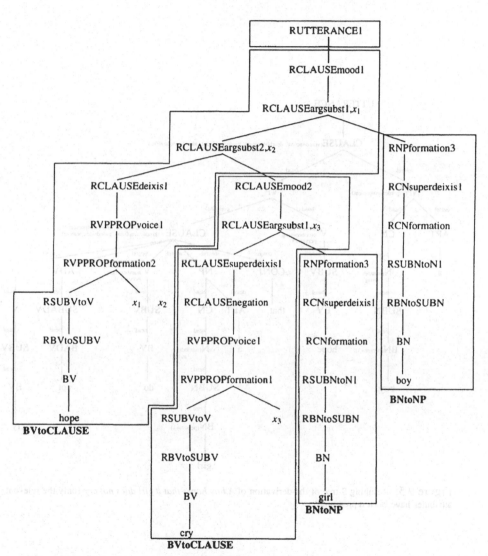

Figure 9.4: D-tree with subgrammar indication for *A boy hopes that a girl does not cry*.

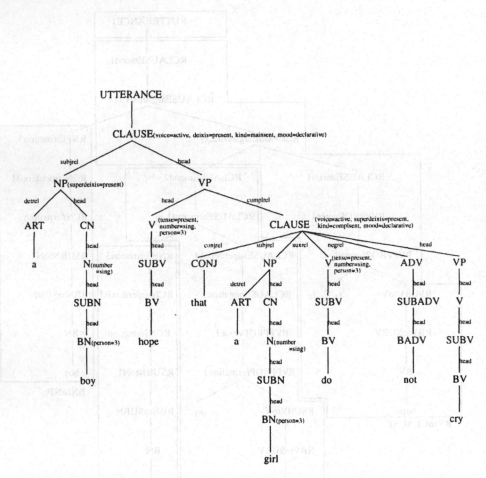

Figure 9.5: Resulting S-tree of the derivation of *A boy hopes that a girl does not cry* (only the relevant attributes have been represented).

Assuming that there are subgrammars for the projection from BD to DP and BADJ to ADJPPROP and a rule RUTTERANCE2 for NP, for example, sentences (2)-(4) can also be derived with the subgrammars above.

(2)   this smart girl cries

(3)   these smart girls hope that a boy cries

(4)   the boy who believes that a smart girl does not cry

Chapter 10

Compositionality and syntactic generalisations

10.1 Introduction

In the preceding chapters a special kind of compositional grammar, M-grammar, has been introduced to describe the form and meaning (or more precisely: translational equivalence) of expressions. The basic idea of compositional grammars, e.g. Montague's PTQ (Thomason (1974)), is that they relate form and meaning in a very direct way. Such grammars usually have a strong semantic bias, in the following sense: in a compositional grammar basic expressions are associated with a basic meaning, and syntactic rules are associated with a meaning operation, and it is the proper composition of the meaning of an expression which determines how many and which syntactic steps to form an expression are distinguished. This semantic bias is essential given the translation method adopted, but it might lead to a grammar which is less adequate from a syntactic point of view.

The introduction of *syntactic transformations* in controlled M-grammars, described and motivated in Chapter 9 makes it possible to overcome this disadvantage. Syntactic transformations have the identity operation as their meaning and are not involved in the isomorphy relation.

This chapter will first supply additional evidence that such transformations are absolutely required to achieve an adequate modularisation of the syntax so that optimal descriptions of syntactic phenomena and their associated meanings can be obtained; second, it will describe and motivate in detail for a number of constructions which rules must be meaningful rules and which rules must be transformations and, third, it will show that the addition of transformations makes the relation between

185

form and meaning considerably more indirect than one might think.

This does not imply that the relation between form and meaning is unclear in the grammar. However, it will turn out that in many cases the rules which account for the form differences are not directly associated to the related meaning operations. Often, the meaning operation is associated with a rule which changes the expression only at an abstract level. Two situations are rather typical, though they do not necessarily exhaust the possibilities: (1) the application of a meaningful rule to an abstract structure leaves a trace, which is used to trigger syntactic transformations that actually perform the relevant operations on the form, and (2) syntactic transformations apply blindly, creating a number of alternative structures, after which meaningful rules check whether the right configurations have been created for them to apply. The form changes performed by these meaningful rules tend to be rather small and often have no direct reflex on the surface.

In short, we attempt to contribute to the search for an optimum in the relationship between syntax and semantics, so that complexity and redundancy can be minimised in syntax, in semantics and in their mutual relationship.

The emphasis in this chapter will be on an investigation into the question of which rules are required to adequately describe certain syntactic constructions and which of these rules must be meaningful rules and which must be transformations. The next chapter will concentrate on how certain transformations must be formulated, which formal operations are required to obtain adequate syntactic descriptions and how the resulting analyses relate to analyses in more theoretically oriented frameworks.

Section 10.2 will introduce the problem in more detail using the syntax of auxiliaries and inversion in English as an illustration. The solution proposed is sketched in general terms and applied to the specific case at hand. The sections that follow show that the kind of problem occurs quite generally and that the kind of solution proposed is applicable to all of these problems. Phenomena relating to mood in Dutch (Section 10.3), variants of sentences which differ only in linear order (Section 10.4), phenomena relating to WH-movement (Section 10.5) and the proper treatment of genericity (Section 10.6) are used to argue for this. The material presented in this chapter is dealt with in more detail in Odijk (1993).

10.2   Auxiliaries and inversion in English

This section introduces the general problem using the peculiar properties of English auxiliaries as examples (Section 10.2.1). A general characterisation of the solution to this kind of problem and an instantiation of this kind of solution specific to the problem at hand will be described in Section 10.2.2.

10.2.1   The problem

Let us start by considering the following two sentences:

(1)   a   He bought a book
      b   Did he buy a book?

At first sight, these sentences appear to be excellent examples for the compositional
approach. The two sentences clearly differ in meaning (declarative sentence versus
yes-no question) and, corresponding to this meaning difference, there is a difference
in form.[1] Sentence (1a) contains a sentence-initial subject followed by an inflected
main verb, while sentence (1b) contains a sentence-initial inflected auxiliary verb,
followed by the subject, followed in its turn by the main verb in its base form.
It is quite straightforward to see how two different rules can be constructed, each
associated with its own meaning and each performing different formal changes to
an input structure. Let us assume that certain rules have derived a structure which
we will represent informally by S(he bought a book). The properties common to
(1a,b) have been expressed in this structure. This structure will be the input for the
rules to form declarative and yes-no interrogative sentences. One rule, let us call
it RDECL, will take this structure as its input and will simply reset the value of the
attribute *mood* of the S-node dominating the structure from *unspecified* to *decl*. The
rule is associated with the meaning of declarative sentences. A second rule, called
RYNQ, takes this structure as input as well and it performs the following changes:
the attribute *mood* of S is changed from *unspecified* to *ynq*, the auxiliary verb *do* is
introduced in a sentence-initial position, the tense features are copied from the main
verb onto this auxiliary and then deleted at the main verb. This rule is associated
with the meaning of yes-no questions.

   If we extend the grammar with additional rules, however, it soon becomes clear
that the simple approach sketched above runs into severe trouble. We will extend
the grammar sketched with a number of rules using the compositional approach as
indicated and we will show in what ways such an analysis is unsatisfactory.

   Consider the following sentence:

(2)   Which book did he buy?

This sentence differs from the sentences discussed above in several respects. Comparing it with (1a), first, there is a semantic difference: (1a) has the meaning of a
declarative sentence, (2) has the meaning of a WH-question (see Groenendijk and
Stokhof (1984) for a semantics of WH-questions in a model-theoretical framework).
Second, corresponding to this semantic difference, there is a formal difference: sentence (2) has a sentence-initial NP, with the determiner *which* instead of the article

---

[1]Here we will ignore details relating to interpunction.

a; this NP is followed by an inflected auxiliary verb, which is followed by the subject, and the main verb in its base form is sentence-final. Again, it is rather straightforward to write a rule for forming such sentences, and to associate this rule with its own meaning. If we assume that the input for the rule is S(he bought which book), the rule, let us call it RWHQ, must perform the following formal changes: the attribute *mood* of the S-node must be reset from *unspecified* to *whq*; the NP *which book* must be preposed to a sentence-initial position, the auxiliary verb *do* must be inserted, the tense features of the main verb must be copied onto this auxiliary verb, and then these tense features must be deleted at the main verb.

Let us add a rule for introducing adverbs. We call this rule RADV. It takes a sentence and an adverb of a certain kind (e.g. *never*) as input and puts the adverb into the sentence right before the main verb. Given S(he bought a book) and the adverb *never* as input we can derive S(he never bought a book). This structure can then be input to the rules introduced earlier to derive the sentences *he never bought a book* and *did he never buy a book* and from a structure such as *he never bought which book* we can derive *which book did he never buy*.

Consider the sentence in (3):

(3)   Never did he buy a book

As before, this sentence differs from the sentences discussed earlier in form and in meaning, or at least in pragmatic aspects (for example topic-comment partitioning). And again, it is fairly easy to write a rule which can take these phenomena into account. We will call this rule RTOP. One possible input for this rule is S(he never bought a book). The rule must perform the following changes: the adverb *never* must be preposed to a sentence-initial position, the auxiliary verb *do* must be inserted to the right of it, the tense features of the main verb must be copied onto this auxiliary verb and then the tense feature of the main verb must be deleted.

We continue to add rules. Let us assume a rule for introducing the adverb *not*. This rule (RNEG) takes a sentence as input, e.g. S(he bought a book), and it performs the following formal changes: the adverb *not* is introduced, the auxiliary *do* is introduced, the tense features are copied from the main verb onto this auxiliary verb and the tense features are deleted at the main verb. The meaning of the rule corresponds to logical negation. The rule derives sentence (4) from a structure such as S(he bought a book):

(4)   He did not buy a book

Finally, let us introduce a rule to form emphatic affirmative clauses. This rule, called REMPH, has the semantics of focusing and it performs the following changes: it introduces the auxiliary verb *do* to the right of the subject, it copies the tense feature from the main verb onto this auxiliary verb and deletes these features at the main verb. The result, when applied to the structure S(he bought a book) is sentence (5):

(5)   He did buy a book

We have now postulated several rules, five of which we want to discuss further: RYNQ, RWHQ, RTOP, RNEG and REMPH. Each of these rules has its own meaning and each performs its own formal operations. They could readily be incorporated into a compositional grammar. Nevertheless, the approach adopted here has serious shortcomings. Notice that certain operations occur in each of these rules:

- introduction of the auxiliary verb *do*,

- copying the tense features from the main verb onto the auxiliary verb *do*, and

- deletion of the tense features on the main verb.

These operations must be described separately in each of these rules. It is clear that this is an undesirable state of affairs. In fact, the situation is worse than described, because the operations were only defined for a limited variety of sentences. As soon as we try to extend the analysis to cover an interesting fragment of English, the common operations must be considerably complicated: different operations must apply if the input already contains auxiliary verbs, the introduction of the auxiliary verb is optional if the main verb is *have* and then the main verb *have* starts to occupy the position where otherwise the auxiliary verb is introduced, etc. The important point here is that all these complications are the same for all the rules introduced. By formulating these rules separately in each rule given above this fact is described as being accidental; a considerable redundancy is introduced into the system; the rule system is unnecessarily large and maintaining and updating the system of rules is made considerably complex. In short, it is clear that a number of linguistic generalisations have been missed.

10.2.2   A solution

It is obvious how the problems sketched in the previous section can be solved: the operations common to all these rules should be factored out. Each individual rule can then be considerably simplified, the grammar as a whole becomes smaller, the common properties are explicitly identified and isolated, and maintainability and updating becomes easier. A future change in an operation that has been factored out will immediately have effects in each of the constructions mentioned, which is clearly a desirable result.

One way to factor out these operations is by writing them as separate grammar rules. This method will be illustrated here and has actually been used in the Rosetta system. It has several advantages. It turns out that most of these operations have properties resembling syntactic rules to a high degree. The method adopted accounts for this fact immediately, it supplies a format and a notation to describe the operations and the modes of interaction with existing rules are determined immediately as well. In addition, it makes it possible to keep the relevant operations local, as will be illustrated in Section 10.5. An alternative method could consist of writing a set of functions which are called by rules, as suggested by Partee (1977), Partee (1979) and Partee *et al.* (1990:318-9). Though we did not compare the methods in detail, the latter method requires additional clarification of the operations allowed, a format and a notation for them and a specification of the possible modes of interaction with rules. In addition, it appears that certain operations cannot be kept local under this approach (see Section 10.5). To our knowledge, this latter method has never been applied in a real large-scale system, whereas the method adopted here has proved its usefulness in the Rosetta system.

Applying this solution to the analysis of auxiliaries in English, we observe that the rule in which the common properties of the preceding rules are described performs operations on auxiliary verbs. It is not at all obvious that a meaning can be associated with this rule. The rule performs a number of the operations needed to form yes-no questions, WH-questions, topicalised constructions, negated sentences and emphatic sentences. Its semantics should be the 'intersection' of the meanings of these constructions, but this intersection is most probably empty. In addition, it is highly unlikely that translation-equivalent rules can be found in other languages. Therefore, this rule must be a *transformation*, a rule which is associated with the identity operation as its meaning. We will call the rule TAUX. The rule is pre-fixed with *T*, in accordance with the convention introduced in Chapter 9 to prefix transformations with *T*.

Considering the rule TAUX in a realistic system, it turns out to be desirable to split it up into two different rules. Note that TAUX introduces an auxiliary verb in all examples, but it should do so in certain cases to the right of the subject (in the constructions for which RNEG, REMPH have been proposed), and in other cases to the left of the subject (in the constructions for which RYNQ, RWHQ, RTOP have been proposed). When some other auxiliary verb is present in the structure, no additional auxiliary verb should be introduced, but in the case of RYNQ, RWHQ and RTOP the auxiliary present must change its position and be put in front of the subject. By isolating and factoring out this operation of inverting the subject and the auxiliary verb the complicated rule TAUX can now be separated into two simpler rules, one which introduces the auxiliary verb *do* if no other auxiliary is present and one which inverts the subject and the auxiliary in certain configurations. The rule of inversion is necessary anyway, to deal with cases of inversion that involve auxiliaries other than the auxiliary verb *do*. This rule can now also be simplified, since it need exclude the auxiliary verb *do* no longer: it can simply state that in certain configurations any auxiliary verb and the subject must be inverted.

In fact, the rules and the whole grammar can be simplified even more if the auxiliary verb is introduced into *all* structures which do not contain an auxiliary verb already and by postulating a rule which copies the tense features from the auxiliary *do* onto the main verb and deletes *do* if, at the end of the derivation, *do* and the main verb are adjacent. This simplifies the rule of auxiliary introduction, it simplifies the rules assigning values to tense attributes (these rules can now refer in all cases to the auxiliary verb) and it simplifies the rule of subject-verb agreement (which also need only refer to the auxiliary verb). The only problem it creates is that this solution will not work for REMPH (in, e.g., *he did buy a book* the auxiliary verb *do* and the main verb are adjacent, but *do* cannot be deleted). This, however, can be solved in a very simple manner, for example, by marking *do* in this construction as [+stressed] and formulate the rule of auxiliary deletion in such a way that it does not apply to [+stressed] elements, or by postulating an abstract element EMPH which occupies the position between *do* and the main verb and which is deleted later in the derivation. This abstract element could be a basic expression and correspond to Dutch *wel* which must occur in translations of this English construction: *he did buy a book - hij kocht* **wel** *een boek*. The analysis of the English auxiliary system sketched here is, of course, based to a large extent on the analysis given originally by Chomsky (1957) and several studies since.

Summarising, the resulting analysis, which has actually been implemented, can be described as follows. There is a transformation which introduces the auxiliary *do* to the right of the subject in all finite sentential structures, unless there already is an auxiliary. The meaningful rules RNEG, REMPH, RYNQ, RWHQ and RTOP still exist, but they have been considerably simplified, since the operations common to them have been factored out. There is an inversion transformation which inverts auxiliary and subject in certain configurations, which are created by the meaningful rules RTOP and RYNQ. And there is a transformation which copies the tense features of the auxiliary *do* onto the main verb and deletes the auxiliary if it is adjacent to a verb.

In the analysis sketched, the relation between the meaning and the form of the sentence has now become very indirect. Though the sentences (6a,b,c) differ formally only with respect to the presence of an auxiliary and with respect to the relative position of the subject and the auxiliary, neither of these formal differences is accounted for by a rule which takes care of the semantic differences.

(6) a He bought a book
     b He did buy a book
     c Did he buy a book?

This situation is typical for most phenomena in natural language. The kind of approach described here, in which common properties of rules are factored out maximally and written as separate transformations, turns out to be useful for many constructions. This will be illustrated by a number of examples in the following sections, which will show that common properties have been factored out of semantically motivated rules and that this leads to operations which operate in a purely formal, syntactic way, making the relation between meaning and form considerably more indirect.

10.3 Mood in Dutch

An account similar to the one given in the preceding section can be given for Dutch as well. Consider the following Dutch sentences:

(7) a Hij koopt een boek
    b Koopt hij een boek?

Here, as before, we have two different sentences: the sentences differ in form and in meaning, and it would be rather straightforward to formulate rules to form each of the sentences and associate each with its own meaning. The formal differences between the two sentences given relate to the position of the finite verb and to the position of the subject. However, when one considers more relevant facts from Dutch, it appears that the simplest description for the facts concerning the placement of finite verbs and subjects in main clauses involves two rules: (1) a rule putting a finite verb into the position of a subordinate conjunction (provided none is present), and (2) a rule preposing the subject in a topic position. The first rule applies in a variety of constructions: in main clauses, in subordinate clauses and even in certain kinds of adverbial clauses. The relevant rule will be discussed in more detail in Chapter 11. It appears impossible to associate this rule with any semantic aspect. For the second rule it also appears to be implausible that a semantics can be attached to it: one might think that this rule plays a role in topic-comment relationships, but in fact the rule also applies to subjects which are completely meaningless grammatical elements such as expletives, the Dutch variants of weather-*it* and extraposition-*it* and idiom chunks, for which topic-comment relations appear irrelevant. And even for semantically non-empty phrases the particular rule does not seem to change topic-comment relations at all: the position of the subject relative to other arguments and adjuncts in the clause does not change. In addition, it is absolutely unclear that this rule can be associated with rules from other languages: there appears to be nothing that could correspond to this rule in English or Spanish, which also makes it difficult (or at least unnatural) to associate a meaning with this rule. Thus again we find a situation where a certain meaning difference is correlated with a formal difference, but where none of the rules taking care of the formal aspects is itself directly responsible for the meaning difference.

In the actual grammar of Dutch in the Rosetta system, the relevant facts are accounted for in the following manner. There is a transformation which optionally puts a subject into a topic position. There is a set of meaningful rules, called Mood rules, which assign a mood to structures (i.e. declarative, yes-no question, imperative, etc.) and which crucially read off from the structure whether this is possible. Thus, the mood rule to form declarative main clauses requires the presence of a [-wh]-phrase as a topic. The mood rule to form WH-interrogatives requires the presence of a [+wh]-phrase as a topic. And the mood rule to form yes-no questions disallows any topic at all. Where appropriate, the mood rules introduce subordinate conjunctions. After the mood rules, transformations apply to put the finite verb in its appropriate position. These transformations apply blindly and put the finite verb in the position of the subordinate conjunction if none is present. So here again, the relation between the form and the meaning is very indirect. The whole grammar is considerably simplified by the approach adopted and linguistically established generalisations have been expressed adequately.

10.4 Order variants

Many sentences have variants in which the phrases have a slightly different relative order, sometimes accompanied by small additional formal differences (e.g. presence of a preposition). Some examples are given in (8). In (8a) the indirect object precedes the direct object, but in (8b) it is the other way around (and the indirect object is accompanied by the preposition *to*). In (8c) the direct object follows the sentential adverb, but in (8d) it precedes this adverb. In (8e) the prepositional complement precedes the verb, but in (8f) it follows. In (8g) the indirect object phrase headed by the preposition *aan* precedes the direct object, but in (8h) it follows. And in (8i) the direct object precedes the beneficiary phrase (headed by the preposition *for*), whereas in (8j) it follows. The problem is that, often (though not in all cases), semantic differences are associated with these different variants, sometimes rather subtle, but in other cases quite large. Thus, the sentences often differ with respect to topic-comment relations and often there are scope differences. Of course, there must be syntactic rules to describe the form differences between these sentences. Since there are meaning differences between these variants as well, the issue arises whether such rules must be meaningful rules and what the corresponding rules are in the other languages dealt with. If the rules to create these order variants are to be associated with meaning operations directly, a number of generalisations will be missed. Each of the relevant rules will have to be tripled, because in certain cases application of the rules does not correlate to any meaning difference, in other cases the meaning difference relates to scope properties and in yet other cases only topic-comment relations are changed. It is very difficult, if not impossible, to describe

(8) a (E) He gave the boy a book

    b (E) He gave a book to the boy

    c (D) Hij heeft waarschijnlijk die jongen gezien

          He has   probably   that boy   seen

          (He has probably seen that boy)

    d (D) Hij heeft die jongen waarschijnlijk gezien

          He has   that boy   probably   seen

          (He has probably seen that boy)

    e (D) Hij heeft naar het programma gekeken

          He has   at   the program   looked

          (He has looked at the program)

    f (D) Hij heeft gekeken naar het programma

          He has   looked   at   the program

          (He has looked at the program)

    g (D) Hij heeft aan de jongen dat boek gegeven

          He has   to   the boy   that book given

          (He has given the boy that book)

    h (D) Hij heeft dat boek aan de jongen gegeven

          He has   that book to   the boy   given

          (He has given that book to the boy)

    i (E) He bought a book for the boy

    j (E) He bought the boy a book

the relevant rules in such a way that the right meaning differences are correctly associated. In addition, the effects of such rules are — so to speak — global. Thus moving a phrase into another position might change its scope relative to some other phrase which does not figure in the rule or its specific application at all. Finally, it is very difficult to set up translation-equivalent rules in other languages: they should have the same semantic effects and apply in the same manner in the corresponding syntactic configurations.

This suggests that the rules responsible for the phenomena indicated should be transformations and the semantic effects should be dealt with by rules which can take the global structure of the sentence into account. Therefore, phrases are not directly introduced into a structure. Instead, *syntactic variables*, i.e. small syntactic trees consisting of exactly one node with a special attribute *index* are initially introduced into the structure. Transformations then apply to yield different orders. And finally, the semantic aspects, e.g. of scope, are taken care of by so-called *substitution rules*. These are rules which substitute a phrase for a variable with a specific index occurring in a syntactic tree. These substitution rules take global aspects of the sentence structure into account, for example, if a certain scope difference is expressed by linear order, they take linear order into account. This approach to scope, with variables and substitution rules, has been adopted directly from Montague (1973). The only difference from Montague (1973) is that there are no syntactic transformations which can apply to syntactic variables in that analysis. See Chapter 16 for a detailed explanation of the treatment of scope in the M-grammar formalism.

A similar approach can be adopted to account for the syntactic realisation of topic-comment relations. Meaningful rules which mark a certain variable as being *topic* or *comment* might be assumed; several transformations can move variables into other positions and the substitution rules which substitute the actual phrases for these variables should take syntactic conditions on topic-comment realisation into account, e.g. they should be applicable only if the variable marked as comment occurs in a specific position. If this were combined with a pragmatic theory of which topic-comment relations in a sentence are appropriate in a specific context, we would have the beginnings of a fully-fledged account of topic-comment relations.

In these examples we see again that certain semantic and pragmatic differences correspond to certain formal differences (i.e. differences in word order). But the rules which are responsible for these formal differences are not themselves directly responsible for these semantic or pragmatic differences.

10.5   WH-movement

Consider the following sentences:

(9) a He can see something
     b He can see what?
     c What can he see?

These three sentences differ semantically and pragmatically: (9a) is a simple declarative sentence, sentence (9b) is an echo question and sentence (9c) is a WH-question. Correspondingly, they also differ in certain formal respects. First, (9a) contains the word *something* as a direct object, and the other two examples contain the word *what* instead. Second, in (9b) the phrase *what* follows the verb, but in (9c) this phrase occupies a sentence-initial position. First, this seems to be an ideal situation for the compositional approach. But again, things will turn out to be slightly more complex than might appear at first sight.

Sentence (9a) and the other two sentences differ because they contain different basic expressions: *something* in (9a), *what* in the other two sentences. It remains to account for the difference between (9b) and (9c). The only difference between these two sentences is the position of the phrase *what*. So, it appears natural to postulate a rule, RMWH, which preposes the phrase *what* from the normal position of direct objects into a clause-initial position and which accounts for the meaning of (9c). In addition, a rule is needed to assign a meaning to (9b).

The first problem for this simple approach, however, is that not only the fact *that* the phrase *what* is preposed to a clause-initial position is relevant, but also *how far* it is preposed. This is illustrated in (10):

(10) a He will know what he can see
      b What will he know he can see?

In both (10a) and (10b) the phrase *what* has been preposed to a clause-initial position, but they clearly have a different meaning. The only difference between the two sentences is the distance over which the phrase *what* has been preposed. So this aspect must be taken into account as well. Second, it has been argued by Chomsky (1977b) that the rule preposing *what* in such sentences plays a role in many constructions, e.g. in relativisation, topicalisation, clefting, pseudo-clefting, tough-constructions, comparative deletion, subdeletion in comparatives, equative constructions, complements to *too*, etc. In all these constructions an operation of preposing is required which obeys exactly the same restrictions in all these constructions.[2] So we would like to analyse all of these constructions as involving the rule RMWH as a suboperation. But now it has become quite difficult to assign a unique meaning to this rule. It cannot have to do with questioning, and in fact we should find a common semantic factor in all of these constructions and show that it has to be associated with this rule (and not with other operations). A third problem is created by languages which can form questions such as (9c) without applying a preposing rule. In such languages the phrase corresponding to *what* can create WH-questions without being preposed. French is an example of this. The sentence *il peut savoir quoi?* can have the meaning of a normal question such as (9c). This would require that in French there is a rule corresponding to English RMWH which performs no formal change.

These arguments suggest that the rule RMWH should be a transformation, and that the difference between (9b) and (9c) should be dealt with in some other manner. From now on, we will therefore call this rule TMWH. In fact, as before, a substitution rule, in combination with the mood rule RWH proposed earlier, can achieve exactly the desired effect. The transformation TMWH preposes [+wh] variables to a clause-initial position. If there is more than one clause-initial position, RWH will, in principle, yield two results. A substitution rule substitutes a WH-phrase for the [+wh] variable which is clause-initial. And the mood rule RWH accounts for the fact that the clause which the interrogative phrase happens to introduce is turned into a WH-question. Thus combination of a substitution rule and the mood rule RWH will automatically control the application of the preposing rule TMWH and account for the relevant semantic aspects, so that rule TMWH need not be associated with a

---

[2]Where there are differences, these can be accounted for by independent factors.

meaning and can apply freely. This is a typical example of the situation mentioned in the introduction, in which transformations apply freely, after which their results are input to meaningful rules, which perform additional form changes and account for the semantic aspects. The approach sketched here is compatible with the semantic analysis of WH-complements as sketched by Groenendijk and Stokhof (1982) and therefore it makes it possible to integrate a well-motivated syntactic analysis of WH-movement with a well-motivated semantic analysis of WH-questions.

If we can show that in all the other constructions mentioned above other rules than TMWH are also required and that the relevant semantics must be associated with these rules rather than with TMWH, we can fully integrate Chomsky's (1977b) insight that the TMWH plays an important role in all these constructions. We think that this can indeed be done and we have actually implemented such analyses for relativisation and topicalisation.

These facts show once again that the relation between form and meaning is rather indirect. The sentences (9b,c) differ in meaning and in form, but the only formal difference which is directly visible (the position of *what*) is accounted for by a rule (TMWH) which itself is not directly responsible for the meaning difference.

The construction dealt with here also supplies us with an argument in favour of the method in which operations which are factored out are written as separate rules and against the method in which functions are called from within rules. The movement operation illustrated here can apply, in principle, over indefinite distances. By formulating the movement operation as a separate rule, the rule can be applied in a successive cyclic manner, so that each application is local. In the alternative approach in which functions are called from within a rule, the function will be called in the rule RWH and the movement will have to be able to apply over indefinite distances. Of course, all other things being equal, local rule applications are to be preferred to global applications, and in addition, there is empirical evidence that the rule involved here must apply in a successive cyclic manner (see Chapter 11).

10.6   Generic sentences

Consider the Dutch sentences in (11).

(11) a Hij zegt dat honden blaffen
         (He says that dogs bark)
      b Hij zegt dat er   honden blaffen
         He says that there dogs   bark   (He says that dogs are barking)
      c Blaffen honden?
         Bark   dogs?   (Do dogs bark?)
      d Blaffen er   honden?
         Bark   there dogs?   (Are dogs barking?)

The subordinate clause in (11a) must be interpreted as describing a generic property of dogs, while the subordinate clause in (11b) must be interpreted as a statement pertaining to a specific situation in which dogs happen to be barking. Similarly, (11c) is a question pertaining to a generic property of dogs and (11d) asks whether — in the particular situation at hand — it happens to be the case that dogs are barking. Corresponding to these semantic differences, there are formal differences: the sentences (11b,d) contain the word *er* which does not occur in the other sentences. Again, we find a situation where a semantic difference appears to correlate rather directly with a formal difference at first sight. It appears straightforward to write rules which account for these facts. However, as before, we will show that the situation is actually far more complex than one might think at first sight. Zwarts (1988) contains an extensive discussion of genericity in the framework assumed here.

If a rule were to be written to deal with sentences (11b,d) directly, then this would be a rule, say RNONGEN, which introduces *er* and relates it to some NP, so that the NP is interpreted non-generically. And an additional rule would be required, say RGEN, which would account for the generic interpretation of this NP. A first problem with such an approach is that it is unclear how the use of *er* in this construction can be related to other uses of *er* in a principled manner. The pronoun *er* is also used in impersonal passives (12a), in passives of verbs with sentential complements (12b), in sentences where the subject must be interpreted non-specifically (12c) and in existential sentences (12d).

(12)   a Er   werd gedanst
           There was   danced   (There was dancing going on)
       b Er   wordt beweerd dat hij ziek is
           There is   said   that he ill   is   (He is said to be ill)
       c Er   kocht iemand een boek
           There bought someone a   book   (Someone was buying a book)
       d Er zijn geen boeken
           (There are no books)

A second problem is that one can show that absence or presence of *er* is not a crucial factor in all cases: In (13) the NP can be interpreted only non-generically, but no *er* is present:

(13)   a Altijd lopen daar mannen
           Always walk   there men
           (There are always men walking there)
       b Altijd spelen in het stadion voetballers
           Always play   in the stadium soccer players
           (In the stadium always soccer players play)

The crucial factor here is a difference in position. And in fact, this holds for the earlier examples as well: the occurrences of the phrase *honden* occupy different positions in (11a,c) and (11b,d) as well. This is shown in (14):

(14) a Hij zegt dat honden altijd blaffen
       (He says that dogs always bark)

   b Hij zegt dat er   altijd honden blaffen
       He says that there always dogs   bark
       (He says that there are always dogs barking)

   c Blaffen honden altijd?
       Bark   dogs   always?
       (Do dogs always bark?)

   d Blaffen er   altijd honden?
       Bark   there always dogs?
       (Are there always dogs barking?)

In (14a,c) the adverb *altijd* follows the phrase *honden*, while in (14b,d) it precedes this phrase. This order is obligatory:

(15) a *Hij zegt dat altijd honden blaffen
         He says that always dogs   bark

   b *Hij zegt dat er   honden altijd blaffen
         He says that there dogs   always bark

   c *Blaffen altijd honden?
         Bark   always dogs?

   d *Blaffen er   honden altijd?
         Bark   there dogs   always?

This suggests that we should consider introduction of *er* to be a purely syntactic transformation and that the rule accounting for the generic or non-generic interpretation of NPs must be formulated in terms of the position the NP occupies. This would make it possible to relate the use of *er* in these constructions to other uses of *er* and it is now also possible to account for the examples where no *er* occurs.

There are, however, reasons to assume that the generic v. non-generic interpretation should not be associated with the different positions of the phrase either, though this is more controversial. First, an account which is formulated purely in terms of positions would be insufficient in two ways: on the one hand, there are many NPs that can never be interpreted generically, whatever position they occupy; and on the other other hand there are NPs that can be interpreted generically or non-generically irrespective of the position they occupy (e.g. bare plurals in direct object position: *he bought flowers* v. *he likes flowers*). So there must be additional rules to specify which NPs can and which cannot be interpreted generically. Second, generic NPs cannot co-occur in just any type of sentence. There are strong restrictions on the aspectual and temporal properties of generic sentences. For example, a generic NP can hardly occur in a sentence with the main verb in perfect tense (unless certain adverbs, e.g. *altijd 'always'* are present): *?Honden hebben geblaft, 'Dogs have barked'.* So there must be conditions on the combination with tense and aspect forms of verbs as well.

In Spanish, generic and non-generic NPs differ in form. The Dutch NP *honden* in its generic interpretation is translated into *los perros* and this NP in its non-generic reading is translated into *perros*. This clearly shows that rules forming NPs must take genericity into account: there must be rules to generate the NP *perros* as an NP which cannot be interpreted generically and the NP *los perros* as one which can. In English the distinction between the generic and the non-generic interpretation is formally encoded here by different tenses of the verb:

(16) a He says that dogs bark
     b He says that dogs are barking
     c Do dogs bark?
     d Are dogs barking?

In order to account for all these facts, we assume that the semantic difference between generic and non-generic NPs must be ascribed only to rules forming NPs. Bare plural noun phrases in Dutch and English are formed by two different sets of rules, one set yielding the generic NP and the other yielding the non-generic NP. The restrictions on the occurrence of generic and non-generic NPs are accounted for by formulating appropriate conditions on the substitution rules that introduce such NPs into a clausal structure. The rules forming NPs account for the right form of the NP and substitution rules check that generic and non-generic NPs are inserted into a structure in the right positions and only if the sentence has specific temporal and aspectual properties. In Spanish, *perros* and *los perros* are formed by different rules and substitution rules check whether they occur in the right environment.

This approach to these phenomena again leads to an indirect relation between form and meaning. Though at first sight it appeared necessary to ascribe the difference between generic and non-generic NPs to the presence of *er*, we soon concluded that this was actually not the relevant factor, though this was the only directly visible formal difference between the initial examples. We shifted the semantics to rules dealing with the positions of NPs in a clause, but again we quite quickly concluded that this would not be sufficient. And finally we decided to ascribe the semantic difference between a generic NP and non-generic NP to rules forming these NPs, leaving the syntactic and semantic conditions which hold with respect to the distribution of such NPs to substitution rules and their corresponding meaning operations. Such substitution rules are meaningful rules, but their semantics does not relate to

genericity or non-genericity of NPs. The resulting situation implies that the difference between (11a,c) and (11b,d) is not to be found in the absence v. presence of *er*
(the only directly visible difference between these sentences), nor in the position that
the NPs occupy (these positions are different, but this cannot be observed directly),
but in a difference between the NPs occurring in these sentences (a difference that is
only visible in abstract intermediate representations of the sentence). This is a clear
example where the relation between form and meaning is very indirect: the rules that
account directly for the visible form differences are not themselves associated with
the meaning differences. Nevertheless, it appears to us to be the simplest analysis
possible and the relation between form and meaning is clear and transparent in the
grammar.

10.7   Concluding remarks

In this chapter we have shown that the controlled M-grammar formalism makes
it possible to find a proper balance between purely syntactic requirements and the
requirements of a compositional grammar in which form and meaning must be
associated in a rather direct way. The M-grammar formalism is a compositional
formalism and therefore has a strong semantic bias. Though such a strong semantic
bias could easily lead to syntactically inadequate analyses, this is compensated by
allowing syntactic transformations, rules which have the identity operation as their
meaning. In this way it is possible to express syntactic generalisations, to simplify
individual rules of the grammar, to reduce the overall size of the grammar, and to
avoid redundancy. In short, it is possible to approach a more modular organisation
of the grammar, so that it becomes easier to maintain and to update.

The combination of meaningful rules and syntactic transformations, each of
which may be relatively simple, increases the amount of rule interaction and makes
the relation between form and meaning rather indirect in the following sense: many
rules which account for form differences should be transformations in a syntactically adequate description, even though the form differences appear to correlate
with meaning differences. Other rules, which often apply to more abstract representations of the sentence and do therefore not have directly visible formal effects on
the surface account for the meaning differences.

The facts discussed show that the relation between form and meaning is a subtle
one and that there is no direct correspondence between meaning aspects and surface
properties of utterances. Note that this does not have negative consequences for the
relation between form and meaning in the grammar. In the grammar this relation
is transparent, which is is a main virtue of compositional grammars, including the
controlled M-grammar framework.

Chapter 11

Incorporating theoretical linguistic insights

11.1 Introduction

This chapter describes some general properties of the syntax, sketches analyses of several constructions, and indicates how these relate to analyses of the same (or similar) constructions in more theoretically oriented approaches. Furthermore, it will show that the method of compositional translation combined with language-specific transformations allows simple and elegant accounts of fairly complex syntactic phenomena. This will be illustrated with a small number of examples of the many phenomena that have actually been implemented. A more detailed account can be found in Odijk (1993).

11.2 General properties of the syntax

This section will indicate globally how aspects of the system are based on certain theoretical approaches or influenced by them. In the subsequent sections this will be illustrated by discussing a number of specific constructions.

The syntax of Rosetta has a rather eclectic character. Aspects from several theoretical frameworks and approaches have been incorporated, though two approaches dominate among these, i.e. *Montague grammar* and *Transformational Grammar* and its direct descendents.

The influence of *Montague grammar* is obvious first and foremost in the global design of the system. This has been discussed extensively in the preceding chapters.

203

The fact that *compositional* grammars are used, and that *derivation trees* play a significant role in the system bear witness to this fact. But the influence of Montague grammar can also be found in other aspects. The treatment of scope is derived directly from the treatment of scope in Montague grammar (see Chapter 16 for an extensive discussion of the treatment of scope).

The influence of *Transformational Grammar* and its direct descendents (i.e. the work done in the framework sketched by Chomsky (1957, 1965, 1970, 1973, 1981, 1986) and others) can be found not only in the fact that M-grammars contain transformations, but also in the analysis of a number of specific constructions. In many cases the derivation of a specific construction in Rosetta resembles the derivation of that construction in (some version of) Transformational grammar to a great extent. This will be illustrated below (cf. Sections 11.3, 11.7). For certain constructions existing analyses have been adopted as a whole, though they have often been refined and extended. An example of this is the treatment of cross-serial dependencies in Dutch, based on the analysis sketched by Evers (Evers (1975)). Most frequently, however, analyses of certain phenomena have been developed purely within the Rosetta grammars, though often some basic insights or ideas from Transformational Grammar have served as a starting point (cf., for instance, the treatment of R-pronouns in Dutch.)

The framework of Transformational Grammar has undergone a number of quite drastic changes in the course of time, and its direct descendent, known as the *Principles and Parameters Approach*, differs substantially from it. For this reason it is necessary to specify somewhat more precisely which version of Transformational Grammar influenced M-grammar most. On the most global organisational level, the syntax resembles work from early Transformational Grammar (Chomsky (1957, 1965)). The fact that controlled M-grammars contain rules and transformations which are both language- and construction-specific and which are applied in a certain order as indicated in a control expression, and the fact that, for instance, traces play no role whatsoever, show this. The organisation of the subgrammars (see Chapter 9 and Odijk (1989)), however, is partly inspired by work from later generative grammar, in particular $\overline{X}$-Theory (Chomsky (1970), Jackendoff (1977)). The central role of so-called *small clauses* finds its inspiration in the work done by Stowell (Stowell (1981,1983)). When looking in more detail at the particular analysis of certain constructions, it can again be seen that insights from later versions of Transformational Grammar play a significant role (for instance, in the treatment of passives, cf. Section 11.3).

The analyses used are usually not direct implementations of existing analyses. Most existing analyses are not sufficiently formalised to be incorporated directly and usually no attempt is made to obtain full coverage of the relevant set of facts. Rather, only a subset of the facts which are expected to yield new insights into certain aspects of a general theory of grammars is analysed. In addition, the analyses within recent versions of descendents of Transformational Grammar tend to be extremely non-deterministic, so that they are computationally barely tractable. For these reasons the existing analyses must be fully formalised, extended to obtain greater coverage and made more deterministic.

In general, certain properties of existing analyses which are crucial to the achievement of descriptive adequacy have been identified and isolated and they have been incorporated (sometimes in a slightly modified form) in an analysis that fits in with the overall grammatical framework used in Rosetta.

We will illustrate these general points with examples from the syntax of Dutch, English and Spanish: passive constructions (Section 11.3), Verb Second in Dutch (Section 11.4), cross-serial dependencies in Dutch (Section 11.5), R-pronouns in Dutch (Section 11.6), unbounded dependencies (Section 11.7) and clitics in Spanish (Section 11.8).

11.3 Passive

The first step in forming a sentence consists of combining a verb with a number of variables into a propositional structure consisting of a predicate and optionally a subject, by so-called Start rules (see Section 3.4.2). The position of the variables and the grammatical relations they bear in this structure correspond to their positions and relations when used in an active sentence. Thus, for instance, the two-place verb *kiss* can be combined with two variables, x_1 and x_2, where x_1 is the subject and x_2 is the direct object in the propositional structure headed by *kiss*.

Voice rules apply to determine the voice of the structure. The rule for Active Voice leaves the structure unchanged, and only changes the value of the voice attribute of the proposition node from *unspecified* to *active*.

The rule for passive voice (called RPASSIVE) changes the value of this voice attribute into *passive*, but a number of other changes are performed as well. The rule RPASSIVE, however, is not really comparable to the traditional *passive transformation* (e.g. as in Chomsky (1957)), but has been decomposed into a number of separate rules and transformations, which together form passive structures. This approach is inspired directly by the treatment of passives in Transformational Grammar and its direct descendents (see e.g. Chomsky (1981)).

In order to illustrate this, we will summarise the differences between a typical passive sentence and the corresponding active sentence, and indicate where and how the differences between them are accounted for:

Voice The attribute **voice** has the value *active* in active sentences, the value *passive* in passive sentences. As pointed out above, the value of this attribute is set in the voice rules.

Subject The first argument of a verb in active sentences is expressed as a *subject*. In passive sentences it is expressed as a complement to the preposition *door* in Dutch, *by* in English or *por* in Spanish. This change is performed in the rule RPASSIVE as well.

Verb form In active sentences the form of the main verb is not fixed. It can be a finite verb, an infinitive, a present participle, a past participle (if an auxiliary verb *hebben* or *zijn* (in Dutch), *have* (in English) or *haber* (in Spanish) is present); in passive structures the main verb is a past participle. The form of the verb is set in the rule RPASSIVE.

Auxiliaries In active sentences no auxiliaries to express voice are present. In passive sentences, however, auxiliary verbs (Dutch: *worden* or *zijn*; English: *be*; Spanish: *ser*) are present. These auxiliary verbs are introduced by rules turning the propositional structure into a clause.

NP-movement One of the NP-arguments inside VP in an active sentence is usually realised as a subject in the corresponding passive sentence. We will call this NP the *moving NP*. It can be a *direct object*, (**The girl** *was kissed*), an *indirect object* (**The man** *was given a book*), a *prepositional object* (**The girl** *was looked at*), the subject of an embedded clause (**The man** *was believed to be ill*) or the subject of an embedded small clause (**He** *was considered a fool*). The operation to turn the moving NP into a subject will be called *NP-movement*. NP-movement is performed by a special transformation.

It is clear that the effects of the traditional passive transformation are performed by the interaction of voice rules, rules to form clauses and transformations to turn NPs into subjects. The reasons for doing this in this way are:

NP-movement This operation is not performed inside the rule RPASSIVE because it is not essential to the passive voice at all:

- There are passive sentences with no VP-internal NP at all (impersonal passives, for instance *Er werd gedanst* (lit. *There was danced*) in Dutch, and passives of verbs that take a sentential complement, for instance *It was said that he was dishonest*). If NP-movement were part of the rule RPASSIVE, a separate rule for such passives would have to be stated.

- In personal passive sentences the moving NP sometimes remains inside VP, and is not turned into a subject. Some relevant examples are: *De mannen werd* **het boek** *gegeven* (lit. *The men was the book given*), *Er werd door hem* **een boek** *gelezen* (lit. *There was by him a book read*), for which it can be argued convincingly that the boldface NPs are objects, not subjects (cf. Den Besten (1981)).

- A distinction is made between *ergative* and *non-ergative* verbs (see Perl-mutter (1978), Burzio (1981), and Den Besten (1981, 1982) and Hoekstra (1984) for Dutch). Ergative verbs are verbs that take an NP as argument but do not realise any of its arguments as an *external argument* (in the sense of Williams (1981), also see Chapter 12). For these verbs there must be a rule to turn an NP into a subject as well, though this involves only active structures. It is natural to use the same rule both in passives and in ergative structures.

- NP-movement must also be performed for NPs that are not yet present in the structure at the moment that the rule RPASSIVE applies. As pointed out above, the first rules to form sentences combine verbs with a number of variables, and it is the case that for a sentence such as *She was considered smart by us* the structure contains a variable for the subject (*we*), and a variable for the 'small clause' *she smart*, but nothing that corresponds directly to the NP *she*, which is the NP to be made the subject the moment that the rule RPASSIVE must apply.

- Control transformations dealing with *obligatory control* (in the sense of Williams (1980)) can be simplified if the object is still an object at the moment that they apply. This makes it easier to account for the fact that a derived subject still can function as a controller, though an NP in the *by*-phrase cannot. Recall here that there are no traces. Some relevant sentences to illustrate the phenomenon are: *She was forced by him to defend herself* v. **She was promised by him to defend himself.*

Auxiliary Verb The auxiliary verb is not introduced in the rule RPASSIVE because there are passive structures where no such auxiliary occurs. This is the case in small clauses with a verb as their head, e.g. *Hij kreeg* **het boek afgeleverd** (*He got the book delivered*), *Hij wist* **zich door hem gesteund** (lit. *He knew himself by him supported, he knew he was supported by him*), *They had* **him killed** .

So the effects of passivisation are achieved by the interaction of a number of rules, some of which are necessary on independent grounds. The analysis sketched here is very much in the spirit of modern Transformational Grammar. The following properties of these analyses have been incorporated: (1) passivisation is *syntactic*, not lexical; (2) no reference to a direct object NP or any NP whatsoever is necessary or desirable; (3) movement of NP is necessary in certain cases, but (4) this movement is independent of passivisation; (5) the presence of the auxiliary is independent of passivisation. The analysis deviates considerably from analyses of the passive construction in most other computational frameworks (e.g. LFG, see Kaplan and Bresnan (1982), or HPSG, see Pollard and Sag (1987)), in which the passive

construction is usually accounted for by a lexical rule that creates a new lexical entry
with new complementation properties from an existing lexical entry. In these latter
analyses, many facts taken into account here, are usually not considered at all (e.g.
ergative verbs, argument of passive verbs that remain direct objects) or are dealt
with in a completely different manner (e.g. small clauses).

11.4   Verb Second in Dutch

In Chapters 2 and 3 the problem of the correct distribution of verbs in Dutch was
introduced, but not solved. This section will sketch the solution that has been
adopted to solve this problem. The solution incorporates the following two assumptions: first, Dutch is a so-called SOV language, and second, Dutch has a rule which
moves the finite verb to a more initial position. Subsection 11.4.1 will explain what
an SOV language is, and will motivate the status of Dutch as an SOV language.
Subsection 11.4.2 will characterise the rule mentioned above in more detail.

11.4.1   SVO and SOV languages

Dutch is a so-called *SOV language*, whereas English and Spanish are so-called *SVO
languages*. This difference will be explained here.

The symbols *S, O* and *V* stand for *subject, object* and *verb* respectively. The
order of these symbols indicates what the relative order of the phrases *subject, object*
and *verb* is. The statement that Dutch is an SOV language entails that a grammar
which adopts this order in the rule which combines the verb with its arguments is
simpler than a grammar which does not adopt this order. The statement *English is
an SVO language* must be interpreted analogously.

The evidence for Dutch as an SOV language is overwhelming. The classical
study on this topic is Koster (1975). We will present one case in which a simplification of the grammar is achieved compared to the assumption that Dutch is an SVO
language.

Let us first state some of the relevant facts. There are sentences which contain
a subject, an object and a verb in SVO order (e.g. *Hij ziet het meisje*, (lit. *He sees
the girl*)) and sentences with an SOV order (*...dat hij het meisje zag*, (lit. *...that he
the girl saw, ...that he saw the girl*). SVO order occurs almost only in main clauses;
SOV order occurs in most subordinate clauses, in infinitival constructions and in
main clauses containing an auxiliary verb. It is not desirable to write separate rules
for each of these constructions, since it would then be necessary to repeat all rules
that express the common properties of sentences with SVO and SOV order. It is
much more natural to describe the common properties of these sentences only once,
and have a special rule to describe the difference. Given this, one has the option

of letting the structures in which the common properties are expressed have SVO order (the SVO hypothesis) or SOV order (the SOV hypothesis).[1]

It is necessary to assume a rule preposing the verb under certain circumstances under the SOV hypothesis, and to assume a rule that postposes the verb under certain circumstances under the SVO hypothesis.

Independently, rules are necessary in Dutch that make it possible to move objects (and other phrases) to a sentence-initial position, e.g. to topicalise phrases, or, if the phrase contains an interrogative pronoun, to form questions. When these rules apply in a main clause, then, in addition to preposing the object, also the (finite) verb must be preposed to a position immediately to the right of the first constituent.

Under the SVO hypothesis this requires an additional rule to prepose the finite verb. Under the SOV hypothesis the existing rule for preposing the verb can be generalised in such a way that it puts the (finite) verb immediately to the right of the first phrase. No additional rule is necessary.

This very simple example shows that it is necessary under the SVO hypothesis to assume the rule to prepose the verb as well. Under the SVO hypothesis two rules are required, under the SOV hypothesis only one. Of course, no conclusions can be drawn from this single example. It is only by comparing two full grammars that conclusions can be drawn concerning their simplicity and elegance. However, many more arguments in favour of the SOV hypothesis and against the SVO hypothesis for Dutch can be provided (see Koster (1975)); the example given here serves only as an illustration.

We have adopted the assumption that Dutch is an SOV language. This assumption also plays a particular role in Chapter 16, which deals with scope and negation.

11.4.2 Verb Second

As we have seen in the preceding section, Dutch is an SOV language, and it is assumed that there is a rule to prepose the finite verb in certain constructions. This rule, and the corresponding phenomenon are usually called the *Verb Second* rule or Verb Second phenomenon. It can be illustrated by the following examples:

(1) a   *hij het boek gekocht *heeft*
          he the book bought   has
     b   hij *heeft* het boek gekocht
          he has   the book bought   (he has bought the book)

---

[1]Of course, other orders are possible as well. They will not be discussed here.

(2) a   ..dat hij het boek gekocht *heeft*
          ..that he the book bought   has   (..that he has bought the book)

     b   *..dat *heeft* hij het boek gekocht
          ..that has   he the book bought

     c   *..dat hij *heeft* het boek gekocht
          ..that he has   the book bought

In the first sentence there are two verbs, a participle form (*gekocht*) and a finite form
(*heeft*). In declarative main clauses such as in (1) the inflected verb must occur in
second position. Hence (1a) is ill-formed and (1b) is well-formed. In subordinate
clauses such as (2) the inflected verb cannot occur in second position (even when
not counting the subordinate conjunction, as in (2c)). Hence (2a) is well-formed,
and (2b,c) are ill-formed.

Though the rule is usually called *Verb Second*, this is a misleading term: the
verb sometimes occurs in sentence-initial position (e.g. in main yes-no questions,
such as *Heeft hij het boek gekocht?*, lit. *Has he the book bought?*), sometimes in
sentence-second position (in normal main declarative sentences) and sometimes
even in sentence-third position (in main declarative sentences with left-dislocated
elements, e.g. *Dat boek, dat heeft hij niet gekocht*, lit. *That book, that has he not
bought*). The correct characterisation of the position of the inflected verb has been
established by Den Besten (1983): the inflected verb occurs in the same position as
subordinate conjunctions (e.g. *dat* (*that*), *hoewel* (*although*).

This generalisation has been incorporated directly by reserving only one position in the S-tree which must be used both by inflected verbs and by subordinate
conjunctions.

Informally, it is often said that Verb Second occurs in main clauses, but not in
subordinate clauses. In fact, however, there is no correlation at all between Verb
Second and main clause status: there are main clauses and subordinate clauses where
Verb Second occurs, and there are main clauses and subordinate clause where Verb
Second does not occur, as illustrated in the following examples:

Main, +V2   Hij is ziek geweest
                 He has ill   been (he has been ill)

Main, -V2   Ziek dat hij geweest is!
                 Ill   that he been   has! (He has been so ill!)

Subord, +V2 Is   hij ziek, dan gaan we niet weg
                 Is   he ill,   then go we not away
                 if he is ill, we will not leave

Subord, -V2 Als   hij ziek is, dan gaan we niet weg
                 If   he ill is, then go   we not   away
                 If he is ill, we will not leave

Verb Second is taken care of by transformations (Tv2) that move the inflected verb into the special position reserved for inflected verbs and subordinate conjunctions. These transformations must apply if no subordinate conjunction is present.

There are two constructions that require some additional clarification. In finite relative clauses (e.g. *(de man)* **die gisteren kwam**, lit. *(the man) who yesterday came, (the man) who came yesterday*) and subordinate interrogative clauses (e.g. *(Hij vroeg)* **wie er kwam**, lit. *(He asked) who there came, (He asked) who came*) Verb Second cannot occur and no conjunction is present, either. For these cases it is assumed that conjunctions are present at the point of application of Tv2. They are deleted after the application of Tv2. For subordinate interrogatives this is the subordinate conjunction *of (if)*, which can remain in the structure (e.g. *(Hij vroeg)* **wie of er kwam**, lit. *(He asked) who if there came*) but is usually deleted; for relative clauses it is the subordinate conjunction *dat (that)*, which is deleted obligatorily. This accounts for all cases mentioned above, and also all other cases of Verb Second in Dutch. For instance, the method adopted is also able to deal with the fact that Verb Second occurs in subordinate clauses such as *Al is hij ziek, we gaan toch* (lit. *al(though) is he ill, we go anyway*) and *Hij mag dan ziek zijn, we gaan toch* (lit. *He may then ill be, we go anyway*). Both sentences mean 'Although he is ill, we will go anyway'). These constructions have not been implemented yet, but when they will be, nothing special will have to be done to make sure that Verb Second occurs in these subordinate clauses. This is automatically taken care of by the analysis of Verb Second.

The analysis sketched incorporates a number of crucial properties of Den Besten's original analysis, i.e. (1) the V2-position is identical to the position of subordinate conjunctions, and (2) there is a movement rule which moves the finite verb into this position. It is much simpler than the complicated gap-threading mechanism used by Van Noord *et al.* (1990) to account for the distribution of verbs in Dutch and Spanish (see also Chapter 8 and Van Noord (1991), in which a different approach to these phenomena is proposed, which does not make use of gap-threading techniques), and it is superior (with respect to descriptive adequacy) to the analysis sketched by Pollard (1990) in which linear precedence rules are used to account for comparable facts of German. See Odijk (1993) for discussion.

11.5   Cross-serial dependencies in Dutch

The treatment of *cross-serial dependencies* in the syntax of Dutch is an almost direct implementation of the analysis given by Evers (1975). In this construction a sequence of argument phrases (NPs, PPs) precedes a sequence of verbs, and if lines are drawn to indicate which argument phrase is an argument of which verb, these lines cross. The number of argument phrases and the number of verbs is in principle unlimited, although the acceptability of such structures decreases as the number of crossing dependencies increases. A relevant example (a subordinate clause, to avoid interference with the phenomenon of Verb Second) is given below:

(3)   ...dat de man de vrouw de boeken zag kopen
      ...that the man the woman the books   saw buy
      (...that the man saw the woman buy the books)

The following is a more complex, but fully grammatical and acceptable example:

(4)   ...dat de man de leraar zijn kinderen Frans had
      ...that the man the teacher his   children French had
      kunnen willen laten leren
      can   want   let   teach
      (...that the man could have wanted to make the teacher
      teach his children French)

The phenomenon of cross-serial dependencies gives rise to structures which can (very abstractly) be characterised as being of the form ωω and it has played an important role in the discussion of whether the syntax of natural languages is context-free (for an overview of this discussion, see Pullum (1991)).[2]

Evers accounts for such structures in the following way. Firstly, he assumes that Dutch is an SOV language and that infinitival complements start out on the left of the verb. Secondly, he supposes that infinitival complements are sentences. Thirdly, he assumes the existence of a transformation, called *Verb Raising* that moves an infinitival verb out of its clause and adjoins it to the right of the embedding verb. Infinitival sentences which have lost their verb by Verb Raising are pruned, i.e. the node S is removed from the structure.

In the Rosetta grammar, these structures are accounted for in almost the same way: all Evers's assumptions mentioned have been implemented, though some slight modifications have been made, especially with regard to the pruning operation.

We will illustrate this by going through the derivation of sentence (3) First, the embedded complement is generated as an infinitival sentence, as illustrated in (5):

(5)

This infinitival sentence is used as a complement to the verb *zien* and put to the left of it (in accordance with the SOV status of Dutch):

---

[2] These structures cannot be described by means of a context-free grammar and, using this fact, it can be proved mathematically that Dutch is not context-free.

(6)

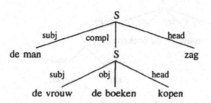

The transformation of Verb Raising is applied to this structure. It raises the verb *kopen* out of its clause and adjoins it to the verb *zag*:

(7)

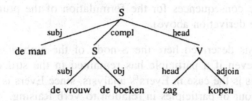

Next, the embedded S-node must be pruned. The S is emptied first, i.e. all nodes dominated by S are moved from under this S-node. In addition, the relations *subj*, *obj* and *indobj* (not occurring in the example structures) are turned into the relation *arg*. This is not really necessary in generation, but it is done to avoid ambiguities in the surface parsing process. This yields:

(8)

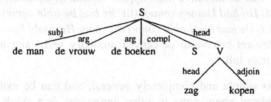

When S does not dominate any nodes any more, it is removed from the structure:

(9)

The subordinate clause can be derived by adding the subordinate conjunction *dat* to the sentence.

There are some differences between the treatment sketched here and Evers's analysis. We will mention them here:

Reversibility Evers's account is not reversible, but the treatment outlined here is. This has specific consequences for the formulation of the pruning operation (see the example derivation above).

Pruning In the analysis described here the S-node of the embedded infinitive is always pruned, even if a participle has remained in the structure. It is not clear whether this is the case in Evers's analysis, since Evers is rather unclear about the behaviour of participles in relation to Verb Raising.

Relations Evers uses a framework in which grammatical relations are not represented. Grammatical relations must be specified in S-trees.

Descriptive detail The treatment has been worked out in full detail, though Evers's analysis leaves a number of aspects of this construction rather vague or completely unspecified. In particular, the behaviour of participles and of particles in such constructions, the so-called *Infinitivus-Pro-Participio* (IPP) effect, i.e. the phenomenon that an infinitive must appear instead of a participle in certain configurations(cf. *Hij had kunnen komen* (lit. *he had be-able come*) v. **Hij had gekund komen* (lit. *He had been-able come*) meaning *He could have come*), and the somewhat deviant behaviour of certain auxiliary verbs and modal verbs are accounted for in full.

The method adopted is simple and completely general, and can be extended quite easily to deal with related phenomena in other languages (e.g. Verb Raising in German, and so-called V-projection raising as in Flemish and Swiss dialects).

This method makes it possible to deal with all relevant sentence types, for instance, sentences containing split verbs and particles (10a), sentences containing a reversed order of past participle and auxiliary verb (10b), sentences containing reversed infinitive plus modal verb (10c), and sentences showing IPP-effects (10a,d):

(10) a Hij zou   de man op hebben willen kunnen bellen
   He would the man up have   want   can   call
   (He would have wanted to be able to call up the man)

   b Hij zou   kunnen worden opgebeld
   He would can   be   called-up
   (He could be called up)

   c ..dat hij die boeken lezen moest
   ..that he those books   read had-to
   (..that he had to read those books)

   d Hij had die problemen op moeten kunnen lossen
   He had those problems   up must   can   solve
   (He should have been able to solve those problems)

The systematic character of the approach becomes evident when even such mon-
strous sentences as the following can be dealt with:

(11)   Hij zou   de man de vrouw de kinderen willen
   He would the man the woman the children   want
   kunnen laten zien leren zwemmen
   can   let   see teach swim
   (He would like to be able to let the man see the woman
   teach the children to swim)

The account sketched makes it possible to deal with these rather complex phenomena
in a simple and elegant way, and also to treat the interaction with other phenomena
such as passivisation and reflexives adequately. The relation with Evers's original
analysis is very transparent: Evers's analysis has been implemented almost exactly.

11.6   R-pronouns in Dutch

The syntax of R-pronouns in Dutch is a notoriously difficult area of Dutch grammar.
The problematic aspects of these words involve their function(s) within a sentence
(most R-pronouns can serve more than one function in a sentence) and their distribution (when and where they can or must occur). The R-pronoun *er* is is the most
difficult one of these R-pronouns. For an extensive discussion of these and related
phenomena, see Bech (1952), Van Riemsdijk (1978) and Bennis (1980, 1986). The
existing analyses of the syntax of R-pronouns have been extended and improved in
the Rosetta grammar, as will be illustrated below.
   We will point out some of the phenomena that must be accounted for. First, the
word *er* can occur in several functions: as an expletive element (as in (12a)), as a
locative adverbial (as in (12b)), as an element that must appear if quantified headless

count NPs occur (quantificational use), as in (12c), and as a form that must appear instead of the pronoun *het* as a complement to prepositions (prepositional use), as in (12d):

(12) a *Er*   werd gedanst
          There was   danced   (There was dancing going on)
      b Hij woont *er*
          He lives   there (He lives there)
      c Hij ziet *er*   twee
          He sees there two   (He saw two of them)
      d Hij kijkt *er*naar
          He looks there-at (He is looking at it)

Many of these functions can be combined in one occurrence of *er* (though not all combinations are allowed), e.g. expletive and prepositional use (13a), quantificational and prepositional use (13b), expletive and locative use (13c), expletive, quantificational and prepositional use (13d), etc. (for a complete overview see Bennis (1986), Model (1991)):

(13) a *Er*   werd naar gekeken
          There was   at   looked   (It was being looked at)
      b Hij beschuldigde *er*   twee van
          He accused   there two   of   (He accused two (of them) of it)
      c *Er*   woont iemand
          There lives   someone (Someone lives there)
      d Werden *er*   twee van beschuldigd?
          Were   there two   of   accused   (Have two (of them) been accused of it?)

The following sentences illustrate combinations (expletive-quantitative and locative-prepositional, respectively) that are not possible:

(14) a *Er   waren twee
          There were   two
      b *Hij legde er   een artikel over
          He put   there an   article about

Furthermore, though the appearance of two occurrences of *er* in one sentence cannot be excluded in general (cf. (15a)), and though they can even occur adjacent to one another in certain sentences (cf. (15b)), many sentences do not allow the presence of two occurrences of *er*, not only when they are adjacent (as in (15c)), but also when there is a certain distance between them (as in (15d)):

(15) a   *Er*   werden *er*   twee gekocht

There were   there two   bought   (Two (of them) were bought)

b   Hij keek *er* erna   naar

He looked there there-after at   (He looked at it afterwards)

c   *Werden *er* *er*   twee gekocht?

Were   there there two   bought?

d   *Er*   werd gisteren ernaar gekeken

There was   yesterday there-at looked

These, and many more problems should be accounted for adequately.

Van Hout (1986) worked out a proposal to deal with R-pronouns in the Rosetta grammar. It is based on a generalisation of Van Riemsdijk's R-position hypothesis (Van Riemsdijk (1978)). The following assumptions are made:

A. There are two special positions in a sentence, the er_Q-position and the R-position. These positions are immediately to the right of other pronominal clitics, though several rules can put phrases between the pronominal clitics and the er_Q-position and the R-position.

B. The er_Q-position can contain one occurrence of *er* in its quantificational use.

C. All other occurrences of *er* must be moved into the R-position if that is possible.

D. R-pronouns in their prepositional function must be moved into this R-position if possible.

E. Prepositional R-pronouns cannot be preposed to the sentence-initial position directly, but must move via this R-position.

F. If more than one R-pronoun ends up in the R-position, amalgamation transformations will turn these R-pronouns into one R-pronoun if possible.

G. Amalgamation is possible only when one of these elements is meaningless (expletive, quantificational *er*), and has only a syntactic function: meaningful elements cannot remain unrealised. If an element is unrealised, its syntactic function must be fulfilled in some other way.

H. If two occurrences of *er* (one in the er_Q-position and one in the R-position) remain adjacent after application of the transformations dealing with Verb Second, deletion transformations delete one of these occurrences.

These assumptions have been implemented. They make it possible to account for all of the facts mentioned above (and many more). We will briefly discuss the examples above.

In (13a) expletive *er* and prepositional *er* are combined in one sentence. Both occurrences of *er* must be put into the R-position (cf. C). This is only possible if they can amalgamate. Amalgamation is possible because expletive *er* is meaningless. It is clear that there is real amalgamation, because the remaining *er* can be topicalised, which is only possible if it has inherited properties of expletive *er* (expletive *er* can, but prepositional *er* cannot be topicalised).

In (13b) quantificational and prepositional *er* are combined. This is possible, since there are two positions, one for quantificational *er*, and one for other *er*s (cf. assumptions A, B and C). Since the two occurrences of *er* become adjacent, they are subject to rule H, hence one of them is deleted.

In (13c) locative and expletive *er* are combined in the same way as prepositional and expletive *er* can be combined (see (13a)).

In (13d) expletive, prepositional and quantificational *er* are combined. Expletive and prepositional *er* can be combined in the manner described for (13a). Quantificational *er* can occur in the sentence independently (cf. A and B). Since both occurrences of *er* are adjacent, they are subject to the rule described in H, so that one of them is deleted.

In (14a) *er* must be expletive and quantificational. Since there is a separate position for quantificational *er*, one occurrence of *er* which is both expletive and quantificational can arise only if expletive and quantificational *er* are adjacent (cf. assumption H). The finite verb *waren* separates the expletive *er* from quantificational *er*. As a consequence, the deletion rule described in (H) cannot apply, and the sentence should contain two occurrences of *er* instead of one. (cf. the well-formed *er waren er twee*)

In (14b) locative *er* and prepositional *er* must both be moved into the R-position, since they can get there (C). This is possible only if they can amalgamate (F), but amalgamation is not possible here (G). Hence the sentence is out.

In (15a) expletive and quantificational *er* are combined in one sentence. This is possible because there are positions in which to put these elements (see A, B and C). Since they happen not to end up next to each other, they cannot be subject to the rule described under H, hence there remain two occurrences of *er* in the sentence.

In (15b) prepositional *er* belonging to *naar* is put into the R-position; prepositional *er* belonging to *na* is not put into this position, because R-pronouns cannot escape from temporal PPs (cf. *hij keek er waarschijnlijk na naar het programma*, lit. *he looked there probably after at the programme*). Hence both occurrences of *er* can occur in this sentence.

In (15c) we have the same structure as in (15b), though here the two occurrences of *er* end up being adjacent, so that the rule described in H must apply and delete one of them. Since this has not been done, the sentence given is ill-formed.

In (15d) prepositional *er* must be in the R-position (cf. C), since it can get there (cf. *hij keek er gisteren naar*). Expletive *er*, however, must be in this position as well. So only one of these words can occur in this sentence. Since there are two occurrences of *er* in this sentence, the sentence is ruled out.

The assumptions made also account for some facts pointed out and analysed by Van Riemsdijk (1978). The R-pronoun *er* and the R-pronoun *waar* can both be used either as a locative adverbial (cf. (16a,b)), or as a complement to a preposition (cf. (16c,d)):

(16) a Hij woont er
     He lives   there
     (He lives there)

    b Waar woont hij
     Where lives   he
     (Where does he live)

    c Hij keek er gisteren naar
     he looked there yesterday at
     (He looked at it yesterday)

    d Waar keek hij gisteren naar
     Where looked he yesterday at
     (What did he look at yesterday)

When both R-pronouns are combined in one sentence, as in (17), one would expect the sentence to be ambiguous, but it is not: in (17) the R-pronoun *waar* can only be interpreted as a locative adverbial and not as complement to the preposition *naar*.

(17)   Waar keek hij er gisteren naar
     Where looked he there at
     (Where did he look at it yesterday)

In the analysis sketched we can account for this fact in the following manner. If we try to derive the sentence under its incorrect interpretation, then locative *er* must be in the R-position (according to assumptions A and C). Prepositional *waar* must be preposed, but cannot be preposed in one step (assumption E). Hence it also gets into the R-position. Since this position is filled already (by locative *er*) and since both elements are meaningful, they cannot amalgamate (in accordance with assumption G), so that the derivation is blocked. Under the other interpretation locative *waar* is simply preposed and prepositional *er* is put into the R-position (in accordance with assumption C), so that the sentence can be derived in this way. As a consequence, the system translates the sentence correctly as *Where did he look at it yesterday?* and not as *What did he look at there yesterday?*.

The same holds if we take the R-pronoun *daar* instead of *waar*, and the system deals with them adequately as well, cf. (18), in a similar manner:

(18) a Daar keek hij er   gisteren naar
      There looked he there yesterday at
      (He looked at it there yesterday)
      b Hij keek er   daar gisteren naar
      He looked there there yesterday at
      (He looked at it there yesterday)

In order to appreciate more fully the complexity of these phenomena, we would like to point out that these examples show that neither the mutual relative order of the R-pronouns *daar* and *er*, nor their distance to the preposition *naar* is a relevant factor in determining these interpretations: in (18a) *daar* precedes *er*, in (18b) *daar* follows *er*; in (18a) *er* is closer to *naar* than *daar*, in (18b) the reverse situation holds. The approach adopted to deal with R-pronouns is elegant and systematic. The systematic character of the approach can also be seen in the fact that a sentence such as (19) in which the R-pronoun *er* combines four functions (expletive, prepositional and twice quantificational) is analysed and translated correctly:

(19)   Hebben er   twee drie van beschuldigd?
       Have   there two   three of   accused?
       (Did two (of them) accuse three (of them) of it?)

The use that is made of transformations, which move R-pronouns into the R-position and amalgamate different R-pronouns, is crucial. The approach adopted is unique: the analysis covers more facts in an elegant way than any other computational approach known to us. Compared with more theoretically oriented approaches, Bennis (1986) attempts to cover the same facts, but he only partially succeeds, and the description in Model (1991) developed much later reaches the same degree of elegance of description, but only for one part of the relevant facts (viz. the distribution of R-pronouns).

11.7   Unbounded dependencies

Unbounded dependencies, as found, for instance, in WH-questioning, relative and topicalisation constructions, are dealt with by transformations that move constituents to other positions. These movements are applied in a successive cyclic manner, as is customary in Transformational Grammar. To illustrate, a sentence such as (20) is derived in the following manner.
(20)   What do you think that Peter would say that she had bought?

First, the most embedded clause is derived. The WH-pronoun *what* is the direct object of the verb *buy*, and prior to the relevant movement rule the clause looks as follows: *[that she had bought what]*. The movement transformation preposes *what*, yielding: *[what that she had bought]*.

In a second step, this clause is used as a complement to the verb *say* on the next cycle:

(21)   [that Peter would say [what that she had bought]].

The movement transformation preposes *what* out of the embedded clause:

(22)   [what that Peter would say [that she had bought]].

Finally, this clause is used as a complement to the verb *think* in the next cycle:

(23)   you think [what that Peter would say [that she had bought]]

In this structure *what* is preposed again, yielding the relevant sentence (after the application of transformations dealing with subject-auxiliary inversion and *do*-support).

In all constructions where unbounded dependencies play a role the same movement transformation can be used. WH-questioning, relativisation and topicalisation have been implemented and some other constructions could be dealt with in this way (comparatives, tough-movement constructions, complements to the adverb *too*), see Chomsky (1977b).

The fact that unbounded dependencies are dealt with by means of transformations that perform actual movements yields interesting results in interaction with certain idiomatic expressions (for the treatment of idiomatic expressions, see Chapter 15, Schenk (1986, 1989) and Landsbergen *et al.* (1989)). In particular, this makes it rather simple to deal with movement of idiom chunks. Consider a Dutch sentence such as (24):

(24)   Welke man heeft zij in de maling genomen?
       Which man has   she in the grind   taken?

Assuming that the Dutch idiomatic expression *iemand in de maling nemen* must be translated into *to pull someone's leg*, this sentence should be translated into (25), in which a part of the idiomatic expression *to pull someone's leg* is in sentence-initial position.

(25)   Which man's leg did she pull?

The system is able to yield this translation, and even the more complex case *Welke man denk jij dat zij in de maling genomen heeft?* (lit. *Which man think you that she in the grind taken has*) is translated correctly into *Which man's leg do you think that she pulled?*, where one part of the idiom (*leg*) is in the main clause and the

other part (*pull*) is in the subordinate clause. In the Dutch sentence the idiomatic
expression is in the subordinate clause as a whole, whereas in the English sentence
the idiom is split over the main clause and the subordinate clause. This discrepancy
can be dealt with without any special measures. In both languages a WH-phrase
must be preposed. In Dutch this WH-phrase is simply a direct object, in English the
WH-phrase is part of a larger NP containing a part of an idiom. The fact that the
whole NP must be preposed, and not the WH-phrase on its own (cf. *Which man's
did she pull leg?*) is a consequence of the normal syntactic rules of English.

Torrego (1984) shows that inversion of verb and subject in Spanish is triggered
by the presence of a certain class of WH-phrases in clause-initial position. This
is illustrated in the examples (26), from Torrego. The relevant subjects have been
italicised. Note that inversion must apply both in main and in subordinate clauses
(see (26c,d)).

(26) a   Con quién vendrá *Juan* hoy?
           (With whom will Juan come today?)
      b   *Con quién *Juan* vendrá hoy?
      c   Es impredecible con quién vendrá *Juan* hoy
           (It is impossible to predict with whom Juan will come today)
      d   *Es impredecible con quién *Juan* vendrá hoy

These facts can be accounted for by assuming a rule which puts WH-phrases in
clause-initial position (WH-movement) and an inversion rule which inverts the subject and the finite verb when preceded by a WH-phrase from the relevant class.
If the WH-movement rule applies before inversion, the relevant sentences can be
derived immediately. Torrego shows that extraction of a WH-phrase out of a deeply
embedded clause requires inversion in each intermediate clause and in the clause
where the WH-phrase ends up. This is illustrated by Torrego with the examples in
(27).

(27) a   *Juan* pensaba que *Pedro* le había dicho que *la revista* había
           publicado ya el artículo
           (Juan thought that Pedro had told him that the journal had published
           the article already)
      b   Qué pensaba *Juan* que le había dicho *Pedro* que había
           publicado *la revista*?
           (What did Juan think that Pedro had told him that the journal had
           published?')
      c   *Qué pensaba *Juan* que *Pedro* le había dicho que *la revista*
           había publicado?

Torrego accounts for these (and many other) facts by, crucially, adopting a successive cyclic application of WH-movement, in combination with a specific assumption

relating to bounding nodes in Spanish. By assuming the simple rules which are required to account for inversion in simple sentences anyway, in combination with successive cyclic application, the relevant facts follow directly from this analysis. If other approaches are adopted to deal with WH-movement, e.g. gap-threading techniques (see chapter 8), or assuming rules which relate WH-phrases to intermediate traces, the rule for inversion must be made more complex to take inversion in intermediate clauses into account. This is a very clear example in which the adoption of a transformation to account for WH-movement makes it possible to keep other rules (inversion) simple, while other techniques to account for WH-movement require that the rule of inversion is made more complex in order to account for all relevant facts. For these reasons an analysis which incorporates these transformations is descriptively more adequate than the alternative analyses. See Odijk (1993) for a more elaborate discussion.

Torrego's analysis has been implemented directly, and the relevant pattern of facts follow directly from it. The WH-phrase is moved step by step from one clause to the next, where it creates the environment for inversion, and after the application of inversion the process is repeated on the next cycle.

Adopting a movement transformation to deal with unbounded dependencies gives a simple and elegant account of very complex facts. In many frameworks the role of movement rules has been taken over by rules relating a phrase and a gap (its trace). This is equivalent in many respects, provided that the relation involves the whole phrase and not just its top node (cf. the idiom chunks), and provided that there are intermediate gaps with the right properties in the right positions (cf. the Spanish inversion facts). In many frameworks the relevant relation is implemented by gap-threading techniques, or by other feature-passing techniques. These are no more than very complicated techniques to simulate movement rules, and they usually do not have the properties just mentioned which are crucial for an adequate description of idioms and inversion in Spanish.

11.8 Romance object clitics

11.8.1 Introduction

One of the most studied areas of Romance linguistics is the grammar of non-reflexive object clitics. *Object clitics* are weak (unstressed) pronouns attached to the verb and related — by agreement of person, gender and number — to the direct and indirect object positions of a sentence; in Spanish, they appear in surface structure in preverbal positions if they are attached to finite verb forms as in *María las ve* (*María them sees*), and glued to the end of the verb if they are attached to the infinitive, as in *María quiere comprarlas* (lit. *María wants to buy-them*), or to the imperative forms. In all these cases, there is a contrast with the corresponding sentences with full object NPs, which appear in object position, as in *María ve* **casas** (*María sees* **houses**) and *María quiere comprar* **casas** (*María wants to buy* **houses**), respectively.

The grammar of object clitics deals with the different aspects of the behaviour of these pronouns. Here we will only discuss one of these aspects, viz. *clitic doubling*. In many languages, the object clitic and the full object NP appear in complementary distribution. In Spanish, however, they may both appear in one sentence in certain syntactic environments. In *María* **le** *da un caramelo* **a Juan** (*María to-him gives a candy* **to Juan**) the indirect object appears as a clitic as well as an complement NP. This co-occurrence is known as *clitic doubling*.

When choosing an adequate approach for the implementation of clitics in a translation system, one should bear in mind that the grammar of clitics and their relation with objects is quite complex. In addition, object clitics are language-specific: they do not appear in all languages. It is possible, in principle, to make a system in which objects are introduced in, for instance, English and Spanish by corresponding rules: in that case the English rule must simply introduce an NP into its correct position, but the Spanish rule must perform much more complicated operations to deal with the correct distribution of clitic pronouns and object NPs. This rule must distinguish between clitic and non-clitic objects, and put the object in a different position depending on its clitic or non-clitic nature. At the same time it must take the presence of other clitics into account. In addition, it must sometimes introduce a clitic accompanying an object to account for the cases of clitic doubling.

Since these operations are quite complex, it is more natural to shift a part of these operations into separate language-specific transformations. This section will describe how this has been done for a small part of the problem. The approach adopted gives a simple and elegant solution for the non-trivial problems that arise when deriving corresponding sentences which contain clitics.

11.8.2   Clitic doubling

The treatment of clitic doubling has been indirectly inspired by the analysis of Romance clitics given by Jaeggli (1982). Although Jaeggli's theory appears to be both descriptively and explanatory adequate for the range of data provided by the distribution of the lexical pair *clitic/object NP*, being able to correctly predict clitic doubling, his approach is strongly non-deterministic. To avoid a combinatorial explosion caused by such an approach, the system of *Clitic Transformations* implemented here has a more deterministic nature. In addition, the clitic rules have been organised in such a way that a sentence is produced for every well-formed derivation tree (for an illustration see the section on *Clitic Combinations* below)

The clitic node

Following Jaeggli (1982), clitics are generated in clitic positions, independently of the elements generated in object position. A transformation that applies at the beginning of a derivation inserts a clitic node — which initially dominates nothing — in every structure. The input for this transformation is characterised by (28a), its output by (28b):

(28) a S[...VP[...*head*/V...]]
     b S[...VP[...*head*/V, *cliticrel*/CLITIC[ ]...]]

In the course of the derivation this clitic node will be filled with several clitics. Since all clitics must occur under this node, co-occurrence restrictions, order restrictions, etc. holding between clitics can be accounted for in a simple and local manner. In addition, this node makes it possible to formulate rules which affect all clitics as a whole in a very simple manner (see the section on *Transformations on the Clitic Node*).

Clitic doubling of direct objects

The presence of the *direct object clitic* in a sentence depends on the syntactic nature of the NP in object position. When the NP is not pronominal, the presence of a direct object clitic leads to ungrammaticality (cf. (29b)).

(29) a   Juan compra *un libro*
          Juan buys   *a* book
     b   *Juan *lo* compra *un libro*
          Juan it buys   a book

On the contrary, if the object NP is pronominal, the *direct object clitic* is obligatory. Furthermore, Romance languages show a strong preference for the clitic above the pronominal NP, and the sentence without *clitic doubling*, as in (30b), is ungrammatical.

(30) a   Juan *los* compra
          Juan them buys
     b   *Juan compra *ellos*
          Juan buys   they

Clitic doubling transformations apply depending on the form of the direct object. They determine the status of the head of the direct object NP: if the head of the direct object NP is *not* pronominal, *clitic doubling* will *not* apply. (However, if the direct object is topicalised, clitic doubling must apply under certain conditions; this will not be discussed here.)

(31)   S[...*head*/V[compra] *cliticrel*/CLITIC[ ] ... *objrel*/NP [**un libro**]...]

On the other hand, if the head of the direct object NP is pronominal, clitic doubling
transformations will apply, introducing the accusative clitic under the clitic node;
this obligatory transformation will apply to (32a) — the structure of the ungrammatical sentence in (30b) —, and yield (32b), which is the correct structure for the
sentence in (30a). In general, the direct object and the corresponding clitic cannot
coexist, so the same transformation also deletes the NP in object position.

(32)   a   [...*head*/V[compra] *cliticrel*/CLITIC[ ] ... *objrel*/NP [**ellos**]...]
       b   [...*head*/V[compra] *cliticrel*/CLITIC[**los**]...]

Clitic doubling of indirect objects

In Spanish, *indirect object clitics* behave differently from *direct object clitics*. The
indirect object clitic can always appear, independently of the syntactic nature of
the indirect object NP. Since they always have the option of being present, indirect
object clitics are inserted by a transformation at the beginning of the derivation, just
after the insertion of the clitic node, in all structures with ditransitive verbs (verbs
with both direct and indirect objects).

(33)   a   ...*head*/V,*cliticrel*/CLITIC[ ]...*indobjrel*/PP[a NPVAR]...
       b   ...*head*/V,*cliticrel*/CLITIC[**le(s)**]...*indobjrel*/PP[a NPVAR]...

Later, *clitic transformations* will optionally delete either the *indirect object clitic*
or the *indirect object NP*, depending on the *pronominal* value of the NP in object
position:

- If the indirect object NP is pronominal, clitic doubling is obligatory, as it is
  with pronominal direct objects; but the indirect object NP can optionally coexist with the clitic; the sentence *Juan gives a book* **to her** (34) corresponds to
  two translations in Spanish: one with the indirect object NP (as in (34a)) and
  one without it (as in (34c)). The corresponding structures will be derived by
  a transformation which applies optionally to a structure like the one in (33b)
  and deletes the *pronominal* indirect object NP, resulting in structure (34b); in
  a second derivation path the transformation will not apply, and (34d) will be
  derived.

(34)   a   Juan *le*   da   un libro *a ella*
           Juan to-her gives a   book to she
       b   [...*head*/V[da] *cliticrel*/CLITIC[**le**] *objrel*/NP[un libro] *indobjrel*/PP[**a ella**]
       c   Juan *le*   da   un libro
           Juan to-her gives a   book
       d   [...*head*/V[da] *cliticrel*/CLITIC[**le**] *objrel*/NP[un libro]...]

• If the indirect object NP is not pronominal, *clitic doubling* is also optional: the clitic and the indirect object can coexist in one sentence. And again the sentence *Juan gives a book* **to María** corresponds to two translations in Spanish: one with the indirect object clitic (as in (35a)) and one without it (as in (35c)). The corresponding structures will be derived by a transformation which also applies optionally to a structure like the one in (33b) and deletes the indirect object clitic if the corresponding NP is *not pronominal*, resulting in structure (35b); in a second derivation path the transformation will not apply, and structure (35d) will be derived.

(35) a Juan *le*   da   un libro   *a*   *María*
      Juan to-her gives a   book to María

    b [...*head*/V[da] *cliticrel*/CLITIC[**le**] *objrel*/NP[un libro]
       indobjrel/PP[**a María**]...]

    c Juan da   un libro *a María*
      Juan gives a   book to María

    d [...*head*/V[da] *cliticrel*/CLITIC[ ] *objrel*/NP[un libro]
       indobjrel/PP[**a María**]...]

Clitic combinations

Since clitics are submitted to a fixed clitic order, cliticisation of both objects will only be possible if the fixed order is preserved. Some clitic combinations will then lead to ungrammaticality; the sentence **ellos* **le te** *recomendaron* (lit. *they to-him you recommended*) is ungrammatical because the third person clitic precedes the second person clitic, which is not possible. In those cases, conditions on the input tree prevent the transformation in (34a) from applying. Instead, alternative transformations will delete the corresponding clitic, licensing the appearance of a pronominal NP without the corresponding clitic, which is ungrammatical in other contexts.

(36)   ellos *te*   recomendaron *a él*
      they   you recommended   to him
      VP[...*cliticrel*/CLITIC[**te**]...*indobjrel*/[**a él**]...]

This example illustrates the point mentioned above: given a well-formed D-tree, some well-formed sentence (with the correct meaning) must be generated by the system, even if the D-tree happens to contain material which would lead to an impossible clitic combination.

    Additional transformations must apply to adapt some clitic combinations: for instance, if two third person clitics occur; the indirect object clitic will change into a SE clitic **María* **le lo** *compra* (lit. *María to-him it buys*) will change into *María* **se lo** *compra*.

Notice that all these co-occurrence relations are restricted to the single clitic node introduced, and can thus be formulated as rules that operate in a very local domain.

Transformations on the clitic node

Once the internal structure of the clitic node has been determined, transformations on the node itself can apply; a single transformation will simply delete the clitic node if it does not have any phonological content; if it does have phonological content, it must be moved into preverbal position if the verb appears in finite form (37a) and glued to the end of the verb if it appears to be in infinitive (37b) (or in the case of imperative forms). Other operations that involve the whole clitic node (e.g. so-called *clitic climbing*, not illustrated here) can also be dealt with easily.

(37) a S[...*cliticrel*/CLITIC[ ], *head*/V...]
    ..*lo* compra..
    ..it buys..

    b S[...*head*/V+GLUE+*cliticrel*/CLITIC[ ]...]
    ..quiere comprar*lo* ...
    ..wants-to buy-it ...

11.9   Concluding remarks

In this chapter we have sketched the analyses adopted for a number of non-trivial syntactic problems from the grammars of Dutch, English and Spanish, and we have shown how these analyses relate to analyses from more theoretically oriented approaches. We have indicated which aspects of existing analyses have been incorporated into the analyses adopted here. Transformations play a significant role. The complex phenomena have been accounted for by the interaction of a small number of relatively simple syntactic transformations, so that simple, elegant and systematic accounts resulted. Allowing transformations makes it possible to incorporate and extend elegant analyses of complex phenomena from theoretical approaches (especially from Transformational Grammar and its direct descendents) in a systematic and rather direct way without being forced to simulate their effects by more complicated methods that make use of feature-passing techniques. These analyses, in combination with other parts of the grammar that are not described here, have yielded powerful, systematic syntactic descriptions of Dutch, English and Spanish, with substantial coverage of a number of core syntactic phenomena. It is relatively easy to extend these descriptions, so that they can form the basis for a real, broad coverage syntax.

Chapter 12
Divergences between languages

12.1 Introduction

Chapter 9 introduced a powerful grammatical framework for the definition of translation relations. The main topic of this and subsequent chapters will be how translation problems can be solved within this framework. As an introduction, this chapter will give an inventory of syntactic divergences between languages which cause translation problems (Section 12.2). A large number of these problems can be solved in a fairly straightforward way in the framework presented in Chapter 9, mainly thanks to the distinction between translation-relevant rules and syntactic transformations. The solutions to translation problems that fit easily within this framework, will be outlined in Section 12.3. For a number of problems a more creative use of the isomorphic method is needed. They will be discussed in the following chapters.

12.2 Syntactic divergence types

Sentences that are perfect translations of each other from a semantic point of view may differ considerably in several other respects: primarily in their lexical units, but also in their syntactic form and structure. It is the latter type of difference, called *syntactic divergence*, that will be discussed here. There are several classifications of such divergences in the literature, e.g. Dorr (1993). We prefer to make a major distinction between divergences with a *structural* source and those with a *lexical* source. Sections 12.2.1 and 12.2.2 will discuss them.

229

12.2.1   Divergences with a structural source

Divergences with a structural source are caused by general syntactic differences between languages. They cannot be treated exhaustively here, but we will give some representative examples.

- Basic word order, reflected, for example, in the so-called SOV versus SVO type of languages. This distinction causes many syntactic differences. Consider for example (1):

  (1) (*E*) I think that I *have seen* the girl
      (*D*) Ik denk dat ik het meisje *gezien heb*
            I   think that I   the girl   *seen*   *have*

The order of the verbs *have/heb* versus *seen/gezien* differs in the subordinate clauses as well as the order of the verbs with respect to the direct object. Some of the differences have already been discussed in Chapter 11. This distinction also causes problems for the preservation of the meaning with respect to scope and negation.

- Occurrence and distribution of pronouns such as R-pronouns in Dutch. Consider for example (2):

  (2) (*D*) *Er*   werden *er*   twee gekocht
            There were *there* two bought
      (*E*) Two (of them) were bought

In English and Spanish an expression such as *er* does not exist.

- Occurrence of the preposition *a* before all human direct objects in Spanish. Consider for example (3):

  (3) a(*S*) Veo *a* una mujer
            I-see *to* a   woman
      b(*S*) Veo una casa
            I-see a   house

This phenomenon does not exist in Dutch and English.

- Behaviour of auxiliary verbs in English, such as, for example, the occurrence of the verb *do* in finite negative and interrogative clause that do not contain another auxiliary verb as illustrated in (4):

(4) a(E) I *did* not see her

    (D) Ik zag haar niet

      I saw her   not

    b(E) *Did* I see her?

    (D) Zag ik haar?

      Saw I her?

Such an auxiliary does not exist in Spanish and Dutch .

- 'Impersonal voice' construction in Dutch and Spanish. In Dutch there is a passive construction as in (5):

  (5) (D) Er   werd gedanst

      There was danced

The sentence in (5) does not contain a (surface) subject. Instead, the R-pronoun *er* must occur. In Spanish such a passive construction does not exist, but a *se*-construction can be used, as in (6):

  (6) (S) Se   bailaba

      'Oneself' was-dancing

Se is a clitic pronoun and the verb is an active verb form. Dutch does not have a *se*-construction of such kind.

Unfortunately, a corresponding construction is not found in English at all. The sentences in (5) and (6) have to be translated into sentences as in (7):

  (7) (E) There was dancing

    (E) They danced

Most divergences with a structural source mentioned in this section can be dealt with easily in the Rosetta framework, due to the existence of language-specific transformations. The solutions for the examples above will be sketched in Section 12.3.1.

12.2.2 Divergences with a lexical source

Divergences with a lexical source are structural differences between translations caused by different syntactic properties of translation-equivalent lexical items. There are various types:

1. conflational divergence

Conflational divergence occurs when a word in one language is translation-equivalent to an expression consisting of two or more words in the other language. These additional words can be seen as meaningless parts of the 'main' expression. The term conflational divergence is taken from Dorr (1993). Examples are:

- reflexive pronouns of reflexive predicates that are not reflexive in the other language, e.g. the Dutch verb **zich** *voordoen* corresponding to the English verb *occur* and the Spanish verb *suceder*;

- particles of particle verbs that correspond to non-particle predicates, for example the Dutch verb **aan**raken corresponding to the English verb *touch* and the Spanish verb *tocar*;

- prepositions of predicates that correspond to 'non-prepositional' predicates. An example is the verb *love* + NP in English that has to be translated into Dutch *houden* **van** + NP;

- idiomatic expressions, e.g. *to pull* (someone's) **leg**, corresponding to the Dutch (iemand) **in de maling** *nemen* and Spanish *tomar* **el pelo** (a alguien).

In these cases, it is more or less natural to see these complex expressions as a whole from a monolingual point of view. But it is also possible that the additional words carry meaning of their own from a monolingual point of view and that the combination of them all together expresses the same meaning as an expression of another language. This phenomenon is also referred to as *translation idiom*, *multiwords* (cf. Thurmair (1990)) or *incorporation* (cf. Sadler *et al.* (1990)). For example, Spanish *madrugar* corresponding to *rise early*. See Chapter 15 for a discussion of the phenomena *idiom* and *translation idiom*.

2. functional divergence

Functional divergence occurs when corresponding arguments of translation-equivalent predicates get a different grammatical function. Dorr refers to them as thematic divergence. We prefer a different terminology, because it is not the semantic roles of these arguments that differ, but their syntactic function. An example of this is (8).

(8) (*E*) I like$_{(1,sing)}$ these apples
     (*S*) Me gustan estas manzanas
            Me like$_{(3,pl)}$ these apples

In the English example, *I* is the subject and *these apples* the direct object, whereas in the Spanish example, *me*, corresponding to *I*, is the indirect object and *estas manzanas* is a kind of subject as it shows agreement with the verb.

3. categorial divergence

Categorial divergence occurs when the syntactic category of translation-equivalent expressions differ. There are several examples:

- **lexical category**: the category of the translation-equivalent basic expressions differs. For example, the verb *like* and its Spanish equivalent *gustar* correspond not only to each other but also to the adverbs *graag* (Dutch) and *gern* (German) as illustrated in (9).

  (9) (E) I *like* swimming (V)
       (S) Me *gusta* nadar (V)
       (D) Ik zwem *graag* (ADV)
       (G) Ich schwimme *gern* (ADV)

- **phrasal category of arguments**: the categories of translation-equivalent argument constituents differ, although the heads of the constituents are of the same category. Consider for example, the ADJPPROP *her intelligent* in (10a) and the CLAUSE *dat zij intelligent is* in (10b). Both have BADJ *intelligent* as head.

  (10) (E) I consider her *intelligent*
        (D) Ik vind   dat zij *intelligent* is
           I   consider that she *intelligent*   is

The source of this kind of divergence is found in the different subcategorisation frames of the predicates. *Consider* requires a small clause as complement, but *vinden* can occur with a finite complement clause.

- **phrasal category of modifiers**: the category of corresponding modifier constituents differs, although the heads are of the same category. Consider for example (11), if *ill* is chosen as a translation for Dutch *ziek*:

  (11) (D) De *zieke* vrouw
           The *ill*   woman
        (E) The woman *who is ill*

The Dutch ADJP *ziek* has to be translated into the relative CLAUSE *who is ill* in English. Both have a head of category BADJ. This kind of divergence is due to the fact that the adjective *ill* in English cannot be used attributively.

- **word or affix status**: in one language the expression is a word and has a normal syntactic category, whereas the translation-equivalent form in the other language is an affix or a syntactic feature. This divergence depends on the fact whether a language deals with a phenomenon in an 'analytic' or a 'synthetic' way (cf. Lyons (1968)) and it often affects grammatical categories such as tense, aspect, voice and mood, but also comparative, superlative and diminutive forms. Givón (1978) calls such problems the 'lexical-versus-syntactic-form' problems which 'involve rather delicate areas of focus and emphasis which one suspects can be got around by using longer, more cumbersome, complex structures to achieve roughly the same effects. They all involve the verbal structure of languages, and in particular the morphemic status of various operators, such as tense-aspect, negation, modal and adverbial markers' (op. cit., p. 265). Examples taken from African languages are given by Givón, e.g. a special tense marker is used to express what is expressed in English as *yesterday* + past tense. An example for the Rosetta languages is the English auxiliary verb *will* expressing future tense that corresponds to the Spanish future tense markers of a verb. Consider for example (12):

> (12) *(E)* *She will* work
>   *(S)* Trabaj*ará*

Another example is the divergence between verbs and particles as in (13):

> (13) *(E)* She would *continue* to work
>   *(D)* Zij zou   *door*werken
>   She would PARTICLEwork

Most divergences with a lexical source mentioned in this section can be dealt with easily in the Rosetta framework, again because of the existence of language-specific transformations. The solutions will be sketched briefly in Section 12.3.2.

Some divergences, however, require special measures and will be discussed in separate chapters:

- lexical and phrasal category divergences are discussed in Chapter 13.

- temporal expressions such as tense and aspect forms of verbs. They are more complicated than 'simple' syntactic word/affix differences. These expressions are discussed in Chapter 14.

- idioms and translation idioms. They are discussed in Chapter 15.

The latter two problem areas additionally involve the question of what should be considered a basic expression and, consequently, of what is considered a basic meaning.

12.3 Solutions

This section sketches solutions for a number of divergences which fit straightforwardly in the framework of Chapter 9. These straightforward solutions can be
achieved by carefully attuning the corresponding subgrammars for Dutch, English
and Spanish to each other. Hence, the subgrammars BVtoCLAUSE for the three
languages have to be isomorphic, the three subgrammars BNtoNP have to be isomorphic, etc. The divergences between languages meant here usually are solved by
using

1. the language-specific definition of S-trees. The structure and attribute-value
   pair specifications are language-specific and can be used to express syntactic
   differences between translation-equivalent expressions;

2. the possibility of having translation-equivalent rules with very different syntactic operations;

3. language-specific transformations. These transformations need not correspond
   to rules or transformations in other grammars and can be added freely in a
   particular grammar to account for language-specific phenomena.

12.3.1 Divergences with a structural source

In this section the solutions for divergences with a structural source will be outlined.
Consider again the examples from Section 12.2.1:

SOV-SVO
The SOV-SVO differences are accounted for by defining different initial S-tree
structures for the different languages: with the V in final position in the VP in
Dutch (SOV) and with the V in initial position in the VP in English and Spanish (SVO) (see also Chapter 11). The translation-equivalent M-rules of the
grammars of the languages take this assumption as to basic order into account
and only because of this they already differ a lot with respect to the syntactic operation from M-rules in the other grammars. Consider, for example, the
perfect tense rule in Dutch and English on simplified S-trees, paraphrased with
strings:

(D) x_1 x_2 zie $\longrightarrow$
        x_1 x_2 gezien heb

(E) x_1 see x_2 $\longrightarrow$
        x_1 have seen x_2

In Dutch this rule transforms the V(*zie*), that is in final position, into a past participle form (*gezien*) and puts an auxiliary verb, V(*heb*) to the *right* of it. In English, it transforms the V(*see*), that is in second position, into a past participle form (*seen*) and puts an auxiliary verb V(*have*) to the *left* of it.

The problems with scope and negation are discussed separately in Chapter 16.

R-pronouns in Dutch

The occurrence and distribution of R-pronouns such as *er* in Dutch is accounted for by language-specific transformations. The phenomenon has been discussed extensively in Chapter 11. Many of the transformations involved do not have equivalents in the other grammars.

preposition 'a' in Spanish

The preposition *a* in Spanish that co-occurs with specific human direct objects is accounted for by a transformation. A transformation TA-INSERTION, for example, operates as follows (leaving out notational details):

$$[x_1 \text{ ver } x_2, (human= true)] \rightarrow [x_1 \text{ ver a } x_2, (human= true)]$$

This rule has no equivalent in the other grammars.

auxiliary verb 'do' in English

The auxiliary verb *do* in English is inserted by a transformation in finite clauses which do not already contain an auxiliary verb. It has person and number agreement with the subject in addition to a tense specification. In certain declarative sentences these specifications are passed on to the main verb and *do* is deleted afterwards. A part of a simplified derivation process for a finite clause expressing the yes-no question *Does Mary work?* is:

M-rule	informal characterisation of result
.....	$[x_1(num=sing, pers=3) \text{ work}]$
TDO-INSERTION	$[x_1(num=sing, pers=3) \text{ do work}]$
RPRESENT	$[x_1(num=sing, pers=3) \text{ do}(tense=present) \text{ work}]$
TAGREEMENT	$[x_1(num=sing, pers=3)$
	$\text{does}(tense=present, num=sing, pers=3) \text{ work}]$
RSUBST,1	$[\text{Mary}(num=sing)$
	$\text{does } (tense=present, num=sing, pers=3) \text{ work}]$
TINVERSION	$[\text{does}(tense=present, num=sing, pers=3)$
	$\text{Mary}(num=sing) \text{ work}]$
.....	.....

See also Chapter 10 for examples. The other grammars do not contain equivalents for *do*-insertion and *do*-deletion.

'impersonal voice'-construction in Dutch and Spanish

In both Dutch and Spanish there are rules that account for 'impersonal voice', but with different syntactic operations. In Dutch these rules make a first step towards a passive construction: the verb form is set to a past participle form and the preposition *door* ('by') is introduced. Subsequent transformations account for the insertion of *er* and the insertion of the auxiliary verb *worden*. An example of a part of the derivation process for *er wordt gedanst* (lit. *there is danced*) is:

M-rule	informal characterisation of result
....	[x₁ dansen]
RPASSIVE	[door x₁ gedanst](*voice=passive*)
TCLAUSEFORMATION2	[door x₁ gedanst worden](*voice=passive*)
RSUBST-EMPTY,1	[gedanst worden](*voice=passive*)
TER-INSERTION	[er gedanst worden](*voice=passive*)
....	....
TVERBSECOND	[er wordt gedanst](*voice=passive*)
.....	......

RSUBST-EMPTY is a substitution rule with the meaning of existential quantification (here: 'there is someone who is dancing'). The result is that the preposition phrase '*door* x₁' in the S-tree disappears. TVERBSECOND puts the last verb into second position in Dutch. See also Chapter 11 for the general treatment of passive. In fact, the impersonal voice is just a subcase of passive voice in Dutch.

In Spanish, the translation-equivalent rule makes the first step towards a *se*-construction,[1] e.g. by marking it as such (voice = *se*). After substitution of the 'empty argument' of the predicate, an abstract element (empty category: 'ec') fills the subject position. It is deleted later by a transformation that also deletes other subject pronouns. Another transformation inserts the clitic pronoun *se* under the clitic node (Chapter 11 discussed the treatment of clitics in Spanish). This is done to account for the interaction of *se* and other clitic pronouns. A simplified derivation process for *se baila* (lit. *oneself dances*) is:

---

[1] Note that a *se*-construction can also be used as a translation of Dutch sentences containing the indefinite pronoun *men*. This is discussed in Chapter 13.

M-rule	informal characterisation of result
.....	[x₁ bailar]
RSE	[x₁ bailar](*voice=se*)
RSUBST-EMPTY,1	[ec bailar](*voice=se*)
.....	.....
TSE-INSERTION	[ec se baila](*voice=se*)
TEC-DELETION	[se baila](*voice=se*)
.....	.....

If the corresponding voice rules and substitution rules are translation-equivalent (and all other translation-relevant rules as well), the Dutch and Spanish examples can be translations of each other. They only differ in the syntactic contents of the rules and in their language-specific transformations.

So, divergences with a structural source can be solved by means of translation-equivalent rules performing different syntactic operations and by means of language-specific transformations.

A solution for the translation of the Dutch and Spanish examples here into the English *There was dancing* with a gerund involves the solution for phrasal category divergences and is discussed in Appelo (1993).

Note that a lot of these divergence examples coincide with cases that have been discussed in Chapters 10 and 11 as these chapters concern syntax and incorporation of syntactic theory.

12.3.2 Divergences with a lexical source

The conflational and functional divergences can often be solved along the same lines as divergences with a structural source, but require an adequate specification of the syntactic properties involved in the lexicon.

1. conflational divergence

Conflational divergences require careful attuning and contrastive research. Two or more words form together one basic expression of which parts are introduced syncategorematically. Conflational divergences are solved in the Rosetta framework by language-specific transformations which are triggered by a property of a basic expression. This property is an indication that parts of the expression are introduced syncategorematically. Some examples:

a. reflexive pronouns

BVs and BADJs in Dutch and Spanish have an attribute *reflexivity* that can have the value *true* or *false*. Transformations take care of the insertion of the correct reflexive pronoun into the syntactic structure in the case of *reflexivity =true*, based on the *person* and *number* value of one of the other arguments, usually the subject. Consider, for example, a Dutch complement sentence with the V *'zich scheren'* which is represented as 'BV scheren (*reflexivity* = *true*)' in the lexicon:

... dat   hij$_{(3,sing)}$ scheren(*reflexivity=true*) $\longrightarrow$
... that   he   shave

... dat   hij$_{(3,sing)}$ *zich* scheren(*reflexivity=true*)
... that   he   *himself* shave

This phenomenon should be distinguished from reflexive arguments as in (14) that occur in all languages. The identity between — in this case — the subject and object is translation-relevant.

(14) (E) She saw *herself* in the mirror
       (D) Zij zag *zichzelf* in de spiegel
            She saw *herself*   in the mirror

b. **particles**

Particles are treated in the same way as reflexives. Particles of BVs are inserted by a transformation if the BV attribute *particle* contains the unique name of the particular particle, such as, for example, *voor*, *aan*, etc. in Dutch. Consider, for example, a Dutch complement sentence with the V *'aankomen'* which is represented as 'BV komen (*particle* = *aan*)' in the lexicon:

... dat   de   koning   kwam (*particle=aan*) $\longrightarrow$
... that   the   king   arrived

... dat   de   koning   *aan*kwam(*particle=aan*)
... that   the   king   PARTICLE-arrived

This phenomenon should be distinguished from *postpositions*, which can behave similarly to *particles*, and *productive particles*. They have a meaning of their own, such as Dutch *over* (across) in (15) and *door* ('through' in the sense of continue) in (16):

(15) a(D) Zij zwom de rivier *over*
              She swam   the river   *across*
       b(D) Zij rende de straat *over*
              She ran   the street   *across*
       c(D) Zij fietste de heuvel *over*
              She cycled the hill   *across*

(16) a(D) Zij werkte *door*   aan de opdracht
        She worked *'through'* on   the order
      b(D) Zij liep   *door*
        She walked *'through'*
      c(D) Zij schreef *door*   aan de brief
        She wrote   *'through'* on   the letter

This kind of divergence is classified as categorial divergence, because
the particle or postposition has to be translated into an expression with
another syntactic category, for example a verb. See Chapter 13.

c. prepositional predicates

Prepositional predicates are predicates that require a prepositional object.
The preposition forms a semantic and syntactic unit with the predicate
(cf. Quirk *et al.* (1972)). The preposition is a feature of the predicate and
the transformation that accounts for the 'predicate pattern' inserts that P
into the S-tree, adjacent to the variable of that argument. An example of
this:

VPPROP[NPvar$_1$
                VP [V(*houd, prep=van*)
                         NPvar$_2$
                ]
        ]
                                  $\longrightarrow$
VPPROP[NPvar$_1$
                VP[V(*houd, prep=van*)
                         PP[P(*van*) NPvar$_2$]
                ]
        ]

d. translation idioms and idiomatic expressions

Translation idioms and idiomatic expressions are treated as *complex basic
expressions*. Since they need some special measures, they are discussed
in a separate chapter, i.e. Chapter 15.

2. functional divergence

Functional divergences are also solved by allowing translation-equivalent rules
to perform different syntactic operations and by using language-specific transformations. Translation-equivalent expressions are always supposed to be of
the same semantic kind and to have the same number of arguments. As only
the semantic role of an argument is important in translation, it should be clear
that its syntactic realisation is a monolingual decision. This holds in fact for
both the grammatical function of that argument and for its syntactic category.
The only thing to be specified is the relation between the semantic role of the

argument on the one hand and its syntactic role and syntactic category on the other.

thetavp = thetavp123: a BV with three arguments. *Arg1* is realised as external argument of the VP. *Arg2* and *arg3* are realised as internal arguments in the VP Example: *give*
thetavp = thetavp120: a BV with two arguments. *Arg1* is realised as external argument of the VP. *Arg2* is realised as internal argument in the VP. Example: *like*
thetavp = thetavp021: a BV with two arguments. Both *arg1* and *arg2* are realised as internal arguments in the VP, in basic order arg2–arg1. Example: *gustar*
thetavp = thetavp010: a BV with one argument. *Arg1* is realised as internal argument in the VP (an ergative or raising verb). Example: *happen*
thetaadjp = thetaadjp120: a BADJ with two arguments. *Arg1* is realised as external argument of the ADJP. *Arg2* is realised as internal argument in the ADJP Example: *able*

Table 12.1: Examples of the representation of the number of arguments of predicates and their syntactic roles.

The semantic roles of arguments of translation-equivalent predicates in Rosetta are not classified as *agent, theme*, etc., but they are ordered, i.e. *arg1, arg2, arg3*, in such a way that the corresponding arguments are given the same numbers. Predicates can also have zero arguments. For each basic expression of a BX-category the lexicon contains an attribute *thetaxp*: thetavp for BV, thetaadjp for BADJ, etc. This attribute specifies indirectly how many arguments there are and whether these arguments are the *external argument* or *internal arguments* in initial S-trees. The *external argument* corresponds to an argument that is realised outside XP, the *internal arguments* correspond to those that are realised inside XP. The format of the value is: *thetaxp'ijk'* where the positions *i,j,k* at the end indicate: *i* =external argument, *j,k* = internal arguments. Each of the three position variables *i,j* and *k* can be replaced by *0,1,2* or *3* where 0 = no argument, 1 = arg1, 2 = arg2 and 3 = arg3. This coding of inherent information is a result of historical factors and Table 12.1 may clarify this rather cryptic notation.

From a monolingual point of view, the *thetavp* of *gustar*, that corresponds to the English *like*, would be *thetavp012*. We have to adapt either the English or Spanish representation. In this case, we have chosen to adapt the Spanish one. Therefore, owing to its correspondence to *like*, the *thetavp* value of *gustar* is *thetavp021*. The external argument of *like*, indicated by *arg1*, corresponds to the second internal argument of *gustar* (in base order), and the first internal arguments of both predicates, indicated by *arg2*, correspond to each other.

Another attribute, called *synxps* (i.e. synvps, synadjps etc.), specifies what the categories of the internal arguments of predicate BX can be and what grammatical relation they bear, such as *direct object, indirect object, prepositional object, directional complement*, etc. A value of *synxps* is related to the positions *j* and *k* of the *thetaxp* value. The attribute *synxps* has a *set* of values, because the internal arguments may be realised in various ways. Examples can be found in Table 12.2. Obviously, not all combinations of *thetaxp* and *synxps* values are possible. There are consistency checks on the lexicon to avoid invalid combinations.

For the translation equivalents *like* and *gustar* the lexicon entries contain:

like:
  thetavp = thetavp120
  synvps = [synDO-NP, synOPEN-TO-INF-CLAUSE]
gustar:
  thetavp = thetavp021
  synvps = [synDO-NP—IO-NP, synOPEN-INF-CLAUSE—IO-NP]

An 'arity' (or 'start') rule that takes as arguments a predicate and zero, one or more variables, depending on the arity of the predicate. It builds an appropriate syntactic structure based on the *thetaxp value*. The syntactic variables are specified for syntactic category and other syntactic information. Xpattern transformations check the categories of the variables with the value of the attribute *synxps* and assign the correct grammatical relation by labeling the branches of the S-tree with the appropriate name of the grammatical relation.

'Arity' rules for different *thetaxp* values can be translation-equivalent if their 'arity' (number of arguments) is the same. For example, *thetavp120* can correspond to *thetavp021*. In this way *like* and basic verb *gustar* in *I like these apples* and *me gustan estas manzanas* (derived from: *gustar estas manzanas a mí*) can correspond to each other. Obviously, not all combinations of *thetaxp* and *synxps* values are possible. There are consistency checks on the lexicon to avoid invalid combinations.

synvps = [synDO-NP, synEMPTY]
the internal argument in VP must be:
- a direct object NP or
- an empty direct object
Example: *eat*.
synvps = [synDO-NP, synOPEN-TO-INF-CLAUSE]
the internal argument must be:
- a direct object NP or
- an infinitive complement sentence that does not realise the subject overtly.
Example: *like*.
synvps = [synDO-NP—IO-NP, synOPEN-INF-CLAUSE—IO-NP]
the internal arguments in VP must be:
- a direct object NP followed by an indirect object NP or
- an infinitive complement sentence and an indirect object.
Example: *gustar*.
synvps = [synCLOSED-TO-INF-CLAUSE]
the internal argument is:
- an infinitive complement sentence with substituted subject.
Example: *happen*.
(The subject of the complement sentence will be raised.)
synadjps = [synOPEN-TO-INF-CLAUSE]
the internal argument is:
- an infinitive complement sentence that does not realise the subject overtly.
Example: *able*.

Table 12.2: Examples of the representation of internal arguments

To summarise, the solution for functional divergence comprises rules for different *thetaxp* values that can differ in their syntactic operation but still correspond to each other as long as the 'arity' and the semantic roles of the arguments are the same. The pattern transformations spell out the different grammatical functions of the arguments required by the predicate and check the syntactic categories of the argument variables that the predicate takes.

3. categorial divergence

The categorial divergences cannot be solved with transformations and different syntactic operations of translation-equivalent rules inside straightforwardly corresponding subgrammars. Basic expressions with different syntactic categories are the head of different subgrammars, and constituents that differ in syntactic category are the exports of different subgrammars. Only a divergence consisting of an NP object argument corresponding to a PP object can be solved by treating them as conflational divergences, resulting in the importing only of NPs. We need special measures for these lexical and phrasal category divergences. They will be discussed in more detail in Chapter 13, where *isomorphic subgrammars within a grammar* will be introduced.

The problems with the divergence in word or affix status which can be considered as a special case of categorial divergence, depending on what counts as a syntactic category. They can be solved by treating the diverging expressions either both as *categorematic* expressions, or both as *syncategorematic* expressions. One of the approaches has to be chosen, as a categorematic introduction of an expression can never correspond to a syncategorematic introduction of the translation equivalent of that expression in the Rosetta framework.

- **categorematic introduction**

  An affix is treated as an abstract basic expression. A transformation incorporates the abstract basic expression into another expression, e.g. as a particle or a feature that is spelled out in the morphological component. For example, in Spanish the abstract modal verb FUTURE is stipulated, corresponding to the verbs *will* in English and *zullen* in Dutch. A transformation accounts for the deletion of this verb and setting the value of the attribute *future* of the adjacent verb to the right to *true*. In the morphological component this is spelled out as a future tense verb form:.

  | María | llegar | + | FUTURE | → | María | FUTURE | llegar |
  | María | arrive | + | 'will' | | María | will | arrive |

  | María | FUTURE | llegar | → | María | llegar(*future=true*) |
  | María | will | arrive | → | María | arrive(*future=true*) |

  | María | llegar(*future=true*) | → | María | llegará |
  | María | arrive(*future=true*) | → | María | will-arrive |

  Note that if the category chosen for this affix is different from the corresponding category in the other language, it is a case of lexical category divergence.

- **syncategorematic introduction**
  A word, an affix or even a combination of the two are treated as syncategorematic expressions and are introduced by corresponding translation-
  equivalent rules (in combination with additional transformations). This
  is often possible as these divergences often concern restricted phenomena such as tense, aspect, mood or voice, comparative, superlative and
  diminutive forms. The example above would then be:

María	llegar	$\rightarrow$	María	llegar(*future=true*)
María	arrive	$\rightarrow$	María	arrive(*future=true*)
María	llegar(*future=true*)	$\rightarrow$	María	llegará
María	arrive(*future=true*)	$\rightarrow$	María	will-arrive

One of the prerequisites to the treatment of divergences in this way is that it
should be clear what the involved meaning concepts and their mappings onto
the linguistic forms in the various languages are. This is not always the case.
In Chapter 14 the case of tense and aspect forms is discussed as an example
of this kind of problem.

Thus, many divergences with a lexical source can be solved by using transformations triggered by a certain property of an expression in the lexicon (conflational and
functional divergence). The syncategorematic solution for a categorial divergence of
the 'word-or-affix' type makes use of the possibility of having translation-equivalent
rules with different syntactic operations. The categorematic solution uses the possibility of stipulating an abstract basic expression in combination with a transformation
that is triggered by that abstract expression.

12.4 Concluding remarks

In this chapter an inventory of translation problems has been given. These problems
are caused by structural differences between translations and they may have a structural or a lexical source. It has been shown that for most of these problems a fairly
straightforward solution is possible within the framework of isomorphic grammars
as introduced in the previous chapters. In particular, the introduction of language-
specific transformations was important. The way in which the Rosetta system deals
with a number of more difficult divergence problems will be discussed in subsequent
chapters.

Chapter 13

Categorial divergences

13.1 Introduction

The topic of this chapter will be the class of translation problems which are called categorial divergences as introduced in Chapter 12. Given the controlled M-grammar framework introduced in Chapter 9, the most obvious way to attune grammars is to attune the corresponding subgrammars of the different grammars per category to each other. The consequence of this straightforward tuning is that words and phrases of a certain syntactic category are always translated into words and phrases of the same category. Thus, isomorphy between BVtoCLAUSE subgrammars assumes that a verb is always translated into a verb and a clause into a clause. Isomorphy between BNtoNP subgrammars assumes that a noun is always translated into a noun and an NP into an NP. This may be preferable, but is not always possible, due to categorial divergences between languages. Some examples of this type of divergence are shown in Table 13.1. In other MT systems, *structural transfer* (cf. Estival *et al.* (1990)) or *complex lexical transfer.* (cf. Thurmair (1990)) is required for these divergences.

This chapter will be organised in the following way: in Section 13.2 two types of categorial divergences will be distinguished: head category divergences and top category divergences. Section 13.3 will introduce the technique of monolingual isomorphic subgrammars, which offers systematic solutions for both types. Section 13.4 discusses a further subdivision of projection subgrammars and Section 13.5 the issue of complete and partial isomorphy of subgrammars. Section 13.6 shows how multiple divergences within one clause can be dealt with. In Section 13.7 a few alternative approaches will be discussed, followed by some concluding remarks in Section 13.8.

247

source language	target language	contrast
(D): zij zwemt *graag* she swims *'with-pleasure'*	(E): she *likes* swimming	ADV - V
(D): de *zieke* vrouw the *ill* woman	(E): the woman *who is ill*	ADJP - S
(E): she has *just* arrived	(S): *acaba* *de* llegar *she-finishes to* arrive	ADV - V
(D): zij werkte *door* she worked *PARTICLE*	(E): she *continued* to work	PART - V
(D): zij *zwom* de rivier *over* she *swam* the river *across*	(S): *cruzó* el río *nadando* *crossed* the river *swimming*	P - V

Table 13.1: Examples of categorial divergence problems.

13.2   Lexical and phrasal category divergence

The issue of translation-equivalent basic expressions with a different syntactic category was discussed first in the context of small free M-grammars in Landsbergen
(1987a) with the example of the adverb *graag* ('*willingly*', '*gladly*') versus the verb
like. The basic assumption was that these expressions should both be treated as
two-place predicates. This is, of course, the most important requirement for translation equivalence: equivalent semantic-type assignment. However, the syntactic
consequences of this assumption were not worked out in that paper. In this chapter
a systematic approach to all kinds of categorial divergences will be given in the
context of controlled and modular M-grammars. The existence of subgrammars,
transformations and rule classes plays an important role in the general solution for
these translation problems in a compositional framework. The approach presented
here is an elaboration of the treatment of so-called *category mismatches* in Appelo
et al. (1987) and Odijk (1989) and it can also be found in Appelo (1993).

Two kinds of categorial divergence have already been distinguished in Chapter 12:
lexical or head category divergences and *phrasal or top category divergences*. We
will discuss them here in more detail.

1. lexical or head category divergences
These are the cases in which translation-equivalent **basic expressions** which are
the head of some constituent, are of a different syntactic category. According to

what has been said in Chapter 9, such basic expressions will be the head of different subgrammars. We refer to these cases as *lexical or head category* divergences. Examples are given in Table 13.2. Note that the examples in this table indicate *possible* translations and that it is not claimed that they are the only ones. This

Dutch	English	Spanish
BADV *graag (willingly, gladly)*	BV *like*	BV *gustar (please)*
BADV *toevallig (accidentally)*	BV *happen*	BADV *acaso (accidentally)*
BV *kunnen* (lit. *'to can'*)	BADJ *able*	BV *poder* (lit. *'to can'*)
BV *kunnen* (lit. *'to can'*)	BADJ *possible*	BV *poder* (lit. *'to can'*)
BV *moeten* (lit. *'to must'*)	BADJ *obligatory*	BV *deber* (lit. *'to must'*)
BV *moeten* (lit. *'to must'*)	BADJ *necessary*	BV *deber* (lit. *'to must'*)
BV *zich schamen*	BADJ *ashamed*	BV *avergonzarse*
(lit. *'to shame oneself'*)		(lit. *'to shame oneself'*)
BADV *weer (again)*	BADV *again*	BV *volver (return)*
BADV *zojuist (just)*	BADV *just*	BV *acabar (finish)*
BADV *langzamerhand (gradually)*	BADV *gradually*	BV *ir (go)* + gerundio
BADJ *woonachtig* (lit. *'resident'*)	BV *reside*	BADJ *residente* (lit. *'resident'*)
BADJ *schuldig (owing)*	BV *owe*	BV *deber (owe)*
P/PART *door- (through)*	BV *continue*	BV *seguir (continue)*
P/PART *over- (across)*	BV *cross*	BV *cruzar (cross)*
BN *honger (hunger)*	BADJ *hungry*	BN *hambre (hunger)*
BV *waaien* (lit. *'to blow'*)	BADJ *windy*	BN *viento (wind)*
BV *misten* (lit. *'to fog'*)	BADJ *foggy*	BN *niebla (fog)*
BADJ *warm (warm)*	BADJ *warm*	BN *calor (warmth)*

Table 13.2: Examples of lexical or head category divergences.

class of divergences covers what Dorr (1993) calls *categorial, promotional* and *demotional* divergences. Lindop and Tsujii (1991) refer to them as *category changes* and *head switching* cases. Kaplan *et al.* (1989) and Sadler and Thompson (1991) talk about *differences in embedding.* Kaplan and Wedekind (1993) refer to them as *head switching* cases again.

2. phrasal or top category divergences:

These are the cases in which the syntactic category of translation-equivalent **constituents** (both arguments and modifiers) differ, while the corresponding head basic expressions are of the same syntactic category. We call them *phrasal or top category divergences.* Table 13.3 gives some examples. The divergences can be attributed to certain language-specific or syntactic properties of lexical heads. For example, adjectives can or cannot be used attributively (cf. the first example), verbs and adjectives take either a finite or an infinitival complement sentence (cf. the second and third examples), and verbs may select a gerund or infinitival complement (cf. the fourth example).

language	category	example
Dutch	adjective phrase	de *zieke* vrouw the *ill* woman
English	relative sentence	the woman *who is ill*
Spanish	adjective phrase	la mujer *enferma* the woman *ill*
Dutch	finite sentence	Ik verwacht *dat zij* zal *vertrekken* I expect that she will leave
English	infinitival sentence	I expect her *to leave*
Spanish	finite sentence	Espero *que partirá* (I-)expect that *(she-)will leave*
Dutch	finite sentence	Het is waarschijnlijk *dat zij zal komen* It is likely that she *will come*
English	infinitival sentence	She is likely *to come*
Spanish	finite sentence	Es probable *que venga* (It-)is likely that *(she-)come*
Dutch	infinitival sentence	Mary houdt ervan dat lied *te zingen* Mary likes of-it that song to *sing*
English	verbal gerund	Mary likes *singing* that song
Spanish	infinitival sentence	A Mary le gusta *cantar* ese canto to Mary her likes *sing* that song

Table 13.3: Examples of phrasal or top category divergences.

In these examples, the properties that vary apply to tense and aspect forms and to control. Translation problems of this type are also discussed in Kaplan *et al.* (1989) in an LFG context.

It is obvious that both types of categorial divergence are a challenge to the isomorphic grammar method. Dealing with the examples above within this framework requires that they be derived in a similar way. The requirement of similarity of derivation in combination with the division in subgrammars argues strongly for a method that systematically relates derivations defined by subgrammars for heads and phrases of different syntactic categories. The development of the systematic treatment of these cases proposed here has been determined largely by the following insight: similarity of derivation applies not only to equivalent utterances in different languages, but also to synonymous expressions within one language, such as the Dutch pair in (1).

(1) (D) a de zwarte piano
             the black   piano
     (D) b de piano die zwart is
             the piano that is   black

If the two forms are to be treated as paraphrases of each other, which means that they are considered to have the same meaning, the subgrammar for tenseless adjectival phrases (cf.(1a)) and for tensed relative clauses (cf. (1b)) have to be isomorphic. If this is realised, transitivity of the isomorphy relation guarantees that the Dutch subgrammars for adjectival phrases and relative clauses are isomorphic to both the subgrammars for English and Spanish adjectival phrases and for English and Spanish relative clauses. In this way a translation relation is defined between the Dutch phrases *de zwarte piano*, *de piano die zwart is*, the English phrases *the black piano*, *the piano that is black* and the Spanish phrases *el piano negro*, *el piano que es negro*.

This extension of the 'possible-translation' relation is exactly what is needed in order to realise similar derivations for the examples in Table 13.3. For example, it defines a translation relation between the Dutch phrase *de zieke vrouw* and the English phrase *the woman who is ill*, while *the ill woman* is ungrammatical. This technique of dealing with categorial divergences by means of isomorphic subgrammars within one language will be elaborated in the sections which follow. For the feasibility of this method the distinction between translation-relevant rules and syntactic transformations, introduced in Chapter 9, is essential. Thanks to that, the isomorphy between subgrammars needs only to concern the translation-relevant rules.

13.3 Isomorphic subgrammars within one grammar

The division of grammars into subgrammars was based on the notion of projection and the sorts of projections along a *projection path* from an S-tree of a head category (of type BX) to an S-tree of an export category (of types XP, XPPROP and CLAUSE) (cf. Chapter 9). This division was inspired by $\overline{X}$-theory. Since in $\overline{X}$-theory the syntactic structures underlying the resulting constituents (more or less corresponding to S-trees) are supposed to be similar, it seems to make sense to investigate the possibility to derive these constituents via similar sets of compositional rules (i.e. assigning them corresponding D-trees). Similarity of derivation is also even more strongly suggested by the fact that most translation-relevant rule classes deal with phenomena that play a role in every subgrammar. For example, rules for valency/semantic relations, substitution of arguments and negation are found in all subgrammars. To solve the *head* or *lexical category divergences*, all subgrammars, each having a different head (categories BV, BADJ, etc.), must be attuned, and to solve the *top* or *phrasal category divergences*, the three different subgrammars starting from S-trees with the same head category (BADJ → ADJP/ADJPPROP/CLAUSE, BV → VP/VPPROP/CLAUSE, etc.) have to be attuned. Consequently, all subgrammars in one M-grammar must be attuned as far as possible. This technique will be referred to as the **isomorphic subgrammar approach**. This tuning takes place within one M-grammar, but the consequence is that it can be used for correspondences between two different M-grammars. If subgrammars A_1 and B_1 of grammar G_1 are isomorphic and if subgrammar A_1 of G_1 and subgrammar A_2 of G_2 are isomorphic, then B_1 and A_2 are also isomorphic.

Obviously, tuning of subgrammars is of a semantic nature. Semantic properties dictate the *possibility* of tuning subgrammars. With respect to this possibility, the subgrammars can be divided into two classes:

1. **non-propositional**: subgrammars that project an S-tree of category type BX to the non-propositional export category type XP. Within this class, there is a large semantic variety, which makes tuning impossible in most cases.

2. **propositional**: subgrammars that project an S-tree of category type BX to the propositional export category type XPPROP or CLAUSE. Within this class a high degree of tuning is possible.

Tuning is impossible between the two classes. Expressions yielded by subgrammars of the first class can never be translations of expressions yielded by subgrammars of the second class for semantic reasons.

The subsections which follow will deal with the class of non-propositional subgrammars (Section 13.3.1) and the class of propositional subgrammars, in particular the ones with non-nominal head and export categories (Section 13.3.2).

13.3.1 Non-propositional subgrammars

Non-propositional subgrammars are subgrammars with head category of type BX and an export category of type XP (see Chapter 9). Typical non-propositional subgrammars are those for nouns (i.e. those that denote entities), determiners, quantifiers, degree modifiers and temporal adverbials, the subgrammars for NP, DP, QP, PP and ADVP, respectively.

Examples of exports of those subgrammars are:

NP: *women, the woman, a woman*, etc.
DP: *that, this, these*, etc.
QP: *every, some, all, more than Mary*, etc.
ADVP: *very, quickly, hard, very hard*, etc.
PP: *for three years, since 1972*, etc.

These expressions are considered to be non-propositional. Hence, they cannot be derived isomorphically to expressions yielded by propositional subgrammars.

In fact, the semantic properties of the XP-subgrammars mentioned above often differ so much that there is no point in making them isomorphic to each other. However, there are exceptions, as is shown by the following examples:

she worked [[*for*]$_P$ [*two hours*]$_{NP}$]$_{PP}$
zij werkte [[*twee uur*]$_{NP}$ [*lang*]$_{ADV}$]$_{ADVP}$

The English PP *for two hours* can be translated into the Dutch ADVP *twee uur lang*. Only a limited amount of tuning is required in order to deal with the translation equivalence. Here, the main translation-relevant rule classes are: valency (zero or one argument), argument substitution and deixis (present or past). The differences are accounted for by transformations and the different syntactic operations of translation-equivalent rules.

13.3.2 Propositional subgrammars

The subgrammars of this type mostly have export categories of type XPPROP or CLAUSE. The head of these subgrammars are the heads of the predicates in subject-predicate relations that could result in a clause or small clause. (See Chapter 9.)

Nouns can also be the head of such predicates, the so-called *nominal* predicates. Nominal predicates are predicates with nominalisations, such as gerunds and derived nominals, and predicative nouns. See Table 13.4 for some examples. Although problematic translation relations between nominal predicates and other - non-nominal - predicates exist (see Table 13.5 for some examples), they will not be discussed in this chapter. This also holds for *complex predicate*-like constructions (consisting of an NP and a 'support verb') that translate into non-nominal predicates. See Table 13.5 for some examples.

Only transformations to derive gerunds from clauses and rules for propositional structures such as *he a fool* in *I considered him a fool* have been implemented in the Rosetta system, but the subgrammars involved have not been attuned to

predicative noun	They are *neighbours*
	He is considered to be *a fool*
gerund	*His going to the opera* surprised me
nominalisation	Hij ging door met *het schrijven* van de brief
	He went PARTICLE with *the write* of the letter
derived nominal	*His destruction* of Rome

Table 13.4: Examples of nominal predicates

subgrammars with a non-nominal head of the same grammar. Other cases have been treated as *translation idioms* (see Chapter 15), but the topic of the tuning of the subgrammars for nominal predicates with other subgrammars and an alternative approach for complex predicates that can be attuned to non-nominal propositional subgrammars is still being investigated. See Appelo (1993) for a discussion.

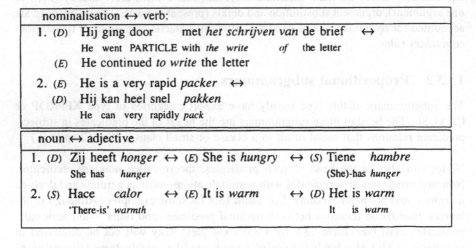

Table 13.5: Categorial divergence problems with nominal predicates and complex predicates.

We will restrict ourselves here to subgrammars with a non-nominal head category, i.e. BV, BADJ, BADV or BP, and discuss the two types of categorial divergence in more detail.

Isomorphic subgrammars with the same head category

An example of expressions that are equivalent with respect to meaning and have heads of the same category, but have a different top category is the pair shown in (2):

(2) a the *smart* girl
     b the girl *that is smart*

These are called *paraphrases*, a term we use for 'translation equivalents within the same language'. To derive (2a) and (2b) the subgrammars for the projection of BADJ to ADJPPROP and BADJ to CLAUSE apply. In the first case the OPENADJPPROP (x_1 smart) is derived and in the second the (relative) OPENCLAUSE(x_1 is smart).[1] Given that they are paraphrases, they only differ in that a transformation deals with the occurrence of the auxiliary verb *be* in the clause case (see Figure 13.1, TCLAUSEFORMATION4). In both cases a rule for present time reference is needed: in the clause case it spells out the tense for the verb *be* (RCLAUSESUPERDEIXIS1[2]); in the adjectival case it seems to be superfluous syntactically, but such a rule can be motivated, if we assume a model-theoretic semantics with a time component that applies to non-verbal phrases as well. Additionally, a 'mood' rule is needed. In the clause case it should be the relative mood rule (RCLAUSEMOOD3).

As mentioned above, this kind of paraphrasing can be helpful if the literal translation is blocked in the other language as is the case with *de zieke vrouw* (lit. *the ill woman*), which cannot be translated into *the ill woman, but has to be translated into *the woman who is ill*.[3]

Isomorphic subgrammars with different head categories

The approach of attuning subgrammars can be extended to subgrammars with different head categories. There exist some monolingual examples, as illustrated in (3), although (3b) is considered very marginal:

---

[1]The prefix *OPEN-* indicates that the S-tree still contains a variable to be substituted.

[2]Note that it is not necessary for this tense to be a *present* tense. That depends on the context. For example, in the sentence *I saw the smart girl, the smart girl* will also correspond to *the girl that was smart*. See also Chapter 14.

[3]The correct relative pronoun is introduced at the moment of substitution. See also the example subgrammars in Chapter 9.

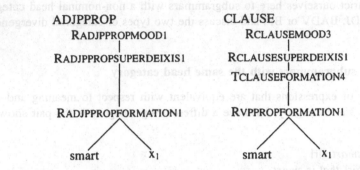

Figure 13.1: Partial, simplified derivation trees resulting from the subgrammars BADJtoADJPPROP and BADJtoCLAUSE.

(3) a   Dit *weegt* drie kilo
        This *weighs* three kilo

    b   ?Dit is drie kilo *zwaar*
        This is three kilo *heavy*

Most arguments are provided by translational problems. From a syntactic point of view, mapping expressions of different categories seems to be a bigger step than tuning subgrammars with the same head category, but it should be stressed that translation equivalence is based on what is postulated as translation-relevant information. The basic expressions which are the heads of these subgrammars and which are taken as each other's translations all denote semantic objects of the same sort. We will discuss three typical examples.

EXAMPLE 1: ADVERB VERSUS VERB:

BV → CLAUSE v. BADV → ADVPPROP

Example: *Mary happened to come* ↔ *Mary kwam toevallig*

In *Mary happened to come* the raising verb *happen* occurs and in *Mary kwam toevallig* the sentential adverb *toevallig*. As these two sentences are considered translations of each other, the subgrammars for BV and BADV should be attuned to each other. This is not obvious from a syntactic point of view, because it is quite natural that the complement of *happen*, i.e [*Mary to come*] is inserted in the clausal S-tree with head *happen*, whereas *toevallig* (the basic expression that corresponds to *happen*) is inserted in the S-tree for the CLAUSE corresponding to [*Mary to come*], i.e [*Mary komen*]:

English: [*happen* [*Mary to come*]]

After application of subject raising, time and agreement rules, this results in: *Mary happened to come.*

Dutch: [*Mary* [*toevallig*] *komen*]

After time, agreement and verb-second rules have been applied: *Mary kwam toevallig.*

Semantically, however, the clause in both cases is the argument of *happen* and *toevallig*:

happen (Mary come)
toevallig (Mary komen)

We follow the 'semantic path' until the moment of substitution and allow for a 'switch of subgrammar' for adverbs at that moment. This means that instead of continuing the projection path in the subgrammar with BADV as head, the parallel path in the subgrammar of the head of the complement (BV, in our example) is continued. Such a switch is possible, if the subgrammars are split into two parts in such a way that the place of this subdivision coincides with the 'switch point', generally a substitution or insertion rule (or transformation). Normally, substitution rules are fairly straightforward rules, but in case of 'switching', the rules take care of all necessary syntactic adaptations, which sometimes results in 'unnatural' rules. Figure 13.2 depicts how the examples *Mary happened to come* and *Mary kwam toevallig* now can be derived isomorphically. In English, syntax and semantics are 'in parallel', so no switching is necessary. In Dutch, instead of following the complete path from BADV to CLAUSE or ADVPPROP, we switch over to the *second* part of the BVtoCLAUSE subgrammar, which means in our example that the verb of the complement, *komen*, takes over the role of syntactic head. RSWITCH-SUBST,i is the 'switch rule'.

Other examples that can be solved analogously are shown in (4)-(6).

(4)   *graag/like*:
       (D) Zij zwom *graag*   ↔ (E) She *liked* swimming
           She swum *with-pleasure*

Mary happened to come

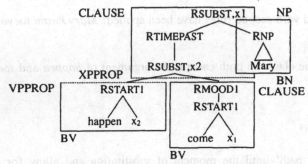

Mary kwam toevallig

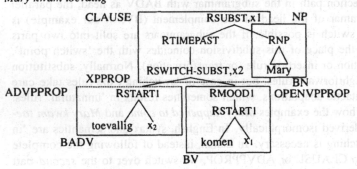

Figure 13.2: Partial and simplified syntactic derivation trees with their relevant subgrammars.

(5)   *weer/again/volver a*:

    (D) Hij kwam *weer* ↔ (E) He came *again* ↔ (S) *Volvió*   *a* venir
       He came *again*   (He-)*returned* to come

(6)   *steeds/keep + -ing of momentary verb*:

    (D) Zij kwam *steeds*   ↔ (E) She *kept* com*ing*
       She came *'always-again'*

The main difference is the syntactic behaviour: adverbs are inserted in the syntactic structure of their semantic argument, whereas the equivalent verbs start as syntactic heads and stay so until the end. The consequence is the 'subgrammar switching' mentioned above. Kaplan and Wedekind (1993), working in an LFG-framework, also assumes that these kinds of problems should be solved by making a monolingual distinction between syntactic and semantic embedding. This approach is justified by the fact that the BADVs and BVs in the examples above share some crucial semantic properties. For example, for both *graag* and *like* the following holds:

- the subject argument has to be animate:

    (7) (D)   *Het huis staat er graag
               The house stands there 'with-pleasure'
      (E)   *The house likes to be there

- it is a two-place argument:

    (8) (E)   *It likes to seem that ...
      (D)   *Het blijkt graag   dat ...
          It   seems 'with-pleasure' that ...

- the Present Perfect Tense[4] without habitual reading is strange, but not with a habitual reading:

    (9) (E)   ?She has liked to work today
      (D)   ?Zij heeft vandaag graag   gewerkt
         She has   today   'with-pleasure' worked

    (10) (E) She has always liked to work here
       (D) Zij heeft hier altijd graag   gewerkt
         She has   here always 'with-pleasure' worked

---

[4] Note that the reading of the Present Perfect Tense in Dutch corresponding to a Simple Past Tense in English is not meant here. See Chapter 14 for the different temporal interpretations of the Present Perfect Tense.

From a syntactic point of view problems may be expected with modification: modifiers of adverbs can have forms other than modifiers for verbs. For example, in English the degree modifier *very* is used with adverbs, but in combination with verbs *very much* is used:

(11) a I like her *very much*
     b I saw her *very* often

In Dutch, *erg* or *zeer* (very) is used with adverbs and *(erg/zeer) veel* ((very) much) with verbs. With the isomorphic subgrammar approach these modifiers should also be derived similarly.

Comparative and superlative forms of adverbs that do not exist for verbs are a similar case:

(12) *(D)* graag   lie ver   *(het)* lief st
           'willingly'   '*more*-willingly' *(the)* '*most-willingly*'
      (E) like   prefer   like best/most

One possibility is not to incorporate comparative and superlative forms of these adverbs (they are often irregular) and stipulate these forms as separate basic expressions that correspond to verbs (*liever-prefer*) or translation idioms (*liefst-like best*). However, a different isomorphic solution is to add corresponding rules to the comparative and superlative rules of the adverb in the BVtoCLAUSE subgrammar where *more* is inserted to form comparatives and *most* to form superlatives. In the example above we get: *like - like more - like most*. In that case *liever* is translated not into *prefer* but into *like more*.

EXAMPLE 2: MODAL (AUXILIARY) VERBS:

Another example that can be seen as a head category divergence is:

main BV → CLAUSE v. auxiliary BV → VPPROP

Examples: *kunnen/poder* ↔ *can*
           moeten/deber ↔ *must*

In Dutch and Spanish modal verbs are main verbs, but in English they form a special auxiliary class. They are translation equivalents, but the auxiliary verbs have a different syntactic behaviour. They cannot occur in all forms, they occupy special positions in the sentence, they cannot combine with other auxiliary verbs, etc. We treat them in the same way as the sentential adverbs above: the auxiliary verbs are inserted into their semantic argument, whereas main verbs are not. The consequence is also the same: 'subgrammar switching' at the moment of substitution of the argument. The head of the argument takes over the role of the syntactic head of the resulting proposition. This solution for the translation problem only works if the other properties correspond. However, this is only partially the case with modal verbs in Dutch/Spanish and English because of the deficient verbal paradigm of the English modal verbs. English modal verbs occur in simple present or past tense, but not as an infinitive or in perfect tense, as illustrated in (13):

(13) a Hij *kon* komen → He *could* come
      b Hij *moest kunnen* werken → *He *must* 'can' work
      c Hij *had kunnen* komen → *He *had* 'could' come

For these cases the correspondences as illustrated in Example 3 are needed:

EXAMPLE 3: VERB VERSUS ADJECTIVE:

BV → CLAUSE v. BADJ → CLAUSE

Example: *kunnen/poder* ↔ *(to be) able / (to be) possible*

In this case we use the path for BADJ to CLAUSE with *be*-insertion as for (2), the example with *the smart girl* and *the girl that is smart*. In this case, however, it will not be a relative OPENCLAUSE but a main CLAUSE. A consequence of this tuning is that in the BADJtoCLAUSE subgrammar an active voice rule has to be added to correspond to the active voice rule of the corresponding verbs. Note that the resulting top category is the same in this case.

Again, problems with this solution can be expected in the area of modification and comparative or superlative forms of adjectives and verbs, but solutions can be found along the same lines as sketched above.

13.3.3 Concluding remarks

The tuning of the propositional subgrammars with head category BV, BADJ, BADV and BP as outlined above has been worked out successfully and has been implemented in the Rosetta3 system.

The tuning of subgrammars is motivated by semantic, not syntactic, similarities. Again, the distinction between translation-relevant *rules* and syntactic, language-specific *transformations* appeared to be very helpful here. The definition of the different rule classes proved useful for establishing the corresponding rules needed. For instance, we had to add time and mood rules to the rules in the BXtoXPPROP subgrammars. The different syntactic behaviour of categories, for instance, in some

cases acting as syntactic heads and in other cases as modifiers, was accounted for by
the possibility of 'subgrammar switching'. This switch is triggered by the categories
themselves. It is therefore unnecessary to make a subdivision into types of lexical
category divergences such as, for example, in Dorr (1993).

13.4   Subdivision of subgrammars

In Section 13.3.2 it has been claimed that the subgrammars have to be split into two
parts for 'subgrammar switching'. In this section this subdivision into parts will be
discussed in greater detail.

The tuning of the subgrammars which have the same head category but different
top categories only affects the second part of the subgrammars involved, as the first
part is the same. In fact, we can collapse the first parts of the subgrammars as
is shown in Figure 13.3. At the point in the derivation where it is decided that
the projected top category will become CLAUSE (by applying the transformation
TCLAUSEFORMATION4) or that it will remain ADJPPROP, the paths diverge.

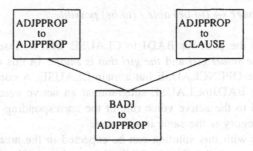

Figure 13.3: Collapse of the first part of the propositional subgrammars with the same head category

For the subgrammars with different head categories, attuning in the first part of
the projection subgrammars for predicates is also necessary. They, too, are divided
into two parts. The natural breaking point is the point of possible switch of subgrammars: the proposition substitution rules. The two breaking points can coincide.
The second part of a subgrammar starts with proposition substitution rules, followed by transformations that determine whether the ultimate export category will
be CLAUSE or XPPROP. These subgrammar parts meet the same requirements as
subgrammars except that the head category need not be a basic category (type BX)
and that the export category of the export S-tree need not be of type XP, XPPROP or
CLAUSE, but may be a top category of an intermediate S-tree during the projection

proces. This category is of type XPPROP and should be distinguished from the original export category type XPPROP which is an abbreviation for OPENXPPROP and CLOSEDXPPROP. We will refer to this type as O/C-XPPROP. These parts of subgrammars are referred to as 'subgrammars' too, as they also account for a well-defined subtask. The difference is that the subgrammars characterised in Chapter 9 account for the whole projection from an S-tree of a basic category (type BX) to an S-tree with a maximal projection top category (type XP, XPPROP or CLAUSE), whereas the parts here only account for a part of that projection. The 'original' subgrammars can be seen as a 'concatenation' or 'composition' of some of these parts with the requirement that the export category of a preceding subgrammar in the concatenation must be the head category of a subsequent subgrammar.

With respect to the definition of subgrammar in Section 9.6.2, some of the conditions given there have to be relaxed. It was stated there that for a subgrammar$_i$,

(a) EXPORTCATS$_i$ ⊆ TOPCATS
(b) HEADCATS$_i$ ⊆ BASICCATS

Condition (a) now only holds for the last subgrammar in a concatenation of subgrammars and condition (b) only for the first subgrammar in such a concatenation. A new condition has to be added:

(c) If subgrammars SG$_i$ and SG$_j$ form a concatenation <SG$_i$,SG$_j$>,
then HEADCATS$_j$ ⊆ EXPORTCATS$_i$

The subdivision of projection subgrammars into two parts has a further advantage: in the CLAUSE case, the second part of the subgrammars is very similar for all categories of type BX. The subgrammars VPPROPtoCLAUSE, ADJPPROPtoCLAUSE, etc. can therefore be collapsed into one subgrammar: XPPROPtoCLAUSE. This means that the set of head categories of this subgrammar, a set that typically contained one element in the case of projection subgrammars, contains more than one element.

Both parts mentioned above have been split into two parts again, the first part into a derivational subgrammar *BXtoX* and the XPPROP formation subgrammar *XtoXPPROP*, because the category X can acquire another value by a derivational morphology rule. The second part has been split into an *XPPROPtoCLAUSE* and a *CLAUSEtoSENTENCE* subgrammar for the clausal path and an *XPPROPtoXPFOR-MULA* and an *XPFORMULAtoO/C-XPPROP* for the XPPROP path. The reason for this division is a practical one. It means that the set TOPCATs, the set of top categories of S-trees that are exported by full projection subgrammars, is now defined more precisely as {XP, SENTENCE, OPENXPPROP, CLOSEDXPPROP} with X = V, ADJ, ADV, P, N, etc.[5]

---

[5]Note that for minor categories such as D (determiner) only XP projection subgrammars exist. How many and what kind of basic categories are distinguished is left to the grammar writers.

To illustrate these adaptations, an example of the adaptations of the example grammar BVtoCLAUSE in Chapter 9 will be given here. This projection subgrammar now will be called: BVtoSENTENCE.

Given that, for example,

TOPCATS = {NP, DP, OPENADJPPROP, SENTENCE} and
BASICCATS = {BN, BD, BADJ, BV}

the projection of BV to SENTENCE is accounted for by a concatenation of four subgrammars:

1. BVtoV
   HEADCATS = {BV}
   EXPORTCATS = {V}
   rules: RBVtoSUBV, RSUBVtoV

2. VtoVPPROP
   HEADCATS = {V}
   EXPORTCATS = {VPPROP}
   rules: RVPPROPformation1, RVPPROPformation2, RVPPROPvoice1

3. XPPROPtoCLAUSE
   HEADCATS = {VPPROP, ADJPPROP}
   EXPORTCATS = {CLAUSE}
   rules: RCLAUSEnegation, RCLAUSEdeixis1, RCLAUSEsuperdeixis1

4. CLAUSEtoSENTENCE
   HEADCATS = {CLAUSE}
   EXPORTCATS = {SENTENCE}
   rules: RCLAUSEargsubst1,i, RCLAUSEargsubst2,i, RCLAUSEmood1,
   RCLAUSEmood2, RCLAUSEmood3

To summarise, Figure 13.4 contains an overview for the complete projection of the propositional subgrammars BVtoSENTENCE, BADJtoSENTENCE, BADVtoSEN-TENCE, BADJtoO/C-ADJPPROP and BADVtoO/C-ADVPPROP with their subgrammar parts. All parts in Figure 13.4 are meant to be isomorphic 'horizontally'. The arrows show the implemented possible concatenations of the subgrammars such as to obtain a full projection. Table 13.6 shows the main translation-relevant rule classes in these subgrammars.

(part of) subgrammar	rule class description
derivation from BX	composition BXtoSUBX and SUBXtoX, derivational morphology
XPPROPformation	valency/semantic relations (including introduction of variables for arguments), voice, Aktionsart, variable introduction for adjuncts, temporal and local modifiers
XPPROPtoCLAUSE	empty and proposition substitution, modification, aspect, deictic aspect, deixis
XPPROPtoXPFORMULA	empty and proposition substitution, modification, aspect, deixis
CLAUSEtoSENTENCE	other substitution/modification/negation (scope-sensitive), mood
XPFORMULAtoXPPROP	other substitution/modification/negation (scope-sensitive), mood

Table 13.6: Main translation-relevant rule classes in the subgrammars.

The top category of a surface tree is UTTERANCE. A special subgrammar puts UTTERANCE on top of S-trees of a category which is an element of TOPCATS. These S-trees represent phrases that can be uttered in isolation. This subgrammar is characterised as follows:

1. **name**: TOPCATStoUTTERANCE

2. **export**: a specification of S-trees of category UTTERANCE. EXPORTCATS = {UTTERANCE}

3. **import**:

   - S-trees of categories that are element of HEADCATS = {NP, ADVP, PP, SENTENCE} are the head;

   - no other S-trees are imported. IMPORTCATS is empty.

4. **rules**: a set of M-rules that put category UTTERANCE on top of S-trees with category XP and SENTENCE.

5. **control expression**: one obligatory rule class with rules disjunctively ordered.

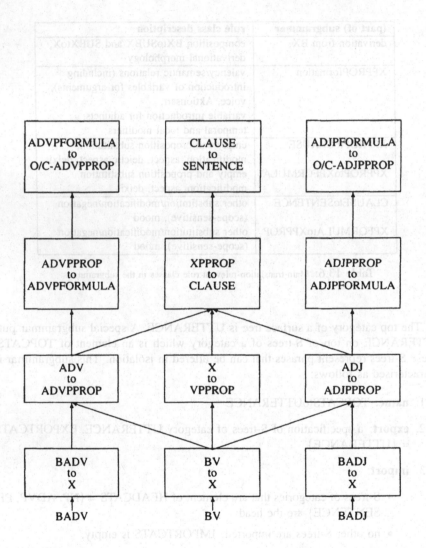

Figure 13.4: Overview of the ways in which propositional subgrammars can be concatenated to form projection subgrammars.

13.5   Partial isomorphy of subgrammars

Many of the divergence problems can be solved by the approach of attuning subgrammars. Subgrammars SG_1 and SG_2 are said to be isomorphic if, for every application sequence of translation-relevant rules in SG_1, there is a corresponding application sequence in SG_2. In that case we call them *completely isomorphic*. However, isomorphic subgrammars have their limits:

- semantic properties of translation-equivalent basic expressions (argument structure, temporal class, modification and voice possibilities etc.) must correspond;

- there are sometimes syntactic restrictions (e.g. limited tense possibilities of auxiliary verbs).

For this reason, it is not always possible to make a subgrammar of one language completely isomorphic with another subgrammar of the same or a subgrammar of another language. However, subgrammars can be made *partially isomorphic*. Two subgrammars are said to be partially isomorphic if not all, but at least one application sequence of translation-relevant rules corresponds. The following cases where not all application sequences correspond are distinguished:

1. w.r.t. corresponding subgrammars with the same head category.
   For example, with BADJtoSENTENCE x_1 *has been nice* and x_1 *is nice* can be derived, but with BADJtoO/C-ADJPPROP only x_1 *nice* can be derived. x_1 *nice* corresponds to x_1 *is nice* and not to x_1 *has been nice*, because *deictic aspect*, in English expressed by a perfect tense (see Chapter 14), only occurs in BADJto**SENTENCE**, or more precisely, in XPPROPtoCLAUSE. *Interrogative, relative* and *imperative* mood are likewise only possible in subgrammars which have top category SENTENCE and not O/C-XPPROP;

2. w.r.t. corresponding subgrammars with different head categories.
   For example, *passive* voice only occurs in subgrammars projecting verbs.

Partial isomorphy may appear not very useful, but one can achieve *complete isomorphy* with *sets* of subgrammars. Two sets A and B of partially isomorphic subgrammars are completely isomorphic if for each application sequence that the control expression of a subgrammar SG out of A allows for, there is at least one corresponding application sequence defined by a control expression of some subgrammar SG' out of B. For example, within one language the subgrammars for BADJtoSENTENCE and BADJtoO/C-ADJPPROP need not be completely isomorphic; neither do those for BADVtoSENTENCE and BVtoSENTENCE. But together, the subgrammars for BADJtoSENTENCE, BADJtoO/C-ADJPPROP, BADVtoSENTENCE and BVtoSENTENCE for Dutch can be completely isomorphic to the same collection of subgrammars for English.

Note that the notion 'strict isomorphy', introduced in Chapter 2, is stronger than what is called 'complete isomorphy' here. Strict isomorphy requires that translation-equivalent rules be applicable in the 'corresponding cases'. The applicability condition is needed to guarantee that corresponding sequences of applied rules yield a result, and that for any sentence that is correct according to one set of subgrammars there is a sentence that is correct according to the other set of isomorphic subgrammars. Proving this applicability condition is not trivial. In practice, a 'high degree' of isomorphy between propositional subgrammars for non-nominal predicates has been achieved. It is found that most differences can be dealt with by syntactic transformations and the 'syntactic operation' of translation-relevant rules.

13.6   Multiple divergence

The examples discussed in the preceding sections contained one categorial divergence per sentence. It is possible for combinations of divergences to occur. Since a general solution for these problems was chosen, the translations in (14) are obtained without problems.

(14)   multiple divergence:

Zij zwom *toevallig graag*	→	She *happened to like* swimming
Het *toevallig verkochte* huis	→	The house *that happens to have been sold*
She *could* expect *them to leave*	→	Zij *kon* verwachten *dat zij zouden vertrekken*
Zij leek te *kunnen* verwachten *dat zij zouden vertrekken*	→	It seemed *to be possible for her* to expect *them to leave*
Rosetta *zal* dit *moeten kunnen* vertalen	→	Rosetta *will have to be able* to translate this
I consider it *necessary for us to leave*	→	Ik vind *dat we weg moeten gaan*

The Dutch-Spanish example in (15), a type of translation problem discussed in the context of other frameworks and MT systems (cf. Isabelle *et al.* (1988) or Sanfilippo *et al.* (1992)) as well, can also be seen as a case of multiple categorial divergence.

(15)   (D) Zij *zwommen* de rivier over

They *swam*   the river   across

(S) Cruzaron   el río *nadando*

(They-)crossed the river *swimming*

It can be solved with isomorphic subgrammars by analysing them as:

zwemmen [zij$_i$, over[x$_i$, de rivier]]
(= swim [they$_i$, across[x$_i$, the river]]) and
nadando [ellos$_i$, cruzar[x$_i$, el río]]
(= swimming [they$_i$, cross[x$_i$, the river]])

The BPtoO/C-PPPROP projection subgrammar is made isomorphic to the BVtoSEN-TENCE projection subgrammar and switching can take place in substitution rules. Dutch *over* is seen as a two-place directional P, the head of a BPtoO/C-PPPROP subgrammar, which is of the type that normally occurs to the right of its object (a so-called *postposition* in Dutch) and can be attached to the verb (like a particle). Most locational and directional arguments are analysed as PPPROPs or ADVPPROPs in the Rosetta grammars. The subject or another argument of the directional or locational predicate of which the PPPROP (or ADVPPROP) is an argument, is assumed to be the same as the subject argument of this PPPROP (or ADVPPROP).

The gerundio form in Spanish is analysed as a two-place verbal 'manner' modifier whose subject argument is the same as the subject argument of the verbal predicate it modifies. The gerundio form, such as *nadando*, indicates that the events occur simultaneously, meaning 'in a swimming way' or 'while swimming'. The simultaneity of the verbs *cruzar* and *nadar* then follows.

A consequence of this approach is that movement verbs such as *zwemmen* must also be two-place predicates. In Dutch these two-place verbs can even be considered ergative predicates because they form perfect tenses with the auxiliary verb *zijn (be)* (cf. Hoekstra (1984)). Two analyses were necessary in Dutch anyway, but they have also to be stipulated in Spanish and English. They can be separate entries in the lexicon or derived from each other. The approach of compositionality of translation only prescribes that the same solution has to be chosen in all languages. The gerundio is analysed similarly to the adverb *graag* in Dutch and, as it corresponds to a verbal head in the other language, this involves subgrammar switching. Note that not only gerundio forms of motion verbs can be analysed in this way, but also gerundio forms of other kinds of verbs referring to the subject of the main event. It corresponds to a present participle analysis in other languages.

(16) (S) Salió llorando
　　　she-left crying
　　(E) She left crying
　　(D) Zij vertrok huilend
　　　She left　crying

The solution sketched here is a general solution that can be applied to all manner-of-motion verbs in combination with directional or goal verbs and prepositions. Tables

13.7 and 13.8 contain examples, taken partially from Sanfilippo *et al.* (1992).

manner-of-motion verbs		
Dutch	English	Spanish
zwemmen	swim	nadar
kuieren	amble	pasear(se)
kruipen	crawl	gatear
drijven	float	flotar
strompelen/hinken	hobble	cojear
rennen	run	correr
lopen	walk	andar
fietsen	cycle	ir en bicicleta

Table 13.7: Examples of manner-of-motion verbs.

direction or goal expressions		
Dutch	English	Spanish
over	across	cruzar/atrevesar (cross)
op	up	subir (ascend)
af	down	descender (descend)
naar/heen	to	alcanzar (reach)
in	into	entrar (enter)

Table 13.8: Examples of directional or goal prepositions and verbs.

The problems of the type of the particle *door-* in Dutch and the English and Spanish verbs *continue* and *seguir* in combination with activity or process verbs in gerund and gerundio form, respectively, can be solved along the same lines.[6]

13.7 Other solutions for categorial divergences

The isomorphic-subgrammar solution is nice, but maybe not always obvious or feasible, because it may turn out that a very complicated rule is needed for a small

---

[6]See Appelo (1993) for more details.

number of cases, no plausible corresponding semantic analysis can be found at first sight, or no agreement on the tuning that is required is reached by the grammar writers. The approach of compositionality of translation in principle allows for other solutions in those cases, for example:

1. abstract basic expressions combined with a generative 'robustness' transformation, a solution that leads to a deviation from the reversibility characteristic of the framework. It is the typical solution for the case where the normal translation method fails or a solution has not yet been agreed on.

2. abstract analysis, a solution that leads to unexpected analyses of phenomena that probably only can be defended in the context of translation. It is typically a 'creative' solution for a small number of cases.

To show that the method of compositional translation is not as rigid as it may appear, an example of these solutions will be discussed briefly.

1. Abstract basic expression with 'robustness transformation'

This approach is meant especially for 'lexical holes': basic expressions in one language for which there are no translation-equivalent basic expressions in the other language.

The essence of this approach comes down to stipulating an abstract basic expression (with the same syntactic category) in the language that is lacking it, and deriving a syntactic structure as if it were a normal basic expression. At a certain point of the derivation, a special transformation, triggered by that abstract basic expression, accounts for the transformation into an acceptable paraphrase in that language. As M-rules are very powerful, this transformation can change the syntactic structures (S-trees) very drastically.

In fact, this approach comes very close to the categorematic treatment of affixes (see Chapter 12), except for the 'missing expression' in the target language. They share the need for an abstract basic expression in combination with a special transformation triggered by that abstract expression, although in the case of an affix this procedure will often be more straightforward. The cases we are referring to here are the ones where the transformation has to change the syntactic structure very drastically. Most of the time, this target language expression can also be derived compositionally with subsequent application of normal rules of the grammar. Therefore, the best strategy is to let the special transformation apply as early as possible in the derivation in order to let the expression under consideration participate in the normal rules as much as possible. Otherwise, there is always a risk that that special transformation has to repeat a lot of rules and transformations that have already been applied at that point of the derivation in the normal case.

An example of such a case is the translation of Dutch *men*, an indefinite pronoun (in German: *man*, in French: *on*, in English sometimes: *one*), in its non-referential interpretation, into Spanish with an impersonal *se*-construction. It is an example of the translation problem area of '*diathesis*' in interaction with voice, arbitrary reference of constituents, certain types of pronominal constructions, and a certain class of morphological reflexives' (cf. Steiner (1990:160)). In the Dutch grammar of Rosetta *men* naturally is considered as a basic expression, whereas *se*-constructions are dealt with by rules in the Spanish grammar of Rosetta.

(17) (*D*) Men verkoopt hier appels
        One sells   here apples

    (*S*) Se   venden manzanas aquí
        'Oneself' sell   apples   here

In Spanish, an NP with an abstract indefinite pronoun is formed which is turned into a construction with the clitic pronoun *se* by a transformation almost at the end of the derivation. This transformation consists in practice of several transformations that account for the different cases. Besides deleting the abstract NP, it must also account, for example, again for subject-verb agreement, interaction with other clitics and the fact that the original object - if present - becomes a kind of subject. These phenomena are normally dealt with by rules and transformations before the special *men*-transformation in Spanish. Some of their results must be undone. The reason for this late application is the fact that the transformation only can be applied after the substitution of the abstract *men*, whereas the other rules and transformations that it repeats apply before substitution. Since the *se*-construction can also be analysed with normal rules, it is not attractive to make these special transformations reversible. In that case, a special transformation will also be needed if we translate in the other direction. In our example a transformation producing *men* in Dutch is needed after the 'normal' correspondence of *se*-constructions with passive constructions.

The conflict between the Dutch and Spanish grammars in the example above is mainly caused by the difference of preference when dealing with these phenomena in a categorematic (Dutch) or syncategorematic (Spanish) way, combined with a rule application order problem.

Another example was suggested in Landsbergen *et al.* (1989) for the example mentioned above with *over, across/cross, cruzar* by stipulating an abstract preposition 'across' in Spanish and a special transformation to derive the structure with *cruzar* + gerundio.

The main disadvantages of this approach in the context of reversible compositional translation are that

(i) a distinction is often made between the use of the grammar as a source or target language grammar: the more these transformations have to repeat preceding rules, the less attractive it is to make such transformations reversible;

(ii) such transformations are often triggered by one specific source language analysis, which — if it is resorted to too quickly — disturbs the strategy of looking for the common semantic properties of translation equivalents; and

(iii) the special transformations are often redundant from a monolingual point of view.

One may argue that the 'Dutch' or the 'Spanish' solution has to be chosen and that the rules should be made reversible, because this is a price to be paid for tuning. However, if this price is considered too high or if one is awaiting an analysis of the phenomena that fits better into an isomorphic approach, the asymmetric approach sketched above can be a possibility. The special transformations can be considered to be 'robustness' measures, i.e. measures taken in case the normal translation method fails. The robustness transformations occur only in generation and are used only with a particular source language.

In general, all head categorial divergences may be solved along these lines if the isomorphic subgrammar solution should be considered not to be feasible. Note that in case of a real lexical or structural gap it will be the only possibility for the generation of some translation.

The robustness transformations are in fact similar to structural transfer rules in other systems. The approach is in agreement with that of Neyt (1988) where it is argued that translation problems have to be solved in generation. But, apart from the deviation from reversibility, the approach is not in contradiction with the compositional translation framework.

2. Abstract analysis

Another method for dealing with difficult translation problems is to look for a more abstract analysis in order to be able to attune the grammars. A characteristic of these analyses is that they tend to be motivated only by contrastive (bilingual or multi-lingual) evidence and would probably not have been proposed outside the context of translation. An example of such an analysis is, for example, an analysis with *weak verbs*.[7] It resembles the complex predicate approach discussed in Chapter 15. Complex predicates consist of two basic expressions, one of which is a verb that can have different forms. It is also-called a 'support verb'.

A variant of this idea is the concept of a 'weak verb'. A weak verb is a verb that can be overruled by another verb of the same type if that other verb modifies the

---

[7]This analysis has not been implemented in the Rosetta system, but serves to illustrate that the framework need not be applied in a dogmatic way.

weak verb. An example of such a verb could be the Dutch movement verb *steken* (*'put'*) that occurs in combination with a particle *over* (*across*). It corresponds to the verbs *cross* in English and *cruzar* in Spanish. If its subject is modified by another movement verb, such as, for example, x_1 *zwemmend* (x_1 *swimming*), *steken* will be optionally replaced by *zwemmen* (*swim*). A condition to be satisfied is that it must have similar semantic properties as *steken*, e.g. being a movement verb. We derive:

(18) Hij *stak* de rivier *zwemmend over* $\rightarrow$ Hij *zwom* de rivier *over*
       He *'put'* the river *swimming across*   He *swum* the river *across*

Other 'weak verbs' in Dutch could be: *gaan* (*go*), *zijn* (*be*), *doen* (*do*). The special transformation is triggered by the 'weak verb'. Note that the 'weak verb' has to be produced in analysis, if this transformation is intended to be reversible.

In the same way we can derive, for example, *hij werkte door* (lit. *he worked PARTICLE*) from *hij ging werkend door* (lit. *he went working PARTICLE*), with the weak verb *gaan* (go), which is a translation for Spanish *siguió trabajando* (lit. *(he)-continued working*) and English *he continued working*, where *doorgaan* (*PARTICLE-go*) would correspond to *continue/seguir*. These 'weak verbs' can also disappear in combination with modals:[8]

(19) (D) Hij wil   naar huis (*gaan*)
              He wants to   home (*go*)
       (S) Quiere   ir a casa
              (He-)wants *go* to home
       (E) He wants to *go* home

(20) (D) Hij moest de rivier *over(steken)*
              He must   the river   *across('put')*
       (S) Debía   *cruzar* el río
              (He-)must *cross*   the river
       (E) He had to *cross* the river

This approach could be useful in cases where one of the languages seems to lack a verb. An advantage is that the intuition of a missing verb is accounted for and that the paraphrase with the verb can also be derived. A disadvantage could be that a deeper analysis is needed for the language in which the 'weak verb' is introduced than would be needed from a monolingual point of view. The framework of compositional translation allows for these abstract analyses but they should only be used if this proves desirable.

---

[8] Actually, the phenomenon illustrated in (19) has been implemented in the Rosetta system.

The *isomorphic subgrammar* solution also uses abstract analyses to a certain extent, e.g. by treating an adverb such as *graag* as a two-place predicate or applying time rules in adjectival subgrammars, but it pursues a common semantic treatment of all syntactic projections that preferably is supported by evidence from all languages. Therefore, it is a more general and powerful attempt to tackle categorial divergences than the occasional abstract analyses for specific phenomena.

13.8   Concluding remarks

Attuning subgrammars within a grammar is a general solution for many categorial divergences. As far as subgrammars with non-nominal categories are concerned, *head category divergence* (isomorphic subgrammars with different syntactic head categories) is only a little more difficult than *top category divergence* (isomorphic subgrammars with the same head category, but different top categories). In addition, the solution is general enough to allow for combinations of divergence.

We have observed that the problem of categorial divergence for non-nominal predicates appears most frequently with modal verbs and adverbs, auxiliaries and semi-auxiliaries, at least in the languages the Rosetta system deals with (Dutch, English and Spanish). In translation systems dealing with, for example, Japanese and English, however, these divergence phenomena are claimed to occur more frequently (cf. Nagao and Tsujii (1986)). The flexibility of the isomorphic subgrammar approach would therefore be very apposite if it were decided to extend the system by adding languages from other families.

Tuning subgrammars is motivated by semantic, not syntactic similarities. The distinction between translation-relevant *rules* and syntactic, language-specific *transformations* is very helpful here. The subdivision into classes in combination with the control expression of subgrammars provides a clear structure for the grammar writers. It increases the clarity and transparency of the grammars in case of translation problems such as with categorial divergence.

In addition to providing an elegant general solution for categorial divergence problems, isomorphic subgrammars within the same grammar also provide a 'translation-relevant' scheme for the composition of non-propositional or propositional subgrammars. This scheme consists of the various translation-relevant rule classes, together with the order and type of application of these classes. It represents the 'ingredients' of a translation or 'paraphrase' relation between two compound expressions.

Other solutions for difficult cases of (multiple) divergence are also allowed in the

Rosetta approach: abstract basic expressions combined with special rules or occasional abstract analyses, for example, as with 'weak verbs'. In some cases such solutions are preferred, for example if the number of cases is small. The disadvantage of those solutions compared to isomorphic subgrammars is that they often only work for two languages or are only applicable to a small number of lexical items, but they are feasible within the framework of compositionality of translation. The grammar writers decide which solution has to be chosen, preferably based on general principles.

Finally, note that the approach with isomorphic subgrammars, which was meant to deal with categorial divergence, has the following side effect. It also operates in cases that a more direct translation, i.e. with the same syntactic category as in the source language, is possible. In these cases, it increases the set of possible translations with a number of paraphrases. In fact, the notion of translation equivalence has been widened. The actual framework does not offer possibilities for expressing a preference for the more direct translation. However, such an extension would be feasible by rating the possible translations, e.g. by rating more direct translations higher than more indirect ones. As a consequence, the question of a more indirect translation will only arise if there is no direct one. Criteria have to be developed for this ranking system. See also chapter 16 for an initial approach.

Chapter 14

Temporal expressions

14.1 Introduction

The topic of this chapter is the problem of *temporal expressions*, i.e. *tensed verbs* and *temporal adverbials*. Translation of these expressions is not a matter of simple correspondence between one language and another language.

Consider the examples in the following tables, in which a tensed verb does not correspond to the expected, similarly tensed verb form in the other language or in which there are several possibilities for the correspondence. They are all considered translations of each other.[1]

DUTCH	↔	ENGLISH:
zij *woont* hier al twee jaar 'simple present tense'	↔	she *has been living* here for two years Present Perfect Progressive
zij *woont* hier 'simple present tense'	↔	she *is living* here Present Progressive
zij *komt* elk jaar 'simple present tense'	↔	she *comes* every year Simple Present
zij *komt* morgen 'simple present tense'	↔	she *will come* tomorrow Future
zij *woonde* daar al twee jaar 'simple past tense'	↔	she *had been living* there for two years Past Perfect Progressive
zij *woonde* daar 'simple past tense'	↔	she *lived* there Simple Past
zij *heeft* daar *gewoond* 'perfect present tense'	↔	she *has lived* there Present Perfect
zij *is* gisteren *gekomen* 'perfect present tense'	↔	she *came* yesterday Simple Past

---

[1]The tables in this section do not show all possible translations, but only the most important ones.

277

Below each sentence, a characterisation of the used *tense* or *aspect* form of the verb is given. The names of the Dutch and Spanish forms have been given paraphrases in English. The first table shows, among other things, that a Dutch 'simple present tense' corresponds to several English tenses.

The next table shows problems with translating the Dutch past tense and the adverb *zojuist* ('just') into Spanish. The adverb *zojuist* corresponds to a verb in Spanish, i.e. *acabar* ('finish'), but, apart from the category mismatch, the tenses do not correspond either.

DUTCH	↔	SPANISH:
zij *kwam* gisteren	↔	*vino* ayer
'simple past tense'		'perfective simple past tense'
zij *kwam* elke dag	↔	*venía* cada día
'simple past tense'		'imperfective simple past tense'
zij *is* zojuist *aangekomen*	↔	*acaba de llegar*
'perfect present tense' + *zojuist*		*acaba de* (present tense) + infinitive form

Between English and Spanish, the Present Perfect Progressive and the adverb *just* cause problems, as is shown in the next table.

ENGLISH	↔	SPANISH:
she *has been living* here for two years	↔	*lleva viviendo* aquí por dos años
Present Perfect Progressive		*lleva* (present tense) + gerund form
	↔	*hace dos años que vive* aquí
		'present tense'
she *has just arrived*	↔	*acaba de llegar*
Present Perfect + *just*		*acaba de* (present tense)
		+ infinitive form

Additionally, problems occur when translating infinitival and participial forms. What the appropriate translation equivalents are also depends on the context. In the next table, there usually is only one correct translation in the language on the right-hand side, in a given context.

de appels *etende* ezel 'present participle'	→ →	the donkey that *eats/is/was eating* apples Simple Present, Present or Past Progressive
de al twee uur appels *etende* ezel 'present participle'	→	the donkey that *has/had been eating* apples for two hours Present or Past Perfect Progressive
het *verkochte* huis 'past participle'	→	the house that *was/has been/had been sold* Simple Past, Present Perfect, Past Perfect
I expect her *to leave* Infinitive	→	ik verwacht dat zij *vertrekt/zal vertrekken* 'simple present tense', 'future tense'
I expected her *to leave* Infinitive	→	ik verwachtte dat zij *vertrok/zou vertrekken* 'simple past tense', 'past future tense'

Other problems involve temporal adverbials. The following table consists of some typical examples in Dutch, English and Spanish:[2]

Dutch	English	Spanish
drie jaar	for three years	por tres años
al drie jaar	for three years	(por) tres años
in twee jaar	within two years	en dos años
binnen een uur	within an hour	dentro de una hora
vijf minuten geleden	five minutes ago	hace cinco minutos
zes jaar geleden	for six years	hace seis años
om drie uur	at three o'clock	a las tres
's morgens	in the morning	por la mañana
's maandags	on Mondays	en lunes/los lunes
hoe laat	(at) what time	(a) qué hora
op haar verjaardag	on/at her birthday	el aniversario natalicio
toen zij kwam	when she came	cuando llegó ella
terwijl zij zong	while she was singing	mientras que cantaba ella

It will be clear that the translation of temporal adverbials is not straightforward, either. In particular, the choice and the absence/presence of prepositions can be difficult.

In any framework for translation one needs an analysis of temporal expressions that is more sophisticated than just mapping of tenses. In this chapter we will present a compositional approach to the translation of temporal expressions. This approach distinguishes 'parts' and rules in accordance with a semantic analysis of tense and aspect.

This chapter will not include discourse phenomena. Because of this, for the time being, the result of a translation process may be a set of possible translations. This means, for example, that *hij woonde daar* will be translated into both *he was living there* and *he lived there*. It is assumed that a choice can be made between these

---

[2]Note again that the table does not show all possible translations.

two sentences if the context of the sentence is used in the source or target language. Besides that, quantification of events will not be discussed in this chapter, which means that some scope phenomena will not be taken into account and that many aspects concerning frequency, habituality or iteration will be left out. The treatment of scope in general is discussed in Chapter 16. Neither will much attention be paid here to the translation problems of temporal adverbials themselves, because a lot of the problems are solved by the solutions presented in the chapters on idioms (Chapter 15) and divergences (Chapter 12 and 13).

We will start with a description of the temporal expressions involved (Section 14.2). Section 14.3 discusses the relation between meaning and form of temporal expressions. The topic of Section 14.4 is the *translation* of temporal expressions. First the compositional approach is explained and then the application in Rosetta is demonstrated.[3] Finally the results are summarised and evaluated in Section 14.5.

14.2   Description of temporal expressions

First of all, a description has to be given of what is meant by *temporal expressions* and some new concepts have to be introduced. There are two main kinds of temporal expressions: *tense* and *aspect* forms of verbs on the one hand and *temporal adverbials* on the other.

14.2.1   Tense and aspect

Tense and *aspect* are the morphological and syntactic markers of verbs or verbal groups that indicate some notion of *time*. There exist a lot of different definitions of *tense* and/or *aspect* and, furthermore, which part of a verb form is considered to be the tense form and which the aspect form differs in the various languages. See, e.g., Comrie (1976) and Comrie (1985). We distinguish between *simple* and *periphrastic* forms.

- *simple* forms: morphological forms of the main verb. Examples of this:

he work<i>s</i>
he work<i>ed</i>

- *periphrastic* forms: combinations of a morphological form of a *temporal auxiliary verb* and 'non-finite' forms of auxiliary verbs and the main verb (participle, infinitive, etc.). Examples of this are:

---

[3]The compositional approach presented here is an extended presentation of Appelo (1986), but a more detailed presentation can be found in Appelo (1993).

> he *has* work*ed*
> he *had* work*ed*
> he *will* work
> he *is* work*ing*

The following tables present an overview of tense and aspect forms of the English verb *work*, the Dutch verb *werken* and the Spanish verb *trabajar*, in third person singular, together with an abbreviation of the name of the tense-and-aspect-form in that language.

Dutch	
werkt	onvoltooid tegenwoordige tijd
werkte	onvoltooid verleden tijd
heeft gewerkt	voltooid tegenwoordige tijd
had gewerkt	voltooid verleden tijd
zal werken	onvoltooid tegenwoordige toekomende tijd
zal hebben gewerkt	voltooid tegenwoordige toekomende tijd

English	
works	Simple Present
is working	Present Progressive
worked	Simple Past
was working	Past Progressive
has worked	Present Perfect
has been working	Present Perfect Progressive
had worked	Past Perfect
had been working	Past Perfect Progressive
will work	Future
will be working	Future Progressive
will have worked	Future Perfect
will have been working	Future Perfect Progressive

Spanish	
trabaja	Presente de indicativo
trabaje	Presente de subjuntivo
trabajó	Pretérito indefinido
trabajaba	Imperfecto de indicativo
trabajara	Imperfecto de subjuntivo
ha trabajado	(Pretérito) perfecto
haya trabajado	(Pretérito) perfecto de subjuntivo
hubo trabajado	Pretérito anterior
había trabajado	Pluscuamperfecto
hubiera trabajado	Pluscuamperfecto de subjuntivo
trabajará	Futuro de indicativo
trabajare	Futuro de subjuntivo
habrá trabajado	Perfecto futuro

Additionally, the past subjunctive forms have an alternative form, e.g. *trabajase, hubiese trabajado*. Apart from these, there are verbal forms that can express a combination of time and modality: when they are used in a main sentence they express 'irrealis' (hypothetical meaning), but when used in a dependent past sentence or context, they are simply the past counterpart of the future tenses:

Dutch	
zou werken	onvoltooid verleden toekomende tijd
zou hebben gewerkt	voltooid verleden toekomende tijd

English	
would work	Past Future
would be working	Past Future Progressive
would have worked	Past Future Perfect
would have been working	Past Future Perfect Progressive

Spanish	
trabajaría	Condicional
habría trabajado	Perfecto Condicional

14.2.2   Temporal adverbials

Temporal adverbials are those phrases (including adverbial sentences) that give some temporal specification. They can be classified in a syntactic and a semantic manner.

- *syntactic*: temporal expressions can be of category NP, PP, ADVP, ADJP and (adverbial) SENTENCE.
  Some English examples:

NP	that day, Sunday afternoon
PP	for two hours, since 1972, during the meeting
ADVP	now
ADJP	next, former
SENTENCE	when he arrived, while he was singing, before he left

- *semantic*: a rather standard way is to distinguish *referential* (when?), *duration* (how long?) and *frequentative or habitual* (how often?) adverbials.
  Some examples of this in English:

referential	now, that day, next summer, before he left
duration	for two hours, in three years
frequentative	three times
habitual	every year, always

14.3 Meaning and form

14.3.1 Modelling time: extending Reichenbach

To explain what temporal expressions mean one can use a time model. The model used for the Rosetta system, like most existing models, has been inspired by the theory of Reichenbach (1947). These models are based on the assumption that time is expressed mainly by tense and aspect forms of verbs and verbal groups. They consist of a time axis with points and/or intervals and relations between them. Within the set of points and intervals three special kinds are distinguished:

- a point or interval E (E = event)

- a point S (S = speech), i.e. 'now'

- a point or interval R (R =reference)

These points and intervals can be ordered on the time axis, as, for example, in the following picture. They can occur *before*, *after* or *simultaneously with* another point or interval.

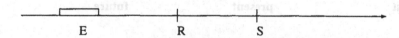

A sentence or clause is associated with an *event* placed in time as an interval E. The event is placed in time, that is, it has a *time reference* with respect to the moment of speech (reading, utterance, etc.) S. E and S are related to each other via a *reference point or interval* R. In Reichenbach's theory each E,R,S combination corresponds to an English tense/aspect form of the verb. The picture above corresponds to the Past Perfect Tense as in *Mary had worked there*.

Reference points R can be considered as representing some 'point of view' that a speaker (or writer) wishes to express. Another option is to consider them 'possible points of speech' (cf. e.g. Oversteegen and Verkuyl (1985)).

In Reichenbach's model each clause or sentence is associated with an E,R,S-combination consisting of one E, one R and one S. In some of its extensions, it is permitted to have a number of points or intervals R involved in the time reference of one event. The Rosetta time model is actually such an extension of Reichenbach's model. Its main difference is that it allows for more than one R and is also suited to other languages than English. If more than one point or interval of type R is involved, we will indicate them with an index: R_x. This implies that apart from relations E–R and R–S, relations R_x–R_y are needed.

Basically, three important kinds of relations between points and intervals E, R and S are distinguished.

- *deixis*, between S and R. We distinguish:

    - *present*: S and R are *simultaneous* or S is located within R (S *is contained in* R)
    - *past*: S is *after* R
    - *future*: S is *before* R

We can represent this in pictures as follows:

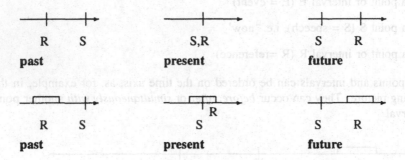

R S	S,R	S R
past	**present**	**future**

R S	S R	S R
past	**present**	**future**

- *aspect*, between E and R. We distinguish:

    - *perfective*: E is within or simultaneous with R. The 'boundaries' of the interval E are assumed to be known.
    - *imperfective*: R is within E. The 'boundaries' of the interval E are not assumed to be known (represented by an arrow in the picture). Only the part that coincides with R is known of E.

Represented in pictures:

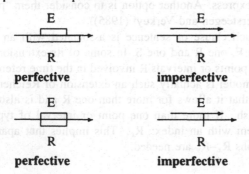

E	E
R	R
perfective	**imperfective**

E	E
R	R
perfective	**imperfective**

- *deictic aspect*, between a point and an interval of type R. The interval has an aspectual relation with E: it is called R_E. The point has a direct or indirect relation with S. We therefore call it R_S here. We distinguish:

  – *retrospective*: R_E lasts until R_S. The left boundary of R_E may be unspecified, representing 'in the past from R_S'.
  This relation can also be called *perfect* aspectual relation and can be characterised as an *after* relation: R_S after R_E, just as in the analyses of, among others, Reichenbach (1947) and Johnson (1981). However, that does not account for the special character of this *after* relation. It is better characterised as 'R_S *is the end of* R_E'. In conformity with Van Eynde (1988) we will use the term *retrospective* aspect for it to distinguish it from the syntactic verbal form *Perfect Tense*.

  In a picture, with the left boundary specified:

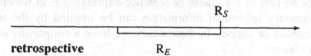

  retrospective R_E

  – *prospective*: R_E begins at R_S. The right boundary of R_E may be unspecified, representing 'in the future from R_S on'. This relation could be characterised as a *before* relation: R_S before R_E, but that does not account for the special character of this *before* relation. It is better characterised as 'R_S *is the beginning of* R_E'. A picture of this, with the right boundary specified:

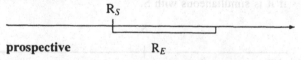

  prospective R_E

The deictic aspectual relation is optional and it can be absent from a figure for a time reference of a given sentence. It is, however, assumed that at least one R is involved. If there is only one R, then that R has an aspectual relation with E and a deictic relation with S.

So, for every time reference of an event, there is at least a deictic and an aspectual relation. The deictic aspectual relation and other relations between other points and intervals R are optional. This means that for every event E, at least one R has to be determined so as to establish a relation between E and S via (one or more occurrences of) R.

Thus, the time model for the Rosetta system consists of a time axis on which point and intervals are defined (i.e of type E, R and S) and several relations between them (of the types deixis, aspect and deictic aspect). They form the elements from which time references of events are composed by relating E to S.

14.3.2   Correspondence between time model and linguistic forms

The Rosetta time model is meant to be used for all languages involved. It has the following properties with respect to the correspondence to linguistic expressions:

- Association of a clause or sentence (an event) with E:
  Every proposition, expressed by a sentence or clause, is associated with an interval or point E in the time model.

- Linguistic expression for every R:
  Every R has to be related to some linguistic form, a temporal expression, except for the cases below. This temporal expression related to an R need not be part of the clause or sentence expressing E to which R is related. The necessary referential information can be implied by the text preceding that sentence or clause. In these cases, we have a *temporally dependent* sentence or clause.

Exceptions:
There are two reference intervals and one point that do not need to correspond to some language form:

1. 'NOW': the moment of speech/reading etc., i.e. S. This also holds for R if it is simultaneous with S.

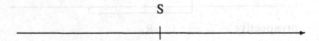

2. 'PAST': the time up to some point R_i.
   It specifies a 'half-open' interval R_E which has a retrospective relation with that point R_i and a perfective relation with E. It means that there is an interval R_E of unspecified length lasting until R_i. That interval contains E (somewhere).

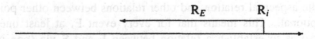

3. 'FUTURE': the time from some point R_i on.
   It specifies a 'half-open' interval R_E that has a prospective relation with

that point R_i and a perfective relation with E. It means that there is an interval R_E of unspecified length beginning at R_i. That interval contains E (somewhere).

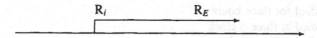

- The *composed* relation between E and S, i.e. the relation between E and S via R, has to be reflected. Most of the time this will be done by verbal *tense* and *aspect* forms. In some languages the parts of the composed relation are reflected (a *tense* form for the deictic part and an *aspect* form for the aspectual part), but in others this is not so clear. See also Section 14.4.1.

14.3.3   Inherent temporal properties

Propositions representing events and adverbials can have temporal properties of their own. Events, for example, have an aspectual nature which is usually referred to as *Aktionsart* or *lexical aspect*. Vendler (1967) distinguished four types:

stative : the event is a state or situation. Its nature is homogeneous and durative.
　　　Examples: *Mary be ill, Mary love films*

activity : the event is a dynamic situation. Its nature is homogeneous and durative.
　　　Examples: *Mary eat, Mary walk, Mary knock on the door, Mary eat apples*

accomplishment : the event is a single completed activity. Its nature is not homo-
　　　geneous and terminative. Internally, the event is durative.
　　　Examples: *Mary eat an apple, Mary walk to the door, Mary build three houses*

achievement : the event is a momentary action. Its nature is terminative.
　　　Examples: *Mary die, Mary win the race, Mary enter the house*

The first two together form the *durative* and the last two the *terminative* Aktionsart in Verkuyl (1972). Another well-known Aktionsart classification is the division of events or situations into *states*, *processes* and *events* (cf. e.g. Bach (1986)). A *process* is equivalent to an activity and an *event* to terminative Aktionsart.
The type of event plays a role in the conditions concerning possible time references, although it is not clear whether these conditions should be considered semantic or pragmatic, since many judgements involve a knowledge of the world or situation. Whether it is appropriate to talk about a *point* or *interval* is not expressed by linguistic means. Is the moment of speech a point or an interval? Should *at three o'clock* be seen as a point? Does an expression such as *within a minute* indicate an interval?

Is the event expressed by the time-neutral sentence *Mary die* considered a point or an interval? The reason we have to consider this topic is that some combinations of events and temporal adverbials are less acceptable. Consider (1):

(1) a ?Mary died for three hours
     b Mary died at three o'clock
     c Mary died within a minute
     d ?Mary was ill at three o'clock
     e Mary was ill for three hours
     f ?Mary was ill within a minute

Additionally, some combinations of events and aspectual relations seem to occur less frequently, e.g. statives and processes are naturally interpreted as imperfective whereas events are interpreted as perfective.

To enable the acceptable sentences to be selected, events and temporal adverbials have been classified with respect to their combination properties in the Rosetta approach. For Aktionsarten, the Vendler classification was chosen. The Aktionsart of an event is considered here to be a semantic property of that event and translation equivalents should have the same Aktionsart.

Statives and activities are both durative and often combine with durative temporal adverbials indicating boundaries or length of the event. These adverbials are called *perfective*, because the boundaries of the event interval are known. Examples are: *for three hours, for years*.

Accomplishments and achievements are both terminative and combine with durative temporal adverbials that can include events. These adverbials are called *imperfective*, because of the analogy with the imperfective relationship between E and R_E where E contains R_E. Examples are: *within a minute, in three hours*.

Most reference temporal adverbials are *imperfective*, except for those that indicate points, e.g. *at three o'clock*. These latter have the property of combining with *achievements* and events that have an *imperfective aspectual relation* with their R_E. Temporal adverbials that specify *retrospective* reference intervals (R_E until R_S) can also be *imperfective*, containing E (e.g. *since 1972*), or *perfective*, setting the boundaries for an E (e.g. *al drie jaar* (lit. *already three year*)).

Apart from aspectual properties, temporal adverbials can have deictic properties. For example, *yesterday* is an adverbial that can only specify an interval situated before the moment of speech.

14.4   Translation of temporal expressions

14.4.1   A Compositional approach to the translation of temporal expressions

The model presented above has been used as a basis for the compositional interpretation and translation of temporal expressions.

It consists of:

(i) intervals and points specified by temporal adverbials (phrases and clauses) and propositions (clauses and sentences without temporal expressions);

(ii) relations between those intervals and points, usually specified by (parts of) tense and aspect forms of verbs

These intervals, points and relations between them form the parts in the derivation. This derivation starts with the proposition (without any temporal expression) specifying the interval E, and ends when the relation with S, the moment of speech, has been established. This derivation (in which OB means obligatory rule, OP optional rule and IT iterative rule) is represented schematically by the following rules:

1. OB: Association of a time-neutral sentence with an interval E and determination of the Aktionsart (i.e. stative, activity , accomplishment or achievement).
   Example: *she work*: activity

2. OP: specification of the length of E.
   Insertion of duration adverbials.
   Example: *she work for three years*
   If not applied, the length of the event is unspecified, which is allowed.

3. OB: specification of the interval R_E and the aspectual relation between R_E and E (i.e. perfective or imperfective).
   The relation is usually expressed by aspect forms of verbs.
   In the case of a temporally dependent clause or sentence, the specification of R_E may depend on a specification in a higher clause or in the preceding context.
   Example: *she be working*: imperfective

4. OP: specification of a point R_i (R_i directly or indirectly related to S) and the relation between R_i and R_E (i.e. retrospective or prospective).
   The relation is usually expressed by perfect or future tenses.
   In the case of a temporally dependent clause or sentence, the specification

of R_i may depend on a specification in a higher clause or in the preceding context.

Example: *she have been working*: retrospective

5. IT: specification of an interval R_i and specification of a relation between that interval R_i and a point or interval R_j (contains, before, after), where R_j is the last point or interval introduced earlier. This relation is not always specified by specific word forms.

   In the case of a temporally dependent clause or sentence, the specification of R_i may depend on a specification in a higher clause or in the preceding context.

   Example: *she be working at five o'clock yesterday*[4]

6. OB: specification of the relation between the last interval or point in the chain R_j and S (i.e. past, present or future).

   The relation is usually expressed by (deictic) tense forms.

   This $R_j = R_E$ in the case of one R.

   Example: *she was working*: past

For compositional translation it is essential that every part of the composition in one language should have a translation-equivalent part in the other language. (cf. Chapter 2).

Although the temporal adverbials involved show some divergences in the various languages with respect to syntactic categories, they do not present serious problems: most of the problematic cases can be solved with the method of *isomorphic subgrammars* (cf. Chapter 13), or by treating them as *translation idioms* (cf. Chapter 15). Discongruencies of tense and aspect forms can also be dealt with, although more abstraction is necessary than just distinguishing parts of tense and aspect *forms* because the parts of a composed or periphrastic verb form do not always correspond directly to the parts of the composition proposed here.

We will subsequently discuss the tense and aspect forms of all Rosetta languages in terms of the model, before looking at the translation relation between them.

As all combinations of the deictic, aspectual and deictic aspectual (including the absence of deictic aspectual) relations should correspond to some tense and aspect form of a verb (simple or periphrastic), there are 18 combinations to examine for every language.

---

[4]It is also possible that there are complex reference adverbials specifying an R, e.g. *yesterday at five o'clock*.

English

The English tense and aspect system is very similar to the proposed compositional time model.[5] The following table represents the correspondences between the several kinds of relations (left column) and the linguistic forms (right column).

Deixis	
present	present tense
past	past tense
future	future tense

Aspect	
perfective	simple tense
imperfective	progressive tense

Deictic Aspect	
retrospective	perfect tense
prospective	future tense

The only problem that occurs is that future + prospective will result in a 'double future tense' (*will* + *will*). But forms with *to be going to* (*is going to, was going to, will be going to*, etc.) can be used for prospective instead of future tense.

Dutch

The Dutch tense and aspect system corresponds less directly to the compositional model than the English system does. In Dutch, there are more possibilities to express a time relation.[6]

Deixis	
present	tegenwoordige tijd
past	verleden tijd
future	toekomende/tegenwoordige tijd

Aspect	
perfective	onvoltooide/voltooide tijd
imperfective	onvoltooide tijd

Deictic Aspect	
retrospective	onvoltooide/voltooide tijd
prospective	tegenwoordige/toekomende tijd

---

[5]The possibility that *future* is expressed by a present tense is left aside here because it also expresses some notion of *near* future that was not taken into account here.

[6]See the tables in Section 14.2 for examples of the use of these tenses.

The distinction between aspect and deictic aspect on the one hand and deixis and deictic aspect on the other hand is not expressed in the composition of the Dutch verb forms. The combination of aspect and deictic aspect or the combination of deixis and aspect is decisive for the verb form, as the table below shows.

perfective	+	retrospective	↔	voltooide tijd ('perfect tense')
imperfective	+	retrospective	↔	onvoltooide tijd ('simple tense')
perfective	+	prospective	↔	onvoltooid toekomende tijd ('future tense')
imperfective	+	prospective	↔	onvoltooid tegenwoordige tijd ('simple present tense')
perfective	+	—	↔	onvoltooide tijd ('simple tense')
imperfective	+	—	↔	onvoltooide tijd ('simple tense')

Moreover, a special possibility in Dutch is:

perfective	+	past	↔	voltooid tegenwoordige tijd ('present perfect tense')

Note that imperfective aspect is always expressed by an 'onvoltooide tijd'.[7]

Spanish

As in Dutch, there is no simple correspondence between the Spanish tense and aspect system and the compositional model.[8] The possibilities to express the relations are presented in the following table.

The problem in Spanish is that there is only a special aspectual form for the past tense:

past	+	perfective	↔	pretérito indefinido ('simple past tense perfective')
past	+	imperfective	↔	imperfecto ('simple past tense imperfective')

---

[7] This does not mean that an 'onvoltooide tijd' cannot express perfective aspect!

[8] Examples of the use of these tenses can be found in the table in Section 14.2.

Deixis	
present	presente
past	pretérito indefinido/imperfecto
future	futuro
Aspect	
perfective	presente/pretérito indefinido/futuro
imperfective	presente/imperfecto/futuro
Deictic Aspect	
retrospective	perfecto/*llevar* + gerundio/
	presente/imperfecto
prospective	futuro

Additionally, we have the same problem as in Dutch:

perfective	+	retrospective	↔	perfecto ('perfect tense')
imperfective	+	retrospective	↔	presente/imperfecto or
				presente/imperfecto of
				llevar + gerundio
				('verb *llevar* + gerund form')

As in English, future + prospective will result in a 'double future tense'. But we can use *ir a* + infinitivo (*go* + infinitive) (*va a, iba a, irá a*, etc.) for prospective instead of future tense.

Overview of the possible combinations

Examples of the 18 possible combinations for deixis, deictic aspect and aspect for Dutch, English and Spanish are given below.

To create a plausible context for the example sentences, the following temporal adverbials are used:

deixis
present: nu, now, ahora
past: gisteren, yesterday, ayer
future: morgen, tomorrow, mañana

aspect
reference perfective: nu, now, ahora
reference perfective: op dat moment, at that moment, en ese/aquel momento
reference imperfective: gisteren, yesterday, ayer
reference imperfective: morgen, tomorrow, mañana
duration perfective: drie jaar/uur, for three years/hours, por tres años/horas

deictic aspect
retrospective perfective: al drie jaar, for three years, tres años/hace tres años que
retrospective imperfective: sinds 1972, since 1972, desde hace 1972
PAST (imperfective): (ooit), (once), (una vez)

prospective perfective: nog twee weken, another two weeks, dos semanas más
prospective imperfective: tot 1993, until 1993, hasta 1993
FUTURE (imperfective): (ooit), (once), (una vez)

The event represented in the examples is an activity event: *zij (hier/daar) werken,
she work (here/there), trabajar (aquí, allí)*. As a consequence, the divergent behaviour of stative events in English and Spanish is not accounted for here. For these
events, progressive forms in English and forms with gerundio in Spanish should not
be applied, but instead the simple forms should be used.

present imperfective
D: o.t.t.   zij werkt nu
E: Pres. Progr.   she is working now
S: presente   trabaja ahora
      pres. estar + ger.   está trabajando ahora
present imperfective retrospective
D: o.t.t.   zij werkt hier nu al drie jaar
E: Pres. Perf. Progr.   she has been working here for three years now
S: pres. llevar + ger.   lleva trabajando aquí tres años ahora
      presente   hace tres años que trabaja aquí
present imperfective prospective
D: o.t.t.   zij werkt hier nog twee weken
E: Fut.Progr.   she will be working here for another two weeks
S: futuro   trabajará aquí por dos semanas más
      fut. estar + ger.   estará trabajando aquí por dos semanas más
present perfective
D: o.t.t.   zij werkt
E: Sim. Pres.   she works
S: presente   trabaja
present perfective retrospective
D: v.t.t.   zij heeft hier (ooit) drie uur gewerkt
E: Pres. Perf.   she has worked here for three years (once)
S: perfecto   ha trabajado aquí por tres años (una vez)
present perfective prospective
D: o.t.t.t.   zij zal (ooit) vier jaar werken
E: Future   she will work for four years (once)
S: futuro   trabajará por cuatro años (una vez)
past imperfective
D: o.v.t.   zij werkte gisteren op dat moment
E: Past Progr.   she was working at that moment yesterday
S: imperfecto   trabajaba en ese/aquel momento ayer
      imp. estar + ger.   estaba trabajando en ese/aquel momento ayer

past imperfective retrospective
D: o.v.t.   zij werkte daar gisteren al drie jaar
E: Past Perf. Progr.   she had been working there for three years
S: imp. llevar + ger.   llevaba trabajando allí tres años
     imperfecto   hacía tres años que trabajaba aquí

past imperfective prospective
D: o.v.t.   zij werkte daar gisteren nog twee weken
E: Past Fut. Progr.   she would be working there for another two weeks yesterday
S: condicional   trabajaría allí por dos semanas más ayer

past perfective
D: v.t.t.   zij heeft gisteren drie uur gewerkt
     o.v.t.   zij werkte gisteren drie uur
E: Sim. Past   she worked for three hours yesterday
S: pretérito indef.   trabajó por tres horas ayer

past perfective retrospective
D: v.v.t.   gisteren had zij daar sinds 1972 drie jaar gewerkt
E: Past Perf.   yesterday she had worked there for three years since 1972
S: pluscuamperfecto   ayer había trabajado allí por tres años desde hace 1972

past perfective prospective
D: o.v.t.t.   gisteren zou zij tot 1993 twee jaar werken
E: Past Fut.   yesterday she would work for two years until 1993
S: condicional   ayer trabajaría por dos años hasta 1993

future imperfective
D: o.t.t.   zij werkt morgen op dat moment
     o.t.t.t.   zij zal morgen op dat moment werken
E: Fut. Progr.   she will be working at that moment tomorrow
S: futuro   trabajará en ese/aquel momento mañana
     fut. estar + ger.   estará trabajando en ese/aquel momento mañana

future imperfective retrospective
D: o.t.t.   zij werkt daar morgen al drie jaar
     o.t.t.t   zij zal daar morgen al drie jaar werken
E: Fut. Perf. Progr.   she will have been working there for three years tomorrow
S: fut. llevar + ger.   llevará trabajando allí tres años mañana

future imperfective prospective
D: o.t.t.   zij werkt daar morgen nog twee weken
     o.t.t.t.   zij zal daar morgen nog twee weken werken
E: Fut. Progr.   she will be working there for another two weeks tomorrow
     Fut. be going + Progr. she will be going to be working there for another two weeks tomorrow
S: futuro   trabajará allí por dos semanas más mañana
     fut. ir a + inf.   irá a trabajar allí por dos semanas más

future perfective
D: o.t.t.   zij werkt daar morgen drie uur
     o.t.t.t   zij zal daar morgen drie uur werken
E: Future   she will work there for three hours tomorrow
S: futuro   trabajará allí por tres horas mañana

future perfective retrospective
D: v.t.t.   morgen heeft zij daar sinds 1972 tien jaar gewerkt
     v.t.t.t.   morgen zal zij daar sinds 1972 tien jaar gewerkt hebben
E: Fut. Perf.   tomorrow she will have worked there for ten years since 1972
S: Perfecto fut.   mañana hará trabajado allí por diez años desde hace 1972

future perfective prospective

D:	o.t.t.	morgen werkt zij daar tot 1 januari
	o.t.t.t.	morgen zal zij daar tot 1 januari werken
E:	Fut. be going + inf.	tomorrow she will going to work there until 1 January
	Future	tomorrow she will work there until 1 January
S:	fut. ir + inf.	mañana irá a trabajar allí hasta el primero del enero
	futuro	mañana trabajará allí hasta el primero del enero

Translation relation

There is a simple correspondence between the model and the English tense and aspect forms, but not between the model and the forms in Dutch and Spanish. But in the latter two cases, the **combination** of the relations between E, (one or more occurrences of) R and S can be reflected. Therefore, it is required that the **composed** relation between E and S is mapped onto tense and aspect forms of verbs. The reason that the steps in between are useful is the requirement of specification of the intervals and/or points involved. This specification has to be the same in translation-equivalent sentences. In that way the problems in Section 14.1 can be solved.

Consider the following examples, which represent some of these problems:

1.

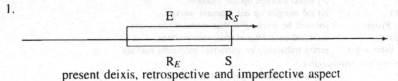

present deixis, retrospective and imperfective aspect

The figure above is meant to be a representation of the temporal aspects of the sentences in (2):

(2) a (D) zij woont hier al   drie jaar
         she lives   here already three year

   b (E) she has been living here for three years

   c (S) lleva viviendo aquí por tres años
         carries living   here for three years

Following the composition prescription, we get:

1. The time-neutral proposition in all three languages, D: *zij hier wonen*, E: *she live here* and S: *(ella) vivir aquí*, is associated with an interval E and the Aktionsart *activity* is determined.

2. There is no specification of the length of E.

3. E has an *imperfective* aspectual relation with an interval R_E which is specified by the retrospective, perfective adverbials D: *al drie jaar*, E: *for three years* and S: *tres años*, respectively.

4. This interval R_E lasts until R_S, which indicates a *retrospective* deictic aspectual relation and R_S is specified by 'NOW' (the moment of speech).

5. No other reference intervals are involved.

6. R_S coincides with S, so there is a *present* deictic relation.

The part of the event referred to is an interval with a *length* of three years *before* the moment of speech.

In Dutch, *present retrospective imperfective* results in a *onvoltooid tegenwoordige tijd* ('simple present tense'). In English, it results in a Present Perfect Progressive Tense and in Spanish in a Presente ('simple present tense') of the verb *llevar* + gerundio ('gerund form'). This, however, is only possible if that retrospective interval has been specified, which means that the retrospective adverbial must be present in the sentence.

2. Consider now the situation without the retrospective interval and the sentences above without that retrospective adverbial:

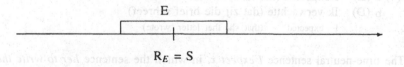

$$R_E = S$$

(3) a (D)   zij woont hier
              she lives   here
   b (E)   she is living here
   c (S)   vive aquí
             lives here

Following the derivation, we get:

1. The time-neutral proposition, D: *zij hier wonen*, E: *she live here* and S: *(ella) vivir aquí*, is associated with an interval E and the Aktionsart *activity* is determined.

2. The length of E is not specified.

3. E has an *imperfective* aspectual relation with a point R_E which is specified by 'NOW' in all three languages (the moment of speech).

4. The deictic aspectual relation is absent. There is only one R: R_E.

5. No other reference intervals are involved.

6. R_E coincides with S, so it has a *present* deictic relation.

The part of the event referred to is the moment of speech.

In Dutch, *present imperfective* results in a *onvoltooid tegenwoordige tijd* ('simple present tense'), like *present retrospective imperfective* (see above). But in
English it results in a Present Progressive Tense and in Spanish, in a Presente
('simple present tense'). These differences are caused by the absence/presence
of the retrospective adverbial in the composition. In this way, the translation
problems with finite tense and aspect forms presented in Section 14.1 can be
solved.

3. Many problems with the infinitival and participial forms (cf. Section 14.1) can
   be solved now, because sentences which contain such verbal forms and which
   do not contain deictic adverbials are always *temporally dependent* sentences,
   which means that the specification of the R interval or point can be found in
   a preceding (matrix) sentence. In the other language this can be spelled out
   as a finite verb form. For example:

(4) a (E)   I expected (her to write that letter)
    b (D)   Ik verwachtte (dat zij die brief schreef)
            I expected   (that she that letter wrote)

The time-neutral sentence *I expect x*, in which the sentence *her to write that
letter* will be substituted for *x*, is associated with an interval E_1 and the Aktionsart *achievement* is determined. E_1 has a *perfective* aspectual relation with
R_{E1}. The interval R_{E1} is specified by the context. R_{E1} is before S, so it has
a *past* deictic relation.

The time-neutral phrase *her to write that letter* is associated with an interval
E_2 and the Aktionsart *accomplishment* is determined. In one of the interpretations, E_2 has a *perfective* aspectual relation with an interval R_{E2}, related to the
time reference of the first event specifying the beginning of R_{E2} (indicated by
R_i below). E_2 therefore inherits the deictic relation from the deictic relation
of E_1, which is *past*.

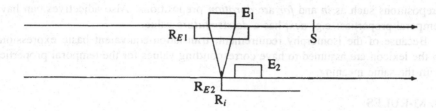

Note that a past future tense in Dutch (o.v.t.t.) would also be possible here.

14.4.2   Application in Rosetta

We will now consider how this approach works out in the Rosetta system. First we will look at main sentences and then - very briefly - at subordinate sentences.

Main clauses and temporal adverbials

Applying this compositional approach to the Rosetta system requires specifying

1. basic expressions with temporal properties

2. (a) rules expressing the relations in the model that

        i.   compose the relation between E and S

       ii.   set the values for temporal attributes of verbs (expressing morphological tense and aspect forms)

     iii.   introduce the necessary temporal auxiliary verbs with the appropriate values for the temporal attributes

    (b) rules that construct temporal adverbials

Therefore, there are:

A. BASIC EXPRESSIONS:

Basic expressions can have temporal properties. For example, verbs have a value for *temporal class* which adds to the determination of the Aktionsart of a sentence. Nouns have a Boolean attribute for *temporal* which indicates whether they can be part of a temporal adverbial: *meeting, year, week*, etc. have temporal=true and *chair, tree, computer* have temporal=false. Some nouns are *unit nouns*, which means that they are part of temporal quantification of length, e.g. *year, week, hour*, etc. Adverbs can be marked for deixis, e.g. *yesterday* has *deixis=past*, and prepositions for aspect, e.g. *in* has *aspect=imperfective* and *for* has *aspect=perfective*. Both can be marked for temporal class: an adverb such as *yesterday* is a *reference* adverb and prepositions such as *in* and *for* are *duration* prepositions. Also adjectives can have temporal properties: e.g. *next* has a *deixis=future* value.

Because of the isomorphy requirement, translation-equivalent basic expressions in the lexicon are assumed to have corresponding values for the temporal properties with the same meaning.

B. M-RULES:

We distinguish (a) rules for the time reference of events expressed by a propositional category, including rules for the calculation of Aktionsart, rules for *tense* and *aspect* forms of verbs and the insertion of temporal adverbials, and (b) rules for constructing *temporal adverbials*.

(a) TIME REFERENCE OF AN EVENT:

The point of departure for these rules is, of course, the scheme presented in Section 14.4.1. For every relation between intervals in the model at least one rule is written. For clauses this means that these rules are part of subgrammars on the path from BX to SENTENCE and will have corresponding rules in other grammars. The rules and the control expressions in the grammar correspond more or less to the scheme presented in Section 14.4.1. Differences are that (i) they are not clustered but spread throughout the various subgrammars on the path from BX to SENTENCE and that (ii) the specifications of the relations and the specifications of the intervals/points are separate. For the intervals/points variables are introduced for which temporal adverbials are substituted later.[9] The presence/absence of the specifications of intervals is accounted for by the presence/absence of the variables. The rules can refer to these variables.

The association with E is done in the transformation class *Aktionsart calculation*. Specification of the length of E is done by introducing a variable for a durative adverbial and substituting the adverbial later. The aspectual relation is specified by the rule class *aspect rules*, the deictic aspectual relation by the rule class *deictic aspect rules* and the deictic relation by the rule class *deixis rules*. The control expression for all rule classes (RC) and transformation classes (TC) for tense and aspect is:

1. iterative RC: Introduction of variables for temporal adverbials
2. obligatory TC: Aktionsart calculation
3. obligatory RC: Aspect rules
4. optional RC: Deictic aspect rules
5. obligatory RC: Deixis rules
6. iterative RC: Substitution of temporal adverbials

---

[9]This has been done for the treatment of scope in Rosetta. This topic will not be discussed here. See Chapter 16.

Step 1 accounts for part of the original steps 2, 3, 4 and 5. Step 2 is the original step 1. Steps 3 and 4 here only take care of a part of the original steps 3 and 4. Step 5 is the original step 6. Step 6 accounts for parts of the original steps 2, 3, 4 and 5.

Aktionsart calculation
The Aktionsart of a sentence is composed from properties of the parts of the sentence: the verb and its complements. Verbs can be classified as *stative, durative, movement, iterative* or *momentary*. Stative, iterative and momentary verbs always lead to stative, activity and achievement Aktionsart, respectively, irrespective of the complements of the verbs. Examples are:

stative: *be, love, possess, have*
iterative: *knock, beat, hit*
momentary: *die, win, reach*

Durative or movement verbs lead to activity or accomplishment Aktionsart depending on the properties of their complements. If the complements are absent or one of them expresses an *unspecified quantity*, the sentence will be classified as activity. If all the non-subject complements express a *specified quantity* (SpecQ), they will be classified as accomplishment.

Unspecified quantities are all those complements that contain a mass or bare plural NP. All others are specified quantities. In case of movement verbs directional phrases should also be taken into account. Examples are:

durative: *sleep, eat*
movement: *walk, push*

The NP, PP or directional arguments are marked for '+SpecQ' or '-SpecQ'. Sentential arguments are considered to be '+SpecQ'.
This Aktionsart calculation has been inspired mainly by Verkuyl (1972).

Aspect, deictic aspect and deixis rules
The aspect, deictic aspect and deixis rules set the values for temporal attributes for verbs and introduce auxiliary verbs such as (in English) *be, have, will*. The morphological component derives the corresponding (auxiliary) verb form from these temporal attribute values. These attributes are *tense, aspect, future* and *modus* in Spanish and *tense* and *modus* in Dutch and English.

Substitution rules

The substitution rules substitute temporal adverbials for the variables. They contain conditions for Aktionsart, deixis and aspect of the sentence to express the restrictions for acceptability indicated in Section 14.3.2. The rules are mixed with the other substitution rules in such a way that interaction between quantified expressions, negation and temporal expressions is taken into account. For example, the fact that negating a sentence implies that the sentence has stative Aktionsart influences which duration adverbial is allowed, depending on the scope relations. Consider (5).

(5) a he built a house in one year
      b he did not (build a house in one year)
      c he (did not build a house) for one year

(b) TEMPORAL ADVERBIALS

Temporal adverbials are constructed in the subgrammars for NP, PP and ADVP or in a rule that introduces a temporal connective into a sentence to form an adverbial sentence in the BVtoSENTENCE subgrammar. Temporal properties from the heads are percolated to the top nodes of S-trees and restrictions on temporal properties of complements are checked in substitution rules. For example, a temporal preposition should be combined with a temporal NP to form a temporal PP. A temporal NP can be formed from a temporal N. Example:

N{temp: true}(*meeting*) → NP{temp: true}(*the meeting*)

P{temp: true, class: ref}(*during*) + NP{temp: true} (*the meeting*) →
PP{temp: true, class: ref}(*during the meeting*)

In case of a temporal adverbial sentence the temporal properties of the connective and the temporal properties of the sentence with respect to deixis, aspect and deictic aspect are decisive. Example:

C{temp: true, class: ref, aspect: imperfective}(*while*) +
SENTENCE{aspect: imperfective}(*he was working*) →
SENTENCE{temp: true, class: ref, aspect: imperfective}(*while he was working*)

Translation-equivalent temporal adverbials should be composed by corresponding translation-equivalent rules. If there are category mismatches, they are solved by the method of *isomorphic subgrammars*, (cf. Chapter 13) or they are treated as *translation idioms*, (cf. see Chapter 15).

We will conclude this section with example derivations for Dutch and English. Consider the following sentences that are translations of each other:

(6) a (D)   Jan woont hier nu al   twee jaar
        Jan lives   here now already two   year

   b (E)   Jan has been living here for two years now

Their derivations with respect to time are given in Figures 14.1 and 14.2, in which the non-terminal nodes are labelled with the names of the rules for the part of the tense or aspect verb form, followed by the semantic part between parentheses.

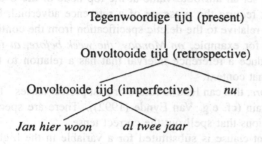

Figure 14.1: Partial derivation tree of *Jan woont hier nu al twee jaar.*

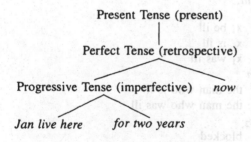

Figure 14.2: Partial derivation tree of *Jan has been living here for two years now.*

Complement, relative and adverbial sentences

Complement, relative and non-temporal adverbial sentences that contain a deictic reference adverbial, are treated just like main sentences. They are *temporally independent*, because the reference of time is specified. Note that this also holds if this reference is the moment of speech S. Examples:

(7) a I see the man *who came yesterday*
    b He said *that Pete is working*

Complement, relative and non-temporal adverbial sentences that do not contain a deictic reference adverbial are *temporally dependent* on the time reference of a preceding sentence or clause. This phenomenon is referred to as *transposition* in the literature. The difference with main sentences is that the rules accounting for deixis are called *superdeixis* rules. They spell out (parts of) tenses in the same way as deixis rules do, but they set an attribute value at the top node of the S-tree to *present* or *past*. They do not require the presence of a reference adverbial, but allow for it. Such adverbials are relative to the deictic specification from the context (e.g. a higher clause), such as, for example, *on Monday, the week before, at two o'clock*. These adverbials introduce a reference interval that has a relation to the time reference specification of that context.

If that relation is *after* or *before*, this can lead to future or past perfect tenses. The time of reference is 'shifted' again (cf. e.g. Van Eynde (1992)). There are special superdeixis rules for these situations that spell out the correct tense.

When a temporally dependent clause is substituted for a variable in the higher clause, it is checked whether its value of superdeixis agrees with the deixis or superdeixis value of that higher clause. In this way we account for the *consecutio temporum* or *transposition* phenomena. See, for example, the simplified derivation scheme for *I saw the man who is ill*:

		x_1 be ill
(i)	Rpresentsuperdeixis	x_1 is ill
(ii)	Rpastsuperdeixis	x_1 was ill

substitution of x_1 by *the man*

(i)	Rsubst,1	the man who is ill
(ii)	Rsubst,1	the man who was ill

substitution for x_2 in *I saw x_2*

(i)	Rsubst,2	blocked
(ii)	Rsubst,2	I saw the man who was ill

Furthermore, the problems with the translation of infinitival and participial forms into finite tense forms can also be solved in this way, because sentences with infinitival and participial forms which do not contain deictic adverbials are considered to be temporally dependent clauses or constituents. Note that in analysis they get a superdeixis value from the higher clause, which can be used in generation to decide on the proper finite tense form. Examples:

(8) a I saw the man *who was ill* ↔ Ik zag de *zieke* man
                      I   saw the *ill*   man

    b I expected *him to leave* ↔ Ik verwachtte *dat hij vertrok*
                      I expected   that *he left*

We have discussed this issue in Chapter 13. See Appelo (1993) for more details.

14.5 Concluding remarks

This chapter has shown how tense and aspect forms that, at first sight, cannot be translated compositionally, can be translated in a compositional framework by using a time model in which the temporal adverbials and Aktionsart of the event are also involved. It accounts for all tense and aspect forms of verbs in Dutch, English and Spanish and the translations between these languages. The crucial points in this approach are the presence or absence of temporal adverbials and the dependency of temporal adverbials in preceding sentences. Infinitival and participial sentences which do not contain deictic adverbials are considered to be temporally dependent on the higher clause. This information can be used to spell out a finite tense in another language, if necessary.

The approach is still limited, because the Rosetta system only deals with 'isolated' sentences at the time of writing. This results in a number of alternatives which have to be disambiguated in the context. The requirement, however, that every reference interval or point has to be expressed can be extended to the context. In fact, in the Rosetta system, we assumed the existence of *abstract reference adverbials* for the composition of isolated sentences such as *John came in*. This sentence would be a very strange start of a normal discourse and the abstract reference adverbial should be seen as a 'place holder' for a reference specification from the context.

Chapter 15

Idioms and complex predicates

15.1 Introduction

This chapter will discuss translation problems that have "translation in context" as a common denominator. The expressions under consideration consist of more than one word. Translation of these words separately yields wrong results. Expressions that fit this denominator are idioms, translation idioms, complex predicates and collocations.

15.1.1 Idioms

Idioms are multi-word expressions, for which a literal interpretation does not yield the correct meaning; consider (1).

(1) a kick the bucket
    b spill the beans
    c read *somebody* the riot act
    d red herring

For example, literally the expression in (1a) means *hit a specific vessel with the foot*. The idiomatic reading is *die*.

Idioms occur in all languages and, in most cases, an idiom in one language has an idiomatic translation equivalent in another. This poses a translation problem, since, as the following examples show, there is no direct correspondence in the surface forms of idioms in different languages. As (4) shows, an idiom may even correspond to one word, since *ditch* is a translation of *laten zitten*.

307

(2) a(E)   Pete kicked the bucket
    b(D)   Pete ging de pijp uit
           Pete went the pipe out
    c(S)   Pete estiró   la pata
           Pete stretched-out his paw

(3) a(E)   Pete spilled the beans
    b(D)   Pete praatte zijn mond voorbij
           Pete talked his mouth past
    c(S)   Pete habló más de la cuenta
           Pete talked much of the bill

(4) a(E)   Pete ditched his wife
    b(D)   Pete liet zijn vrouw zitten
           Pete let his wife sit
    c(S)   Pete dejó en la estacada a su mujer
           Pete left in the stockade to his wife

15.1.2   Translation idioms

A translation idiom is a complex expression that - like an ordinary idiom - is translation-equivalent to a dissimilar expression in another language, but that still has a compositional interpretation from a monolingual point of view. Examples of translation idioms are given in (5-6). The primitive expression *cocinar* in (5a) has to be translated into the complex expression *prepare a meal* (5b), which is a translation idiom.

(5) a cocinar
    b prepare a meal

(6) a madrugar
    b rise early

Translation idioms and idioms have in common that in both cases compositional translation is impossible or only possible by means of highly ad hoc grammars. The techniques developed to treat idioms can also be used for translation idioms.

15.1.3   Collocations

Collocations are expressions in which an open class head selects a word (a collocate) from a restricted class. In addition to the normal semantic restrictions, there is also a lexical restriction on the collocate. Examples of collocations are given in (7). The adjective *strong* in (7a) is selected by the noun *liquor*. The idiosyncratic nature of collocations with respect to translation is also illustrated: while *strong* in (7a) has to be translated into *sterke* in (7b), the translation of *strong* in (7c) in the context of *tobacco* is *zware*, cf. (7d).

(7) a (E)   strong liquor
    b (D)   sterke drank
    c (E)   strong tobacco
    d (D)   zware shag

In the present system, only a specific subclass has been dealt with, i.e. complex predicates. Complex predicates are expressions that consist of a verb and a noun. Examples are given below in (8).

(8) a   give a demonstration
    b   make progress
    c   give *somebody* a kick
    d   pay attention to

The verb in complex predicates does not contribute very much to the meaning of the sentence, such a verb is commonly called a 'light' verb. The noun is used in its normal meaning.

While, in the case of the idiom types, the surface structures differ across languages, the surface structures of complex predicates have comparable geometries. Another difference between idioms and complex predicates is that the latter have a normal compositional semantics and idioms do not, as we will argue below. Both in the case of idioms and complex predicates there is almost always a literal translation for the expressions, which gives rise to ambiguities.

Idioms and translation idioms will be discussed in Section 15.2, and complex predicates in Section 15.3.

15.2   Idioms

Our approach to the idiom problem is to treat idioms as non-compositional, i.e. the meaning of an idiom is not derived compositionally from its parts. This implies that the parts of an idiom do not carry meaning. (This claim has been made by several linguistic researchers, for instance Chomsky (1981), Fraser (1970), Katz (1973).)

In the following we will argue that an idiom does not have an internal semantics, by looking at one of the classic problems with idioms, i.e. its deficient syntactic behaviour. Then we will discuss the translation relation between idioms and their translation equivalent and the lexical representation of idioms.

An alternative opinion is that idioms can be treated as if they were compositional, i.e. some exceptional, idiomatic interpretation is assigned to the idiom and its parts.

In this case the meaning representation of the idiom is some complex expression. Such an approach is defended in, for example, Gazdar *et al.* (1985). We will not discuss this approach; we will merely show that our approach gives a correct account of the data.

15.2.1   Syntactic behaviour

Idiomatic expressions can undergo syntactic transformations and can therefore not be treated as a fixed string of words.

(9) a Pete broke Mary's heart
    b Mary's heart was broken by Pete
    c It was Mary's heart that Pete broke
    d It was Pete that kicked the bucket
    e It was Pete that broke Mary's heart
    f At whose door did Pete lay his failure
    g Whose heart did Pete say that Mary broke
    h Mary's heart Pete broke
    i The beans seem to have been spilled by John

For example, the idiom in (9a) has a 'passive' counterpart in (9b). It can be 'clefted' with the direct object as focus, as in sentence (9c). 'Clefting' with the subject as focus as in both (9d) and (9e) is permitted. In (9f) the PP *at whose door* and in (9g) the NP *whose heart* is subject to 'wh-movement'. In (9h) the NP *Mary's heart* is 'topicalised'. In (9i) the idiom has been 'passivised' after which the NP *the beans* has been subject to 'raising'. There are also restrictions on the behaviour of idiomatic constituents, cf. the examples in (10). All these sentences are grammatical when read literally.

(10) a *The bucket was kicked by Pete
     b *The piper tries to be paid (by John)
     c *The bucket Pete kicked
     d *It was the bucket that Pete kicked
     e *The beans John spilled were astonishing
     f *The bucket John kicked was astonishing
     h *Which bucket did John kick?

'Passivisation' in (10a), 'subject control' in (10b), 'topicalisation' in (10c), 'clefting' in (10d), 'relativisation' in (10e-f) and 'wh-questioning' in (10h) are ungrammatical in the idiomatic reading.

The central problem dealt with in this section is that while syntactic transformations are applicable to idiomatic expressions in principle, the restrictions on the syntactic behaviour of idiom parts have somehow to be accounted for. As stated above, we assume that idiom parts do not carry meaning. We will now consider other expressions that are generally assumed to have no meaning, i.e. expletives, e.g. *it*, as used in sentences that describe a circumstance such as the weather or in sentences with extraposition, and existential *there*. We will show that in relevant aspects they have the same distribution as idiom parts. We will consider three syntactic operations. Two of these operations, i.e. raising and control, exhibit a strong resemblance in surface structure and the third, i.e. topicalisation, is an example of long distance movement. 'Pied-piping' will be discussed in the section on topicalisation, which gives a good illustration of the fact that meaningful elements are moved under topicalisation. The conclusions that we will draw hold for other operations, such as wh-questioning, relativisation, pronominal reference, clefting, etc., and for all languages.

Raising

In the examples below *believe* is a 'raising-to-object' verb and *tend* a 'raising-to-subject' verb. Raising-to-object moves the subject of the subordinate clause to the object position in the main clause and raising-to-subject moves the subject of the subordinate clause to the subject position in the main clause. In (11a) *these dogs* and in (12a) *dogs* have semantic content; existential *there* in (11b) and (12b) and expletive *it* in (11c) and (12c) are non-referential.

(11) a John believes these dogs to be ill
    b John believes there to be ghosts
    c John believes it to rain

(12) a Dogs tend to be ill in California
    b There tends to be a lot of rain in California
    c It tends to rain a lot in California

So the examples with expletives show that raising applies regardless of the semantic content of the constituent to be raised. The assumption was that idiom parts did not carry meaning. The prediction is that this does not impose restrictions on the raising of idiom parts. This is borne out by the facts, cf. (13a) and (14a) in which the idiomatic NP *the beans* is meaningless, (13b) and (14b) in which the NP *the roof* does not carry meaning and (13c) and (14c) in which the NP *Mary's leg* only partially carries meaning.

(13) a John believes the beans to have been spilled
    b John believes the roof to have caved in on Pete's dreams
    c John believes Mary's leg to have been pulled

(14) a   The beans tend to be spilled
     b   The roof tends to cave in on John's dreams
     c   Mary's leg tends to be pulled

So raising is always possible. The transformation is the same for meaningful and
meaningless expressions. Other syntactic operations that show a similar behaviour
are, for example, verb second in Dutch, and object-to-subject in English and Dutch.

Control

In this subsection a phenomenon will be discussed in which two meaningful elements
are related, i.e. the control constructions. At the surface, the control structures are
similar to the raising structures. There are two types of control structures. The first
is the object control structure in (15a-b) in which the object of *instruct* (*the dog* and
it, respectively) is the subject of *fetch*. The second is the subject control structure in
(16a-b) in which the subject of *try* (*the dog* and *it*, respectively) is also the subject
of *eat*.

(15) a   John instructs the dog to fetch the newspaper
     b   John instructs it to fetch the newspaper
     c   *John instructs it to rain
     d   *John instructs there to be people

(16) a   The dog tries to eat
     b   It tries to eat
     c   *It tries to rain
     d   *There try to be people

As (15c-d) and (16c-d) illustrate, the control structures are ungrammatical if the
target of control does not carry meaning. In (15c) and (16c) the target is weather *it*
and in (15d) and (16d) existential *there*. Control is only possible under identity of
the two targets. This identity does not exist with expletives and it also cannot exist
with idioms, since idiom chunks are non-referential. This is borne out by the facts
(cf. (17-18)).

(17) a   *John instructs the beans to be spilled
     b   *John instructs Mary's leg to be pulled
     c   *John instructs the piper to be paid
     d   *John instructs the cat to get his tongue

(18) a   *The beans try to be spilled
     b   *Mary's leg tries to be pulled
     c   *The piper tries to be paid
     d   *The cat tries to get his tongue

Topicalisation

This paragraph gives an example of long distance movement, i.e. topicalisation. Under this operation a constituent is moved to a position at the front of the sentence. Consider the following examples.[1]

(19) a He saw John
     b John he saw

(20) a He believes the unicorns to be there
     b There he believes the unicorns to be

(21) a He believes this man to have won the race
     b This man he believes to have won the race

(22) a   He believes there to be unicorns
     b *There he believes to be unicorns

In the (b) sentences variants of the (a) sentences are given in which part of the sentence is topicalised. In (19) the object *John* is topicalised, in (20) the locative adverbial *there* and in (21) the subject of the subordinate clause *this man*. In (22) topicalisation of existential *there* is not allowed. This is not due to the fact that *there* cannot be topicalised at all, cf. (20), nor is it due to the fact that elements cannot be topicalised out of these positions, cf. (21). Existential *there* does not carry meaning and therefore it cannot be the focus of topicalisation.

The prediction is that idiom parts behave in the same way and this is borne out by the facts. Consider the following sentences:

(23) a Pete read the riot act to the class
     b To the class Pete read the riot act

(24) a John spilled the beans
     b *The beans John spilled

(25) a John believes Mary's heart to be broken
     b Mary's heart John believes to be broken

---

[1]No examples are given to show that meaningless *it* cannot undergo topicalisation, since *it*, even if it is meaningful, cannot be the focus of topicalisation at all, cf.:

a   John gave it to Mary
b *It John gave to Mary

(26) a Pete broke Mary's heart
     b Mary's heart Pete broke

In (23) the object *to the class* is topicalised; this is a free argument of the idiom
and has meaning. In (24) the object *the beans* has no meaning and therefore cannot
be topicalised. In (25) the subject of the subordinate clause and in (26) the object
Mary's heart is topicalised; *heart* is an idiom part and has no meaning. The NPs
do, however, contain a free argument, i.e. *Mary* which has semantic content. The
fact that *Mary* in (25) and (26) is a free argument makes it possible to topicalise
out of these positions, while it is impossible to topicalise constituents out of these
positions if such constituents do not contain a meaningful subpart.

This is an example of a general phenomenon, since in these configurations, if
a subpart of an expression is the focus of topicalisation, a larger constituent has to
be moved according to the principle of so-called pied-piping (cf. for instance Ross
(1967)). In (27), if *Pete* is the focus of topicalisation, the NP *Pete's book* has to be
moved, cf. the ungrammaticality of (27c-d).

(27) a   John bought Pete's book
     b   Pete's book John bought
     c   *Pete John bought book
     d   *Pete's John bought book

For a more elaborate discussion of the deficient syntactic behaviour of idioms and
types of expressions that behave similarly, cf. Schenk (1992).

15.2.2 The syntactic treatment of idioms

In the foregoing sections it has been argued that the deficient syntactic behaviour of
idioms is accounted for if we assume that idiom parts do not carry meaning. We
have shown this by comparing the distribution of expletives with that of idiom parts
and we have shown that the distribution is similar. So the general rule scheme that
is necessary for expletives is also used for idiom parts.

Generatively speaking, the rule scheme is as follows (analysis is the reverse).
After the start rules and verb pattern rules, there is a canonical structure for the sentence that is to be derived. In Section 15.2.3, we will give examples of the canonical
structure of idioms and how it is generated in the lexicon. In this canonical structure,
the argument positions are variables like NPVAR, PPVAR, ADJPVAR, etc., except
for idiom parts and expletives. In the case of idioms and expletives, the meaningless constituents are fully specified constituents with categories like NP, PP, ADJP,
etc. Rules and transformations are applicable to this canonical structure in a certain
order and eventually the substitution rules are applicable that substitute a variable
by an S-tree (cf. Chapter 3). Rules and transformations that are applicable before

the substitution rules are, for example, raising, equi, topicalisation, verb second, questioning, etc. The transformations and rules in the grammar are made sensitive to the different category types in order to capture the different behaviour of meaningless and meaningful constituents. In this way the deficient syntactic behaviour of expletives and idiom parts is accounted for. The rule scheme is more general, since expletives are restricted to occurrence in subject and object positions and idiom parts can also occur in other positions. Consider the examples in (28). These sentences are grammatical when read literally, but not in the idiomatic interpretation.

(28) a *Yvonne put the cart before the brown horse
     b *How dry did Alexander keep his powder?
     c *Before the horse Stefanie put the cart

15.2.3   Translation relation and lexical representation

Translation relation

As shown in Chapter 2, every basic expression is mapped onto a basic meaning. The basic expressions discussed there are syntactic primitives. In the case of idioms, a semantic primitive does not coincide with a single word. For example, the idiom *kick the bucket* has the idiomatic primitive meaning *die*, but the syntactic primitives are *kick*, *the* and *bucket*. An idiom is treated as a complex basic expression, i.e. an expression with an internal structure, which has a primitive meaning (cf. Schenk (1986)). In analogy to simple basic expressions, the translation relation between a complex basic expression (an idiom) in one language and a basic expression in another language, which may be simple or complex, is established by relating the basic expressions in the different languages to a basic meaning.

There is a difference in use between an idiom and its literal paraphrase, since an idiom and its paraphrase cannot always be interchanged. This can be accounted for by assuming style levels, cf. (29).

(29) a(D)   John verliet zijn vrouw
            John left   his wife
     b(E)   John ditched his wife
     c(D)   John liet zijn vrouw zitten
            John let his   wife sit
     d(D)   John gaat de pijp uit
            John goes the pipe out
     e(E)   John kicks the bucket

Simple expressions like *left* and *ditched* cannot be interchanged, because they are not on the same style level. Style levels play an important role in translation, for idioms even more so than for words. *Ditch* is a translation of the idiom *laten zitten*, because they have the same style level. So style levels are necessary for simple words and can also be used for idioms. Also consider (29d-e); the idiomatic expression *de pijp uitgaan* can be translated into *kick the bucket* because they have the same style level. This is accounted for in Rosetta by establishing a translation relation between words that have the same style level.

Lexical representation

Generatively speaking, syntactic rules and transformations are applicable to the canonical structure of an idiom (cf. Section 15.2.2). As an example, the canonical syntactic representation of the idiom *kick the bucket* is given in Figure 15.1. A syntactic representation is canonical when no syntactic transformations or rules have been applied to that structure. For example, if there is a passive transformation, the active form is canonical. The NP dominating *the bucket* is fully specified to account for the syntactic behaviour. Note that the structure in Figure 15.1 is simplified, for example the attribute-value pairs at the nodes have been omitted. There are several

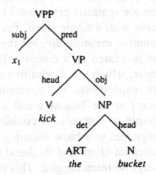

Figure 15.1: Syntactic representation of *kick the bucket*.

reasons why the idiom should not be represented in the dictionary as a syntactic representation. The main reason will be discussed here. For a further elaboration cf. Schenk (1989).

As shown above, the syntactic representation has to be comparable to non-idiomatic structures, because idioms can undergo syntactic operations. More generally, the representation has to be similar to non-idiomatic structures with roughly the same form in relevant aspects, i.e. it is constructed with existing lexical items and with existing syntactic rules. If a syntactic structure like Figure 15.1 were listed in the dictionary as such, the grammar would have no control over the structure and there would be no guarantee that such a structure is correct according to the grammar. Therefore, in Rosetta, a set of 'idiom derivation trees' is specified in the dictionary. Every element in this set defines the syntactic representation of a specific idiom. An idiom derivation tree specifies which rules have to be applied to which basic expressions to form the syntactic representation of a specific idiom. As an example, the idiom derivation tree for *kick the bucket* is given in Figure 15.2. The tree is simplified for expository reasons. In Figure 15.2, a start rule RSTARTV2 is

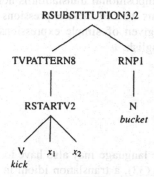

Figure 15.2: Idiom derivation tree for *kick the bucket*.

applicable to a verb, in this case *kick*, that takes two arguments, and it specifies that the first argument has to be realised in subject position yielding (30a). A verb pattern rule TVPATTERN8 specifies that the second argument has to be represented as an object in the verb phrase, giving (30b). A substitution rule RSUBSTITUTION3 substitutes the NP *the bucket*, represented in (30c), which is made by rule RNP1 on the basis of the noun *bucket*, for the variable with index 2, yielding (30d), which was also represented in Figure 15.1. The article *the* is introduced syncategorematically in rule RNP1 of Figure 15.2. The rules are taken from the existing set of syntactic rules and the lexical elements are taken from the syntactic lexicon.

(30) a $VPP[subj/x_1, pred/VP[head/V, arg/x_2]]$
   b $VPP[subj/x_1, pred/VP[head/V, obj/x_2]]$
   c $NP[det/ART, head/N]$
   d $VPP[subj/x_1, pred/VP[head/V, obj/NP [det/ART, head/N]]]$

Furthermore, there are the simple entries in the syntactic lexicon that are necessary for this idiom, i.e. *the*, *bucket* and *kick*, cf. Chapter 7. These are the normal entries for these words.

15.2.4 Translation idioms

The techniques developed for establishing the translation relation between idioms described above can also be used to solve other translation problems, particularly if a word in one language does not correspond to a single word in another language, but to a larger expression. This larger expression does not have to be an idiom from a monolingual point of view, since it may have a compositional semantics. In spite of the compositional semantics a compositional translation is not possible. Because of the technical similarity with idioms we call these expressions *translation idioms*.

In (31) and (32) examples are given of simple expressions in Spanish corresponding to translation idioms in English.

(31) a cocinar
      b prepare a meal

(32) a madrugar
      b rise early

Of course, a translation idiom in one language may also have to be translated into a complex expression in the other. In (33), a translation idiom in Dutch corresponds to a simple expression in Spanish and an idiom in English. In (34), an example is given of a correspondence between two complex expressions; the combination of a verb, an object and a prepositional object has to be translated into a combination of a verb, an object and a subordinate clause in which the verb takes an object.

(33) a(D)   verliefd worden
          in love   become
     b(S)   enamorarse
     c(E)   fall in love

(34) a(E)   send *somebody* for *something*
     b(S)   mandar a *alguien* a buscar *algo*
          ask   to someone to get   something

Expressions like these are listed in the dictionary as if they were idioms, as a syntactic derivation tree. The translation relation is established similarly to idioms.

A compositional translation of the translation idiom is always possible and, in several cases, even necessary, cf. (35-37). *Prepare a meal* can be translated into both *cocinar* and *preparar la comida*. In (36), the translation into *cocinar* is not possible, because the NP *the meal* is modified. A similar argument holds for (37).

(35) a(E)   Jan prepares a meal
     b(S)   Jan cocina
     c(S)   Jan prepara una comida

(36) a(E)   The meal Jan prepares is nice
   b(S)   La comida que Jan prepara es buena

(37) a(E)   Jan rises early
   b(S)   Jan madruga
   c(S)   Jan se levanta temprano

Despite the fact that there is always a compositional translation for a translation idiom, the technique is necessary, because, if the source language is Spanish, for example the expression *madrugar* can only be translated into *rise early* in English.

15.2.5 The recognition of idioms

As illustrated in Section 15.2.3, an idiom is a basic expression with an explicit constituent structure. In the lexicon it is represented as a syntactic derivation tree that specifies how the canonical constituent structure of the idiom can be derived.

Obviously, this way of representing idioms is only one part of the solution. The grammars have to be organised in such a way that they can deal with these complex basic expressions. Therefore we will go into the organisation of the Rosetta grammars as far as is necessary to clarify the treatment of idioms. In this section we discuss the grammars from the *analytical* point of view and show in particular how a basic expression corresponding to an idiom can be isolated during syntactic analysis.

We will illustrate the relevant aspects of the Rosetta grammars by showing a part of the analysis process of the English sentence *Did he kick the bucket?*, which has both a literal and an idiomatic reading.

The first rules that apply to a sentence in analysis are the Mood rules, i.e. rules that determine whether the sentence is interrogative, imperative or declarative, etc., and whether the sentence is a main or subordinate clause. For the sentence to be analysed it is determined that it is a main clause and a yes-no question, and the structure is changed in such a way that the syntactic aspects expressing this (inverted order of the auxiliary and subject) disappear. The result of applying this rule is S(*he did kick the bucket*).

Next, the substitution rules must apply. In analysis, these rules 'desubstitute' elements from a sentence. They apply iteratively, i.e. zero or more times, the maximum being determined by the number of arguments in the sentence. A condition on the application of these rules guarantees that an argument is desubstituted only if no occurrences of variables to the right of it exist. In the sentence being dealt with here there are two potential arguments, i.e. *he* and *the bucket*. The following ways to proceed with the analysis process are now possible:

- no substitution rule is applied at all: S(*he did kick the bucket*)

- only *the bucket* is desubstituted: S(*he did kick* x_2)

- only *he* is desubstituted: S(x_1 *did kick the bucket*)

- first *he* is desubstituted, and after this *the bucket* is desubstituted:
  S(x_1 *did kick* x_2)

Other options are not available, e.g. it is not possible to first desubstitute *the bucket* and after that *he*, because in that case a variable occurs to the right of *he* at the moment it is desubstituted. The NPs desubstituted from these structures (*he*, *the bucket*) are analysed themselves, and are found to be well-formed NPs of English.

The analysis process is continued for all four options. Tense and Aspect rules apply to determine the tense and aspect of the sentence and they undo the syntactic and morphological encoding of these properties (the past tense of the auxiliary verb *do* in the example being discussed). This yields the following four structures:

- S(*he do kick the bucket*)

- S(*he do kick* x_2)

- S(x_1 *do kick the bucket*)

- S(x_1 *do kick* x_2)

Next, rules apply that turn the structures given into a propositional unit with a verb as its head (called VPPs). These rules remove the auxiliary verb *do*. Voice is determined (the sentences are in active voice). This yields:

- VPP(*he kick the bucket*)

- VPP(*he kick* x_2)

- VPP(x_1 *kick the bucket*)

- VPP(x_1 *kick* x_2)

The verb pattern rules are applied to these structures. They check whether the arguments of a verb are realised syntactically in the right way. Among the verb pattern rules there is a rule which states that a transitive verb (as the verb *kick* is) must realise its two arguments as a subject and a direct object. All four structures satisfy this requirement.

After application of the verb pattern rules the start rules are applied. These start rules break the structure down into a basic expression and a number of syntactic variables. For the four structures mentioned the following candidate results can be formed:

- candidate basic expression *he kick the bucket* + zero variables

- candidate basic expression *he kick* + x_2

- candidate basic expression *kick the bucket* + x_1

- candidate basic expression *kick* + x_1 + x_2

These results will be found to be well-formed if the candidate basic expressions occur in the basic lexicon as actual basic expressions. Remember that we presented the rules in a simplified notation and that the candidate basic expressions in fact have the form of constituent structures. The candidate basic expression in the fourth example (*kick*) is a single word and it can easily be recognised as an actual basic expression by looking at whether it exists in the basic lexicon. It does, and this implies that an analysis has been found for the literal interpretation of the sentence. For the other three candidate basic expressions, a check is made of whether there is a idiom in the basic lexicon, i.e. whether there is a syntactic derivation tree that derives one of these expressions. The result of this process is that the candidate basic expression in the third example is recognised as a basic expression (the idiom *kick the bucket*), but the first and second example are not and so the corresponding analysis paths are rejected.

Notice the role that variables play in this treatment. They indicate the number of free arguments taken by the basic expressions. In the literal interpretation of the sentence two variables occur (x_1 and x_2), corresponding to the fact that the verb *kick* takes two free arguments. In the idiomatic interpretation one variable occurs (x_1), corresponding to the fact that the idiom *kick the bucket* takes one free argument.

15.2.6   Fixed idioms

Some idioms and translation idioms can be treated as strings. These expressions, which we call *fixed idioms*, consist of several words, the order of which cannot be changed by syntactic operations. Also, no other words can intervene between the words of the fixed idiom. Furthermore, it is possible to assign a lexical category to expressions of this type, like noun or adjective. These idioms are treated in Rosetta as though they were simple words without any relevant internal structure and are listed in the dictionary as strings. For example *red herring* is represented in the dictionary as a noun. Some examples are given below in (38). It is permitted to apply morphological operations to them, for example for deriving the plural form *red herrings*. Fixed idioms can be non-compositional, as in (38a), or a translation idiom, as in (38e).

(38) a(E)   red herring
     b(D)   kant en klaar
             lace and ready (ready-made)
     c(E)   by and large
     d(E)   to and fro
     e(E)   naar huis[2]
             to   house (home)

Note that the notion 'fixed idiom' is merely technical. From a linguistic point of view there does not seem to be sufficient motivation to treat these expressions as one word. It is always possible to represent a fixed idiom with the techniques for the 'flexible' idioms described above. There are two reasons, however, to treat fixed idioms as strings. The first is simplicity. A second reason is that, in some cases, it is not very appealing to treat these expressions as flexible idioms. Consider (39): the suffix *er* in *goeder* is a remnant of Dutch grammar rules that have ceased to exist. If this expression were to be treated as a flexible idiom, this implies that rules that deal with these phenomena would have to be added to the grammar. This is not very efficient, however, since these rules are not productive.

(39) a(D)   te goeder trouw
             to goodaffix faith
     b(E)   in good faith

15.3   Complex predicates

Two aspects of complex predicates will be discussed: first, the way the translation relation is established between complex predicates, and second, the problem of the so-called 'argument merge'.

15.3.1   Translation relation and the dictionary

A complex predicate consists of a verb and a noun. The noun has its 'normal' interpretation, but the verb is not used in its regular meaning. We will argue that translation of complex predicates can be done in a compositional way. The parts of a complex predicate cannot be translated in isolation, however, because there are differences between the light verbs of a complex predicate in for example English and Dutch, given a certain complement, e.g. *have a bath* and *have a shower* are translated into *een bad nemen* (*take a bath*) and *een douche nemen* (*take a shower*)

---

[2]This type of construction is very productive in Dutch and English cf. *naar school (to school), in school, per trein (by train).* It is not fully productive, however, cf. *naar de universiteit (to the university),* **naar universiteit.* The principles underlying this semi-regularity are unknown.

and not literally into *een bad hebben* and *een douche hebben*. Note that the *nemen*-equivalents do exist in English, cf. *take a bath* and *take a shower*. Another illustration of the idiosyncratic nature of the phenomenon is that while *make a journey, make a bow, make an appeal* and *make an attempt* belong to the same class in English, according to Cattell (1984), only the former two are translated into Dutch in *maken* (*make*) + complement, cf. *een reis maken* and *een buiging maken*; the latter two have to be translated into *doen* (*do*) + complement, i.e. *een verzoek doen* and *een poging doen* and not *een verzoek maken* and *een poging maken*.

In a complex predicate, the noun selects the light verb. This is represented in CP-DICT. The dictionary entries for a complex predicate are as follows. If a noun is part of a complex predicate, two attributes are specified (apart from the standard attribute value pairs of the noun):

1. The syntactic key of the light verb that is part of the complex predicate.

2. The complement of the noun, i.e. the arguments that are in the subcategorisation pattern of the noun. This can be done in two ways:

   (a) A set of noun patterns is specified. This is the case when there is no verb corresponding to the noun.

   (b) Reference is made to the verb that corresponds to the noun and a mapping is made from the set of patterns of the verb to the set of noun patterns. This is necessary to account for the direct relation between the patterns of the verb and the noun, cf. (40). The direct object of the verb *demonstrate* in (40a) is realised as an *of* PP in (40b) and the *to* PP in (40a) is realised as part of the NP in (40b), but cf. argument merge in Section 15.3.2.

   (40) a John demonstrated Rosetta to the students
        b John gave a demonstration of Rosetta to the students

   Another example is (41). Normally the verb *give* can take two arguments in the VP. Sentence (41d) is ill-formed though, because the corresponding verb *sneeze* does not take an argument in the VP, cf. (41c).

   (41) a   John sneezed
        b   John gave a sneeze
        c   *John sneezed to Mary
        d   *John gave a sneeze to Mary

At the entry for the verb a syntactic key is specified, which is the key of the light verb in the complex predicate. This light verb key corresponds to a meaning key. For example, the meaning key for *make* in *make a blunder* corresponds to the syntactic key for *maken* if the noun is *blunder* in Dutch and to *slaan* if the noun is *flater*.

As sketched globally in Figure 15.3, the translation relation is established as follows. If in M-PARSER in a sentence there is the possibility of a complex predicate, the key of the verb is compared with the specification at the dictionary entry of the noun. If they match, the expression is considered to be a complex predicate and the key of the verb is replaced by the syntactic key of the light verb. This key is then mapped on the meaning key for the light verb in A-TRANSFER. The correspondence between this key and the syntactic key of a light verb in another language is established in G-TRANSFER. In M-GENERATOR, this key is replaced by a normal syntactic key on the basis of the specification at the dictionary entry of the noun.

Syntax language 1

Syntactic Verb Key + Syntactic Noun Key

Syntactic Light Verb Key + Syntactic Noun Key

Semantics (Interlingua)

Semantic Light Verb Key + Semantic Noun Key

Syntax Language 2

Syntactic Light Verb Key + Syntactic Noun Key

Syntactic Verb Key + Syntactic Noun Key

Figure 15.3: Translation relation between complex predicates.

15.3.2   Argument merge

Argument merge is the technique that is used to account for the observation that the arguments in the subcategorisation pattern of the noun can also be realised in the VP as shown in (42). Cattell (1984) observed that it is possible for the *to* complement of the noun to surface as a *to* PP under the VP and as an indirect object under the VP. Cattell's examples are given in (42b-c) (his (50a-b), p. 66).

(42) a The demonstration to the students was given by Harry
     b Harry gave a demonstration of the new technique to
       the students
     c Harry gave the students a demonstration of the new
       technique

However, Cattell overlooked the fact that a PP such as *to the students* can also be part of the NP *the demonstration*. (42a) shows that the *to* PP is a modifier of the noun *demonstration*. In (42a) the PP *to the students* is moved to subject position as a part of the NP, so the NP *the demonstration* and the PP *to the students* have to be one constituent. In (42b-c), the indirect object occurs in the two dative positions due to dative shift. These dative positions have to be inside the VP. So we have to assume that the following three structures, in Figures 15.4, 15.5 and 15.6, are the representation of the complex predicate.

Looking at it from a generative point of view, this is accounted for in Rosetta as

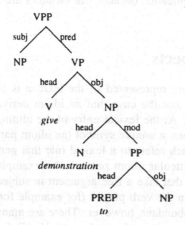

Figure 15.4: *Give demonstration*; complement is modifier of NP.

follows. In the start rule, in which the complex predicate is created, if the noun has a non-empty subcategorisation pattern, the arguments are realised not only in the noun phrase, but also in the verb phrase. For the complex predicate *give demonstration*, for example, this results in the structures of figures 15.4, 15.5 and 15.6. False paths which are created here[3] are eliminated in the substitution rules, since none of the

---

[3]This is the theoretical account. In the actual implementation, a technique is used in the start rule that creates the complex predicate, such that false paths are not created. We will not discuss this here.

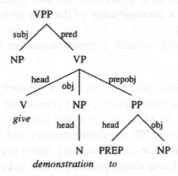

Figure 15.5: *Give demonstration*; complement is prepositional object NP.

substitution rules will be applicable, because the variables are at the wrong levels in the S-tree.

15.4   Practical aspects

The way in which idioms are represented in the lexicon is more economical than was suggested above. It is not the case that an idiom derivation tree is given in the lexicon for every idiom. At the lexical entry of the idiom, next to the syntactic keys of the words in an idiom, a unique symbol (an idiom pattern) for the syntactic derivation tree is given, which refers to a lexical rule that generates (or parses) the syntactic structure for a particular idiom pattern. An example of an idiom pattern is the pattern for all idioms that take a free argument in subject position and a verb and an object noun phrase in the verb phrase (for example for *kick the bucket*).

Practical problems are abundant, however. There are many idioms and collocations, in every language. A count, performed on the Van Dale Contemporary Dutch dictionary, shows that there are tens of thousands of Dutch idioms. Since there are no lists of idioms and collocations in a form that could be transformed automatically into a form that can be used in a natural language processing system, collection of these expressions has to be done for the larger part manually on the basis of specifications in paper dictionaries. The two main problems are:

1. Paper dictionaries give no clear definition of idioms and collocations. This implies that idioms and collocations are not easy to find.

2. Usually, in paper dictionaries, the expressions are given in examples. For

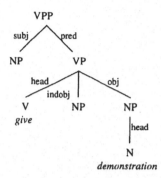

Figure 15.6: *Give demonstration*; complement is indirect object NP.

instance, an idiom like *read somebody the riot act* is represented in an example, e.g. *John read the class the riot act*. It is impossible to extract the idiom from such a representation automatically.

15.5 Concluding remarks

In this chapter we have discussed a number of translation problems, which we have solved compositionally and systematically. The power of the solutions is illustrated by the fact that no grammatical components other than the syntactic lexicon have to be adapted to accommodate the different types. This means that it is not necessary to refer to the idiomatic or collocational status of an expression in morphology, syntax or semantics. In the syntactic component, the rule scheme that was necessary for the treatment of the deficient behaviour of idiom parts was already necessary for expletives.

An elegant treatment of a phenomenon related to complex predicates that has remained unnoticed in the linguistic literature until now, i.e. argument merge, has been presented.

Chapter 16

Scope and negation

16.1 Introduction

One of the translation-relevant phenomena which a machine translation system has to deal with is the phenomenon of *scope*. Characteristic of scope bearing elements is the possibility that a combination of two or more of them has two or more interpretations. For example, (1) has at least two interpretations, one with *every man* having wide scope and one with *a woman* having wide scope:

(1)   *Every man* loves *a woman*

The two corresponding logical expressions are:

(2) a $\forall x[man(x) \rightarrow \exists y[woman(y) \wedge love(x,y)]]$
   b $\exists y[woman(y) \wedge \forall x[man(x) \rightarrow love(x,y)]]$

These expressions can be read as follows:

  a For all x holds that if x is a man then there exists a y such that y is a woman and x loves y, or, less formally, *all men love some woman*.

  b There exists a y such that y is a woman and for all x holds that if x is a man then x loves y, in other words, *there is a woman who is loved by all men*.

The quantificational expressions *every man* and *a woman* are called scope bearing elements.

This chapter is concerned with the translation of two classes of scope bearing elements:

329

1. *Q-phrases.* This class consists of NPs and adverbials containing a quantifier[1] like:

	DUTCH	ENGLISH	SPANISH
NPs	veel kinderen	many children	muchos niños
	een vis	a fish	un pez
Adverbials	vaak	often	muchas veces
	in sommige gevallen	in some cases	en algunos casos

2. *NEG,* containing both the adverbs *niet* (Dutch), *not* (English) and *no* (Spanish), and quantifiers with morphologically incorporated negation, such as *niets* (Dutch), *nothing* (English) and *nada* (Spanish).

For reasons of clarity and space, only Q-NP and NEG examples will be discussed here; other Q-phrases, however, can be treated in a similar way.

The following sections will explain what kind of scope phenomena and Q-phrases exist (Section 16.2), how scope in the Rosetta approach can be dealt with in general (Section 16.3), which translation problems remain (Section 16.4), and how these problems have been solved (Section 16.5). Finally, Section 16.6 contains some concluding remarks.

16.2   Scope and negation

This section discusses what kind of scope and negation phenomena have to be dealt with. First, a principle that we will call *Jackendoff's principle* will be discussed (Section 16.2.1), then quantifiers with a negative counterpart (Section 16.2.2) and non-scope-sensitive quantifiers (Section 16.2.3) will be described. Finally, a subdivision of quantifiers will be given (Section 16.2.4).

16.2.1   Jackendoff's principle

As already explained above, sentences with more than one scope bearing element can have more than one interpretation. An example of an analysis accounting for this systematic ambiguity is Montague's PTQ (see e.g. Thomason (1974), Dowty *et al.* (1981), Montague (1973)). Following the PTQ approach, it would be natural to assign all interpretations to sentences with Q-phrases. For sentence (1), for example, this would result in two derivation trees in which the 'scope domain' of a Q-phrase within a sentence is indicated by the order of substitution, as is illustrated in Figure 16.1. The later (or higher) a Q-phrase is substituted, the wider its scope is.

---

[1]The notion of quantifier is used here in a rather restricted sense. Determiners that occur in so-called referring expressions, such as definite articles, and possessive and demonstrative pronouns, are excluded from it.

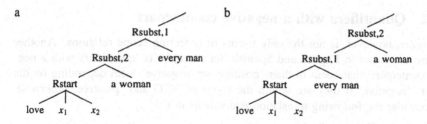

Figure 16.1: Partial and simplified derivation trees for *Every man loves a woman*.

The two interpretations for sentence (1) are not equally plausible, however. The interpretation with *every man* having wide scope, (2a), is far more natural. Although judgements are often unclear, most of the time the surface order of scope bearing elements reflects the intended scope relations: the leftmost element has wide scope. If this preference exists in all languages, then it is preserved in translation if the word order of Q-phrases is preserved.

We will assume that this preference exists in all the languages dealt with here and, therefore, we will make the simplifying assumption that *surface order* in principle represents the most *plausible* scope order of Q-phrases and NEG *within a clause*. This is in accordance with Jackendoff's principle (cf. Jackendoff (1972)):

> *A Q/NEG element has scope over the Q/NEG elements on its right and is itself inside the scope of the Q/NEG elements on its left.*

Thus, the *scope domain* of a Q/NEG element consists of all elements on its right within a clause. Note that this principle implies that other important factors are not taken into consideration, such as:

- *Intonation*, which is not visible in a written text. Therefore, all sentences will be considered under neutral intonation here.

- *Context*. Currently, only isolated sentences will be taken into consideration.

The essential claim now is that, even if we assume that a sentence like (1) is ambiguous because there are two scope readings, both this sentence and its translations into Dutch and Spanish will have the same *most plausible reading* as long as the Q-phrases have the same surface order. Furthermore, only this 'most plausible reading' will be taken into account and it will be the basis for the scope treatment in the Rosetta approach. So only Figure 16.1a will be accepted as a derivation tree of sentence (1).[2]

---

[2]Note that this may turn out to be a problematic approach in case of an extension from translating isolated sentences to texts because the other interpretation could be needed.

16.2.2   Quantifiers with a negative counterpart

Word order, however, is not the only means of reflecting scope relations. Another phenomenon found in English and Spanish, for example, is 'quantifiers with a negative counterpart' that occur in their 'positive' or 'negative' form depending on the context: 'negative' if they are within the scope of NEG and 'positive' otherwise. Now consider the following translation equivalents in (3):

(3) a(D) Jan heeft *iemand   niet* gegroet
       Jan has   somebody not greeted
   b(S) Jan *no* ha saludado *a alguien*
       Jan not has greeted   to somebody
   c(E) Jan did *not* greet *somebody*

In the Dutch sentence (3a) the *word order* (iemand – niet) expresses the scope in the sentence. In Spanish and English, (3b,c), the word order of scope elements is not the same as in Dutch (no – alguien / not – somebody). In this case the quantifier is clearly outside the scope of the negation despite the word order. *Alguien* and *somebody* are inherently 'positive', i.e. outside the scope of the negation, irrespective of their position in the sentence. In (4) their 'negative counterparts', which are inherently inside the scope of the negation, are used:

(4) a(D) Jan heeft *niemand*[3] gezien
       Jan has   nobody   seen
   b(S) Jan no ha visto *a nadie*
       Jan not has seen   nobody
   c(E) Jan did not see *anybody*

In the Spanish and English sentences, *nadie* and *anybody* have to be used in this interpretation, respectively, instead of *alguien* and *somebody*.

It should be noted that these sentences with NEG are not ambiguous with respect to scope in contrast to many sentences like (1) containing only Q-NPs as scope bearing elements. In Dutch, the word order of Q-phrases with respect to NEG determines the scope order unambiguously most of the time. In English and Spanish only a combination of NEG and quantifiers that have a negative counterpart determines the scope without any ambiguity.

16.2.3   Non-scope-sensitive quantifiers

For certain types of Q-phrases the surface order with respect to NEG is not crucial for the interpretation; these phrases always have wide scope, regardless of their po-

---

[3] We treat *niemand* as a morphological contraction of *niet + iemand*. Morphological contraction is a phenomenon that occurs in Dutch and English: at surface *niet/no* + certain Q-NPs adjacent to NEG contract to one word. E.g. *niet + iemand → niemand* in Dutch, *not + anybody → nobody* in English.

sition. For example:

DUTCH	ENGLISH	SPANISH
sommige N	some N	algunos/algunas N
de meeste N	most N	los/las más N

However, these phrases do contain a quantifier and there is clearly a strong preference for a surface order which reflects the scope. Therefore, (5b) is a much more natural word order than (5a), although both sentences have in fact the same meaning. (For some speakers (5a) is even out).

(5) a(*D*)*Niemand* gelooft *sommige opmerkingen*
      Nobody   believes some   remarks

  b(*D*)*Sommige opmerkingen* gelooft *niemand*
      Some   remarks   believes nobody

16.2.4 Subdivision of quantifiers

To get to grips with all these kinds of quantifiers, we divided the terms involved in the following way (only NPs are taken into account here):

(1) Q-NPs: NPs containing a quantifier.
    They are marked *[+Q]*. They can be subdivided:

    (1.A) Q-NPS SENSITIVE TO SCOPE.
        For these NPs and for NEG surface order is crucial for the interpretation. These scope-sensitive Q-NPs are marked *[+S]* . For languages that have quantifiers with a negative counterpart again a subdistinction can be made which will be marked by the feature *[P]* (P from 'polarity'). We will refer to them as *[P]*-quantifiers. They can have two values:

        (1.A.a) POSITIVE.
            The form that occurs in 'positive' contexts (i.e. without a NEG) and in case the quantifier is outside the scope of NEG.
            They are marked *[+P]* .
        (1.A.b) NEGATIVE.
            The form that occurs in a 'negative' context (i.e. containing a NEG) in case the quantifier is inside the scope of NEG.
            They are marked *[-P]*.

        Note that this subdistinction is language-specific.

    (1.B) Q-NPS NOT SENSITIVE TO SCOPE.
        The surface order of these Q-NPs and NEG is not crucial for the interpretation; these NPs always have wide scope, irrespective of their position. They are marked *[-S]*.

(2) NON Q-NP: NPs that do not contain a quantifier.
   The surface order is irrelevant for scope interpretation.
   Such NPs have the features *[–S] [–Q]*.

It will be clear that the [Q] and [S] values of expressions are translation-relevant,
but the [P] value is language-specific and not relevant for all expressions. For NPs,
the [P] value exists in English and Spanish, but not in Dutch, and is only relevant
for some of the expressions with value [+S][+Q]. In Table 16.1, for a number of
quantifiers the values of these features are presented.

	DUTCH	ENGLISH		SPANISH	
[+S] [+Q]	iemand	somebody	*[+P]*	alguien	*[+P]*
		anybody	*[–P]*	nadie	*[–P]*
	iets	something	*[+P]*	algo	*[+P]*
		anything	*[–P]*	nada	*[–P]*
	iedereen	everybody	-	todo el mundo	-
	veel N	many N	-	muchos/as N	-
	alle N	all N	-	todos/as los/las N	-
	twee N	two N	-	dos N	-
[–S] [+Q]	sommige N	sóme N		algunos/as N	
	de meeste N	most N		los/las más N	
[–S] [–Q]	Jan	John		Juan	
	jullie	you		vosotros/vosotras	
	de vele N	the many N		los/las muchos/as N	
	het boek	the book		el libro	

Table 16.1: Subdivision of quantifiers.

16.3   Application in Rosetta: Right-Left Substitution

As a basis for the treatment of scope and negation in Rosetta, we adopted a combination of the PTQ approach and Jackendoff's principle, explained in Section 16.2.1.

16.3.1   Scope

Consider (6b), which is a simplified part of the syntactic derivation tree of (6a)
which contains two Q-NPs.

(6) a *Iedereen* leest *twee boeken*
   Everybody reads two   books
   b

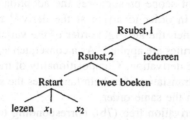

```
                          Rsubst,1
                         /        \
                 Rsubst,2          iedereen
                /        \
          Rstart          twee boeken
         /      \
    lezen   x₁   x₂
```

In this tree, *twee boeken* and *iedereen* are abbreviated syntactic derivation trees for NPs in (6b).

The derivation process takes place bottom-up. The moment of substitution of a Q-phrase indicates its scope domain. In (6b) *iedereen* is substituted later than *twee boeken*, so it has wider scope. In other words, for the most plausible reading of a sentence the Q-phrases are substituted from right to left in generation (*Right-Left Substitution*). There are conditions on the applicability of substitution rules and negation rules forcing this surface order, basically following conditions (I) and (II) below.[4] Note that variables, like e.g. variables for NPs, have features such as [S], [Q], etc. A Q-NP can only be substituted for a variable with the same feature values. These feature values are maintained during translation.

(I) An argument-substitution rule (*Rsubst,x*) for a Q-phrase with value [+S][+Q] only applies if there are no free variables (from now on VARs) with value [+S][+Q], to the right of the variable to be substituted.

(II) A negation rule (*Rneg*) only applies if there are no free VARs with value [+S][+Q] to the right of the position where NEG is inserted.

For (6a) this means that the output of the rules is as follows (details are omitted):

   Rstart: x_1[+S][+Q] x_2[+S][+Q] lezen
   Rsubst,2: x_1[+S][+Q] twee boeken leest
   Rsubst,1: iedereen   twee boeken leest

(Note that to derive (6a), rules for person and tense of the verb, and a rule to put the verb in second position (Dutch is an SOV language: Chapter 11) have to apply additionally.)

Rsubst,1 cannot apply before *Rsubst,2* under condition (I) stated above, since x_2, a free [+S][+Q] VAR to the right of x_1, has not been substituted for yet. In other

---

[4]But see Section 16.5 for modifications.

words, application of *Rsubst,1* is blocked in this case.

An advantage of a derivational account of scope is that D-trees can represent the scope order of Q-phrases and NEG for the most plausible reading of a sentence in a natural way. This treatment of scope presupposes the adoption of variables for elements that can bear scope. In order to arrive at the derived relation between substitution order and surface order, the left-right order of the variables must be established before the substitution rules are applied. As a consequence, the substitution rules are applied at the end of the derivation. Compositionality of translation implies that scope can be maintained in translation if in both languages the substitution rules and negation rules are applied in the same order.

Consider now the English derivation tree (7b), corresponding to the Dutch one (6b):

(7) a *Everybody* reads *two books*
    b

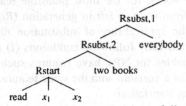

The output of the relevant rules is as follows:

Rstart: x_1[+S][+Q] read x_2[+S][+Q]
Rsubst,2: x_1[+S][+Q] reads two books
Rsubst,1: everybody reads two books

In this example, the construction of an isomorphic derivation for English (or Spanish) is easy, because the order of Q-phrases is the same as in Dutch. The corresponding trees ((6b) and (7b)) have exactly the same geometry.

16.3.2   Negation

As has already been stated above, the negation rule *Rneg* can apply if there are no free [+S][+Q] VARs to the right of the position where NEG is inserted (condition II). In the implemented version of Rosetta, syncategorematic introduction of NEG was chosen. Consider, for instance, (8a) and its derivation tree (8b):

(8) a Many girls do not read all books

   b

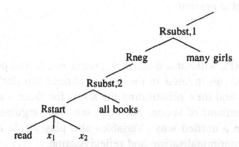

Rstart: $x_1[+S][+Q]$ read $x_2[+S][+Q]$
Rsubst,2: $x_1[+S][+Q]$ read   all books
Rneg: $x_1[+S][+Q]$ do not read all books
Rsubst,1: Many girls do not read all books

Only sentence negation is dealt with in this chapter, but this includes many cases of apparent negation of other constituents at the surface level. In these cases, the negation element has to be incorporated into the constituent to its right. In (9a) the position of NEG is syntactically inside the NP. It will be put in this position (generatively) by means of a transformation, cf. (9b), where *Rneg* applies at sentence level rather than NP level:

(9) a Not every man walks

   b

Rstart: x_1 walk
Rsubst,1:   (every man)   (walks)
Rneg: not (every man)   (walks)
Tneg: (not every man)   (walks)

Similarly, (10a) and (11a) can simply be translated into (10b) and (11b), respectively:

(10) a (D) *Niemand* kwam
        Nobody   came
     b (E) *Nobody* came

(11) a(D) *Veel* mensen krijgen *geen   kado*
      Many people get   'no + a' present
    b(E) *Many people* do *not* get *a present*

16.3.3   Remarks

In Rosetta, all terms, including NPs without a quantifier, proper nouns and personal pronouns (i.e. [–S][–Q]-elements), are treated in the way Q-phrases are dealt with, i.e. by first introducing variables and then substituting the terms for these variables. This is not necessary for the treatment of scope, but there are other arguments for treating NPs and other phrases in a unified way. Variables also play a role in rules that govern anaphora, control, pronominalisation and reflexivisation.

The *Right-Left Substitution* strategy avoids spurious ambiguities in analysis, but may seem to be too rigid in generation. For non Q-phrases, however, we can deviate from it without problems, if the translation relation requires this. An example of this is (12b), with the direct object (a non-Q-phrase) and NEG switched, leading to a correct translation of (12a):

(12) a(D) De kinderen aten *de snoepjes niet* op
      The children ate   the sweets   not up
    b(E) The children did *not* eat *the sweets*

This also holds for Q-phrases that always have wide scope, the [–S][+Q]-elements. We can deviate from Right-Left Substitution in the same way as with [–S][–Q]-elements, because they will always have wide scope regardless their position. Note that this can only be done if the [–S][+Q] values of these Q-phrases are the same in all languages.

It should be noted that phenomena such as *topicalisation* and *passivisation* change the order of arguments. This is done by transformations most of the time (see Chapter 11) *before* the substitution rules. Therefore, these phenomena interact desirably in a fully automatic manner with the Right-Left Substitution approach to scope.

16.4   Translation problems

In most cases, the Right-Left Substitution strategy works fine, but there are some phenomena for which it is inadequate. In general, these inadequacies will occur whenever monolingual syntactic constraints cause differences between the surface ordering of the Q-phrases in the translational equivalents. Two examples will be discussed, namely *argument switch* and *quantifiers in a negative context*.

16.4.1 Problems with switch of arguments

Problems arise if at the surface level the order of the arguments in one language is not the same as the order of arguments in the other language. Consider, for instance, the following verb patterns:

Spanish: x_1 dar x_2 x_3
Dutch: x_1 x_3 x_2 geven

If surface order reflects scope order, (13a) and (13b) cannot be seen as translation equivalents, although they are.

(13) a(D) Jan geeft *iedereen een boek*
    Jan gives everybody a book
    b(S) Jan da *un libro a todo el mundo*
    Jan gives a book to everybody

In one of the languages the order of the Q-phrases has to be switched somehow. This means that, in order to get a semantically correct translation (i.e. with the same surface order of scope-sensitive Q-phrases), the syntactic form has to be changed.

16.4.2 Quantifiers in negative context

Rosetta translates between two types of languages, namely the SOV type (Dutch) and the SVO type (Spanish and English). For more details on SOV and SVO, see the chapter on the application of theoretical linguistics in this framework, Chapter 11. This SOV versus SVO character has important consequences for the expression of scope, especially in a negative context. We claim that in both types of language the position of NEG for sentence negation is as close to the left of the verb in basic position as possible. It only precedes possible Q-phrases that are within the scope of NEG (cf. Van Munster (1985, 1988)).[5]

Consider the following scheme, in which S = subject, O = object, (OARG) = optional other arguments, NEG = negation element and V = verbs, and which reflects the *basic* word order in Dutch, English and Spanish with NEG as close to the *left-hand* side of the verb as possible:

Dutch: S O   (OARG) NEG–V
English/Spanish: S NEG–V O   (OARG)

---

[5] Although in the development of the Rosetta system only these three languages have been investigated, we claim that the theory will hold for other Western-European SVO and SOV languages, e.g. Italian and French (SVO) and German (SOV), too.

In an SOV language the verb (in basic position) is in sentence-final position, while in an SVO language the verb is in second position. Consequently, in an SVO language only two elements (one in subject position and one in *'shift-position'*, i.e. the first position in the sentence[6]) can precede NEG and be outside the scope of NEG; the object and the other arguments are to the right of the verbs - and therefore to the right of NEG - in basic position and they are all inside the scope of NEG. In SOV languages like Dutch, however, the object and other arguments are to the left of NEG in basic position and they are all outside the scope of NEG. In principle, there is no restriction on the number of elements that can appear to the left of NEG in Dutch. Note that NEG can occur at more positions to the left, for example, in Dutch:

S   O   NEG–(OARG) V
S   NEG–O   (OARG)   V
NEG-S   O   (OARG)   V

In Spanish and English only one alternative is possible:

NEG-S V   O   (OARG)

Therefore, an SOV language seems to be more 'suited' to the expression of scope through word order than an SVO language, especially if the sentence contains a NEG.

So, problems are to be expected in the case of translation between languages of a different type, especially from SOV to SVO. The SVO languages English and Spanish, however, have 'quantifiers with a negative counterpart' to express some of the different scope relations. We will first look at quantifiers without such a negative counterpart and then at quantifiers with a negative counterpart.

Quantifiers without a negative counterpart

Consider e.g. (14), where (14a) and (14b) cannot be treated as translation equivalents since the relative order of NEG and the Q-phrase is not the same:

(14) a(D) De kinderen aten *veel snoepjes niet* op
            The children ate   many sweets   not up
     b(E) The children did *not* eat *many sweets*

The corresponding syntactic derivation trees are given in Figure 16.2.
Schematically, the output of the rules in generation is:
Dutch:

---

[6]This is also the position for wh-elements and topicalised constituents.

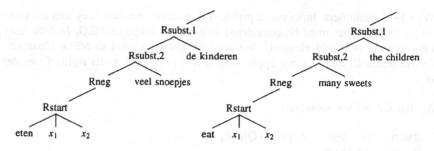

Figure 16.2: Derivation tree for *De kinderen aten veel snoepjes niet op* and its English equivalent.

Rstart: x_1 x_2[+Q]   eet
Rneg: x_1 x_2[+Q]   niet aten
Rsubst,2: x_1 veel snoepjes niet aten
Rsubst,1: de kinderen veel snoepjes niet aten

English:

Rstart: x_1 eat x_2[+S][+Q]
Rneg: (blocked)

Since x_2 is to the right of the verb (and thus to the right of the NEG position), *Rneg* is blocked because of condition II. Note that this blocking is justified: without blocking the result of applying the English rules would be (14b), which is not a correct translation of (14a). In other words, the wrong output is blocked but the question is: how can a correct translation be obtained? Most problems arise if NEG follows a non-subject Q-phrase in Dutch.

Quantifiers with a negative counterpart

In Section 16.2.2 we saw that certain quantifiers in English and Spanish have a 'negative counterpart', e.g. *alguien* [+P], *nadie* [–P] and *somebody* [+P], *anybody* [–P]. The negative forms must occur within the scope of NEG, i.e. to the right of NEG. We repeat example sentence (4) here as (15).

(15) a(*D*) Jan heeft *niemand* gezien
       Jan has   nobody   seen
     b(*S*) Jan no ha visto a *nadie*
       Jan not has seen   to nobody
     c(*E*) Jan did not see *anybody*.

These [–P]-quantifiers do not cause problems for Right-Left Substitution; after substitution the sentence can be marked to indicate that *Rneg* must apply.

With [+P]-quantifiers, however, a problem does arise, because they can occur to the right of NEG, but must be considered outside the scope of NEG. In fact, they behave like the [–S][+Q] elements, but then only with respect to NEG. However, under condition II, *Rneg* cannot apply with a free [+P] VAR to its right. Consider (16).

(16) Jan did not see *somebody*

Rstart: x_1 see x_2 [+S][+Q][+P]
Rneg: (blocked)

16.5 Solutions

A lot of scope translation problems seem to be solved by allowing a larger variety of syntactic forms. One could consider changing the syntactic form in such a way that the relative order of the Q-phrases would be maintained during translation. Consider again the English translation of the Dutch sentence (14a)) and two possible ways to change the syntactic form:

(14) a(D) De kinderen aten *veel snoepjes niet* op

1. With topicalisation of the Q-phrase.
    In the English sentence the object can to be shifted to the 'shift-position', i.e. the first position in the sentence, in order to get the same scope relations as in the Dutch sentence (14a):[7]

    (14) c(E) *Many sweets* the children did *not* eat

    This is, of course, also a translation of:

    (14) d(D) *Veel snoepjes* aten de kinderen *niet* op

    where the arguments have been switched with respect to the basic order, also because of topicalisation.

2. With passivisation of the sentence:

    (14) e(E) *Many sweets* were *not* eaten by the children

    This is, of course, also a translation of the passive Dutch sentence

---

[7]Note, however, that such a topicalisation is quite stylistically marked in English. An alternative would be: *There were many sweets the children did not eat.*

(14) f (D) *Veel snoepjes* werden door de kinderen *niet* opgegeten

In both (14c) and in (14e) the relative order of NEG and the Q-phrase is the same as in the Dutch sentences (14a,d,f).

Thus, the semantically correct translation could be a translation that differs in syntactic form. But then, it usually corresponds to another expression as well. An objection to this kind of tolerance, clearly, is that it will work out everywhere, because of the fact that the translation relations and the rules are local. For example, consider (17):

(17) a (D) Jan leest de bijbel
     Jan reads the bible
    b (E) The bible is read by Jan

Sentence (17a) is an active sentence, whereas sentence (17b) is a passive sentence. This kind of translation is not what is pursued in general. Tolerance with respect to syntactic form only should be allowed in the cases where it is necessary. The translations show that translation is not a simple matter of right or wrong, but that there are differences in quality (which are in fact outside the scope of this book, see Chapter 1). Our priority is *meaning preservation* and therefore we accept form differences if they are inevitable. As the rules are local and the inevitability of syntactic differences obviously appear on a more global level, we need a new mechanism: a *preference* or *bonus* system.

In Section 16.5.1 a solution is presented in which on the basis of the division of quantifiers in Section 16.2.4, [+Q]-arguments are shifted only in case it is desirable. This solves the problems with switch of arguments and the [+S][+Q] and [+S][+Q][−P] quantifiers in a negative context. For the remaining problems, those with [+S][+Q][+P] quantifiers, a solution is presented in which condition II on substitution is *loosened* (Section 16.5.2). For the cases for which a solution with 'syntactic tolerance' is not possible, a *negative bonus* or *penalty* system is added to yield a certain order of the output set of translations, indicating the degree of deviance.

16.5.1 Optional [+Q]-shift

One of the solutions already suggested above was shifting a Q-phrase to the 'shift-position'. To avoid unnecessary tolerance with respect to syntactic form, two points of departure have been chosen:

1. the basic syntactic order of arguments should be preserved as much as possible. Note that this order is in principle language-specific.

2. the subsitution order of the *source* language will dictate the scope order of Q-phrases and NEG.

Note that a perfect translation relation is symmetric, but an 'imperfect' one is not. Therefore we cannot discuss this approach purely symmetrically and relationally as we have done until now. We have to discuss it with respect to the process of translation in which a source language and a target language are distinguished.

VARs have all features of the arguments that will be substituted for them. So they can be characterised by $[\alpha Q]$,[8] $[\alpha S]$ and, for certain languages, $[\alpha P]$. In the *shift-transformations*, where VARs are shifted, $[+Q]$ VARs are shifted to shift-position (which is to the left of the subject position) under certain conditions. These transformations are optional, which means that two paths are always created during generation. Since not both paths end up as well-formed surface trees, these are *temporary paraphrases*. In fact, this is the point where the tolerance is effectuated. Only one of these paths is meant to have a result.

Since there is only one shift-position, only one VAR can be shifted per clause. The shift-transformations can be subdivided into two cases:

1. The $[+Q]$ VAR is shifted over a $[+Q]$ VAR.

   This type of shift is necessary to get the correct scope relations when syntactic differences of languages cause a different word order. A negation in the sentence is not necessary.

   For (13), here repeated as (18), in which both arguments are $[+S][+Q]$, this means that the shift-transformations render two surface orders of VARs in the target language, e.g. Spanish:

   (18) a(D) Jan geeft *iedereen een boek*
   Jan gives everybody a   book
   b(S) Juan da *un libro a todo el mundo*
   Juan gives a   book to everybody

   (path i) x_1 dar $x_2[+Q]$ $x_3[+Q]$
   (path ii) shift/$x_3[+Q]$ x_1 dar $x_2[+Q]$

   Later on, only (path *ii*) offers the correct input for a successful application of substitution rules, since x_2 has to be substituted first (*Right-Left Substitution*, see Section 16.3).

2. the $[+Q]$ VAR is shifted over a $[-Q]$ VAR.

   This type of shift is not necessary for SOV languages, since all Q-NPs can precede NEG without shift (see Section 16.4.2). For SVO languages this shift

---

[8] α stands for either + or -.

is necessary in order to put a [+Q] argument in a position to the left of NEG, i.e. to get the correct scope relations. Consider again the Dutch sentence (14a), repeated here as (19a) with its Spanish and English translation (19b,c):

(19) a (*D*) De kinderen aten *veel snoepjes niet* op
        The children   ate   many sweets   not up

    b (*S*) *Muchas dulces los niños no* comieron
       Many   sweets the children not ate

    c (*E*) *Many sweets* the children did *not* eat

Now consider again the output of the English rules for (14) (or (19)):

Rule	Output			
Rstart:	$x_1[-Q]$		eat	$x_2[+Q]$
Tshift:	(i) $x_1[-Q]$		eat	$x_2[+Q]$
	(ii) shift/$x_2[+Q]$		$x_1[-Q]$ eat	
Rneg:	(i) (blocked)			
	(ii) shift/$x_2[+Q]$ $x_1[-Q]$		not	eat
Rsubst,2:	(ii) many sweets $x_1[-Q]$		not	eat
Rsubst,1:	(ii) many sweets the children not		eat	

(Final result: - Many sweets the children did not eat)

16.5.2   Adaptation of condition II

As explained earlier, in the SOV language Dutch it is easier to express scope by word order than in English and Spanish, especially if the sentence contains a negation (see Section 16.4.2). In this section we will explain how condition II on substitution, stated in Section 16.3, can be loosened in order to solve the problems with the [+S][+Q][+P] quantifiers. We will repeat this condition here:

(II) A negation rule (*Rneg*) only applies if there are no free [+S][+Q] VARs to the right of the position where NEG is inserted.

Now, we add to this condition that, if the VAR is [+S][+Q][+P], then *Rneg* may apply. This, conversely, does not hold for *Rsubst*. If a [+S][+Q][+P] variable is substituted for, the sentence must be marked that *Rneg* may no longer apply. It is marked, for example, with [pos]. So, the new condition is:

(II)' A negation rule (*Rneg*) only applies either if there are no free [+S][+Q] VARs to the right of the position where NEG is inserted, unless it is a [+S][+Q][+P] VAR, or if the sentence has not been marked with [pos].

This relaxation of condition II and the addition of a marker solves the problems with the positive counterparts of some quantifiers with negation, e.g. (16), here repeated as (20), where *somebody* is a quantifier NP with features [+S][+Q][+P]:

(20) Jan did not see *somebody*

16.5.3   A bonus system

A lot of problems can be solved with 'argument-shift to shift-position', but the scope order cannot always be maintained, since there is only one shift-position. For example, if in Dutch the NEG is preceded by two Q-NP arguments, only one of the corresponding arguments can be moved to the first position in the English translation:

(21) Wij lezen *aan twee kinderen drie verhalen niet* voor
      We read to two children three stories not for

Either *two children* or *three stories* can be topicalised, but not both constituents; one Q-NP has to remain to the right of NEG.

Also, if the subject in (14a) were a Q-NP, the object cannot move to first position, since the order of Q-elements would change. Neither the English sentence (22b), without topicalisation, nor (22c), with *many sweets* being topicalised, has the same scope order (i.e. surface order of Q-elements) as the Dutch sentence (22a):

(22) a(*D*) *Twee kinderen* aten *veel snoepjes niet* op
        Two children ate many sweets not up

      b(*E*) *Two children* did *not* eat *many sweets*

      c(*E*) *Many sweets two children* did *not* eat

Although it is beyond the scope of this book (see Chapter 1), this section will indicate how the best possible translation in those cases can be generated with a so-called *bonus system*. The formalism is extended with the possibility for an S-tree to receive a bonus value which can be increased or decreased by every rule application. The default case is that rules do not change this bonus value and that the S-tree has a bonus value *0*. Under certain conditions this value may change. In the end, if there is more than one output, the difference in bonus merely determines the *order* in which the output sentences appear.

[+Q]-shift

In case two [+S][+Q] VARs should be shifted but only one can be shifted, a free [+S] VAR remains to the right. In that case the bonus application[is as follows, where n and i have to be specified for a particular grammar and be positive:

1. Application of *Rneg* with a free [+S] VAR to the right decreases the bonus with n.

2. Application of *Rsubst,x* with a free [+S] VAR to the right decreases the bonus with (n + i).

In other words, a deviation in the order of NEG and [+S]-elements is preferred to a deviation in the order of [+S]-elements mutually.

Now consider the Dutch sentence (22a), here in (23) together with its Spanish translation:

(23) a Twee kinderen aten veel snoepjes niet op
　　　Two　children　ate　many sweets　not　up
　　b

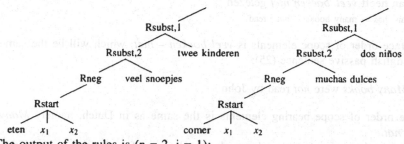

The output of the rules is (n = 2, i = 1):

Rule	Output				Bonus
Rstart:	x_1[+Q]		comer	x_2[+Q]	0
Tshift:	(i) x_1[+Q]		comer	x_2[+Q]	0
	(ii) shift/x_2[+Q]		x_1[+Q]	comer	0
Rneg:	(i) x_1[+Q]	no	comer	x_2[+Q]	-2
	(ii) shift/x_2[+Q]		x_1[+Q] no	comer	0
Rsubst,2:	(i) x_1[+Q]	no	comer	muchas dulces	-2
	(ii) muchas dulces no		x_1 [+Q] no	comer	-3
Rsubst,1:	(i) dos niños	no	comer	muchas dulces	-2
	(ii) muchas dulces dos niños no		comer		-3

The output sentences are:
(1) Dos niños no han comido muchas dulces (*path (i)*)
(2) Muchas dulces dos niños no han comido (*path (ii)*)

The corresponding output for English is:
(1) Two children did not eat many sweets (*path (i)*)

(2) Many sweets two children did not eat (*path (ii)*)

Note that the scope order is not the same in either of the output sentences as it is in Dutch. The limit of scope translation through word order has been reached.

In general it can be said that, while SOV languages are more suited to expressing scope through word order, in SVO languages the *intonation* of the sentence may play a crucial role in the expression of scope.

Passivisation

As stated above, another way of maintaining the correct scope order is by means of passivisation. Since the passive construction is more marginal in Spanish, an example of a translation into English will be given. Consider (24):

(24)   Jan heeft *veel boeken niet* gelezen
       Jan has   many books   not read

The surface order of scope elements is *veel boeken – niet*, which will be the same in the English passive sentence (25):

(25)   *Many books* were *not* read by John

Here the order of scope bearing elements is the same as in Dutch, namely *Many books – not*.

How can these two sentences be made translations of each other? Again this can be done by way of the *bonus system*, but now in the *generative transfer rules*. The Dutch active rule corresponds both to the English active and passive rule, the passive assigning a lower bonus (-m). If the passive translation renders the correct scope order, as in (24), and we choose m < n, the passive translation will be the preferred output sentence.

The output for the rules for (24) is (n = 2, i = 1, m = 1):

Rule		Output				Bonus
Rstart:		x_1		read	$x_2[+Q]$	0
Rvoice:	(i)	x_1		read	$x_2[+Q]$	0
	(ii)	$x_2[+Q]$		read	by x_1	-1
Rneg:	(i)	x_1	not	read	$x_2[+Q]$	-2
	(ii)	$x_2[+Q]$	not	read	by x_1	-1
Rsubst,2:	(i)	x_1	not	read	many books	-2
	(ii)	many books	not	read	by x_1	-1
Rsubst,1:	(i)	John	not	read	many books	-2
	(ii)	many books	not	read	by John	-1

The output sentences are:
(1) Many books were not read by John (*path (ii)*)
(2) John did not read many books (*path (i)*)

Note that the output with '[+Q]-shift' would be preferred with this bonus assignment: *Many books John did not read* (bonus = 0). The examples already indicate that the ultimate bonus value is the result of a ranking of deviations. This ranking has been rather arbitrary so far and is still a topic of investigation.

16.6   Concluding remarks

In this chapter we have dealt with the application of the principle of compositionality of translation to scope phenomena.

The Rosetta approach is somewhat similar to the Montague Grammar (or PTQ) approach, in that the level where scope is represented is the same, i.e. the D-tree level. There are also differences. First, only one scope reading is chosen, which implies that there are no quantificational ambiguities in Rosetta. Second, all terms are treated as Q-phrases, in the sense that they are all substituted for variables, but they are not subject to the Right-Left Substitution conditions concerning +Q variables. Q-phrases that always have wide scope (the [+Q][−S] phrases) are treated as non-Q-phrases in the latter respect.

The Rosetta approach differs from some versions of TG-theory, because in those theories scope is encoded in a representation which is more like S-tree representations rather than to a representation of the derivation of a sentence.

The approach to scope and negation presented here is strongly based on the adoption of Jackendoff's principle, which does not work out well in all cases of translation, especially from an SOV language into an SVO language. It was shown how translation problems with respect to scope that result from this approach can be solved to a certain extent by means of shift-transformations and passivisation.

Since a solution is not always possible if we want to strictly maintain the surface order of Q-phrases (and since, on the other hand, sentences are ambiguous anyway, particularly in SVO languages like English and Spanish), rules which break scope-order prescriptions do in fact apply, but they assign a lower bonus. This bonus influences the output order of sentences. In fact, this preference system is beyond the scope of this book and has only been incorporated to show how more pragmatic or practical solutions could be added within this framework. The preference system can also be used to order sets of possible translations as for example in (26) and (27), and cases of categorial divergence as treated in Chapter 13, by using a bonus assignment in the transfer component.

(26) a de *mooie* vrouw
      the beautiful woman
      b 1. the *beautiful* woman
         2. the woman *that is beautiful*

The translation with an adjective (*beautiful*) is preferred to one with a relative sentence (*that is beautiful*).

(27) a zij *kan* komen
      she can come
      b 1. she *can* come
         2. she is *able* to come

The translation with a verb *can* is preferred to one with an adjective (*able*). The bonus system accounts for this.

The preference system can also be used to rank stylistic preferences to avoid, for example, passive constructions in Spanish or certain topicalisations in English. All in all, the approach to scope presented in this chapter does not always seem to be the most ideal solution. We already mentioned the problems with the 'scope-through-word-order' assumption and the necessity of a bonus system. The treatment of scope also faces certain technical problems in defining the notion of 'substitution from right to left'. The formulation 'substitute only if there is no [+S][+Q] variable to the right', given earlier, works fine if all phrases are introduced by substitution rules, but it fails if some phrases are introduced in other ways.[9] Negation, for instance, is not introduced by substitution. In the structure [...NP...Neg...] nothing prevents *Neg* from being removed first in analysis, and only NP after that: there is no [+S][+Q] variable to the right of *Neg*, and there is none to the right of NP, but this leads to the wrong scope relations if wider scope corresponds to a position more to the left. This problem has been solved in the actual system by introducing so-called place-markers: When *Neg* is removed in analysis, a marker is introduced on the position of *Neg*, marking the fact that *Neg* has been there in an earlier stage of the (analytical) derivation. Special rules remove these markers later in the (analytical) derivation, after the application of all substitution rules. This problem indicates that scope rules which link S-tree properties to scope relations cannot be rules which simply introduce elements: there must be place-markers, or other ways to indicate (in analysis) which position the relevant phrase occupies in the structure, so that this can be seen even after application of the scope rule applying to this element.

Some of the other problems we met should not remain unmentioned either, although they cannot be explained in detail here:

---

[9] We know of no alternative formulation. One must bear in mind that the structure can contain phrases which are parts of idioms or phrases which are introduced syncategorematically and which, consequently, are never substituted.

1. Sometimes it is not clear in which subgrammar a variable should be substituted. For example, must *him* in *I consider* **him** *funny* be substituted in the ADJPPROP subgrammar or in the CLAUSE subgrammar with head *consider*?

2. Substitution rules apply late in the derivation. A consequence of that is that the internal structure of phrases will also be known late. This is too late for NP-internal reflexives and reciprocals and inalienable possession constructions. An example of this is the interpretation of *me* in:

(28) *(S)* Me ha   lavado las manos
　　　　Me he-has washed the hands
　　(E) He has washed my hands

Because of these problems other approaches such as, for example, encoding scope in attribute-value pairs in combination with early substitution and checking the order of phrases afterwards should be investigated within this framework.   However, it should be stressed that the approach along the lines sketched here turned out to be feasible and efficient in a lot of cases and, therefore, investigating and implementing it was worthwhile.

1. Sometimes it is not clear in which subgrammar a variable should be substituted. For example, must Aim in A consider him, many be substituted in the ADJPREDP subgrammar or in the CLAUSE subgrammar with head consider?

2. Substitution rules apply late in the derivation. A consequence of that is that the internal structure of phrases will also be known late. This is too late for NP-internal reflexives and reciprocals and inalienable possession constructions. An example of this is the interpretation of me in:

> (26) (a) Me ha / lavado las manos.
> Me he-has washed the hands
> (c) He has washed my hands

Because of these problems other approaches such as, for example, encoding scope in attribute-value pairs in combination with early substitution and checking the order of phrases afterwards should be investigated within this framework. However, it should be stressed that the approach along the lines sketched here turned out to be feasible and efficient in a lot of cases and, therefore, investigating and implementing it was worthwhile.

Chapter 17

The formal definition of M-grammars

17.1 Introduction

In preceding chapters the notion of M-grammar has been introduced informally and step by step. Chapter 2 introduced compositional grammars with rules operating on symbol strings. In Chapter 3, linguistic considerations led to the introduction of M-grammars with rules operating on S-trees. The relation between lexical S-trees and strings is provided by a separate morphological component, which was discussed in Chapter 6. In order to solve problems associated with writing large grammars, in Chapter 8 the original notion of an M-grammar as a free production system has been refined with notions like subgrammars, rule classes, transformations and control expressions.

   The purpose of this chapter is to recapitulate all this in a systematic way and to define the various components of M-grammars and their relation to the modules of the Rosetta system more precisely than we did in the previous chapters. The emphasis will be on the syntactic component of M-grammars and on the definition and properties of the modules M-PARSER and M-GENERATOR.

   This chapter is divided into two major parts. The first part formally defines *free M-grammars* that were introduced in Chapter 3. The syntactic rules of free M-grammars constitute a uniform set. There are no restrictions on the order of rule applications. We discuss various properties of the modules defined by free M-grammars and we show how to build a translation system from two free isomorphic M-grammars. In the second part we discuss the consequences of the modifications introduced in Chapter 8 and define *controlled M-grammars*. In particular, we show

how the notions connected to subgrammars influence the architecture of the translation system. Control over rule applications predominantly affects the modules M-PARSER and M-GENERATOR, and controlled versions of these modules are discussed in detail.

17.2 Trees: terminology and formalisation

First we characterise the objects the M-grammar formalism deals with, in particular the different kinds of trees that play a role. The main distinction is that between S-trees and derivation trees. Both kinds of trees have several subclasses that are listed here as well.

17.2.1 S-trees

The syntactic rules of an M-grammar operate on S-trees, i.e. their arguments are S-trees and the result of a successful rule application is an S-tree. An *S-tree* is an ordered labelled tree, formally defined as follows:

An *S-tree* is

- a node N, or

- an expression of the form

$$N[r_1/t_1,\ldots, r_n/t_n] \qquad (n>0)$$

where N is a node, the r_is represent syntactic relations and the t_is are S-trees.

We will often use this kind of recursive definition: the second - recursive - part of the definition indicates that S-trees may have arbitrary, but finite, depth; the first part shows how the recursion terminates: the leaves of the trees are always (terminal) nodes.

A node N is defined as a syntactic category followed by a tuple of attribute-value pairs $(a_i:v_i)$.

$$N = C\{a_1:v_1,\ldots, a_k:v_k\} \qquad (k\geq0)$$

For each syntactic category there is a fixed set of attributes that each have a (generally finite) set of possible values. So, given a set of syntactic relations and a set of syntactic categories with the corresponding attributes and values, the set of possible S-trees is defined. This set is called T: the domain of S-trees. So the general form of an S-tree t is

$$t = C\{a_1:v_1,\ldots, a_k:v_k\} [r_1/t_1,\ldots, r_n/t_n].$$

C is called the syntactic category of t.

Four kinds of S-trees play a special role:

Basic S-trees. They are the starting point for the derivation of a sentence and are specified in a lexicon: B-LEX. Basic S-trees usually consist of one node, with idiomatic expressions as the obvious exception (cf. Chapter 15). The terms basic expression and basic S-tree are used synonymously, although strictly speaking the concept of basic expression is more general.

Abstract S-trees. These are basic S-trees that do not correspond to words. Among the abstract S-trees are the syntactic variables. Syntactic variables are the only S-tree nodes that have an attribute (the index of the variable) that has no bounded range of values. This makes the number of basic S-trees infinite. In theory this is important for the power of the formalism. The infinite number of available variables causes no serious practical complications.

Full S-trees. These are the final result of a derivation and can be distinguished by the category of the top node: UTTERANCE. The category UTTERANCE only appears at the top nodes of S-trees. Full S-trees are the surface structures of complete utterances, e.g. sentences.

Lexical S-trees. These are subtrees of full S-trees corresponding to the words of the utterance. The usual perception of a surface structure is that the leaves, i.e. the terminal nodes, ordered from left to right, represent the utterance. This perception is still valid, but with the complication that the lexical S-trees need not be terminal nodes. In fact, they usually consist of more than one node. The category of a lexical S-tree (the category of its top node) is a member of the set LEXCATS, which includes ART, N, V, CONJ, ADV. This is illustrated in Figure 17.1.

S-trees not belonging to any of these classes may occur as intermediate results of rule applications during the derivation process, they are called *intermediate S-trees*.

17.2.2   Derivation trees

The process of application of rules, starting with basic expressions and finally yielding a full S-tree, is made explicit in a syntactic derivation tree.

A *syntactic derivation tree* is a labelled ordered tree. The ordering of the syntactic derivation tree is related to the order of the arguments of the rules. This ordering is not related to the surface order, but to the ordering of the arguments of the rules, which is arbitrary except for the convention that the head is always the first argument (cf. Chapter 9).

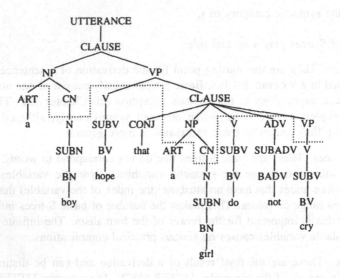

Figure 17.1: An S-tree. Relations and attributes are not displayed. The top nodes of lexical S-trees are just below the dotted line.

An example of a derivation tree is Figure 17.2. In general some of the basic expressions of the derivation tree will be syntactic variables and some of the rules, the substitution rules, are parametrised by these variables. The indices of variables may be renamed systematically without altering the meaning of the derivation tree. A convenient choice of indices is given by the prescription that a substitution rule is always parametrised by a variable with index equal to the *level* of the substitution rule. This level is the length of the path from the substitution rule to the top of the derivation tree. Derivation trees with this property are called *canonical*.

We distinguish *well-formed syntactic derivation trees*, which have the property that the recursive application of the rules yields one or more S-trees, and *ill-formed syntactic derivation trees* containing rules that are not applicable.

A *full syntactic derivation tree* is a well-formed syntactic derivation tree that specifies that a special rule, the utterance rule, is the last rule to be applied. The result of applying the rules of a full syntactic derivation tree is a full S-tree. The tree of figure 17.2 is a full derivation tree if R_1 is the utterance rule.

Up to now, the terms D-tree and derivation tree were used synonymously. At this point we make a subtle distinction between the two: a D-tree is a *representation* of derivation trees. As we will see below, such a representation is not unique.

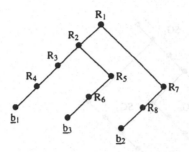

Figure 17.2: A derivation tree.

Formally, a *D-tree* is
- the name b of a basic expression, or
- an expression of the form $R_i <d_1,\ldots,d_n>$,   (n>0),
  where R_i is a rule name and $d_1,\ldots,d_n$ is a (non-empty) sequence
  of D-trees.

Semantic derivation trees are the meaning representations of sentences. A *semantic derivation tree* is a labelled ordered tree, with the same topology as syntactic derivation trees. However, the leaves are labelled by basic meanings and internal nodes are labelled with names of semantic rules.

A *well-formed semantic derivation tree* corresponds to a well-formed syntactic derivation tree, according to the semantic component. So there is no independent criterion of well-formedness at the semantic level.

17.2.3   δ-trees

In controlled M-grammars, derivation trees are annotated with the subgrammar structure, as in Figure 17.3. The annotation maps each node to a subgrammar, except terminal nodes. However, the terminal nodes may be taken to belong to a special subgrammar that exports basic S-trees; let us call this subgrammar SG_{blex}. SG_{blex} is introduced for technical reasons (to simplify the algorithms below) only: it is not a subgrammar to a linguist. A convenient way to include subgrammar information in a tree is by replacing the tree of Figure 17.3 by the one in Figure 17.4. Trees like the latter are called δ-*trees*. In a δ-tree a new kind of node (the square ones) is used which is labelled with subgrammar names. Whereas in the D-tree representation of derivation trees all arguments of an M-rule are treated equally, in a δ-tree the distinction between the *head* argument (the first one) and the other arguments of an

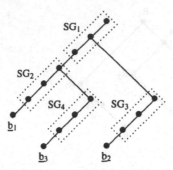

Figure 17.3: A schematic derivation tree with subgrammar structure annotation.

M-rule is made explicit. From the figure and the way it was constructed we conclude that a δ-tree has the following structure. The top of a δ-tree is a subgrammar node. The first daughter of a subgrammar node is a δ-tree, from which the head argument for the subgrammar's first rule application can be derived. The other daughters of a subgrammar node are called λ-trees: trees with a rule name at the top. If this name corresponds to a unary rule, the λ-tree consists of only one node. If the top of a λ-tree is labelled by an n-ary rule, this node has n-1 daughters, which are again δ-trees and correspond to the non-head arguments of the rule. Formally, the above amounts to the following definition.

A *δ-tree* is

  -an expression $SG_{blex} < \underline{b} >$, with b a basic expression, or

  -an expression of the form $SG_i < \delta, \lambda_1, \ldots, \lambda_k >$, where $\lambda_1, \ldots, \lambda_k$ are expressions of the form $R_j < \delta_1, \ldots, \delta_n >$. The symbols δ, $\delta_1, \ldots, \delta_n$ denote δ-trees, R_j is an M-rule name and SG_i is a subgrammar name. The sequence $\delta_1, \ldots, \delta_n$ is possibly empty (if R_j is unary rule). The sequence $\lambda_1, \ldots, \lambda_k$ is required to have at least one element (an application of a subgrammar involves at least one rule application).

We will often refer to the top node of a λ-tree. For this purpose we adopt the following convention: if λ is expression $R_j < \delta_1, \ldots, \delta_n >$ then R_λ denotes the rule R_j. A λ-tree has an intuitively appealing interpretation: it is the name of a unary function on S-trees associated with R_λ. Function λ is obtained from R_λ by partial parametrisation. Fixing all arguments except the first one of the generative function associated with R_λ leaves a function on the first argument. Expressed as a formula,

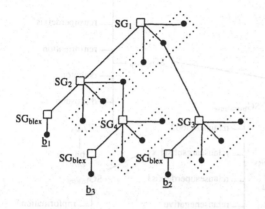

Figure 17.4: A δ-tree representation of the derivation in Figure 17.3

the function $R_\lambda < \delta_1, \ldots, \delta_n >$ applied to S-tree t is defined as follows (generatively, R_λ needs n+1 arguments).

$$R_\lambda < \delta_1, \ldots, \delta_n >(t) =_{def} \{ s \mid s \in F_\lambda(t, t_1, \ldots, t_n), \text{ where } t_1 \text{ can be generated from }$$
$$\delta_1, t_2 \text{ can be generated from } \delta_2, \text{ etc.} \}$$

Here F_λ is the generative function that corresponds to M-rule R_λ.

Figure 17.4 shows one possible way to display δ-trees. Figure 17.5, for instance, displays a realistic derivation in another format. It will be clear that one unique D-tree corresponds to each δ-tree. It is not difficult to find a recursively defined mapping from δ-trees to D-trees. To avoid unnecessary formalities we leave this to the reader.

The nodes of semantic derivation trees defined above are labelled by basic meanings or semantic rule names. If subgrammar information is considered translation relevant, as in the current Rosetta system, this is conveniently encoded by a semantic δ-tree with semantic subgrammar names at the nodes that are labelled by syntactic subgrammar names in the corresponding syntactic δ-tree. We shall come back to this at the end of this chapter.

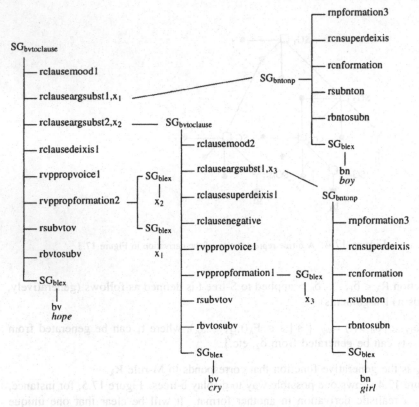

Figure 17.5: A stylised δ-tree representation of a realistic derivation tree.

17.3   Free M-grammars

17.3.1   Informal introduction

A *free M-grammar* consists of

- a syntactic component, consisting of two parts: the central part, which is the M-syntax and a 'secondary' part, the surface grammar, which is only needed for analysis purposes;

- a semantic component;

- a morphological component.

The task of a (free) M-grammar is, first, to define a language, i.e. the set of well-formed utterances and, second, to relate each well-formed utterance to one or more surface structures, one or more syntactic derivation trees and one or more semantic derivation trees. The first task is automatically fulfilled if the second task is fulfilled, because we consider an utterance well-formed if it is related to a syntactic derivation tree by the M-grammar.

The M-grammar defines the objects of Section 17.2 and various relations between them.

1. The syntactic component defines

    (a) the set of possible S-trees (full S-trees, lexical S-trees, basic S-trees, intermediate S-trees);

    (b) the set of well-formed S-trees.

2. The semantic component specifies a set of semantic rules and a set of basic meanings, a mapping from syntactic rules to semantic rules and a mapping from basic S-trees to basic meanings. In other words, it defines the set of possible semantic derivation trees and a relation between syntactic derivation trees and semantic derivation trees.

3. The morphological component defines a relation between sequences of lexical S-trees and written utterances.

The syntactic component is the central part of the M-grammar. The other two components are in a sense dependent on this. The semantic component relates semantic derivation trees to all well-formed syntactic derivation trees. The morphological component assigns a string to each sequence of lexical S-trees that is yielded by a full S-tree.

17.3.2 The syntactic component

The syntactic component of an M-grammar defines

- The domain T, the set of possible S-trees. This is the domain in which the syntactic rules operate and, as the general format of S-trees is fixed (see Section 17.2), it is defined by enumerating the syntactic relations, the categories and the corresponding attributes and values. In practice there are many extra conditions on allowable S-trees. Many relationships between attribute values at one node or between the values of attributes of a node and the values of attributes of its daughters. Severe restrictions exist on allowable orderings of relations in S-trees. Such linguistic restrictions, however, have not been formalised.

- The set T_M of well-formed S-trees, a subset of T. T_M consists of the surface trees of sentences that are well-formed according to the grammar. T_M is defined by specifying:

1. a set B of basic S-trees;
2. a set of syntactic rules, called M-rules;
3. a special category: UTTERANCE.

ad 1. The set of basic S-trees is a subset of T (the basic lexicon). A basic S-tree b has a unique name, denoted $\underline{b}$.

ad 2. An M-rule R_i defines a generative function F_i from tuples of S-trees to finite sets of S-trees. So application of R_i to a tuple $t_1,\ldots,t_n$ yields a set $F_i(t_1,\ldots,t_n)$. The set is empty if the rule is not applicable. As was explained in Chapter 4, M-rules are reversible, i.e. each M-rule corresponds not only to a generative function but also to an analytical one. Notationally, M-rule R_i defines not only function F_i, but also its reverse, the function F_i':

$$t \in F_i(t_1,\ldots,t_n) \iff (t_1,\ldots,t_n) \in F_i'(t).$$

S-trees are constructed by applying M-rules recursively, starting from basic expressions, The set T_M is the set of S-trees that can be derived in this way and that have the category UTTERANCE.

On the basis of the syntactic component of an M-grammar the functions M-GENERATOR and M-PARSER can be defined. M-GENERATOR is applied to a D-tree and yields a set of S-trees; M-PARSER is applied to an S-tree and yields a set of D-trees. As the definition of D-trees consists of two cases, the definitions of M-GENERATOR and M-PARSER consist of two sets:

$$\text{M-GENERATOR}(d) =_{def}$$
$$\{ t \mid \exists\, b \in B: d=\underline{b} \text{ and } t=b \}$$
$$\cup\ \{ t \mid \exists\, t_1,\ldots,t_n,\ d_1,\ldots,d_n,\ i :$$
$$d = R_i <d_1,\ldots,d_n> \text{ and }$$
$$t_1 \in \text{M-GENERATOR}(d_1) \text{ and }$$
$$\ldots$$
$$t_n \in \text{M-GENERATOR}(d_n) \text{ and }$$
$$t \in F_i(t_1,\ldots,t_n) \}$$

In this definition d, $d_1,\ldots,d_n$ are D-trees, t, $t_1,\ldots,t_n$ are S-trees, B is the set of basic S-trees, b is a basic S-tree, $\underline{b}$ is the name of a basic expression.

M-PARSER(t) $=_{def}$
$$\{ d \mid \exists\, b \in B: t = b \text{ and } d = \underline{b} \}$$
$$\cup \ \{ d \mid \exists\, t_1, \ldots, t_n, d_1, \ldots, d_n, i :$$
$$(t_1, \ldots, t_n) \in F'_i(t) \text{ and}$$
$$d_1 \in \text{M-PARSER}(t_1) \text{ and}$$
$$\ldots$$
$$d_n \in \text{M-PARSER}(t_n) \text{ and}$$
$$d = R_i <d_1, \ldots, d_n > \}$$

Here we abstract from the fact that rules can be parametrised. In particular, substitution rules are parametrised with syntactic variables. It is not difficult to define a variant of M-PARSER that takes account of rule parameters, in particular the index parameters of substitution rules, in such a way that only canonical D-trees are produced.

From the set-theoretic definitions of the functions M-PARSER and M-GENERATOR recursive algorithms can be derived in any programming language. Given the reversibility of the M-rules, it is easy to prove that

$$t \in \text{M-GENERATOR}(d) \Longleftrightarrow d \in \text{M-PARSER}(t).$$

Note that M-PARSER and M-GENERATOR can both be used to define the set T_M of well-formed S-trees. T_M can be defined as the set of S-trees (of category UTTERANCE) that can be derived by applying M-GENERATOR to all possible derivation trees. T_M can also be defined as the set of S-trees (of category UTTERANCE) for which M-PARSER yields at least one derivation tree. The equivalence of both definitions of T_M follows from the reversibility of the grammar.

The M-PARSER need not always be effective. Assuming that M-rules define effective functions, M-PARSER is effective if and only if an M-grammar obeys the *measure condition*, which requires that a measure, a function from S-trees to natural numbers, exists such that if t is the result of a generative M-rule applied to $t_1, \ldots, t_n$, then t is bigger according to this measure than each of the arguments $t_1, \ldots, t_n$. Then, analytically, M-rules produce ever smaller results, so that the recursion in M-PARSER is finite. The measure condition is the weakest possible restriction on M-grammars. If there is any proof that M-PARSER terminates for a given M-grammar, a measure for this M-grammar can be deduced that satisfies the measure condition: for each S-tree this measure is the length of the maximal sequence of M-rules that may be applied to it recursively. This length is always finite. If it were not, M-PARSER would not be effective.

The S-trees produced by M-GENERATOR represent utterances. The mapping from these S-trees to sequences of words happens in two steps. First the function LEAVES maps an S-tree into a sequence of lexical S-trees and subsequently each lexical S-tree is mapped onto a word or a sequence of words, by the function G-MORPH. LEAVES is defined as follows:

$$\text{LEAVES}(t) =_{def}$$
$$\{ <t> \mid t.cat \in \text{LEXCATS} \}$$
$$\cup \ \{ c \mid \exists \ N, r_1 \dots r_n, t_1 \dots t_n : \text{not } t.cat \in \text{LEXCATS and}$$
$$t = N[r_1/t_1, \dots, r_n/t_n] \text{ and}$$
$$c = \text{concatenate}(\text{LEAVES}(t_1), \dots, \text{LEAVES}(t_n)) \}$$

We may now define the set C of sequences of lexical S-trees, defined by an M-grammar:

$$C =_{def} \{ c \mid \exists \ d : c \in L(d) \}, \text{ where}$$

$$L(d) =_{def} \{ c \mid \exists \ t : t \in \text{M-GENERATOR}(d) \text{ and } c \in \text{LEAVES}(t) \}.$$

From the definition of L it follows that the function L^{-1}, defined by

$$L^{-1}(c) =_{def} \{ d \mid c \in L(d) \}$$

yields a non-empty set of D-trees for each sequence in C. In order to be able to effectively compute L^{-1} we assume that there exists a set of surface rules that allow the building of a full S-tree on top of a sequence of lexical S-trees. Surface rules can be considered as a context-free grammar with lexical S-trees as terminals (see Chapter 8 for details). The module that applies the surface rules is called S-PARSER and is a unidirectional reverse of LEAVES:

$$t \in \text{S-PARSER}(c) \Rightarrow c \in \text{LEAVES}(t)$$

if c is a sequence of lexical S-trees. The set T_S of S-trees that can be produced by S-PARSER, is defined as follows (s is a sentence):

$$T_S =_{def} \{ t \mid \exists \ c,s : c \in \text{A-MORPH}(s) \text{ and } t \in \text{S-PARSER}(c) \}$$

where A-MORPH is the analytical morphological module, see below. Now we assume that the morphological and surface rules are written in such a way that the condition $T_M \subseteq T_S$, named the *surface syntax condition*, is satisfied. This condition states that during analysis, S-PARSER must construct at least all correct S-trees for each sentence. It may generate too many S-trees, producing wrong ones as well. If $T_M \subseteq T_S$, the function L^{-1} can be effectively computed according to

$$L^{-1}(c) =_{def} \{ d \mid \exists \ t : t \in \text{S-PARSER}(c) \text{ and } d \in \text{M-PARSER}(t) \}$$

17.3.3   The semantic component

The semantic component consists of

1. a set of names of basic meanings and a set of names of meaning rules;

2. a relation ϕ that associates a set of (names of) basic meanings with each (name of a) basic expression. Syntactic variables are related to logical variables with the same index;

3. a relation ψ that associates one meaning rule with each meaningful M-rule. M-rule parameters are related to parameters of meaning rules. Here, too, syntactic variables are related to logical variables with the same index.

The functions A-TRANSFER and G-TRANSFER are defined in terms of ϕ and ψ, as follows:

$$\text{A-TRANSFER}(d) =_{def}$$
$$\{ \, m \mid d \text{ is the name of a basic expression and } (d,m) \in \phi \, \}$$
$$\cup \{ \, m \mid \exists \, R_i, d_1, \ldots, d_n, M_i, m_1, \ldots, m_n :$$
$$d = R_i <d_1, \ldots, d_n > \text{ and}$$
$$(R_i, M_i) \in \psi \text{ and}$$
$$m_1 \in \text{A-TRANSFER}(d_1) \text{ and}$$
$$\ldots$$
$$m_n \in \text{A-TRANSFER}(d_n) \text{ and}$$
$$m = M_i <m_1, \ldots, m_n > \}$$

$$\text{G-TRANSFER}(m) =_{def}$$
$$\{ \, d \mid m \text{ is the name of a basic meaning and } (d,m) \in \phi \, \}$$
$$\cup \{ \, d \mid \exists \, R_i, d_1, \ldots, d_n, M_i, m_1, \ldots, m_n :$$
$$m = M_i <m_1, \ldots, m_n > \text{ and}$$
$$(R_i, M_i) \in \psi \text{ and}$$
$$d_1 \in \text{G-TRANSFER}(m_1) \text{ and}$$
$$\ldots$$
$$d_n \in \text{G-TRANSFER}(m_n) \text{ and}$$
$$d = R_i <d_1, \ldots, d_n > \}$$

Obviously, A-TRANSFER and G-TRANSFER are each other's reverse:

$$m \in \text{A-TRANSFER}(d) \Longleftrightarrow d \in \text{G-TRANSFER}(m).$$

17.3.4   The morphological component

The morphological modules A-MORPH and G-MORPH have already been discussed in some detail in Chapter 6. A-MORPH maps each word onto a set of lexical S-trees, and hence each sentence onto a set of sequences of lexical S-trees. The function G-MORPH reversely maps each sequence of lexical S-trees onto a written sentence. The two modules are each other's reverse:

$$c \in \text{A-MORPH}(s) \iff s \in \text{G-MORPH}(c).$$

The morphological modules comprise only part of what is usually called morphology: the definition of the correct words of a language. We have seen that the set C of correct sequences of lexical S-trees is determined by the syntactic component. The possible values of the individual lexical S-trees that are elements of such sequences are thus also determined by the syntactic component alone.

17.3.5   Conditions on M-grammars

Above, we have seen how the syntactic component defines not only the modules M-PARSER and M-GENERATOR, but also leads to specifications of other modules.

The requirement that the syntactic component defines all and nothing but correct sentences entails, as specification for the module G-MORPH, that it must map *all* lexical S-trees that are produced by M-GENERATOR to a string: it may not act as a filter.

The requirement of reversibility led to the surface grammar condition. If A-MORPH is the reverse of G-MORPH, the surface grammar condition can be satisfied by writing suitable surface rules. In other words, if the morphological modules are reversible, the surface grammar condition is a specification for S-PARSER. The demands on the morphological modules and on S-PARSER should be interpreted as guidelines. The rule writer should set out to satisfy them, but in general it will not be possible to formally prove that a given S-PARSER satisfies the surface grammar condition, or that G-MORPH does not act as a filter.

The whole grammar is reversible, if each generative module is the reverse of the corresponding analytical one. Literally, this requirement is not fulfilled, because S-PARSER and LEAVES are not each other's reverse. However, if the surface grammar condition holds, S-PARSER followed by M-PARSER (L^{-1}) is the reverse of M-GENERATOR followed by LEAVES (L). If we define the functions analysis and generation as analysis(s) $=_{def}$ {m | ∃ c,t,d:

        c ∈ A-MORPH(s) and

        t ∈ S-PARSER(c) and

        d ∈ M-PARSER(t) and

        m ∈ A-TRANSFER(d)}

generation(m) $=_{def}$ {s | ∃ c,t,d:

        d ∈ G-TRANSFER(m) and

        t ∈ M-GENERATOR(d) and

        c ∈ LEAVES(t) and

        s ∈ G-MORPH(c)}

reversibility of the grammar means

    m ∈ analysis(s) ⟺ s ∈ generation(m).

In other words, if a string can be analysed and leads to a semantic derivation tree m, then the same string can be generated from this m.

A last point is about termination conditions. A sufficient condition for the system to terminate is that each module terminates. Morphological rules should abide by a measure condition in order to guarantee that the morphological modules terminate (see Chapter 6). Surface rules are a kind of context-free grammar, and general parsing algorithms may be used to implement S-PARSER, without termination problems. The termination of the modules A-TRANSFER and G-TRANSFER follows from the fact that the relations ψ and φ associate only finitely many meanings with each basic expression and to each M-rule, and vice versa. M-GENERATOR terminates if the M-rules are effective functions. M-PARSER terminates if, in addition, M-rules satisfy a measure condition, as discussed above. Finding one measure for all M-rules is very difficult for realistic grammars. In the case of controlled M-grammars, termination conditions are easier to formulate: we shall come back to this at the end of this chapter.

17.3.6 Isomorphic M-grammars

As explained above, reversibility holds within an M-grammar: if the analysis of a sentence associates a semantic derivation tree to it, this sentence can also be generated from the same semantic derivation tree. In the context of translation such reversibility is convenient, especially if it is extended across languages. Let us assume two M-grammars, G and G′. For grammar G the functions analysis and generation are constructed, and for grammar G' the functions analysis' and generation'. The translation relation $TR_{G,G'}$ is defined for sentences, as

$$(s,s') \in TR_{G,G'} =_{def} \exists \, m: m \in analysis(s) \text{ and } s' \in generation'(m)$$

which states that s' can be generated as a translation of s.

From the reversibility of G and G' it follows that an alternative definition is

$$(s,s') \in TR_{G,G'} =_{def} \exists \, m: m \in analysis'(s') \text{ and } s \in generation(m),$$

which states that s is a translation of s'. Hence, if sentence A is a translation of sentence B, then B is a translation of A. This is nice, but in itself not necessarily very useful. Note, for instance, that reversibility also holds if one of the grammars does not generate any sentence. To make reversibility practical, we must demand that if according to grammar G a semantic derivation tree is well-formed (in other words, a sentence can be generated from it) it is also well-formed according to G'. To achieve this, M-grammars G and G' must be *attuned* to each other. As already described in Chapter 2, attuned grammars are isomorphic.

M-grammars G and G' are called **isomorphic** if and only if

- Every basic expression of G has at least one translation-equivalent basic expression in G', with which it shares at least one basic meaning, and vice versa.
- For every meaningful rule of G there is at least one translation-equivalent rule in G', with which it shares at least one meaning, and vice versa.

If G and G' are isomorphic, then for each syntactic derivation tree for one grammar one can construct at least one derivation tree for the other grammar that consists of translations of the rules and basic expressions. This does not yet mean that for each well-formed derivation tree of one grammar one can construct at least one well-formed derivation tree of the other grammar. If this is the case, two M-grammars are called *strictly* isomorphic.

M-grammars G and G' are **strictly isomorphic** if and only if

$$\forall m : (\exists s : s \in generation(m)) \Leftrightarrow (\exists s' : s' \in generation'(m))$$

The status of strict isomorphy is like that of the surface grammar condition, in that it can not been proven for two arbitrary M-grammars. The problem is that, because M-rules are partial functions that are unrestricted apart from the reversibility requirement and measure conditions, there is only one general way to prove that a derivation tree is well-formed: apply M-GENERATOR to it. Because there are infinitely many derivation trees, this is not a finite procedure.

17.4   Controlled M-grammars

Controlled M-grammars differ from free M-grammars in two respects. Firstly, in a controlled M-grammar the rules are divided into two groups: meaningful rules and transformations. Meaningful rules have an associated meaning rule, transformations have not. Meaningful rules may have more than one argument, transformations always have exactly one argument. In derivation trees only meaningful rules occur. Secondly, a controlled M-grammar consists of a number of subgrammars.

A *subgrammar* SG_i is defined by stipulating

- a set of meaningful rules and a set of transformations;
- export specifications, in the form of a set *exportcats$_i$* of syntactic categories. Only generated S-trees with category in this set are admissible for export to other subgrammars;
- import specifications. These consist of
  1. a set *headcats$_i$* of syntactic categories, which are the categories of S-trees that are allowed as the head of the subgrammar, and
  2. for each rule an import specification of the non-head arguments. This will not be formalised in this chapter (it has not been implemented, either);
- a control expression that indicates what sequences of rule applications are possible, from imported head to exported result.

A control expression is a restricted regular expression over rule names (meaningful ones and transformations), that is restricted in two ways:

1. It is a sequence of rule classes.
2. Each rule may occur only once in a control expression.

An example of a control expression is

$$(R_1).[R_2|R_3].\{R_4|R_5\}.(T_1|T_2).(R_6)$$

which is also used in Chapter 9. The allowed sequences of rules are the instances of the regular expression, such as

$$R_1R_2R_4T_1R_6,$$
$$R_1T_1R_6,$$
$$R_1R_4T_1R_6,$$
$$R_1R_2R_4R_5T_2R_6,$$
etc.

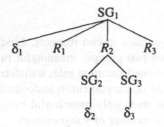

Figure 17.6: A controlled δ-tree; the tree is correct only if the sequence $R_1R_2R_3$ is allowed by the control expression of subgrammar SG_1.

The set of all instances of the control expression of SG_i is called *control$_i$*. If the control expression involves iteration, this set is infinite.

A control expression of a controlled M-grammar may be viewed as a restriction on allowable derivation trees. This restriction can be formulated most easily on δ-trees. Consider the sequence $\lambda_1,\ldots,\lambda_k$, as it occurs in the definition of δ-trees. The corresponding sequence $R_{\lambda_1},\ldots,R_{\lambda_k}$ of rules must be an instance of the control expression of the subgrammar that dominates this sequence, where transformations in these instances must be neglected; see Figure 17.6. If a δ-tree satisfies such constraints for all subgrammars that appear in it, it is called *controlled*.

The formal definition of the notion of controlled δ-trees reads:

A *controlled δ-tree* is

- an expression $SG_{blex} < \underline{b} >$, with b a basic expression, or
- an expression of the form $SG_i < \delta, \lambda_1,\ldots,\lambda_k >$, where $\lambda_1,\ldots,\lambda_k$ are expressions of the form $R_j < \delta_1,\ldots,\delta_n >$, where $\exists \beta_0,\ldots,\beta_k :$ $\beta_0 R_{\lambda_1}\beta_1 R_{\lambda_2}\beta_2,\ldots,R_{\lambda_k}\beta_k \in control_i$. Here $\delta, \delta_1,\ldots,\delta_n$ are controlled δ-trees, R_j is a meaningful rule, SG_i a subgrammar name, and variables β_i denote sequences of transformations.

Below we will keep to the convention that β_i are sequences of transformations. Variables α_i are used for arbitrary sequences of M-rules, that is, without restrictions on the kind of M-rules. For reasons of elegance, we assume (without losing generality) that each rule sequence in $control_i$ begins with a rule T_i^{init} and ends with T_i^{final}. Both T_i^{init} and T_i^{final} are transformations equal to the identity function on S-trees.

Control expressions are used for generation as well as analysis. In generation the allowed rule sequences are applied from left to right; in analysis they are applied from right to left. Let us first study generation: how a subgrammar is applied, given some δ-tree. Let the δ-tree be $SG_i < \delta, \lambda_1,\ldots,\lambda_m >$. Suppose that the tree δ produces an S-tree t. The rules $R_{\lambda_1}\ldots R_{\lambda_m}$ must be applied in this order. However, such a sequence of meaningful rules will not be an instance of the control expression: it must be interleaved with transformations. First T_i^{init} is applied to t, then there could be other transformations before it is the turn of R_{λ_1}. More completely, a rule sequence

$$T_i^{init}\beta_0 R_{\lambda_1}\beta_1\ldots R_{\lambda_m}\beta_m T_i^{final}$$

in control$_i$ must be found and applied. The transformations T_i^{init} and T_i^{final} need not really be applied, of course, because they are identity functions. We write the application of such a complete instance of the control expression as

(1)
$$t \xrightarrow{\beta_0\lambda_1\beta_1\ldots\lambda_m\beta_m} s .$$

The sequence $\beta_0\lambda_1\beta_1\ldots\lambda_m\beta_m$ should be interpreted as a sequence of unary rules: the transformations in the sequences β_i, to be viewed in the generative sense, and the λ functions obtained from R_λ by partial parametrisation, as explained in Section 17.2.3. Then, (1) means that these unary rules, applied in this order, transform t into s. To implement M-GENERATOR recursively, it is convenient to consider rule sequences from T_i^{init} to T_i^{final} as a special case of sequences between two arbitrary rules or transformations, R_1 and R_2. In this more general case, we look for sequences $\alpha_1 R_1\beta_{j-1} R_{\lambda_j}\beta_j\ldots R_{\lambda_k}\beta_k R_2\alpha_2$ that are in control$_i$ and compute

$$t \xrightarrow{\beta_{j-1}\lambda_j\beta_j\ldots\lambda_k\beta_k} s.$$

Such computations, for fixed R_1 and variable R_2, are performed by the following function:

$$\text{generator}_i(t,R_1,<\lambda_j,\ldots,\lambda_m>) =_{def}$$
$$\{(s,R_2,<\lambda_{k+1},\ldots,\lambda_m>) \mid \exists\ \alpha_1,\alpha_2,\beta_{j-1},\ldots,\beta_k :$$
$$j - 1 \le k \le m \text{ and}$$
$$t \xrightarrow{\beta_{j-1}\lambda_j\ \beta_j\ldots\lambda_k\beta_k} s \text{ and}$$
$$\alpha_1 R_1\beta_{j-1} R_{\lambda_j}\beta_j\ldots R_{\lambda_k}\beta_k R_2\alpha_2 \in \text{control}_i \}$$

This definition is such that

$$(s,T_i^{final},<>) \in \text{generator}_i(t,T_i^{init},<\lambda_1,\ldots,\lambda_m>)$$

means that the relation between s and t is given by (1). The function generator$_i$ can be used to implement of M-GENERATOR for controlled M-grammars. The function is called M-GENERATOR$_c$, with the c of control:

M-GENERATOR$_c(\delta) =_{def}$
$\quad \{ s \mid \exists\, b \in B: \delta = SG_{blex} < \underline{b} > \text{ and } s = b \}$
$\quad \cup \{ s \mid \exists\, i, t, \delta_1, \lambda_1, \ldots, \lambda_m :$
$\qquad \delta = SG_i < \delta_1, \lambda_1, \ldots, \lambda_m > \text{ and}$
$\qquad t \in \text{M-GENERATOR}_c(\delta_1) \text{ and}$
$\qquad t.cat \in \text{headcats}_i \text{ and}$
$\qquad (s, T_i^{\,final}, <>) \in \text{generator}_i(t, T_i^{\,init}, < \lambda_1, \ldots, \lambda_m >) \text{ and}$
$\qquad s.cat \in \text{exportcats}_i \}$

This expresses the meaning of a subgrammar, as was explained above. If $\delta = SG_i < \delta_1, \lambda_1, \ldots, \lambda_m >$, M-GENERATOR$_c$ is recursively applied to δ_1 to obtain trees t on which the rules of subgrammar SG_i are applied, if t.cat $\in$ headcats$_i$. Going from T_i^{init} to T_i^{final}, applying all the rules of the δ-tree, interleaved with transformations, S-trees s are computed. A final check (s.cat $\in$ exportcats$_i$) is performed to see whether s has a correct category.

The control expression of SG_i is fully determined by the *successor* function:

$$\text{succ}_i(R) =_{def} \{ R' \mid \exists \alpha_1, \alpha_2 : \alpha_1 \, R \, R' \, \alpha_2 \in \text{control}_i \}.$$

For this to be true it is crucial that each rule appears only once in a control expression. The implementations of generator$_i$ below will be formulated in terms of successor functions. So, from a formal point of view, it is the successor function that counts, and the control expression is but a practical, albeit linguistically motivated, way to specify this.

With the successor function, a recursive definition of generator$_i$ can be derived from the one above:

generator$_i(t, R_1, < \lambda_j, \ldots, \lambda_m >) =_{def}$
$\quad \{ (s, R_2, < \lambda_{k+1}, \ldots, \lambda_m >) \mid$
$\qquad k + 1 = j \text{ and } s = t \text{ and } R_2 \in \text{succ}_i(R_1) \}$
$\quad \cup \{ (s, R_2, < \lambda_{k+1}, \ldots, \lambda_m >) \mid \exists\, u, t_1, \ldots, t_n, \delta_1, \ldots, \delta_n, R_{\lambda_j} :$
$\qquad \lambda_j = R_{\lambda_j} < \delta_1, \ldots, \delta_n > \text{ and}$
$\qquad \text{meaningful}(R_{\lambda_j}) \text{ and}$
$\qquad R_{\lambda_j} \in \text{succ}_i(R_1) \text{ and}$
$\qquad t_1 \in \text{M-GENERATOR}_c(\delta_1) \text{ and}$
$\qquad \ldots$
$\qquad t_n \in \text{M-GENERATOR}_c(\delta_n) \text{ and}$
$\qquad u \in F_{\lambda_j}(t, t_1, \ldots, t_n) \text{ and}$
$\qquad (s, R_2, < \lambda_{k+1}, \ldots, \lambda_m >) \in \text{generator}_i(u, R_{\lambda_j}, < \lambda_{j+1} \ldots \lambda_m >) \}$

$\cup \; \{ \; (s,R_2,< \lambda_{k+1}, \ldots, \lambda_m >) \; | \; \exists \; u, \; R_l \; :$
    transformation(R_l) and
    $R_l \in$ succ$_i(R_1)$ and
    $u \in F_l(t)$ and
    $(s,R_2,< \lambda_{k+1}, \ldots, \lambda_m >) \in$ generator$_i(u,R_l,< \lambda_j \ldots \lambda_m >) \; \}$

The three sets in this definition arise from the following three situations that can occur in derivations $t \xrightarrow{\beta_{j-1} \lambda_j \beta_j \ldots \lambda_k \beta_k} s$:

1. No meaningful rules and no transformations are applied: $j-1 = k$, so that $t \xrightarrow{\beta_{j-1}}$ s, and β_{j-1} consists of zero transformations. This means that $s = t$, whereas the condition $\alpha_1 R_1 \beta_{j-1} R_{\lambda_j} \beta_j \ldots R_{\lambda_k} \beta_k R_2 \alpha_2 \in$ control$_i$ reduces to $R_2 \in$ succ$_i(R_1)$.

2. At least one rule is applied and the first rule is a meaningful one: β_{j-1} is empty and $k \geq j$. This means that

$$t \xrightarrow{\beta_{j-1} \lambda_j \beta_j \ldots \lambda_k \beta_k} s \equiv t \xrightarrow{\lambda_j} u \xrightarrow{\beta_j \lambda_{j+1} \beta_{j+1} \ldots \lambda_k \beta_k} s.$$

The function λ_j is applied to t by using F_{λ_j} (for the interpretation of λ_j as a function, see Section 17.2.3). The first argument of F_{λ_j} is t, whereas the other ones are supplied by M-GENERATOR$_c$ (defined below). The derivation from u to s corresponds to the recursive call of generator$_i$.

3. At least one rule is applied and the first rule is a transformation: $\beta_{j-1} = R_l \beta'_{j-1}$. This means that

$$\xrightarrow{\beta_{j-1} \lambda_j \beta_j \ldots \lambda_k \beta_k} s \equiv t \xrightarrow{R_l} u \xrightarrow{\beta'_{j-1} \lambda_j \beta_j \ldots \lambda_k \beta_k} s.$$

The derivation from t to u is performed by computing $F_l(t)$ and the derivation from u to s again corresponds to a recursive call of generator$_i$.

The predicates *meaningful* and *transformation* check whether their arguments are a meaningful rule or a transformation, respectively.

To implement M-PARSER, we need the reverse of generator$_i$:

$parser_i(s, R_2, < \lambda_{k+1}, \ldots, \lambda_m >) =_{def}$
$\{(t, R_1, < \lambda_j, \ldots, \lambda_m >) \mid \exists\ \alpha_1, \alpha_2, \beta_{j-1}, \ldots, \beta_k :$
$j - 1 \leq k \leq m$ and
$t \xrightarrow{\beta_{j-1}\lambda_j\ \beta_j\ldots\lambda_k\beta_k} s$ and
$\alpha_1 R_1 \beta_{j-1} R_{\lambda_j} \beta_j \ldots R_{\lambda_k} \beta_k R_2 \alpha_2 \in control_i \}$

Reversibility between $generator_i$ and $parser_i$ means that

$(s, R_2, < \lambda_{k+1}, \ldots, \lambda_m >) \in generator_i(t, R_1, < \lambda_j, \ldots, \lambda_m >)$

is equivalent to

$(t, R_1, < \lambda_j, \ldots, \lambda_m >) \in parser_i(s, R_2, < \lambda_{k+1}, \ldots, \lambda_m >).$

In both cases there is a sequence of generative rule applications that map t onto s. The applied rules form a path through the control expression of SG_i from R_1 to R_2, excluding R_1 and R_2 themselves. The meaningful rules in the path are $R_{\lambda_j}, \ldots, R_{\lambda_k}$. As $j \leq k + 1$, $\lambda_{k+1}, \ldots, \lambda_m$ is a subsequence of $\lambda_j, \ldots, \lambda_m$: $generator_i$ 'eats' λs and $parser_i$ produces them.

M-PARSER$_c$ is defined analogously to M-GENERATOR$_c$ as

$\text{M-PARSER}_c(s) =_{def}$
$\{ \delta \mid \exists\ b \in B: s = b \text{ and } \delta = SG_{blex} < \underline{b} > \}$
$\cup \{ \delta \mid \exists\ i, t, \delta_1, \lambda_1, \ldots, \lambda_m :$
$\quad s.cat \in exportcats_i \text{ and}$
$\quad (t, T_i^{\ init}, < \lambda_1, \ldots, \lambda_m >) \in parser_i(s, T_i^{\ final}, <>) \text{ and}$
$\quad t.cat \in headcats_i \text{ and}$
$\quad \delta_1 \in \text{M-PARSER}_c(t) \text{ and}$
$\quad \delta = SG_i < \delta_1, \lambda_1, \ldots, \lambda_m > \}$

To implement $parser_i$ we note that reading a control expression from right to left, it is not only characterised by a successor function, but also by its reverse, the *predecessor* function

$pred_i(R) =_{def} \{ R' \mid \exists \alpha_1, \alpha_2 : \alpha_1 R' R \alpha_2 \in control_i \}.$

Function $parser_i$ can be defined in a recursive fashion analogously to $generator_i$:

$\text{parser}_i(s, R_2, < \lambda_{k+1}, \ldots, \lambda_m >) =_{def}$
$\quad \{ (t, R_1, < \lambda_j, \ldots, \lambda_m >) \mid$
$\qquad\qquad j = k + 1 \text{ and } t = s \text{ and } R_1 \in \text{pred}_i(R_2) \}$
$\quad \cup \{ (t, R_1, < \lambda_j, \ldots, \lambda_m >) \mid \exists\, u, t_1, \ldots, t_n, \delta_1, \ldots, \delta_n, R_{\lambda_k} :$
$\qquad\qquad \text{meaningful}(R_{\lambda_k}) \text{ and}$
$\qquad\qquad R_{\lambda_k} \in \text{pred}_i(R_2) \text{ and}$
$\qquad\qquad (u, t_1, \ldots, t_n) \in F'_{\lambda_k}(s) \text{ and}$
$\qquad\qquad \delta_1 \in \text{M-PARSER}_c(t_1) \text{ and}$
$\qquad\qquad \ldots$
$\qquad\qquad \delta_n \in \text{M-PARSER}_c(t_n) \text{ and}$
$\qquad\qquad \lambda_k = R_{\lambda_k} < \delta_1, \ldots, \delta_n > \text{ and}$
$\qquad\qquad (t, R_1, < \lambda_j, \ldots, \lambda_m >) \in \text{parser}_i(u, R_{\lambda_k}, < \lambda_k \ldots \lambda_m >) \}$
$\quad \cup \{ (t, R_1, < \lambda_j, \ldots, \lambda_m >) \mid \exists\, u, R_l :$
$\qquad\qquad \text{transformation}(R_l) \text{ and}$
$\qquad\qquad R_l \in \text{pred}_i(R_2) \text{ and}$
$\qquad\qquad u \in F'_l(s) \text{ and}$
$\qquad\qquad (t, R_1, < \lambda_j, \ldots, \lambda_m >) \in \text{parser}_i(u, R_l, < \lambda_{k+1} \ldots \lambda_m >) \}$

The above recursive definitions of M-PARSER$_c$ and M-GENERATOR$_c$ are clearly each other's opposites. This follows immediately from the fact that generator$_i$ and parser$_i$ are each other's reverse. Algorithmically, the definitions of M-PARSER$_c$ and M-GENERATOR$_c$ are not maximally efficient. Removal of superfluous computation is simple but it affects the elegance of the algorithms and the manifest reversibility between M-PARSER$_c$ and M-GENERATOR$_c$.

Constructors of a translation system on the basis of the M-grammar formalism must choose either to work with D-trees or with δ-trees. Section 17.3 defined the functions analysis and generation in terms of syntactic and semantic D-trees. For M-grammars without control this is the natural thing to do. In the case of controlled M-grammars the option to keep working with D-trees exists, if the subgrammar structure is considered irrelevant for translation. In such a system the above algorithms for M-PARSER and M-GENERATOR need substantial revision. Especially in the case of M-GENERATOR, working with D-trees is more complicated than working with δ-trees. A D-tree is more ambiguous than a δ-tree: a priori it has many possible subgrammar annotations, and all these must be investigated. In Chapter 18 the problem of defining M-GENERATOR in terms of D-trees, for controlled M-grammars, is solved by translating the task of M-GENERATOR into a formal parsing task.

The other option is to build a translation system with δ-trees. Then the subgrammar structure is considered relevant for translation and the transfer modules must be revised to operate at the level of δ-trees. This is technically easy: A-TRANSFER not only replaces names of basic expressions by names of basic meanings and names of M-rules by names of meaning rules. It also replaces every (syntactic) subgrammar name by a semantic subgrammar name and G-TRANSFER does the reverse.

In the current Rosetta system the subgrammar structure is considered relevant. We have two groups of subgrammars: the ones that export S-trees with non-propositional categories (XP) and those that export S-trees with propositional categories (XPPROP, CLAUSE, SENTENCE). These correspond to semantic subgrammar names SG_{XP} and SG_{XPPROP}, respectively.

Two isomorphic M-grammars have corresponding rules and basic expressions, according to the above definition. In the controlled case, the subgrammars in which corresponding rules occur are required to be isomorphic to each other, as far as meaningful rules are concerned. This is explained in Section 9.6.

As has been mentioned before, to prove that M-PARSER always terminates for free M-grammars one needs to construct a measure on S-trees. In a large grammar it is very difficult to find a measure such that the outputs of analytical rules are always smaller than their inputs. The situation is different in controlled M-grammars. The freely applied parts of these grammars are subgrammars, not rules. This means that a measure must be constructed to make sure that the outputs of subgrammars are smaller than their inputs, in analysis. In practice a subgrammar application typically consists of many rule applications, and finding an appropriate subgrammar measure is no problem. However, such a measure does not yet guarantee termination of M-PARSER: the subgrammars themselves must also terminate. Because the rule applications are controlled, termination problems in subgrammars are localised: they can only occur in the iterative parts of control expressions. Suppose that a control expression contains an iterative rule class, i.e. it contains an expression $\{B\}$, where B is a set of rules. Then a measure must be found such that application of each rule in B analytically decreases the measure. The introduction of transformations causes a minor complication that does not exist in the uncontrolled case. Because transformations are not included in derivation trees, M-GENERATOR$_c$ no longer necessarily terminates: if the subgrammar allows iteration over transformations only, a measure is needed to guarantee that there can not be an infinite sequence of successful generative applications of such transformations.

Summarising, it may be said that termination problems for controlled M-grammars are more manageable than they are for free M-grammars, because they are localised and different measures may be defined to deal with each problem.

17.5 Concluding remarks

Formal requirements like the surface grammar condition and strict isomorphy between M-grammars can not be proved. Violations of these requirements will occur regularly during the creation of a translation system. However, such problems are easily recognised and are, in any case, negligible compared to other, empirical, translation problems. The unprovability of the formal requirements associated with M-grammars is related to the status of the M-grammar formalism. It is not a theory about language, but rather a practical and powerful methodology for writing large grammars. With the current state of the art in (computational) linguistics, we advocate a practical attitude towards writing grammars. In particular, we prefer restrictive usage of a powerful formalism to being confined in a restricted formalism.

One of the big problems in computational linguistics is the maintainability of large grammars. Our formalism offers a modularisation mechanism to make it possible to write and understand large grammars: the division of the grammar into subgrammars. Subgrammars, however, still lack a number of properties of real modules, as they exist in programming languages. First, the head and the import and export conditions should be more refined than they are now. Second, the current concept of subgrammars lacks encapsulation of data. If a subgrammar uses an S-tree produced by another subgrammar, every property of the S-tree is accessible: information is never hidden. New research and experiments are needed to find out to what extent grammars for natural language may be written in a genuinely modular way.

Chapter 18

An attribute grammar view

18.1 Introduction

Controlled M-grammars, defined formally in Chapter 17, are essentially different
from M-grammars without control. The set of well-formed derivation trees is defined
at two levels instead of one. The control expressions define a superset of this set
of derivation trees, and M-rule applications filter out the ill-formed ones from this
superset. The difference is not one of formal power. A controlled M-grammar can
be translated into one without control (cf. Chapter 19), and of course free grammars
can be changed into controlled ones by adding a sterile control expression: a regular
expression that generates the set of M-rules. Rather, the difference is one of grammar
organisation. Control expressions function as the backbone of the grammar, and in
some sense form an easy-to-grasp grammar summary. This makes the existence of
control important for the design, development and maintenance of the grammar.

In Chapter 19 it will be shown that M-grammars can be interpreted as algebras.
This algebraic view hides the control aspect of M-grammars and also abstracts from
the way M-rules are specified. Instead of hiding control and rule notation one
can also take these aspects of M-grammars as primary concepts, and this leads to
additional links between M-grammars and standard computational formalisms. If one
takes the specification format of M-rules as the primary concept, one may depict
M-grammars as term rewriting systems (Huet and Oppen (1980)), apart from minor
details of our M-rule notation. Indeed, the heart of the M-rule notation, explained
in Chapter 3 is formed by its S-tree models. Models are S-tree templates, and are
naturally interpreted as terms of a term rewriting system. Because of its limited
practical value, we will not pursue this view of M-grammars.

If one takes the control aspect of M-grammars as the primary concept, one is led
to the attribute grammar perspective (Rous (1991)). A major virtue of the transla-

379

tion of M-grammars into attribute grammars is that it provides a way to implement the modules M-PARSER and M-GENERATOR with standard generation and parsing algorithms for attribute grammars. As we will derive them, these versions of M-PARSER and M-GENERATOR work with D-trees instead of δ-trees (see the discussion at the end of Chapter 17). The attribute grammar view is very natural if the set of derivation trees defined by the control expressions contains only few ill-formed ones. In the opposite case, i.e. if the control expressions allow many ill-formed derivation trees, the translation of M-grammars into attribute grammars is correct but rather artificial. In the Rosetta M-grammars, the importance of control is somewhere in between. It would therefore be misleading to conclude from the existence of a translation of M-grammars into attribute grammars that M-grammars are attribute grammars in disguise.

The M-grammar formalism is not the only Rosetta formalism that can be translated into attribute grammars. The surface grammar formalism (see Chapter 8) is obviously very close to attribute grammars. Surface grammars consist of context-free rules with (synthesised) attribute evaluation. The only deviance from normal attribute grammars results from the fact that the right-hand side of a rule is a regular expression over categories, rather than a sequence of categories. This causes complications because the attribute evaluation must be specified for each path through the regular expression. The parameter mechanism (see Chapter 8) was devised to deal with this. Of course, regular expressions can be eliminated at the cost of extra non-terminals. This chapter will show how to rewrite regular expressions such that the parameters of the original rules map onto attributes of the extra non-terminals, thereby mapping surface grammars onto attribute grammars. The mapping provides a cubic parsing algorithm for S-PARSER.

The role of regular expressions in surface grammars is quite analogous to the role of control expressions in M-grammars. In surface grammars they define a superset of S-trees, filtered by attribute evaluation. In M-grammars they define a superset of derivation trees, filtered by M-rule applications. This analogy will be used to explain the translation of M-grammars into attribute grammars.

18.2   Surface grammars

To review the surface grammar formalism, explained in Chapter 8, a small example rule will be considered that defines a noun phrase as a determiner followed by an arbitrary number of adjectives, followed by a noun:

$$NP \rightarrow DET/1.\{ADJ/2\}.NOUN/3.$$

Associated with the rule is a sequence t of parameters and five functions. One is the parameterless function *init* that assigns an initial value to the parameters. In the example of Chapter 8 all parameters are Booleans with initial value *false*. The categories on the right hand side are indexed with integers (1, 2, 3 in our example, 1...9 in the example of Chapter 8). For each index value i there is a partial function act_i that takes the attributes of the category with index i and a parameter sequence and produces a set of parameter value sequences. As was explained in Chapter 8, these functions are defined in terms of condition-action pairs. Conditions operate on the input, the attribute and parameter values, and the actions stipulate the output, in terms of alterations to the input values of the parameters. The last function, *final*, is also set-valued and maps the parameters to attributes of *NP*. It is defined in terms of condition-action pairs, also. The functions act_i and *final* may produce the empty set (if the conditions do not apply), which signals the rejection of a particular application of the rule.

The attributes of *NP* for a given sequence of categories that is defined by the regular expression, are specified in terms of the functions act_1, act_2, act_3, and *final*. For example, suppose the sequence is *DET ADJ ADJ NOUN*, with attributes *DET.atts*, $ADJ^1.atts$, $ADJ^2.atts$, *NOUN.atts*, respectively. Then the following prescription yields the possible values of the attributes of *NP*:

$$NP.atts \in final(t_4), \text{ where } t_4 \in act_3(NOUN.atts, t_3),$$
$$\text{where } t_3 \in act_2(ADJ^2.atts, t_2),$$
$$\text{where } t_2 \in act_2(ADJ^1.atts, t_1),$$
$$\text{where } t_1 \in act_1(DET.atts, init). \tag{18.1}$$

The parameter mechanism provides a dynamic kind of attribute grammar. The parameters can be seen as a kind of variables the values of which are changed at each step in a path through the regular expression (here these values are $init$, t_1, t_2, t_3 and t_4) and the final values are used to calculate the attributes of the left-hand side of the grammar rule (here *NP.atts*). How this kind of attribute grammar can be transformed into a standard, declarative, format, will be explained below.

A conventional syntax for attribute grammars with synthesised attributes is illustrated by the following example. If one has a rule $A \rightarrow BC$ then

$$\left[\begin{array}{l} A{<}a{>} \rightarrow B{<}b{>} \; C{<}c{>} \\ a = \phi(b, c) \end{array} \right.$$

stipulates that the attributes a of A can be evaluated from the attributes b of B and c of C, with the function ϕ. A useful extension, that combines applicability conditions and nondeterminism, is obtained by arranging that ϕ is set-valued:

$$\left[\begin{array}{l} A{<}a{>} \rightarrow B{<}b{>} \; C{<}c{>} \\ a \in \phi(b, c) \end{array} \right.$$

If $\phi(b, c)$ has more than one element, the rule is to be applied in more than one way and is equivalent to a number of rules with the same context-free rule $A \rightarrow BC$ that have a unique attribute evaluation. If $\phi(b, c)$ yields the empty set, the rule is not applicable. Without its attributes, the above surface rule can be replaced by

$$NP \rightarrow I\ NOUN, \quad I \rightarrow I\ ADJ, \quad I \rightarrow DET,$$

where I is some non-terminal that did not exist before. The attribute calculation may be added by writing

$$\left[\begin{array}{l} NP{<}a{>} \rightarrow I{<}s{>}\ NOUN{<}n{>} \\ a \in final(t), \text{ where } t \in act_3(n, s) \end{array} \right.$$

$$\left[\begin{array}{l} I{<}t{>} \rightarrow I{<}s{>}\ ADJ{<}a{>} \\ t \in act_2(a, s) \end{array} \right. \tag{18.2}$$

$$\left[\begin{array}{l} I{<}t{>} \rightarrow DET{<}d{>} \\ t \in act_1(d, init) \end{array} \right.$$

Here the attributes of the extra non-terminal I are of the same type as the parameters of the original rule. The intermediate values t_1, t_2 and t_3 in the above calculation (18.1) of $NP.atts$ appear in the transformed grammar as the attribute values of instances of I in the derivation of the NP:

$$NP{<}NP.atts{>} \rightarrow I{<}t_3{>}\ NOUN{<}NOUN.atts{>}$$
$$I{<}t_3{>} \rightarrow I{<}t_2{>}\ ADJ{<}ADJ^2.atts{>}$$
$$I{<}t_2{>} \rightarrow I{<}t_1{>}\ ADJ{<}ADJ^1.atts{>}$$
$$I{<}t_1{>} \rightarrow DET{<}DET.atts{>}$$

The relations between the attributes that appear in this derivation are determined by the stipulations in the attribute grammar (18.2) and coincide with (18.1). For instance, the first rule applied in this derivation is an instantiation of the first rule in (18.2) with $a = NP.atts$, $s = t_3$, and $n = NOUN.atts$. According to (18.2) the attributes satisfy

$$NP.atts \in final(t), \text{ where } t \in act_3(NOUN.atts, t_3),$$

which agrees with the first line of (18.1) after t is renamed t_4.

The example illustrates the general picture. Regular expressions can be replaced by regular subgrammars, involving a number of extra non-terminals. The dynamic surface rule way of attribute evaluation is translated into conventional static attribute evaluation, the extra non-terminals functioning as carriers of parameter values. Because there are only synthesised attributes, a bottom-up parsing algorithm can be used that evaluates the attributes as a matter of course. Moreover, as the rules of the rewritten grammar contain at most two non-terminals at their right hand sides, the CYK parser (Aho and Ullman (1974)), enriched with attribute evaluation, is a natural choice. If the attributes have finite sets of values, which is the case in surface grammars, this parser will run in cubic time.

It is clear how to obtain the S-trees described by a surface grammar from the syntax trees according to the rewritten grammar: just eliminate the non-terminals that were added while rewriting the grammar. Figure 18.1 displays the correspondence for an example in which the S-tree can be obtained by eliminating three instances of I, or alternatively, by viewing them as auxiliary nodes in a linked-list implementation of the daughters of the NP.

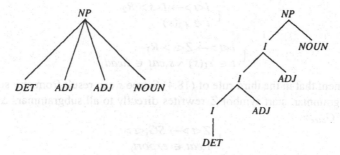

Figure 18.1: S-tree and corresponding derivation in rewritten grammar.

18.3 M-grammars

Chapter 17 gave the formal definitions of controlled M-grammars. An M-grammar consists of a set of subgrammars. Each subgrammar has a control expression, head specifications and export specifications. As in Chapter 17, SG_{blex} is taken to be a special subgrammar without a control expression, with keys of basic expressions as head, and with all basic categories as export. Suppose subgrammar SG_1 has control expression $R_1.\{R_2\}.R_3$, isomorphic to the surface rule in Section 18.2. Suppose for the moment that all rules are unary. Then the rule sequence $R_1 R_2 R_2 R_3$ produces S-trees t such that

$$
\begin{aligned}
&t \in r_3(t_4), \text{ where } t_4 \in r_2(t_3), \\
&\text{where } t_3 \in r_2(t_2), \\
&\text{where } t_2 \in r_1(t_1), \\
&\text{where } t_1 \text{ comes from another subgrammar and } t_1.cat \in head_1.
\end{aligned}
\tag{18.3}
$$

$t.cat$ denotes the category of S-tree t and $head_i$ is the set of head categories of subgrammar SG_i. The functions r_i are the generative versions of the M-rules R_i. Prescription (18.3) is analogous to (18.1): the categories $DET, ADJ, NOUN$ are replaced by names of M-rules (to which no attributes are associated), and S-trees take the place of the parameters. The above computation can be encoded in an attribute grammar, as in the previous section. For each subgrammar a non-terminal with an attribute of the type S-tree is introduced. An attribute grammar segment analogous to (18.2) can be written to represent subgrammar SG_1:

$$
\left[\begin{array}{l} SG_1\!\triangleleft t\!> \rightarrow\ I\!<\!s\!>\ R_3 \\ t \in r_3(s) \end{array}\right.
$$

$$
\left[\begin{array}{l} I\!\triangleleft t\!> \rightarrow\ I\!<\!s\!>\ R_2 \\ t \in r_2(s) \end{array}\right. \tag{18.4}
$$

$$
\left[\begin{array}{l} I\!\triangleleft t\!> \rightarrow\ Z\!<\!s\!>\ R_1 \\ t \in r_1(s) \wedge s.cat \in head_1 \end{array}\right.
$$

To implement that in the third rule of (18.4) S-tree s can result from any subgrammar of the M-grammar, start symbol Z rewrites directly to all subgrammars SG_i, among which is SG_{blex}:

$$
\left[\begin{array}{l} Z\!\triangleleft t\!> \rightarrow\ SG_i\!\triangleleft t\!> \\ t.cat \in export_i \end{array}\right.
$$

Here $export_i$ is the set of export categories of SG_i, as in Chapter 17. The above only works in this way if the rules are unary. Otherwise, if the rules are n-ary, extra arguments of the M-rules must be supplied. These arguments can in general result from arbitrary subgrammars. A straightforward way to express this in the attribute grammar is by adding $n-1$ start symbols Z to the right of each occurrence of the name of an n-ary M-rule in the attribute grammar, and using the attributes of Z as the extra arguments of the M-rule. For instance, if R_2 is ternary, we change the second rule in (18.4) into

$$
\left[\begin{array}{l} I\!\triangleleft t\!> \rightarrow\ I\!<\!s_1\!>\ R_2\ Z\!<\!s_2\!>\ Z\!<\!s_3\!> \\ t \in r_2(s_1, s_2, s_3) \end{array}\right.
$$

In this way, arbitrary control expressions containing M-rules with arbitrary arity are encoded in an attribute grammar. The only missing subgrammar is SG_{blex}, which is encoded with a rule

$$
\left[\begin{array}{l} SG_{blex}\!\triangleleft t\!> \rightarrow\ key \\ t = blex(key) \end{array}\right.
$$

for each basic expression key. The function *blex* retrieves the appropriate basic S-tree for every key.

The left tree in Figure 18.2 is a syntax tree according to an attribute grammar that contains subgrammar SG_1, with R_2 a ternary rule. The d_is refer to partial syntax trees with some subgrammar name at the root. The tree clearly is homomorphic to a D-tree expected from the control expression. The non-terminals I and SG_1 must be identified with their second daughters (rule names) and every instance of Z with its only daughter to get the standard D-tree format, which is the right tree in Figure 18.2. Here the d_i's are the D-trees obtainable from the trees d_i by a similar mapping. D-trees can be recovered not only by a homomorphism on the syntax trees according to the attribute grammar, but also, and even better, by an isomorphism on the language generated by the attribute grammar. This language consists of sequences of M-rule names and keys of basic expressions. Such a sequence approximately represents its own derivational history. To make it completely isomorphic to a D-tree, the attribute grammar must be altered slightly.

The first change involves transformations, which are omitted in D-trees. It is a simple matter to remove transformation names from the attribute grammar as well. For instance, if R_3 in our control expression is a transformation, the first rule in (18.4) is changed into

$$[\begin{array}{l} SG_1<t> \to I<s> \\ t \in r_3(s) \end{array}$$

keeping the transformation for the purpose of attribute evaluation, but deleting its name from the grammar rule.

The second change is necessary because the sequences of M-rule names and keys not always encode the derivational history uniquely. For instance, the sequence $key_1R_2key_2R_4key_3R_5$ corresponds to either one of the attribute grammar syntax trees (that abstract from labels like I, Z, SG_i) of Figure 18.3.

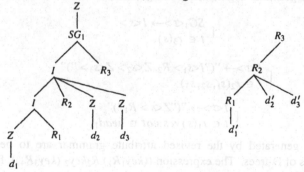

Figure 18.2: Attribute grammar syntax tree and corresponding D-tree

This problem is solved by generating bracketed sequences of M-rule names and keys, so that the first of the above syntax trees would correspond to $(key_1R_2(key_2R_4)(key_3R_5))$, and the second to $(key_1R_2((key_2R_4\ key_3)\ R_5))$. The required bracketed sequences are generated by a revised attribute grammar, in which each grammar rule that contains

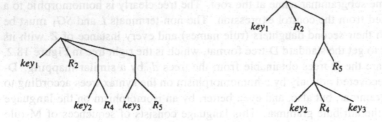

Figure 18.3: Alternative attribute grammar syntax trees with same leaves.

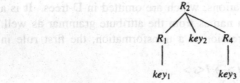

Figure 18.4: D-tree equivalent of $((key_1 R_1)R_2 key_2 (key_3 R_4))$.

an M-rule name starts and ends with the terminal symbols "(" and ")", respectively. For the example subgrammar, defined by control expression $R_1.\{R_2\}.R_3$, with R_1 a unary rule, R_2 a ternary rule, and R_3 a transformation, the following is the associated revised attribute grammar segment, replacing (18.4):

$$\left[\begin{array}{l} SG_1 <\!t\!> \rightarrow I <\!s\!> \\ t \in r_3(s) \end{array} \right.$$

$$\left[\begin{array}{l} I <\!t\!> \rightarrow \text{"("} I <\!s_1\!> R_2\ Z <\!s_2\!> Z <\!s_3\!> \text{")"} \\ t \in r_2(s_1, s_2, s_3) \end{array} \right.$$

$$\left[\begin{array}{l} I <\!t\!> \rightarrow \text{"("} Z <\!s\!> R_1 \text{")"} \\ t \in r_1(s) \wedge s.cat \in head_1 \end{array} \right.$$

The sequences generated by the revised attribute grammar are to be viewed as direct encodings of D-trees. The expression $((key_1 R_1)\ R_2 key_2\ (key_3 R_4))$, for example, corresponds to Figure 18.4.

As the attribute grammar generates encodings of D-trees, the algorithm that implements M-GENERATOR may be specified as the solution to a *parsing* problem. Its input is a D-tree d, and its output consists of the possible values of the S-tree attribute t of the start symbol Z, such that $Z <\!t\!>$ derives d:

$$\text{M-GENERATOR}(d) =_{def} \{t \mid Z <\!t\!> \xrightarrow{*} d\}$$

A standard bottom-up parsing algorithm (Earley (1970), Leermakers (1992), Leermakers (1993)) may be used for this purpose.

Reversely, M-PARSER is implemented with a top-down D-tree *generation* algorithm. Its input is the attribute of the start symbol, and the D-trees that can be generated from it form its output:

$$\text{M-PARSER}(t) =_{def} \{d \mid Z\langle t\rangle \overset{*}{\to} d\}$$

Here all attribute evaluations must be applied in reverse order. This is possible because M-rules and the function *blex* are reversible.

At first sight it may be surprising that the attribute grammar perspective on M-grammars leads to a parser-generator dualism: what is conceived to be a parser in the M-grammar framework turns out to be a generator if the grammar is written as an attribute grammar. Conversely, an M-grammar generator corresponds to an attribute grammar parser. However, M-GENERATOR naturally does have a parsing-like task. The D-tree that is input for M-GENERATOR is only a partial prescription for generating S-trees. Transformations have to be added between meaningful rules according to the control expressions of the grammar, and this indeed constitutes a parsing problem.

18.4   Concluding remarks

One might have thought that the implementation of the Rosetta modules would call for Rosetta-specific algorithms. This chapter, however, shows that the algorithmic problems of the modules S-PARSER, M-PARSER, and M-GENERATOR are related to standard ones. Because the modules LEAVES, A-TRANSFER and G-TRANSFER can be implemented according to their specification (see Chapter 17) in a straightforward way, the above solves the implementation problems for all components of the Rosetta system, except for the morphological components. The detailed specifications and implementations of the morphological components are not dealt with in this book. This should not be taken to imply that the implementation of morphological components is trivial or that the formalism for morphology is not worthy of detailed discussion. Such a discussion would have been too elaborate, however, given that the emphasis of this book is on translation. The compositional translation method can be used in conjunction with different formalisms for morphology.

The functions M-PARSER and M-GENERATOR as defined above need not terminate. Only if M-rules satisfy appropriate measure conditions, as discussed in Chapter 17, is termination ensured. In that case, the theoretical complexity of M-PARSER and M-GENERATOR is an exponential function of the length of the sentence. In practice though, at least in our experience, they run in linear time. That is, the time M-PARSER takes for one S-tree is a linear function of the size of that

S-tree, and similarly the time needed by M-GENERATOR for one D-tree is a linear function of the size of that D-tree. It should be born in mind, however, that the number of S-trees produced by S-PARSER, to be processed by M-PARSER one at the time, in worst cases is an exponential function of sentence length. The fact that M-PARSER and M-GENERATOR run in linear time reflects that, on average, M-rules do not use the full power offered by the formalism. For example, rules may produce arbitrarily big sets of results. In principle these sets might grow with the size of the M-rule arguments (the S-trees), but in practice rules have typically 0, 1 or 2 results, independently of S-tree sizes.

Chapter 19

An algebraic view

19.1 Introduction

The principle of compositionality of translation, introduced in Chapter 2, is the main principle of the Rosetta method and constitutes an important theme of this book. A mathematical model of compositional translation will be developed in the present chapter. The character of this chapter is somewhat different from the two previous chapters. Chapters 17 and 18 provide a formal treatment of the Rosetta system from two different perspectives, whereas the present chapter is more remote, in the sense that it does not primarily deal with the system, but with its method. The model that will be presented will be abstract, using several notions from universal algebra, but the main example of this model will, of course, be the Rosetta system.

Developing a mathematical model of compositionality has several advantages. To mention some:

1. It gives a new perspective on the Rosetta system, in which other facets become interesting. The algebraic point of view links the Rosetta framework with Montague grammar and with model theoretic semantics.

2. It relates the Rosetta method to well-investigated mathematical theory. Thus it is possible to use tools from mathematics and to prove results concerning the method. It makes it possible to investigate whether additions made to the ideas of Chapter 2 (e.g. control, introduced in Chapter 9) constitute a relaxation of the method or not (see Section 19.4).

3. It describes what are the essential ingredients for a compositional translation system, and it abstracts from aspects that are specific to the Rosetta system.

389

Thus it becomes possible to recognise the compositional method in other situations; for instance, when other syntactic theories are used, or, when the languages involved are not natural languages (see Section 19.5).

4. It offers a framework for the investigation of the power of the method and to answer questions such as: does compositionality form a restriction on the languages that can be dealt with? Or: what is the role of reversibility and of the measure condition? (see Section 19.6).

This chapter is organised as follows. Basic universal algebra is presented in Section 19.2, and this is used in Section 19.3 to develop an algebraic model for compositional translation. In section 19.4 the Rosetta system is considered in the perspective of this model, and other instances of the model are mentioned in section 19.5. Finally, Section 19.6 discusses aspects related to the formal power of the method.

19.2   Basic universal algebra

This section will introduce several notions from universal algebra, the main ones being *algebra, generator, term, homomorphism*, and *isomorphism*. These notions will be used in the next section to define a mathematical model of compositional translation. The definitions in this section are standard (see e.g. Graetzer (1986)), except for the definition of homomorphism, which deviates slightly from the usual one.

19.2.1   Algebras

An algebra is, intuitively speaking, a set with some operations defined on it. The relevant terminology is given in the following definitions.

Definitions:

An *algebra* A consists of a set A, called the *carrier* of the algebra, and a set of operators F defined on that set. So an algebra A is a pair $\langle A, F \rangle$, where A is a set and for each $f \in F$ holds $f \subset A^n \times A$. The *elements* of the algebra are by definition the elements of its carrier. An *n-ary operator* is an operator that takes n arguments, and a *partial operator* is an operator that is not defined on the whole carrier.

The notion of 'set' is a very general notion, and so is the notion 'algebra' which depends on it. In order to get used to this abstract notion, some examples of a different nature will be given below.

1. The algebra with as carrier the finite strings formed from $\{a, b, ..., z\}$ with concatenation of two strings as operation.

2. The algebra with as carrier the natural numbers $\{0, 1, 2, ...\}$ and with addition and division as operators. Here division is a partial operator since 3 cannot be divided by 2 if only natural numbers are available.

3. The algebra of all points in the $X - Y$ plane with as operation the assignment to three points of the point that is equidistant from all three points. Its operation is a 3-ary, and it is a partial operator since it is only defined for three points that do not lie on one straight line.

In order to avoid the misconception that everything is an algebra, an example of a non-algebra might be useful. Consider the first example: an algebra with finite strings as carrier, and with concatenation as operation. Add an operator that determines the length of a string. Then the result is no longer an algebra, since the lengths (natural numbers) are not elements of the carrier.

19.2.2 Generators

Often, the elements of an algebra can be obtained from a small subset using operations of the algebra. For instance, in the algebra of strings with concatenation as operation every string can be obtained starting from $\{a, b, .., z\}$ by application of the concatenation operator. These symbols are called the *generators* of the algebra, and the set $\{a, b, ..., z\}$ is called a *generating set*. In the algebra $\langle N^+, + \rangle$ of positive natural numbers with addition as operation the set $\{1\}$ is a generating set since $1 + 1 = 2$, $(1 + 1) + 1 = 3$, etc..

Starting with the set $\{a, b\}$ and using only the concatenation operator, the set of all strings of as and bs is obtained. This is an algebra, too, because the concatenation of two strings consisting of as and bs is again a string consisting of as and bs. Because its carrier forms a subset of all strings over $\{a, b, ..., z\}$, it is called a subalgebra of the algebra of all strings. An algebra which has a generating set B and a collection of operators F is denoted as $\langle [B], F \rangle$. So $\langle [\{a, b\}], concatenation \rangle$ is the algebra of all strings over $\{a, b\}$. And $\langle [\{2\}], + \rangle$ is the algebra of even numbers.

Definitions:

Let $A = \langle A, F \rangle$ be an algebra, and H be a subset of A. Then $\langle [H], F \rangle$ denotes the smallest algebra containing H, and is called the *subalgebra generated* by H. If $\langle [H], F \rangle = \langle A, F \rangle$, then H is called a *generating set* for A, its elements are called *generators of A*.

19.2.3   Terms

It often is important to know in which way an element is formed. In some kinds of
algebra it seems difficult to describe this process, in particular when the elements are
abstract (e.g. points in the plane). The general method of representing a generation
process is as follows. Names for the generators are introduced (say, $a_1, a_2, \dots$) and
names for the rules (say, $f_1, f_2, \dots$). Suppose f_1 is the name for a binary operator.
Then the expression $f_1\langle a_1, a_2 \rangle$ denotes a derivation where f_1 is applied to a_1 and a_2.
Such an expression is called a term. This term can occur as a subterm in a larger
expression, for example in $f_2\langle f_1\langle a_1, a_2 \rangle, a_3 \rangle$. This term can also be represented as a
tree as in Figure 19.1.   The terms (derivations, derivational histories) themselves

Figure 19.1: A tree representation of a term.

form an algebra. The carrier consists of all the terms. The operators of this algebra
combine small terms into larger ones. To continue the example given above, there
is an operator F_{f_1}, which takes as inputs the terms a_1 and a_2 and yields the term
$f_1\langle a_1, a_2 \rangle$. So for each operator in the original algebra there is precisely one operator
in the algebra of terms. Hence, given an algebra A there is a corresponding term
algebra (denoted as T_A). A term corresponds with an element in the original algebra
in the obvious way (apply the corresponding operators to the arguments obtained).
In a term algebra the operations are defined on the whole carrier, whereas operators
in the corresponding algebra may be partial.

Definition:

> Let $A = \langle [B], F \rangle$ be an algebra. Introduce for each element in B a distinct
> symbol b, and for each operator in F a distinct symbol f. Then $T_{B,F}$, the set
> of terms over $\langle [B], F \rangle$, is defined as follows:
>
> 1. for each element in B the corresponding symbol $b \in T_{B,F}$
> 2. if f corresponds with an n-ary operator, and if $t_1, t_2, \dots, t_n \in T_{B,F}$, then
> $f\langle t_1, t_2, \dots, t_n \rangle \in T_{B,F}$.
>
> In case we do not want to be explicit about the set of generators we may use
> the algebra itself as subscript (as in T_A).

19.2.4   Homomorphisms and isomorphisms

A homomorphism h from an algebra A to an algebra B is, intuitively speaking, a mapping which respects the structure of A in the following sense. If in A an element a is obtained by means of applying an operator f to an element a' then the image of a can be obtained in B by application of an operator corresponding with f to the element corresponding with a'. The structural difference that may arise between A and B is that two distinct elements of A may be mapped onto the same element of B, and that two distinct operators of A may correspond with the same operator in B. An isomorphism is a homomorphism for which such a structural difference does not arise, so an isomorphism has an inverse that also is a homomorphism.

Definitions:

   Let $A = \langle A, F \rangle$ and $B = \langle B, G \rangle$ be algebras.
   A mapping $h : A \cup F \to B \cup G$, where $h(A) \subseteq B$ and $h(F) \subseteq G$ is called a *homomorphism* if for all $f \in F$ and all $a, ..., a_n \in A$ holds: $h(f(a_1, ..., a_n)) = h(f)(h(a_1), ..., h(a_n))$.
   An *isomorphism* $h : A \cup F \to B \cup G$ is a homomorphism such that there is a homomorphism $g : B \cup G \to A \cup F$ with the property that for all $a \in A : g(h(a)) = a$.

The above definitions of homomorphism and isomorphism differ slightly from the definitions in the literature. Here, the correspondence of the rules is incorporated in the notion of homomorphism: it is standard to assume this correspondence as given. The two types of definition differ in case two different homomorphisms are defined on the same algebra, a situation that will not arise here. An advantage of the given definition is that it makes sense to speak about the image of an operator (and in later sections about the translation of a rule).

   Homomorphisms (and, consequently, isomorphisms) have a property that is very important in applications, and which will be appealed to several times. It is the property that a homomorphism is uniquely determined by its value for the operators and generator. This means that a homomorphism on an infinite domain can be defined by finite means. This is expressed in Theorem 1.

Theorem 1   *Let $A = \langle A, F \rangle$ and $B = \langle B, G \rangle$ be algebras, where D is the generating set of A.*
   Let $h : A \cup F \to B \cup G$ be such that $h(D) \subset B, h(F) \subset G$, and suppose that for each f its image $h(f)$ has the same number of arguments as f. Then there is a unique extension of h from D to A.

Sketch of Proof Suppose h_1 and h_2 are extensions of h. Then it can be shown by induction that for all $a \in A : h_1(a) = h_2(a)$.
End of Proof

19.2.5 Polynomials

It is useful to have a method available to introduce new operations in an algebra using already available operations. A simple example is composition: if f and g are operators which take one argument, then $f \circ g$ is defined by first applying f to the argument, and next applying g to the result. So for all $a: f \circ g(a) = g(f(a))$.

Another example concerns the algebra of natural numbers with $+$ and $\times$ as operators. The new operator takes two arguments and is represented by the expression $x_1 \times x_1 + x_2 \times x_2$ (or equivalently, $x_1^2 + x_2^2$). The operator assigns to the arguments 1 and 2 (given in this order) the value $1 \times 1 + 2 \times 2$, i.e. 5, and it assigns to the arguments 2 and 3 the value $2 \times 2 + 3 \times 3$, i.e. 13. An expression like $x_1^2 + x_2^2$ is called a polynomial. Given two arguments, the value yielded by the polynomial $x_1^2 + x_2^2$ is obtained by substituting the first argument for x_1, the second argument for x_2, and performing the calculations which are indicated in the expression.

This method of defining new operations by means of polynomials can be used in every algebra, the relevant formal definitions are given below.

Definitions:

A *polynomial* is a term in which indexed variables for elements of the algebra may occur (terms are special polynomials: polynomials without variables). A polynomial symbol p defines a *polynomial operator*: its value for given arguments is found by evaluating the term that is obtained by replacing x_1 by the first argument, x_2 by the second, etc.

Given an algebra $A = \langle [B], F \rangle$, and a set P of polynomial symbols over A, we obtain a new algebra $\langle [B], P \rangle$ by replacing the original set of operators by the set of polynomial operators defined by P. An algebra obtained in this way is called a *polynomially derived algebra*.

19.3   An algebraic model for compositional translation

19.3.1   Introduction

This section will give a mathematical model which characterises the essential aspects of a compositional translation system. The starting point of the discussion is the principle of compositionality of translation from Chapter 2. For ease of discussion it is repeated here:

Principle of compositionality of translation

Two expressions are each other's translation if they are built up from parts which are each other's translation, by means of translation-equivalent rules.

The mathematical model will be introduced step by step, and will be illustrated by string grammars resembling those given in Chapter 2, but now in an algebraic fashion.

19.3.2 Syntax

The compositionality principle speaks about *parts*, and the mathematical model should have a formal definition of this notion. Since the rules of the syntax determine how expressions are formed, we let the syntax determine what are the parts of an expression. For this purpose, the rules should take inputs and yield an output, and we define the *parts* of an expression E as those expressions from which E is formed by means of some rule. This means that the rules of syntax can be regarded as operators in an algebra.

The parts of an expression can again be expressions, and the principle is intended to hold for these parts as well. So there can be a chain of 'parts of parts of parts...'. Since the principle is intended to give a constructive approach to translating, this chain should have an end. These final parts can be taken as the generators of the algebra.

Summarising the above discussion: in a compositional translation system the syntax of source and target language are generated algebras. The parts of an expression E are the expressions that can be used as input for an operator yielding output E.

As an example the grammar $G_{English}2$ from Chapter 2 will be presented as an algebra. For convenience's sake, the grammar is repeated here:

$G_{English}2$:
1. Basic expressions:
   N(*girl*), N(*boy*), ADJ(*intelligent*), ADJ(*brave*),
   IV(*cry*), IV(*laugh*)
2. Rules:
   R_E1: N(α) + ADJ(β) $\Rightarrow$ NP(β αs)
   R_E2: IV(α) $\Rightarrow$ VP(α)
   R_E3: IV(α) $\Rightarrow$ VP(*do not* α)
   R_E4: VP(α) + NP(β) $\Rightarrow$ S(β α)

The carrier of the algebra $A_{English}2$ consists of strings (e.g. N(*boy*) or S(*intelligent boys cry*)), its generators are the basic expressions, and its operators are the rules. For instance, rule R_E1: N(α) + ADJ(β) $\Rightarrow$ NP(β αs) can be considered as a partial operator that takes two strings of a certain form as arguments, and yields one string as output. Using the algebraic notation introduced before, we may represent the algebra as:

$$A_{English}2 = \langle [\ N(girl),\ N(boy),\ ADJ(brave), IV(cry),\ IV(laugh)],$$
$$\{R_E1,\ R_E2,\ R_E3,\ R_E4\}\rangle,$$

where the effects of R_E1, etc., are as defined above.

19.3.3 Translations

The principle of compositionality states that the way in which expressions are formed from basic parts gives the complete information needed for determining its translation. In algebraic terminology it means that the terms over an algebra form the domain for the translation relation. The principle also states that the translations of an expression are formed in an analogous way from the translations of parts. So the range of the translation relation also consists of terms. An example of a term over the algebra $A_{English}2$ (see Section 19.3.2), is

$$R_E4\langle R_E3\langle IV(laugh)\rangle,\ R_E1\langle\ N(girl), ADJ(brave)\rangle\rangle,$$

which represents the derivation of S(*brave girls do not laugh*). The D-tree for this sentence is given in Chapter 2 and gives precisely the same information (viz. which basic expressions are used, and which rules).

Next we consider the *nature* of the translation relation between two languages A and B. For clarity's sake, we assume for the moment the simplification that in A and B each basic expression and each rule has precisely one translation. So there are no synonyms or ambiguities on the level of terms, and the translation relation between T_A and T_B is a function. Structural or derivational ambiguities of expressions of A and B are still possible.

Let us consider a simple example: algebra A, with a two-place operator f, and an algebra B in which the operator g corresponds with f. Let Tr_{AB} denote the translation function from T_A and T_B. Then the principle of compositionality of translation tells that the translation of the term $f\langle a1, a2\rangle$ is obtained from $Tr_{AB}(a_1)$ and $Tr_{AB}(a_2)$ by means of the operation g. So

$$Tr_{AB}(f\langle a_1, a_2\rangle) = g\langle Tr_{AB}(a1), Tr_{AB}(a2)\rangle =$$
$$Tr_{AB}(f)\langle Tr_{AB}(a_1), Tr_{AB}(a_2)\rangle$$

This means that Tr_{AB} is a homomorphism.

The same argument holds for the reverse translation. So Tr_{BA}, the reverse translation function, is a homomorphism as well:

$$Tr_{BA}(g\langle b_1, b_2\rangle) = Tr_{BA}(g)\langle Tr_{BA}(b_1), TrBA(b_2)\rangle.$$

Note that a translation followed by a reverse translation yields the original term:

$$Tr_{BA}(Tr_{AB}(f\langle a_1, a_2\rangle)) = Tr_{BA}(Tr_{AB}(f)\langle Tr_{AB}(a_1), Tr_{AB}(a_2)\rangle) =$$
$$Tr_{BA}(Tr_{AB}(f))\langle Tr_{BA}(Tr_{AB}(a_1)), Tr_{BA}(Tr_{AB}(a_2))\rangle = f\langle a_1, a_2\rangle$$

A homomorphism of which the inverse is a homomorphism as well, by definition is an isomorphism. Hence Tr_{AB} is an isomorphism.

We may summarise the formalisation obtained so far as follows. For a compositional translation system without synonyms and ambiguities at the level of terms holds: the translation relation is an isomorphism between the term algebra over the source language and the term algebra over the target language.

As an example we will consider a translation into Dutch of the expressions that are generated by $A_{English}2$. In order to obey the assumptions made in this section (no ambiguities on the level of terms) the grammar $G_{Dutch}2$ from Chapter 2 is modified in one respect: there is only one translation for *cry* viz. *huilen*. This grammar ($G_{Dutch}5$) is as follows:

$G_{Dutch}5$:
1. Basic expressions:
    N(*meisje*), N(*jongen*), ADJ(*dapper*), IV(*huilen*), IV(*lachen*)
2. Rules:
    R_D1: N(α) + ADJ(β) $\Rightarrow$ NP(βe αs)
    R_D2: IV(α) $\Rightarrow$ VP(α)
    R_D3: IV(α) $\Rightarrow$ VP(α *niet*)
    R_D4: VP(α) + NP(β) $\Rightarrow$ S(β α)

An algebraic presentation of this grammar that is isomorphic with the algebra $A_{English}2$ given in Section 19.3.2 is $A_{Dutch}5 = \langle[$ N(*meisje*), N(*jongen*), ADJ(*dapper*), IV(*huilen*), IV(*lachen*)], \{R_D1, R_D2, R_D3, R_D4\}$\rangle$, where the effects of R_D1, etc. are as defined above. The first generator of $A_{Dutch}5$ corresponds with the first of $A_{English}2$, the second generator with the second, etc., and the same goes for the operators. Hence the translation isomorphism maps the term

$$R_E4\langle R_E3\langle IV(laugh)\rangle, R_E1\langle N(girl), ADJ(brave)\rangle\rangle$$

on the term

$$R_D4\langle R_D3 \langle IV(lachen)\rangle, R_D1\langle N(meisje), ADJ(dapper)\rangle\rangle.$$

Figure 19.2 illustrates the isomorphism between term algebras for $A_{English}2$ and $A_{Dutch}5$ by indicating the values for some of the terms in these algebras.

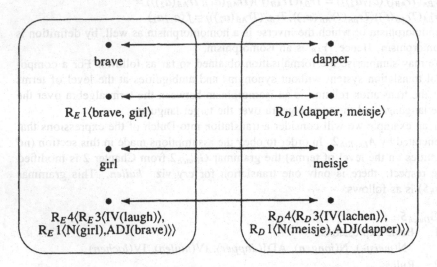

Figure 19.2: A translation isomorphism between some terms in $T_{English} 2$ and in $T_{Dutch} 5$.

19.3.4 Sets of synonymous translations

Next we allow that there are synonyms of basic expressions and of rules. The translation relation is then not a function from T_A to T_B, because a term may have several translations. But we can view the relation as a function yielding a set of synonymous terms. The same can be done in the source language algebra, and then the translation relation relates sets of synonymous terms in T_A with such sets in T_B. These collections of sets have the structure of an algebra. The result of the application of a set of operators to a set of terms is defined as the union of application of all operators to all terms. Figure 19.3 shows the situation that arises if the grammar from Figure 19.2 is extended with the synonyms *courageous* for *brave* and *moedig* for *dapper*. One may notice that in Figure 19.3 for the sets of synonymous terms the same situation arises as in Figure 19.2 for the terms themselves. This suggests that *the translation function is an isomorphism between the algebras of synonymous terms in T_A and T_B*. The suggestion can be proved to be correct using a theorem on isomorphisms that is not presented in the previous section: since synonymy is a congruence relation, it induces an isomorphism on the corresponding quotient algebra (see Graetzer (1986)).

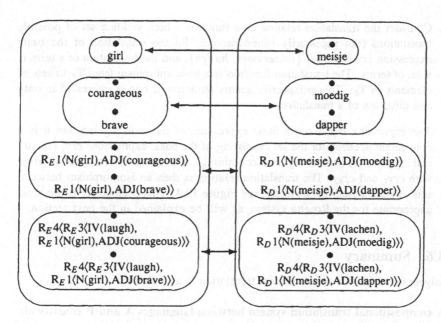

Figure 19.3: A translation isomorphism between some sets of synonymous terms in $T_{English}2$ and in $T_{Dutch}5$.

19.3.5 Ambiguities in translations

Finally, the consequences of ambiguous basic expressions and rules are considered. The introduction of ambiguities on the term level is an essential difference from the traditional situation in Montague grammar (e.g Montague(1970, 1973) where the terms uniquely determine the meaning of an expression and form an disambiguated language. However, a more recent development (called 'flexible Montague grammar') allows for ambiguous terms as well. See, for example, Partee and Rooth (1983), Hendriks (1987), and Groenendijk and Stokhof (1989).

Ambiguous basic expressions and rules may disturb the symmetry between source language and target language because an ambiguity in the one language needs not to correspond to an ambiguity in the other language. An example in the grammar $G_{English}2$ from Chapter 2 is *cry*, which can be translated into Dutch by *schreeuwen* (meaning *shout*) and *huilen* (*weep*). We consider three ways to conceive ambiguous terms in algebraic perspective:

1. The ambiguities of basic expressions (and of rules) form an exception to the situation that the grammars of source and target algebra are isomorphic algebras. This point of view might be useful if there are few exceptions.

2. Consider the translation relation as a function which yields a set of possible translations (not necessarily synonymous). So the translation of the basic expression *cry* is the set {*schreeuwen, huilen*}, and the translation of a term is a set of terms. The translation function is a homomorphism from T_A to sets of elements in T_B. This perspective seems attractive if one is interested in only one direction of a translation.

3. The expression *cry* is not a basic expression of the term algebra, but it is a convenient notation for the set consisting of the basic expressions cry_1 (*shout*) and cry_2 (*weep*), and every term containing *cry* is a notation for a set of terms with cry_1 and cry_2. The translation relation is then an isomorphism between sets of such unambiguous terms, see Figure 19.4. This perspective is the most appropriate for the Rosetta system, as will be explained in the next section.

19.3.6 Summary

The algebraic model for compositional translation is as follows:

A compositional translation system between languages A and B consists of:

1. Generated algebras as syntax for A and B. The parts of an expression E are the expressions that can be used as input for an operator yielding output E.

2. A translation relation that is defined between T_A and T_B and consists of an isomorphism between sets of synonymous terms in T_A and such sets in T_B.

19.4   Rosetta and the algebraic model

The present section will show that the grammars of Rosetta form an instance of the algebraic model. Furthermore, it will discuss some issues that are interesting from the algebraic point of view. The attention is restricted to the kernel of the grammar: the syntactic component and to the translation relation, whereas morphology and surface grammar are not considered.

19.4.1   Free M-grammars as algebras

The formalisation of the principle of compositionality of translation requires that the syntax of the languages in the system is organised as an algebra. This is the case for free M-grammars: they form an algebra, with the set of all possible S-trees as the carrier, and the M-rules as its operators. The incorporation of control will be

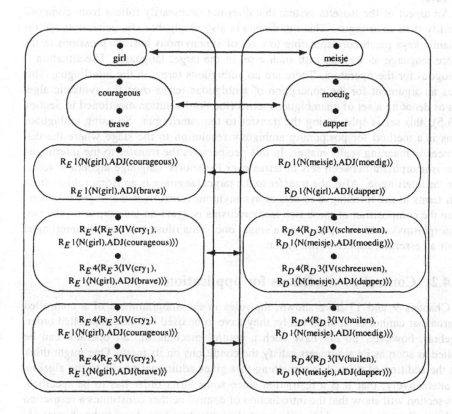

Figure 19.4: The translation isomorphism between some sets of synonymous terms after resolution of the ambiguity of cry.

considered in Section 19.4.2. The generators of the Rosetta algebra are its basic expressions; we will consider them in more detail in Section 19.4.4.

The formalisation of compositional translation requires that the translation relation is defined on the level of terms over the syntactic algebra. The syntactic D-trees are a representation of the terms, and the translation relation is indeed defined on this level.

An aspect of the Rosetta system that does not necessarily follow from compositionality is its interlingua. This interlingua is also an algebra. Its generators are the semantic keys (each corresponding to a set of synonymous basic expressions in the source language as well as with such a set in the target language. The situation is analogous for the operators. There are no ambiguous terms in the interlingua. This gives an argument for the conception of ambiguous terms over the syntactic algebras as denoting a set of unambiguous terms (the third solution mentioned in Section 19.3.5): this set is split during the transfer to the interlingua. So using ambiguous terms is a method for postponing ambiguity resolution to the stage where the differences in meaning really matter. In this perspective, the transfer to the interlingua is an isomorphism between sets of terms over the source language algebra to terms over the interlingua. Also, the transfer to the target language is an isomorphism from such terms in the interlingua to sets of synonymous terms over the target language. Since the composition of these two isomorphisms is again an isomorphism, the two isomorphisms could be replaced by a single one. This illustrates that the interlingua is not an essential aspect of the system.

19.4.2 Control as conditions for application

As Chapters 9 and 17 have shown, the rules in the subgrammars of a controlled M-grammar cannot be applied freely; they have to be used in some controlled order. Algebras, however, do not have such a control mechanism: an operator can be applied as soon as its arguments satisfy the conditions on its input. One might think that the addition of control is something that gives additional power to the algebra, or, alternatively, that it is a restriction since some strict order has to be specified. This section will show that the introduction of control neither constitutes a restriction on the algebra nor gives additional power. For this, two facts have to be shown: (1) that an algebra without control can be seen as a special algebra with control, and (2) that an algebra with control can be formulated as one without control.

First, consider an algebra without control, i.e. with free order of application of the operators. Suppose the algebra has operators $R_1, R_2, ..., R_n$. Then free application is described by the control expression $\{R_1|R_2|, ..., |R_n\}$. Thus, 'without control' is a special case of 'with control'.

Consider next an algebra with control. With this, the same effects can be obtained as without control. The idea is to extend the elements with information concerning their position in the course of the controlled generation process. Then the application conditions of the operators take care of the rule ordering. This idea is worked out in the following example.

Suppose we have, as in M-grammars, an algebra in which the elements are trees. We will enrich the top node with an attribute for control. Suppose the following control expression is given:

(1) $(R_1).\{R_2\}.[R_3]$

The possible values of the attribute are all strings which can be obtained by inserting a * somewhere in this control expression. The initial value of the attribute for control is

(2) $*(R_1).\{R_2\}.[R_3]$

The operator R_1 is only applicable to inputs that have this initial value for the control attribute. By application of R_1 the value of the attribute is changed into

(3) $(R_1) * \{R_2\}.[R_3]$

For R_2 two operators are introduced, R_{2a} and R_{2b}. Both require (3) as input value. Then R_{2a} applies R_2 and leaves the value of the attribute unchanged, whereas R_{2b} only changes it into

(4) $(R_1).\{R_2\} * [R_3]$

For R_3 we introduce two operators, viz. R_{3a} and R_{3b}. The effect of R_{3a} is the effect of applying R_3 and changing the control attribute into

(5) $(R_1).\{R_2\}.[R_3]*$

The effect of R_{3b} consists in changing the control attribute into (5), without application of R_3.

This example shows that an algebraic grammar with a control expression can be simulated by an uncontrolled one. In M-grammars the situation is somewhat more complex, because there is a control expression for each of the subgrammars. In order to incorporate the subgrammar structure, the attribute for control has to be enriched with information about the subgrammar this control expression originates from. The result can then be recognised as such, and may be imported into other subgrammars. Furthermore, in a free grammar each rule has to satisfy the measure condition, whereas in a controlled M-grammar this only holds for the iterative rules.

So a measure has to be designed together with the above construction. For this purpose we might take an unorthodox measure, which for the non-iterative rules looks at the position of the * in the attribute for control (the more to the right, the more complex), and for iterative rules in addition uses the measure given with such a rule. This point completes the discussion of the example that illustrates that a controlled grammar can be simulated by a free grammar.

19.4.3 Rules and transformations as polynomials

Syntactic transformations were introduced in Chapter 9 . These have no semantic effects on expressions, and are not relevant for defining the translation. Therefore they are ignored in the definition of isomorphism between source language derivations and target language derivations. This suggests that the introduction of transformations is a relaxation of compositionality of translation. Somers (1990b), quoting Carroll (1989), even stated that the introduction of transformations makes 'a complete mockery' of the statement that grammars are isomorphic. However a change of perspective shows that it fits perfectly into the algebraic framework, and hence it is an instance of the compositional approach.

The simplest solution would be to assume that for each transformation in the source language algebra there is an operation in the target language algebra which gives its input unchanged as output: a syntactic identity rule. The same would be done in the source language for all transformations from the target language algebra (see Chapter 9). Mentioning these rules explicitly in the translation relation does not yield any interesting information, therefore they can be omitted. This perspective is completely in accordance with the formalisation of compositionality of translation as given before, but it introduces another problem.

If a syntactic identity rule is applied, it might be applied indefinitely many times. So an expression can have infinitely many derivations, and obtaining all derivation trees is impossible. Hence parsing is impossible. A related objection is that the identity rules do not obey the measure condition (because the complexity of the output of the rule equals the complexity of its input). This measure condition, together with reversibility, is a prerequisite for the parsing method of M-grammars. Since the measure condition is not satisfied, the solution with the identity rules is not in accordance with the restrictions imposed on the Rosetta grammars. But another perspective on transformations is possible in which the measure condition is not violated.

The second method is based upon polynomially derived algebras. This is illustrated by means of a simple example. Suppose that source algebra *A* has the following control expression:

$$R_1.[T_1].R_2.\{T_2\}$$

where R_1 and R_2 are rules and T_1 and T_2 are transformations. Then consider this algebra with control, as an algebra A' without control, derived from A, and where the operators are defined by the polynomial symbols

$$R_1, R_1T_1, R_2, R_2T_2, R_2T_2T_2, R_2T_2T_2T_2, \ldots$$

As a result, the transformations have been connected with the preceding rules to form a polynomial operator. This choice is arbitrary, we might as well connect them with subsequent rules. If the control expression is more complicated, e.g. with more transformation classes mentioned between R_1 and R_2, then these classes define a set of possible sequences of applications of transformations. Each of these sequences can be connected with R_1 to form a polynomially derived operator.

In the target algebra we will use the same method to define new operators. Suppose the control expression is

$$T_3.R_3.[T_4].R_4$$

Here R_3 is the rule that corresponds with R_1, and R_4 with R_2. This control expression defines the derived operators:

$$T_3R_3, T_3R_3T_4 \text{ and } R_4.$$

The derived algebras have a correspondence of operators: all derived rules containing R_1 correspond with all rules containing R_3, and all derived rules containing R_2 correspond with all rules containing R_4.

In this perspective, the control expression is a finite method to define an infinite set of polynomial operators of the derived algebra A'. If the transformations and rules the polynomial operators are composed of, satisfy the reversibility and measure condition, the polynomials do so as well. This shows that the transformations are not a relaxation of compositionality: they are a method for defining a derived algebra with polynomial operations.

It might not be clear that the derived algebra can be parsed because, in the above example, the transformation T_2 is responsible for an infinite number of derived operators. However, only a finite number of derived rules has to be applied. Each application in analysis of a transformation decreases the complexity by at least 1. So if an input expression has complexity measure m, only sequences $R_2T_2T_2\ldots T_2$ with length $\leq m$ have to be tried, and this is a finite number of derived rules. Note that in M-grammars there is another situation in which an infinite number of rules is available for parsing. When a variable has to be introduced in analysis by a substitution rule, there are in principle infinitely many variable indices possible. Here a related solution is used: the rule is only applied for one new (conventionally determined) index.

19.4.4   Lexicon as generating set

The formalisation of compositionality requires that some suitable subset of expressions is selected as the set of generators. In mathematics it is often required that a generating set is *minimal*, or *finite*. These two properties will be considered below. Furthermore, the definition of lexicon for idioms will be looked at.

A generating set is *minimal* if no elements of the set can be missed. In some applications one aims at using minimal generating sets, for instance in geometrical applications, because the dimension of the object in some cases equals the minimal number of generators. The generating set of the Rosetta algebras is not minimal. The grammars produce, for instance, an S-tree for *John kicked the bucket* from two different sets of generators. Either from the elements {*John, bucket, kick*} in S-LEX, or from *(kick the bucket)* in ID-DICT and *(John)* in S-LEX. If the idiom were not in the lexicon, then still the same S-tree could be formed. This is done because in the translation process idioms are considered as basic expressions.

In applications one often aims at a finitely generated algebra, because such an algebra can be specified by finite means. The generating set of the Rosetta algebra is infinite, because an unlimited number of variables is available. This infinity causes no problem for a finite specification of the translation relation because the translation of these infinitely many elements is completely regular (a variable is translated into a variable with the same index). There are infinitely many different analyses of a sentence which differ only with respect to the choice of a variable. As indicated in Section 19.4.3, this causes no serious problems.

It is interesting to see that idioms and translation idioms are defined in the lexicons by polynomial symbols. For instance, the translation idiom *cocinar* is translated into *prepare a meal*, and this complex expression is defined by giving the keys of the basic expressions and of the rules which form it, hence by giving the term which describes the derivation of the complex expression. Idioms with an open position give rise to polynomials with variables (e.g. *to pull* x*'s leg*). Representing idioms by means of polynomials is done for a practical reason: to guarantee that the S-trees that are assigned to them are suitable input for later rules (see Chapter 15).

19.4.5   The translation relation as a homomorphism

The translation relation in a system for compositional translation is a homomorphism (in fact a special one: an isomorphism). Due to the properties of homomorphisms, there are several advantages.

1. A homomorphism is fully determined by its values for the generators and operators. This justifies the way in which the Rosetta system translations are defined: by giving the translations of generators and operators. Thus the infinite translation relation is reduced to a finite relation between grammars.

2. The translation is defined for the same operators and generators as used in the syntax to define the language. Thus it is guaranteed that if an expression is generated in the syntax, it is automatically accepted as input for the translation. This situation contrasts with a situation in which the generated language is defined by one mechanism and the translation by another. Then there is no guarantee that a generated expression is suitable as input for translation (cf. the intersection problem discussed in Chapter 5).

3. The last, but important, advantage concerns the correctness of the translations. As was already explained in Chapter 2, generators and rules of the Rosetta grammars are designed in such a way that they represent a (basic) meaning or an operation on meanings. So there is an (implicit) algebra of meanings, and the assignment of a meaning to terms is a homomorphism. Hence the meaning of a term is uniquely determined by the meanings of generators and operators. Furthermore, the generators and operators of the target language have the same meaning as the corresponding generators of the source language. So the algebra of meaning for the source language is identical to the algebra of meanings for target the language. Consequently a term of the target language has the same meaning as the corresponding meaning in the source language. So, due to the fact that translation is a homomorphism, the correctness of the translation follows from the correctness of the translations of the generators and operators.

19.4.6   Conclusions

We have considered several aspects of the Rosetta system from an algebraic perspective. It turned out that M-grammars satisfy the algebraic model, even in those cases where this was not at first evident (e.g. control and transformations).

19.5   Other examples of compositional translation

19.5.1   Related work

The algebraic model as described above, can be found outside the context of the Rosetta system. In some cases this is not surprising since there is a common background, such as Montague Grammar and compositionality, or other ideas originating from Rosetta publications. Below we mention some examples where the same algebraic model is used, most of them have already been mentioned in Chapter 5 in another context.

1. Dowty (1982) noticed the analogy of derivation trees for small fragments of English, Japanese, Breton and Latin, and proposed such derivation trees for translation. For Latin (a language with free word order) the grammar would not generate strings (or structures), but (unordered!) sets of words.

2. Tent (1990) used Montague grammar to give a method for investigating a typology of languages. She does so by comparing grammatical rules in different languages for the same meaning operation. In fact she designs (very small) isomorphic grammars or English, Japanese, Indonesian and Finnish.

3. Rupp (1986) attempted to write isomorphic grammars for a machine translation system with generalised phrase structure rules.

4. The CAT framework of Eurotra is a proposal (not implemented) for the design of the Eurotra system, the translation project of the EC (e.g. Arnold *et al.* (1985), Arnold *et al.* (1986), Des Tombe(1985) and Arnold and Des Tombe(1987)). This proposal is based upon a variant of the principle of compositionality of translation, viz. *The translation of a compound expression is a function of the translations of its parts.* This formulation of compositionality is also given by Nagao (1989). The algebraic model of this principle gives rise to a model in which translation is a homomorphism (see Janssen (1989)). It can be turned into an isomorphism by introducing sets in the way indicated in Section 19.3.5.

19.5.2 Other proposals that are compositional

For some proposals it might not be immediately obvious that the compositional approach is followed. Then an algebraic reformulation of a proposal might make the analogy evident. Two examples of this are given below.

A TAG grammar is a tree grammar: its basic expressions are trees, and the operations are operations on trees. Such an operation may for instance replace, under certain conditions, an internal node by a subtree. Abeillé *et al.* (1990) proposed the use of synchronised TAG grammars for translating. A synchronised TAG grammar consists of two TAG grammars. The basic trees of the two grammars are given in pairs: a tree in one grammar with the corresponding tree in the other grammar. The positions in which the expansions may take place are 'synchronised': for each node that may be expanded in one tree, a link with a node in the other tree is given. A derivation starts with two coupled basic expressions, and continues by expanding two linked nodes. This means that the grammars are isomorphic and derivations are made in parallel. Thus, synchronised TAG grammars are an instance of compositional translation.

Some theories of language do not have constituent structures as a notion in their theory. For instance, Dik's functional grammar (Dik (1978)) is inspired by logic: predicate frames constitute the skeleton of the syntax and rules operate on such frames (e.g. attaching a modifier or substitution of an argument). Van der Korst(1989) proposed a translation system based upon functional grammar, and, to a large extent, this can be seen as a compositional translation system. The predicate frames filled with arguments, and with modifiers attached, can be considered terms in an algebra, where the frames and modifiers are operations.

That these rather divergent theories fit into the algebraic framework may give rise to the misconception that this holds for all syntactic theories. A counterexample is given by the approach which says that the strings of a language have a structure and that this can be any structure that meets certain well-formedness conditions. So there are no rules, only conditions. Such a system was proposed by McCawley (1986). Since there are no rules, there is no algebra with operations, and a compositional translation system in the sense of the principle cannot be designed.

A somewhat similar situation arises in the theory of 'Principles and Parameters', because, there too, the conditions are the central part of the theory. Formally, the situation is slightly different because the crucial part of the grammar is a rule (called move-α) which can move any constituent to any position, and this movement is controlled by many conditions. An algebraic formulation of this theory is possible, with as most important operator the partial operator corresponding with move-alpha. In this case, the algebraic approach is not interesting because the syntactic algebra hardly has any structure, and it is unlikely that a compositional translation system can be based upon this algebra. Note that many generalisations are used in M-grammars which were proposed within the 'Principles and Parameters' theory, but in a much more structured way than with one movement rule.

19.5.3 Other applications of compositional translation

Besides natural languages there are programming languages and logical languages. Translations are made between such languages, as well. We will consider some examples of this, illustrating that the compositional approach, which is innovative for translations between natural languages, is accepted and more or less standard for other kinds of translations.

1. *From logic to logic.*

In logic, translations are frequently used to investigate the relation between different kinds of logic, for instance their relative strength or their semantic relation. The standard method of translation is the compositional method. An example is the Gödel translation: this translates intuitionistic logic into modal logic. For instance the intuitionistic implication $\phi \to \psi$ is translated into $\Box(\phi' \to \psi')$, where ϕ' and ψ' are translations of ϕ and ψ, respectively. Therefore, the translation of the implication is a polynomial symbol over the syntactic algebra of modal logic.

2. *From natural language to logic.*

The aim of Montague grammar is to associate meanings with natural language expressions. This is done by translating natural language into intensional logic. The methodological basis of Montague Grammar is the principle of compositionality of meaning, and, therefore, this translation has to be compositional. In many cases a syntactic operator is translated into a compound expression over the logic. For instance, verb phrase disjunction is translated as $\lambda x[\alpha(x) \vee \beta(x)]$, where α and β are the translations of the verb phrases.

3. *From programming language to programming language.*

Computers have to execute programs written in some programming language, and for this purpose the programming language is translated into machine code. The compiler is the part of the computer software which performs this translation. Often, one instruction from the programming language has to be translated into a compound of machine code instructions. A standard method to perform the translation is the so called 'syntax directed translation'. This method can be seen as a form of compositional translation. The power of the compositional approach is used by Thatcher *et al.* (1979) to design a method which allows a proof of the correctness of such a compiler. Following the compositional approach, the problem of proving correctness of an infinite set of possible programs is reduced to proving the correctness of translating the generators and the syntactic constructions.

In all these examples the source algebra and the target algebra were not designed in connection with each other, but with independent motivations. It is, therefore, not surprising that in all cases the source language and the target language have algebraic grammars that are not isomorphic with each other. Nevertheless, the translations are isomorphisms. This is possible because in all cases the translation covers only a subset of the target language. Furthermore in all cases only a subset of the target language arises as output of the translation. For this subset a new algebra is designed using polynomials over the original target language algebra. This derived algebra is then isomorphic to the source language algebra, and a compositional translation is obtained.

19.6 Power of compositional translation

19.6.1 Generative power

This section considers the power of the framework with respect to the generated language. We will first look at compositional grammars in which the rules are unrestricted. The theorem below shows that the unrestricted compositional grammars have the same power as Turing machines. The simulation method used in the proof is interesting because it stimulates the discussion in the next section, in which the role of the reversibility and the measure condition are investigated.

Theorem 2 *Any recursively enumerable language can be generated by a compositional grammar.*

Proof In order to prove the theorem we will simulate a Turing machine by means of a compositional grammar. For this purpose we take a non-deterministic Turing machine that starts on an empty tape. The machine halts when no instruction is applicable and the string of symbols (neglecting the blanks) is the generated string. The set of all strings it can generate is the language generated by the machine. Our aim is to design a compositional grammar for the same language.

We assume that the Turing machine is of the following type. It operates on a tape that has a beginning but no end, and the machine starts on an empty tape filled with blanks, with its read/write head placed on the initial one. The machine acts on the basis of its memory state q and of the symbol read by the head. It may move to the right (R), to the left (L) or print a symbol, together with a change of memory state. So, two examples of instructions are:

1. $q_1 s q_2 R$ (= if the Turing machine is in state q_1 and reads an s, then the state changes to q_2 and the head moves to the right);

2. $q_1 s q_2 t$ (= if the Turing machine reads an s when in state q_1, then it goes into state q_2 and writes a t).

A compositional grammar is of another nature. It has neither memory, nor an infinite tape. But these features of a Turing machine can be encoded by a finite string in the following way. In any stage of the calculations, the head of the Turing machine has passed only a finite number of positions on the tape. That string determines the whole tape, since the remainder is filled with blanks. The current memory state is inserted as an extra symbol in the string on a position to the left of the symbol that is currently scanned by the head.

Each instruction of the Turing machine will be mimicked by an operation of the algebra. Below, this will be done for the two examples mentioned before. Besides this, some additional operations are needed: Operations that add additional blanks to the string if the head stands on the last symbol on the right and has to move to the right, and operations that remove at the end of the calculations the state symbol and the blanks from the string. We will not describe these additional operations in detail.

The first example of the simulation of a Turing machine instruction concerns the instruction q_1sq_2R (moving to the right). The corresponding operator F is defined for strings of the form $w_1q_1sw_2$ where w_1 and w_2 are strings consisting of symbols from the alphabet and blanks. The effect of F is defined by $F(w_1q_1sw_2) = w_1sq_2w_2$. The second example concerns writing: q_1sq_2t (replace s by t). The corresponding operator G is defined for strings of the form $G(w_1q_1sw_2) = w_1q_2tw_2$. Since the algebra imitates the machine, the generated language is the same.
End of Proof

The recursively enumerable languages form the class of languages which can be generated by the most powerful kinds of grammars (unrestricted rewriting systems, transformational grammars, Turing machine languages, etc.), or, more generally, by any kind of algorithm. Theorem 2 shows that if a language can be generated by any algorithm, it can be generated by a compositional grammar. Thus, compositional grammars can generate any language that can be generated by the other grammars. This means that the method of compositionality of translation does not restrict the class of languages that can be dealt with. This conclusion, however, does not apply to M-grammars because they are not arbitrary compositional grammars, as explained in Section 19.6.2.

19.6.2 Reversibility and complexity

In order to make parsing possible, the rules of an M-grammar have to obey two restrictions which originate from Landsbergen (1981). For free grammars these conditions are (see also Chapter 4):

1. Reversibility
   For each rule R there is a reverse rule R' such that R'(y) is finite and

   $y \in R(x_1, x_2, ..., x_n)$ *if and only if* $(x_1, x_2, ..., x_n) \in R'(y)$

2. Measure condition
   There is a computable function that assigns to an expression a natural number: its measure. The output expression of a generative rule has a measure that is greater than the measures of its input expressions.

The combination of the two conditions guarantees that the output expression of an analytical rule has smaller measure than its input expressions. For controlled M-grammars the measure condition is more complicated (see Chapter 17).

The parsing algorithm for M-grammars is based upon the above two conditions. Condition 1 makes it possible to find, given the output of a generative rule, potential inputs for the rule. Condition 2 guarantees termination of the recursive application of this process. Since this parsing algorithm is available, it follows that the generated languages are decidable languages. A well-known result of formal language theory is that the decidable languages form a subset of the class of the recursively enumerable languages. Hence, in the light of Theorem 2 it follows that the two restrictions are not only restrictions on the kind of grammars, but also decrease the generative power of the grammars.

Let us investigate the proof to see where the restrictions play a role. The kernel of the proof is the simulation of the Turing machine instructions. The rules which do this are reversible. For instance, if the rule simulating a move of the head to the right, then the reverse rule simulates a move to the left. And if the rule makes the head replace the symbol t by the symbol s, the reverse rule overwrites an s with a t. Therefore, the reversibility condition is satisfied. It is difficult, however, to imagine in which respect the string becomes more complex when the head moves to the right or when a symbol is overwritten. And indeed, if such a measure did exist, the generated language would be decidable (the parsing algorithm sketched above could then be used).

As we have just seen, the grammar used in the proof obeys the reversibility condition but not the measure condition. So, either the combination of the two conditions is responsible for the decrease of generative power, or only the measure condition. The following theorem shows that it is the measure condition.

Theorem 3 *Let G be a free algebraic grammar with a finite number of generators and rules. Suppose G satisfies the measure condition. G then generates a recursive language.*

Sketch of Proof. An algorithm deciding whether an expression belongs to the language is as follows. Determine the complexity of the given expression. Then try all generations that are possible with the given grammar, but stop as soon as the generated (intermediate) results have a complexity greater than the complexity of the given expression. Since the grammar satisfies the measure condition, this process terminates.
End of Proof

This theorem can, under certain conditions, be generalised to infinite sets of generators and for rule schemes. One might, for instance, require that only a finite number of generators of a given complexity is available.

In a controlled M-grammar not all the rules need to satisfy the measure condition. However, a variant of the theorem expressing that an expression can be parsed by generation still holds. There is a measure condition on the relation between import and export conditions of subgrammars that restricts the generation on the level of subgrammars. Within the subgrammars the generation is restricted by the control and the measure for iterative rules.

The results presented in this section show that the measure condition is responsible for the decrease in generative power of the compositional grammars. The reversibility condition is only a restriction on the kind of rules used in the grammar, but is not a restriction on the power. It is a restriction that makes an attractive parsing algorithm possible. It would even be incorrect to claim that the reversibility condition guarantees efficient parsing: both with the algorithm sketched in the proof, and with the algorithm based upon reversibility, the running time can be exponential in the length of the input.

19.6.3 Translation power

Next, we investigate the power of the framework with respect to the relation between source language and target language. The first result shows that by means of unrestricted compositional grammars 'any' language can be translated into 'any' language.

Theorem 4 *Let L be a recursively enumerable language, and $Tr : L \to M$ a computable translation function of the expressions of L into M. We will show that there are isomorphic compositional grammars for L and M such that Tr is an isomorphism.*

Sketch of Proof In the proof of Theorem 2 the existence of an algebra as syntax for the source language L is proved. For the target language we take a copy of this algebra and extend it with rules that perform the translation. This is possible for the following reason. Since the function Tr is computable there exists a Turing machine computing Tr, and this Turing machine can be simulated by an algebraic grammar. These rules which perform the translation, are considered as transformations of the target language algebra. So, when an expression is generated in the source language algebra, its translation is generated isomorphically in the target language algebra.
End of Proof

This result shows that compositionality does not restrict the possibilities of translation. It is, of course, good to know this, but the above theorem does not help to find such a translation, because Tr is assumed to be given. The present book argues that a good method is to design isomorphic grammars. The above theorem does not apply to M-grammars because of the reversibility conditions and measure conditions, but the method might be used to obtain a related result for Turing machines satisfying these two conditions.

The last question concerns the problem of proving strict isomorphy (proving that two grammars are not only isomorphic but that they also obey the stronger condition of defining a translation for all the sentences they generate - see Chapter 17). Formulated in the algebraic terminology the problem is: given two algebras with partial rules, and an isomorphism between the term algebras, is it decidable whether the term for the source language yields an expression if and only if this is the case for the target language? The answer is negative, as is shown below.

Theorem 5 *It is undecidable, given two algebras $\langle A, F \rangle$ and $\langle B, G \rangle$ and a isomorphism $h : A \cup F \rightarrow B \cup G$, whether for all $a \in A, f \in F : f(a)$ is defined if and only if $h(f)(h(a))$ is defined.*

Proof Let TM_1 and TM_2 be arbitrary Turing machines. Consider the algebras $A = \langle \{0, 1\}^*, \{f\} \rangle$ and $B = \langle \{0, 1\}^*, \{g\} \rangle$, where

$$f(w) = \begin{cases} 1 & \text{if } TM_1(w) \text{ is defined} \\ \text{undefined} & \text{otherwise} \end{cases}$$

and

$$g(w) = \begin{cases} 1 & \text{if } TM_2(w) \text{ is defined} \\ \text{undefined} & \text{otherwise} \end{cases}$$

Let the isomorphism $h : A \rightarrow B$ be defined by $h(f) = g$, $h(0) = 0$ and $h(1) = 1$. Suppose that it is decidable whether $f(w)$ is defined if and only if $g(w)$ is defined. Then it would be decidable whether TM_1 and TM_2 accept the same language. This is known to be undecidable (the problem can be reduced to the halting problem by taking for one of the machines a Turing machine that accepts all strings). Therefore there cannot be a general method to decide whether for two corresponding algebras the one yields an expression if and only if the other does.
End of Proof

Of course M-grammars have no rules of which the applicability conditions depend on a Turing machine that generates a recursively enumerable language. The conditions in the rules of the M-grammars are intended to be decidable, but there is no formal restriction guaranteeing this yet. This means that assuming decidable conditions would not be a good model. Furthermore, also for Turing machines that accept decidable languages, equivalence is not decidable.

Since the notion of strict isomorphy is linked so closely to the equivalence of Turing machines, it is unlikely that strict isomorphy can be proved for two grammars if the conditions are independent in the two languages. Only if applicability conditions for corresponding rules (or rule classes) of different languages are in a well defined connection, might such a proof be possible. For some examples where strict isomorphy is proved, see Landsbergen (1987a). All the examples can be seen as many sorted algebras with total rules.

19.7   Concluding remarks

This chapter has presented a mathematical model of compositional translation systems. This model has given us a new point of view on Rosetta, more in particular, an algebraic one. The model was helpful in evaluating certain aspects of the Rosetta system the compositionality of which might be doubted. Some of these turn out to be direct instances of the model (e.g. compound basic expressions), for other aspects (e.g. the measure condition in combination with transformations) results from universal algebra were needed to show their compositional nature. Ambiguous basic expressions (and rules) could be viewed in such a way that the translation remains an isomorphism. The model was also useful to give a characterisation of what are the essential aspects of the compositional method, and to recognise the compositional method of translation in other contexts. It has been shown that several fields of science that deal with translations accept compositionality as standard method. Finally, the power of compositional translation and the effects of the restrictions on M-grammars have been investigated.

Chapter 20

Software engineering aspects

20.1 Introduction

The formal specifications of the Rosetta modules do not fully determine the algorithms that implement them. This leaves ample room for consideration about performance optimisation or subjective criteria such as elegance to influence the actual algorithms. Decisions must be made about the algorithms in each of the Rosetta modules. These algorithms, some of which were discussed in the previous chapter, are not the only subject of design decisions that have to be made, nor are they the most important ones. Many questions must be posed and answered while building a system like Rosetta. What does the user interface look like? What debugging facilities must be offered for developing linguistic software? What are the most convenient interfaces between the Rosetta modules, and what do S-trees, syntactic derivation trees (D-trees), semantic derivation trees and dictionaries look like? Can a translation system be run as one process, or is it better to split it into several subsystems? Each module of the Rosetta system produces a set of results. How does one represent such sets if they are very large? In what order do we process their elements? What programming language is chosen? Is linguistic data written in this language or in a special-purpose language that is subsequently translated into the programming language? Many of these problems can be dealt with in various ways. Their solutions are a matter of taste rather than of principle and do not deserve a detailed discussion here. The design of user interfaces is the subject of another discipline and is also beyond the scope of this book. Below we touch upon issues of software engineering that either involve a problematic aspect of the formalism or have proved to be essential in building our translation system.

417

20.2   Design decisions

The existing implementation of the Rosetta system is intended to be a research ve-
hicle. The system can be run in two modes. One is the batch mode, in which it
produces all possible translations of a sample of sentences. In the interactive mode
the system translates one sentence at a time. The user has various options for in-
teracting with the system during the translation process. Debugging facilities are
offered for each module of the system. Interfaces and other data structures may
be inspected and edited. A notable option is the interaction during the analytical
transfer to disambiguate the sentence lexically. This interaction is the only way to
make the system produce only one translation, and is therefore important for the
system as a potential product.

The most important design decisions probably concern the architecture of the
system in terms of modules and processes and the way ambiguities are processed.
At the specification level, a Rosetta system is composed of eight modules, and this
structure should be preserved in its implementation. How the modules are put together in processes and the details of the interaction between modules are open to
choice. According to the specifications, every Rosetta module produces a set of results, each result being input for the next module. For instance, A-MORPH produces
a set of sequences of lexical S-trees. Each sequence is input for S-PARSER, which
produces a set of S-trees. Each S-tree is input for M-PARSER that produces a set
of D-trees for this S-tree, etc., etc. The formal specifications do not determine the
exact order in which computations are to be performed. For instance, if an S-tree
is found it may in principle be processed directly by M-PARSER, but this may also
be postponed until all S-trees are determined for a given sentence.

In a sequential program, there are two extremes with respect to computation ordering. In the first, so-called *breadth-first*, approach each module is invoked only once
for each sentence. Hence, the morphological module calculates the full set of sequences of lexical S-trees, next S-PARSER calculates all S-trees for every sequence,
then M-PARSER processes each S-tree, and so on. In the second, *depth-first*, approach the morphological module produces one sequence of S-trees, next S-PARSER
produces one S-tree for this sequence, next M-PARSER produces one D-tree, that
is processed further. When this first D-tree has been processed by A-TRANSFER,
M-PARSER tries to find another one for the same S-tree, and if it does not exist,
S-PARSER is asked for another S-tree for the same sequence of lexical S-trees. If
this S-tree does not exist either, the morphological module is re-invoked to give an
alternative sequence of lexical S-trees for the same sentence. This process is called
backtracking. It should be noted that the distinction between breadth-first evaluation
and depth-first evaluation can only be made if the algorithms are implemented in a
programming language that determines the order of computation exactly. In certain
functional languages, in particular the ones that use *lazy evaluation* strategies, algo-

rithms that are intuitively conceived as being breadth-first may well be executed in depth-first order.

One may also consider parallel implementations. M-PARSER, for instance, could process all S-trees produced by S-PARSER in parallel. Another possibility would be to implement Rosetta as the parallel composition of eight processes, one process for each module in the translation system.

The current implementation of Rosetta is a combination of several strategies: it is partially breadth-first, partially depth-first, and it consists of several processes. There is one process, called *analysis*, that contains the four analytical modules and one process, *generation*, with the four generative modules. Analysis and generation communicate with a third process, called *control*, that takes care of the user interface and starts and stops the analysis and generation processes. The main advantage of this architecture is that one needs only two executables for each language, instead of one for each pair of languages.

The choice between depth-first computation order and breadth-first computation order is influenced by the following considerations. The interaction with the user during A-TRANSFER, to resolve ambiguities, involves the comparison of various readings of the sentence. This implies that, ideally, before entering this interaction all readings of the sentence must have been determined, and hence that analysis as a whole should be a breadth-first process. In generation, assuming that analysis produced one interlingua expression, possibly after interaction, a depth-first calculation of the translations yields the first translation as quickly as possible. Hence, we implemented generation in a depth-first manner.

Some circumstances make it impractical to implement analysis as a breadth-first process. The surface grammar potentially is very ambiguous, and word ambiguities only add to this. In the worst case, the number of S-trees for a given sentence is an exponential function of the sentence length. Many of these S-trees will be ill-formed according to the M-grammar, but they have to be processed by M-PARSER to find that out. Despite the exponential number of S-trees, the output of S-PARSER can be calculated in a breadth-first way with cubic time complexity, representing the set of S-trees as a so-called parse forest with a size that also is a cubic function of the input. The ambiguity problem becomes urgent and sometimes prohibitive in M-PARSER. This module cannot process the parse forest in polynomial time and space. Because M-rules are unrestricted reversible functions, referring to arbitrary properties and combinations of properties of individual S-trees, in principle each S-tree must be analysed separately by M-PARSER, and polynomiality is lost. Although the current implementation still evaluates all D-trees for each sentence, it seems inevitable that in a practical system some selection of a small number of S-trees must be made after being processed by S-PARSER. This selection has to be such that well-formed S-trees are selected most of the time, and it must be much faster than M-PARSER, which of course performs a similar selection. The rules underlying such selection are inevitably heuristic: they must predict the results of the M-grammar with far less power. If, in M-PARSER or from the dialogue with the user, it is found that the selection contains no acceptable S-trees, a new selection can be made after returning to S-PARSER. Summarising, to obtain a practical system with a reasonable efficiency, it is appropriate to switch from a breadth-first strategy to some depth-first strategy after S-PARSER.

20.3 Lingware

The creation of a translation system is a complex and laborious task. Once completed it contains an implementation of the translation method and a representation of a huge amount of linguistic information. Whereas in principle the translation method may be fixed once and for all, the linguistic information will change continually during the construction of the system. Of course, the linguistic information also depends on the languages to be translated, whereas the translation method presented in this book does not.

A good principle of software engineering is to clearly separate modules which it is expected will change over time from modules that will not. The fixed modules can be programmed as efficiently as possible in low-level languages such as C, Pascal or Modula-2. The modules that are amenable to change must not be specified in such low-level languages. It is every programmer's experience that changing old, and thus only partially understandable, software is dangerous and leads to errors. Besides, even if one knows which aspects of the modules are the ones that are likely to change, it might not be possible to separate these aspects from the constant parts of the module. It is therefore wise to invent a specification language (SpecL, for short) tailored to the application, in which only the changeable aspects of modules are described, and generate the low-level language modules automatically from specifications written in SpecL. The fixed modules together with the SpecL compiler(s) form a system *generator* that generates a system for every specification written according to SpecL. In the case of a natural language processor it is customary to refer to such specifications as *lingware*. In a Rosetta system, lingware is present to specify dictionaries, morphological rules, surface rules, the M-rules, transfer rules, the domains of S-trees and the interlingua. Each kind of specification is written in its own notation and compiled separately into low-level programming language modules (in our case, the language is a modular variant of Pascal) and data files.

At the level of Pascal, we distinguish three kinds of software: a module is classified as either language-independent, language-specific or operating-system dependent. The separation of operating-system dependent software from the rest facilitates a transfer from one computer to another. Examples of operating-system dependent software are window management, process creation and file I-O. Language-independent modules contain the general algorithms, e.g. parsers, that implement the Rosetta modules. Language-specific software consists of the Pascal representation of linguistic information. It is generated from the (language specific) lingware by SpecL compilers. This architecture is depicted in Figure 20.1.

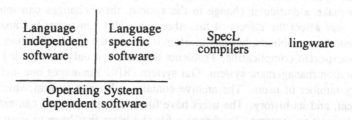

Figure 20.1: Architecture of the Rosetta system

A similar strategy may be followed for the SpecL compilers . Assuming that the syntax and semantics of the lingware notation is subject to occasional change, it is wise to make use of a good compiler generator and generate the compilers from attribute grammars.

The use of special high-level languages to express linguistic information has a number of interesting properties:

- All (in practice: many) implementation details that are not relevant to linguists can be hidden from them.

- The SpecL definitions form a natural interface between computer scientists and linguists.

- Conversion to another low-level language is relatively easy: only the handwritten code and the code generation part of the attribute grammars that specify the SpecL compilers have to be rewritten.

- Programming languages such as Lisp and Prolog, which are popular in computational linguistics, offer no real advantage when used as low-level implementation languages. Clearly, the lingware compilers that translate lingware into Prolog can be much simpler than compilers that translate lingware into C. However, if the translation to C is done in a smart way, the resulting system will run much faster than a corresponding Prolog system.

20.4   Configuration management

All in all, the only thing linguists need to do to produce a Rosetta system is to create lingware. This is very convenient, but if there are many linguists modifying the same system, some software engineering problems still arise. If two people wish to make a particular change to the system, these changes can interfere: one change may affect the effects of the other one. This can occur because of human communication problems, but just as often it will be the result of failing to perceive some unexpected complication. Problems like this can only be handled by using a configuration management system. Our system (RBS[1]) manages one archive and an arbitrary number of users. The archive contains a Rosetta system which is always consistent, and its history. The users have files of their own and can create private (local) translation systems. To change a file the users first have to *grab* it from the archive. This means that a private copy becomes available in which they can edit freely. RBS allows a file to be grabbed only if it has not already been grabbed by someone else. Changed grabbed files, together with archival files, specify a new Rosetta system. After having tested this private system a satisfied user may want to upgrade the archive. The RBS environment then sees to it that the revised system has been consistently built out of all sources, and tests the new translation system by running it in batch mode on a fixed corpus of sentences. If everything is all right, the archival system is replaced by the revised one, and all sources that were grabbed become ungrabbed again. Only one user at a time can upgrade the archive, so that in case two users want to upgrade the archive with interfering changes, only the first upgrade is performed. Hence, it may happen that a perfectly tested local system is rejected by RBS because between testing and upgrading someone else changed the archive in a critical way. A corpus consisting of sentences and their translations is used to check the system. The idea is that it contains all phenomena that can already be translated adequately. Growing bigger and bigger as the translator develops, such a corpus guarantees in a systematic way that the functionality of the program remains at least constant.

20.5   Concluding remarks

Without suggesting that we have produced an optimum solution to our software engineering problems, it is fair to say that we have succeeded in creating a workable environment for the construction and maintenance of a large Rosetta system. This was done by a team of 12 people on average, of different backgrounds, over several years. We did not run into any software crises or lingware crises. Despite the large size of the current system, it can still be grasped and improved. The system was

---

[1]RBS stands for Rosetta Beheerssysteem, or, in English, Rosetta Control System.

developed on a VAX computer under the operating system VMS. Subsequently, it was transported, without any serious problems, to a UNIX machine with a rather different version of the Pascal language.

developed on a VAX computer under the operating system VMS. Subsequently, it was transported, without any serious problems, to a UNIX machine with a rather different version of the Pascal language.

Chapter 21

Conclusion

21.1 Introduction

This book has presented a compositional way of dealing with the linguistic aspects of translation. The scope of the book has been described as the development of computational methods to define the set of 'linguistically possible' meaning-preserving translations of sentences. In this final chapter we will first summarise and evaluate the results achieved, according to the following subdivision:

- the translation method, the concept of compositional translation and its elaboration as the isomorphic grammar method (section 21.2),

- The M-grammar formalism (Section 21.3),

- The lingware developed in this formalism (Section 21.4),

- The implementation (Section 21.5),

Section 21.6 proposes an alternative system design, which avoids some of the problems of interlingual systems. Finally, Section 21.7 enumerates a number of research topics outside the linguistic scope of this book, but which are important for practical application of the results.

21.2 The method

21.2.1 Results

The primary result of the book is the development of the isomorphic grammar method, an elaboration of the idea of compositional translation. This method has

425

proved to provide a nice framework for research on machine translation. Its main virtues are:

- correct sentences of the source language are translated into correct sentences of the target language;

- preservation of meaning is guaranteed;

- other translation relevant information can be preserved as well;

- translation is defined in a generative way, by a relation between generative grammars, but, thanks to the reversibility of the grammars, a translation system can be derived from this relation (cf. Chapter 4);

- the 'subset problem' with interface structures is avoided (cf. Chapter 5).

After the illustration of the method by means of simple string grammars in Chapter 2, Chapter 3 and subsequent chapters have pointed out that application of the method to large language fragments requires a more sophisticated grammar formalism. This has led to the definition of controlled M-grammars, which fulfill this requirement while maintaining the abovementioned virtues. The isomorphic grammar method has been elaborated for this grammar formalism and the combination has proved to be extremely fruitful for the clear description and the solution of a wide range of translation problems. However, the method is not dependent on this formalism. In fact, as shown in Chapter 19, the method is compatible with any grammar that has the structure of an algebra.

21.2.2 Problems

The main objection raised against the method is that the isomorphy requirement will lead to a 'pollution' of the grammars: they may contain rules that would not be needed in a purely monolingual grammar. This point has already been discussed in Chapter 5, where it was argued that the number of extra rules for the tuning of the grammars is very small and that this should be compared with the problems caused by structural transfer rules.

There is another objection, which is often confused with the first one. It concerns a more serious problem, which relates not specifically to the Rosetta system but to interlingual systems in general. In an interlingual system the translation between two languages will sometimes be unnecessarily complicated because the peculiarities of a third language have to be taken into account in the interlingua. If the translation between a particular pair of languages requires that certain meaning distinctions are made in the interlingua, these distinctions have to be taken into account for other language pairs, too, even if they are superfluous for these pairs. This type of redundancy will occur most frequently in the lexicon, because in the intermediate language all distinctions between word meanings have to be made that are needed for any of the language pairs involved. The same problem will arise for the structural meaning aspects. For example, in an interlingual system based on isomorphic grammars, the additional rules needed for tuning a particular pair of grammars will propagate to grammar pairs for which they are unnecessary. This problem is not caused by the isomorphic grammar method, but it is an inevitable consequence of the interlingual approach. If the ultimate goal is the development of a real interlingual system, where the analysis module of one language can be coupled freely to the generation module of any other language, the abovementioned redundancy is simply the price that has to be paid. But if the main motive for choosing an interlingual architecture is the economic development of a number of bilingual systems which translate via an explicit meaning representation, an alternative design is possible. This will be outlined in Section 21.6.

From a formal point of view, the main weakness of the translation method is that (strict) isomorphy cannot be proved. In fact, this is not a weakness of the method itself, but of the combination of the method with M-grammars. Isomorphy can be proved for more restricted types of grammars (cf. Landsbergen (1987a) for examples). A challenge for future research will be to find grammar formalisms with adequate descriptive power on the one hand, but also sufficiently restricted for making the isomorphy proof possible. Up till now, establishing the isomorphy has been entirely the responsibility of the grammar writers. Because of the complexity of the grammars, this is not an easy task. Occasional errors are made, with the consequence that a sentence that can be analysed, sometimes cannot be translated into the target language.

21.3 M-grammar formalism

21.3.1 Results

The free M-grammar formalism introduced in Chapter 3 obeys the principle of compositionality of meaning of Montague Grammar. Its rules are 'powerful', they operate on constituent structures that are called S-trees, and are able to perform various operations on these trees. The notation of the M-rules limits the power of the rules somewhat, but in fact the rule notation is not at all essential. It has been adjusted to the needs of the grammar writers several times in the course of the project and it may change again in the future. The characteristics of the grammar are not a consequence of the rule notation but result from the conditions that the rules have to obey. These conditions are (i) the reversibility of the rules, (ii) the measure condition, and (iii) the surface grammar condition. Any notational variant of M-grammar that obeys these conditions is effectively reversible and thus can be used for both generation and analysis. Grammars with this property can be conceived from a constructive/generative point of view and can then be used for analysis as well. This way of designing grammars has worked very well in practice.

Presumably, the power of the M-grammar formalism is greater than is formally required for describing natural languages or translation relations. But searching for the most restricted formalism was not the goal of the project. We preferred to have a flexible and powerful tool.

In Chapter 9 it was argued that the free M-grammar formalism had to be extended in several ways. It turned out that writing large grammars with a group of people required more structure in the grammars and more ways to control rule applications than the original free M-grammars offered. Some of the algebraic elegance had to be sacrificed to manageability. The extensions are: (i) the subdivision of the grammar into subgrammars in a linguistically motivated way, (ii) the organisation of semantically related rules in rule classes, (iii) the distinction between meaningful rules and syntactic transformations, and (iv) the explicit control of rule applications in a subgrammar by means of control expressions. From a purely mathematical point of view these extensions do not add to the power of the grammars (cf. Chapter 19), but they considerably enhance the transparency and manageability of the grammars. Although the extensions were partially motivated by the needs of translation, we expect controlled M-grammars to be useful for any application for which non-trivial compositional grammars have to be developed. One of the main achievements of the Rosetta project is the development of a grammar formalism that makes the semantically motivated Montague framework syntactically feasible and thus enables to incorporate results from theoretical linguistics.

The Rosetta project is a fairly rare combination of fundamental research and large-scale development of grammars. Thanks to this large scale we could arrive at the insight that striving for linguistic generalisations in a compositional framework enforces a less naive view on compositionality. The rules that carry the meaning cannot usually be the same as the rules that have the formal effects. The latter rules are usually syntactic transformations triggered indirectly by the meaningful rules. This insight in the trade-off between compositionality of meaning and syntactic generalisations was discussed extensively in Chapter 10.

Chapters 18 and 19 showed that we can look at controlled M-grammars in two different ways. From the algebraic perspective, presented in Chapter 19, they are a reformulation of the free M-grammars. So the grammars are still algebras, but in disguise. This view reflects the way the grammar formalism developed in actual history. The alternative perspective, presented in Chapter 19, is to view control as the essential aspect. It is then more natural to consider controlled M-grammars as special kinds of attribute grammars, which suggests an elegant implementation in a well-known computational framework.

A final aspect of M-grammars that should be mentioned is the reversible morphological component, which has proved to be a powerful tool, enabling us to describe inflection, derivation and other morphological phenomena in a transparent way (cf. Chapter 6).

21.3.2 Problems

Having made these points, it is worth noting that the current grammar formalism leaves several wishes unfulfilled.

1. In the first place, the notation of the M-rules is not yet fully, reversible. The rules still contain parts that have to be spelled out separately for analysis and generation. In practice, this has never been a problem, because it is easy to establish the reversibility of the individual rules. Moreover, in the meantime a fully reversible notation has been developed, which can be used in future versions of the system.

2. We have already noticed that the measure condition has to be checked manually. This is no problem in practice after the introduction of controlled M-grammars, but it would be more elegant if the grammar compilers could perform this test automatically.

3. A more important problem is that the surface grammar has to be derived by hand, without any supporting tool that helps to establish the relation between the surface grammar and the M-grammar.

4. A problem of considerable practical significance is the insufficient formalisation of the notions of import and export of subgrammars. Currently there is only a partial formalisation, by means of syntactic categories, of the export and part of the import, the head. In actual practice, grammar writers make use of much more detailed information about the kinds of expressions that have to be imported into and exported from subgrammars. A further formalisation of this information is desirable, especially if substantially larger grammars are to be developed in the future.

21.4   Lingware

21.4.1   Results

The M-grammar formalism has been used successfully to describe very large parts of Dutch, English and Spanish and their translation relation, as has been shown extensively in Chapters 10 – 16. Some of the most interesting results of the linguistic research are enumerated here:

1. The linguistic work was a test of the feasibility of the isomorphic grammar method and of the 'ease of use' of the M-grammar formalism and the related software tools. After having made the adjustments described in the book, the judgment was very positive, although we came to the conclusion that a further modularisation of the grammars is desirable. With the current tools it was possible to write grammars of more than 1000 M-rules each, where an average rule (e.g. the example M-rule in Chapter 8) takes more than one page of text. The morphological components fully cover the inflection of the three languages, and some derivational phenomena.

2. We could only arrive at the abovementioned fundamental insights into the relation between compositionality of meaning and syntactic generalisations after the large effort in grammar writing.

3. Insightful descriptions have been provided for a number of linguistic phenomena. An example is the description of R-pronouns, for which a description has been given which is superior to existing analyses in the literature. Another example is the treatment of temporal expressions, which is applicable to a number of languages and which shows that a high level of abstraction is needed to describe the subtle interplay between tenses and time adverbials. Another aspect in which the grammars are unique is their ability to deal with idiomatic expressions, by treating them as basic expressions with an internal syntactic structure. The research provided new insights into the syntactic behaviour of idioms, in particular the similarity in deficient behaviour of idiom parts and expletives.

4. In many cases a thorough monolingual treatment of linguistic phenomena supports a natural definition of the translation relation as well, due to the possibility of language-specific transformations. A number of structural divergences stemming from structural and lexical sources could be dealt with in this way, for example differences in word order, differences in the use of auxiliaries or pronouns, and the translation relation between prepositional, phrasal or reflexive predicates and simple predicates.

5. Thanks to the introduction of isomorphy between subgrammars within the same grammar, it was possible to give a systematic solution for a number of other difficult divergence problems, caused by differences in lexical and phrasal categories.

For the design of the grammars the following strategy was pursued:

1. First, we made a long list of language constructs. We decided which of them would have to be dealt with by the system to be developed and for which the treatment would be postponed until a later stage. To the latter class belonged both 'uninteresting' constructs (e.g. clock times and parentheticals) and a few very difficult constructs (e.g. coordination with ellipsis).

2. Then we designed a general isomorphic scheme for the grammars of the three languages, including subgrammars and rule classes.

3. Finally, the grammars were developed and tested step by step. During the development a test corpus was maintained, containing sentences with the constructs that the grammar should deal with at that moment.

Obviously, there was feedback and iteration during this development process. In the initial phase of grammar writing the feedback has even caused changes in the M-rule notation.

This development strategy contrasts with another possible strategy, often used in machine translation projects: the use of a corpus of example texts representative of the type of text the final system has to translate. Without doubt such a corpus is very useful, but we decided to make a system with a firm and general linguistic foundation first, and to make use of a text corpus only in a second phase, when a decision about the application would have to be made.

21.4.2   Evaluation

There is no generally accepted objective way of measuring the coverage of grammars. So our intuition that these grammars - and certainly the grammar for Dutch - are unique in their precision and coverage cannot be proved to be correct.

However, we performed an evaluation of the Dutch grammar that we would like to report here. By the end of 1990, the Dutch Eurotra group made a Dutch test suite for testing its Dutch grammar. This was a Dutch version of the well-known Hewlett Packard test suite for English (cf. Flickinger et al. (1987)). The Dutch HP-NL test suite contained 1246 both well-formed and anomalous sentences. It covered most linguistic phenomena of Dutch (although, due to its English origin, some typically Dutch phenomena got insufficient attention, e.g. R-pronouns, which the Rosetta grammars can handle so well).

We performed the following test. A Dutch-Dutch translation system was constructed by coupling the Dutch analysis and generation modules. For well-formed sentences the test was considered successful if the analysis module was able to construct a semantic derivation tree for it and the generation module produced a set of 'translations' for this semantic derivation tree consisting of the original input sentence and a number of semantically equivalent paraphrases. For anomalous sentences the test was considered successful if they were not accepted by the analysis module. The system had been developed without any knowledge of this test suite and it was not adjusted before the test was done, except that a few content words which were in the Eurotra lexicon but not in ours were added to our lexicon. The result of the test was that the system correctly dealt with 57 % of the sentences in the corpus, a substantially better score than for the Eurotra system. Phenomena for which the system scored rather well are: lexical dependencies, relative clauses, questions, imperatives, negation, NPs and tense and aspect. Unsurprisingly, the scores for the phenomena that we had decided not to deal with yet, for example coordination with ellipsis, clefts, parentheticals and direct quotations, were poor.

Since the test was performed, the grammars have been extended and improved, but repeating it with the same test suite would not be very informative, now that it has already influenced the grammar development.

21.4.3 Problems

There still is a lot of linguistic work to be done before we come close to a 100 percent coverage of well-formed sentences. Much mundane work must be carried out in order to deal with constructs that linguists do not find interesting but that may occur rather frequently in actual texts. A more onerous task will be the solution of a number of classical syntactic problems, such as the treatment of ellipsis. Presumably, the grammar formalism will have to be extended somewhat to deal with the latter.

Besides these grammatical deficiencies there is a large class of translational phenomena that have not been studied sufficiently. In Chapter 15 they were indicated as 'translation idioms'. In fact, this notion stands for all cases where the smallest translatable units are larger than the smallest meaningful units from a monolingual point of view. Although in principle the techniques developed for monolingual idioms can be put to use for these cases too, it is not clear that this approach can be maintained in practice for the large variety of cases that can be expected here. They are a challenge for machine translation that still has to be met.

In Chapter 7 we have already discussed the problem of acquiring the necessary lexical data, which have to be more precise and more complete than what is provided by printed dictionaries.

21.5 Implementation

Relatively little attention has been paid to implementation in this book. This does not mean that implementation is considered unimportant. Many of the insights described in the other sections would not have been arrived at without a running system. The large grammars could never have been developed without a number of software tools and the facilities for testing the results. The main reason for not going deeply into implementational aspects is that the functionality of the translation system can be understood on the basis of the formal definition of isomorphic M-grammars. (Historically, there has been some influence of the implementation on the formalism, especially on the rule notations, but this need not bother us here.) Certainly, there were several degrees of freedom for the implementors. Some of them have been discussed in Chapter 20. They concern matters of representation, the choice between breadth-first and depth-first, etc. The implementors' most important task was to implement the eight modules in an efficient way, especially with respect to time.

Indeed, we succeeded in designing efficient algorithms for all eight modules of the Rosetta system. This is also the case for the module S-PARSER, even if it has to parse long and ambiguous sentences and thus may produce hundreds of surface trees. However, there is a snag here. All eight modules are efficient in the sense that for one input expression they produce the output set of results in at most a few seconds and often less than a second (on a 10 MIPS SUN). But this does not imply that the system as a whole is efficient, because a module may have to deal with a very large set of input expressions. This occurs especially at two places in the system: between S-PARSER and M-PARSER, and between G-TRANSFER and M-GENERATOR.

- Because a meaning rule usually relates to a large set of M-rules of the target language, G-TRANSFER usually produces an enormous set of syntactic derivation trees. Fortunately, they do not have to be spelled out and inspected by M-GENERATOR one by one. They are represented in one 'hyper-tree' with sets of rules at the nodes and M-GENERATOR can make the selection locally at the nodes, in an efficient way.

- Thus far, we have not been able to find a similar solution for the interface between S-PARSER and M-PARSER. Even if M-PARSER takes less than one second for an average S-tree, this becomes a problem if S-PARSER produces hundreds of S-trees, which, in practice, often happens for long sentences. In fact, this is not an implementation problem, but a problem of the formalism or of the way it is used by the grammar writers. Future research will have to provide a fundamental solution for this or otherwise we will have to move to a heuristic approach, as has already been indicated in Chapter 20.

Finally, some information about the size. The total size of one instance of the Rosetta system, i.e. the object code, for Dutch to English, is approximately 30 MB. Figure 21.2 outlines the design of the Dutch - English system with its eight modules in a somewhat different way than usual. It is the well-known picture (compare Figure 3 in Chapter 4), but here the relative sizes of the rectangles represent the amount of lingware in the actual modules. The picture is instructive, because it illustrates the amount of linguistic effort needed for the various components of the grammar and also shows the difference in size between the Dutch and the English grammar. This can be partially explained by the fact that the Dutch grammar has been developed in somewhat more detail than the English one (and the Spanish one), but it also seems that the English grammar is inherently simpler. This is most obvious for the morphological component.

21.6   Alternative system design

In Section 21.2 it was pointed out that interlingual systems cause certain problems that one would like to avoid if the goal is the development of a set of bilingual systems, while on the other hand one would like to maintain the advantages of the interlingual architecture. This is possible if, during the development of isomorphic grammars for a set of languages, a clear distinction is made between the aspects that all the grammars have in common and the aspects that relate to one particular language pair.

Singling out the aspects that are specific for one language pair is, of course, the philosophy behind transfer systems, but there it is related to a specific design, where the system consists of an analysis module, a transfer module and a generation module, to be applied in that order (see the left part of Figure 21.1). For an interlingual system like Rosetta a transfer version can be designed as follows (see the right part of Figure 21.1). The analysis module that translates from the source language into the intermediate language consists of two parts: a general part that is used for all languages under consideration and a specific part for each particular target language; analogously, the generation module consists of a general part and a specific part for the source language. The specific part may contain both rules and lexical entries, which are interleaved with general rules and general lexical entries, so it is not a separate module that is applied before or after the general part.   The result is a 'parameterised' interlingual system, which has the abovementioned advantages of economic development and explicit meaning representation, but does not involve the complications of full interlingual systems.

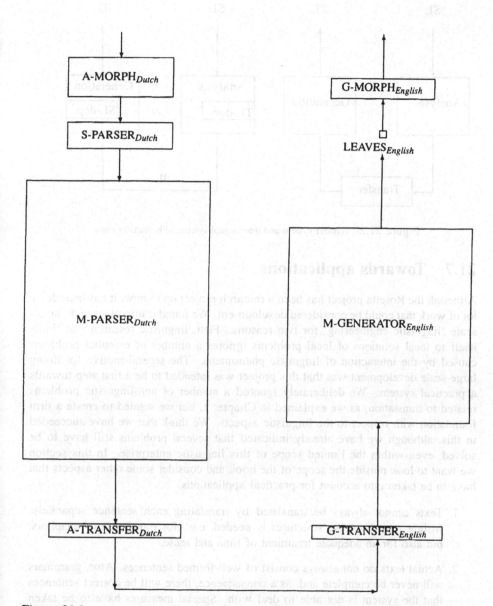

Figure 21.1: Global design of the Rosetta system for Dutch - English. The size of the rectangles reflects the size of the lingware in each module.

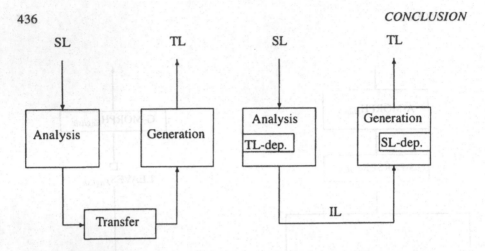

Figure 21.2: Transfer system and interlingual system with 'transfer parts'.

21.7   Towards applications

Although the Rosetta project has been a research project up to now, it has included a lot of work that could be considered development. We found it important to do large-scale 'linguistic engineering' for two reasons. First, linguistic research that limits itself to local solutions of local problems ignores a number of essential problems caused by the interaction of linguistic phenomena. The second motive for doing large-scale development was that this project was intended to be a first step towards a practical system. We deliberately ignored a number of non-linguistic problems related to translation, as we explained in Chapter 1, but we wanted to create a firm foundation with respect to the linguistic aspects. We think that we have succeeded in this, although we have already indicated that several problems still have to be solved, even within the limited scope of this linguistic enterprise. In this section we want to look outside the scope of the book and consider some other aspects that have to be taken into account for practical applications.

1. Texts cannot always be translated by translating each sentence separately. Insight into discourse structures is needed, e.g. for translation of anaphors, but also for an adequate treatment of time and tense.

2. Actual texts do not always consist of well-formed sentences. Also, grammars will never be complete and, as a consequence, there will be correct sentences that the system is not able to deal with. Special measures have to be taken in these cases, depending on the type of system that is envisioned. For fully automatic translation of texts 'robustness measures' will be needed to make a partial translation in such a situation. In an interactive system a good strategy

may be to tell the user that he has passed the borders of the language fragment that the system can cover, and to indicate how he should reformulate the text.

3. As has already been stated in Section 21.5, it may turn out that an approach where all intermediate results are considered systematically is not feasible, because of the combinatorial explosion. In such situations we may have to resort to statistics in order to get an insight into the frequency of phenomena and to make the system select on the basis of this information.

4. Usually, a translation system will be expected to give one correct translation, correct in a certain context, instead of a set of linguistically possible translations. In order to make a selection, one needs an insight into the text on the basis of world knowledge. Because we do not expect systems to acquire this type of insight in the foreseeable future, we opted for interactive translation. But even in that case the system will have to solve a substantial part of the ambiguities, possibly on the basis of a rough semantic classification of the objects in the domain, by means of semantic features. This approach has a greater chance of succeeding if the subject domain is small.

5. Interactive disambiguation may work well for selecting a particular word meaning, but the question is still open how syntactic ambiguities can be explained to a linguistically naive user.

6. We restricted our research to sentences for which a semantically perfect translation is indeed possible. In many cases only imperfect translations are possible, for example if a word has to be translated into a word with a wider or a narrower meaning. A human translator is able to judge whether the difference is relevant in the context, a translation machine is not. Problems like this will be very hard to solve, but fortunately they are not equally crucial for all applications. In technical texts this type of problem does not often arise.

7. In principle, translation via derivation trees offers the possibility to convey other than purely semantic information, e.g. stylistic information, but more insight in the role of these types of information will be needed in order to make fruitful use of this possibility.

We have already indicated that not all these problems have to be solved for every application. Interactive translation of technical texts seems to be within reach, if the user is the author of the text and is willing to stay inside some kind of 'controlled' language.

There are also possible applications where a system that provides all linguistically possible translations is exactly what is needed. An example would be a 'phrase translator', which fulfills a role similar to that of a bilingual dictionary, but now for short phrases instead of words.

The results of the Rosetta project can also be utilised for applications other than translation. This holds for all applications that require detailed grammars, for example grammar checkers and intelligent editors, but in particular for applications that require a clear relation between syntax and semantics. If the meaning operations associated with the syntactic rules are expressed in a logical language, the analysis module of the Rosetta system can be extended to a system that translates sentences into logical expressions. This can be used for natural language interfaces, for example for querying data bases.

A very attractive application of this work can be expected in the area of computer aided language learning. These systems can become much more flexible if they contain an explicit grammar of the language fragment to be learned. One of the interesting features of isomorphic grammars that is relevant in this context is the possibility to perform transformations within one language. If the syntactic derivation tree yielded by the Dutch analysis module is slightly changed, for example by replacing the rule for active voice by the rule for passive voice, and this is given as input to the Dutch generation module, the result is a system that transforms active sentences into passive sentences. Similarly, declarative sentences can be turned into interrogative sentences, affirmative sentences into negative sentences, sentences with a singular subject into sentences with a plural subject, etc. In this way a large variety of exercises can be generated.

21.8 Final remarks

We want to conclude with expressing our hope that this book has made at least the following two points: (i) compositional translation is a fine framework for linguistic research on translation of which the possibilities have not been exhausted yet, and (ii) in the Rosetta project a major step has been made in the direction of reliable interactive translation systems.

Bibliography

[Abeillé et al., 1990] A. Abeillé, Y. Schabes, and A.K. Joshi. Using lexicalized TAGs for machine translation. In H. Karlgren, editor, *Proceedings COLING 1990*, volume III, pages 1–6, Helsinki Finland, 1990.

[Ades and Steedman, 1982] A.E. Ades and M.J. Steedman. On the order of words. *Linguistics and Philosophy*, 4(4):517–558, 1982.

[Aho and Ullman, 1974] A.V. Aho and J.D. Ullman. *The theory of parsing, translation, and compiling*. Prentice Hall Inc., Englewood Cliffs N.J., 1974.

[Akkerman et al., 1985] E. Akkerman, P.C. Masereeuw, and W. J. Meijs. *Designing a Computerized Lexicon for Linguistic Purposes*. Rodopi, Amsterdam, 1985.

[Alistar, 1986] A. Alistar. Unification and computational analysis. *Computers and Translation*, 2(2):67–76, 1986.

[Allegranza et al., 1991] V. Allegranza, P. Bennett, J. Durand, F. Van Eynde, P. Schmidt, and E. Steiner. Linguistics for machine translation: The Eurotra linguistic specifications. In C. Copeland, J. Durand, S. Krauwer, and B. Maegaard, editors, *The Eurotra Linguistic Specifications*. Commission of the European Communities, Luxembourg, 1991.

[Alonso, 1990] J. A. Alonso. Transfer interstructure: Designing an 'interlingua' for transfer-based MT systems. In *Proceedings of the Third International Conference on Theoretical and Methodological Issues in Machine Translation of Natural Language*, Austin, Texas, 1990.

[Appelo and Landsbergen, 1986] L. Appelo and J. Landsbergen. The machine translation project Rosetta. In *Proceedings First International Conference on State of the Art in Machine Translation, Saarbrücken*, pages 34–51, 1986.

439

[Appelo *et al.*, 1987] L. Appelo, C. Fellinger, and J. Landsbergen. Subgrammars, rule classes and control in the Rosetta translation system. In *Proceedings of European ACL Conference, Copenhagen*, 1987.

[Appelo, 1986] L. Appelo. A compositional approach to the translation of temporal expressions in the Rosetta system. In *Proceedings of the 11th Conference on Computational Linguistics, August 25 - 29*, Bonn, 1986.

[Appelo, 1993] L. Appelo. *Categorial Divergences in a Compositional Translation System*. PhD thesis, University of Utrecht, Utrecht, 1993.

[Arnold and des Tombe, 1987] D. Arnold and L. des Tombe. Basic theory and methodology in EUROTRA. In S. Nirenburg, editor, *Machine Translation. Theoretical and Methodological Issues*, pages 114–134. Cambridge University Press, 1987.

[Arnold and Sadler, 1990] D. Arnold and L. Sadler. The theoretical basis of MIMO. *Machine Translation*, 5(3):195–222, 1990.

[Arnold *et al.*, 1985] D.J. Arnold, L. Jaspaert, R.L. Johnson, S. Krauwer, M. Rosner, L. des Tombe, G.B. Varile, and S. Warwick. A MU1 view of the CAT framework in EUROTRA. In *Proceedings of the Conference on Theoretical and Methodological Issues in Machine Translation of Natural Languages*, pages 1–14, Hamilton, NY, 1985. Colgate University.

[Arnold *et al.*, 1986] D.J. Arnold, S. Krauwer, M. Rosner, L. des Tombe, and G.B. Varile. The CAT framework in EUROTRA: a theoretically committed notation for MT. In *Proceedings of Coling 1986*, pages 297–303, 1986.

[Bach, 1986] E. Bach. The Algebra of Events. *Linguistics and Philosophy*, 9:5–16, 1986.

[Bar-Hillel, 1960] Y. Bar-Hillel. The present status of automatic translation of languages. *Advances in Computers*, 1:91–163, 1960.

[Bear, 1986] J. Bear. A morphological recognizer with syntactic and phonological rules. In *Proceedings of COLING 1986*, pages 272–276, 1986.

[Bech and Nygaard, 1988] A. Bech and A. Nygaard. The E-framework: A formalism for natural language processing. In *Proceedings of COLING 1988*, pages 36–39, 1988.

[Bech, 1952] G. Bech. Über das niederländische Adverbialpronomen *er*. In *Traveaux du Cercle Linguistique de Copenhague, 8*, pages 5–32. Copenhague/Amsterdam, 1952. Also appeared in Hoogteijling (1969, 147-174).

[Bennett and Slocum, 1985] W.S. Bennett and J. Slocum. The LRC machine translation system. *Computational Linguistics*, 11(1):111 – 122, 1985.

[Bennis, 1980] H. Bennis. *Er*-deletion in a modular grammar. In S. Daalder and M.Gerritsen, editors, *Linguistics in the Netherlands 1980*, pages 58–68. North-Holland, Amsterdam, 1980.

[Bennis, 1986] H. Bennis. *Gaps and Dummies*. Foris Publications, Dordrecht, 1986.

[Besten, 1981] H. den Besten. Government, Syntaktische Struktur und Kasus. In M. Kohrt and J. Lenerz, editors, *Sprache: Formen und Strukturen*, pages 97–107. Max Niemeyer Verlag, Tübingen, 1981. Linguistische Arbeiten 98.

[Besten, 1982] H. den Besten. Some remarks on the ergative hypothesis. *Groninger Arbeiten zur Germanistischen Linguistik*, 21:61–82, 1982.

[Besten, 1983] H. den Besten. On the interaction of root transformations and lexical deletive rules. In W. Abraham, editor, *On the Formal Syntax of the Westgermania. Papers from the "3rd Groningen Grammar Talks", January 1981*, volume 3 of *Linguistik Aktuell*, pages 97–107. John Benjamins, Amsterdam/Philadelphia, 1983.

[Boguraev and Briscoe, 1989] B. Boguraev and E. Briscoe, editors. *Computational Lexicography for Natural Language Processing*. Longman Group UK Limited, Harlow, England, 1989.

[Boitet, 1990] C. Boitet. Towards personal MT: general design, dialogue structure, potential role of speech. In H. Karlgren, editor, *Proceedings of the International Conference on Computational Linguistics (COLING-90), Helsinki, Finland, August 1990*, pages 30–35, 1990.

[Bresnan, 1982] J. Bresnan. Control and Complementation. In Joan Bresnan, editor, *The Mental Representation of Grammatical Relations*, pages 282–391. MIT Press, Cambridge, Mass, 1982.

[Brown et al., 1988] P. Brown, J. Cocke, S. della Pietra, F. Jelinek, R. Mercer, and P. Roosui. A statistical approach to language translation. In *Proceedings of COLING 1988*, pages 71–76, 1988.

[Brown et al., 1990] P. Brown, J. Cocke, S. Della Pietra, V. Della Pietra, F. Jellinek, J. Lafferty, R. Mercer, and P. Roosin. A statistical approach to machine translation. *Computational Linguistics*, 16(2):79–85, 1990.

[Burzio, 1981] L. Burzio. *Intransitive Verbs and Italian Auxiliaries*. PhD thesis, MIT, 1981.

[Carnap, 1947] R. Carnap. *Meaning and Necessity: A Study in Semantics and Modal Logic*. The University of Chicago Press, Chicago, 1947.

[Carroll, 1989] J.J. Carroll. *Graph Grammars: an approach to transfer-based MT exemplified by a Turkish-English system*. PhD thesis, Centre of Computational Linguistics, UMIST, Manchester, 1989.

[Cattell, 1984] R. Cattell. *Composite Predicates in English*, volume 6 of *Syntax and Semantics*. Academic Press, 1984.

[Chevalier *et al.*, 1978] M. Chevalier, J. Dansereau, and G. Poulin. *TAUM-METEO: description du système*. TAUM, Montreal, 1978.

[Chomsky and Lasnik, 1977] N. Chomsky and H. Lasnik. Filters and control. *Linguistic Inquiry*, 8(3):425–504, 1977.

[Chomsky, 1957] N. Chomsky. *Syntactic Structures*. Mouton, The Hague, 1957.

[Chomsky, 1965] N. Chomsky. *Aspects of the Theory of Syntax*. MIT Press, Cambridge, Massachusetts, 1965.

[Chomsky, 1970] N. Chomsky. Remarks on nominalization. In R.A. Jacobs and P.S. Rosenbaum, editors, *Readings in English Transformational Grammar*, pages 184–22. Georgetown University Press, Washington DC, 1970.

[Chomsky, 1972] N. Chomsky. *Language and Mind*. Harcourt Brace Jovanovich, New York, 1972. Extended edition.

[Chomsky, 1973] N. Chomsky. Conditions on transformations. In Stephen R. Anderson and Paul Kiparsky, editors, *A Festschrift for Morris Halle*. Holt, Rinehart and Winston, New York, 1973. Reprinted in Chomsky (1977a).

[Chomsky, 1977a] N. Chomsky. *Essays on Form and Interpretation*. North-Holland, New York, 1977.

[Chomsky, 1977b] N. Chomsky. On wh-movement. In P.W. Culicover, T. Wasow, and A. Akmajian, editors, *Formal Syntax*, pages 71–132. Academic Press, New York, 1977.

[Chomsky, 1980] N. Chomsky. On Binding. *Linguistic Inquiry*, 11(1):1–46, 1980.

[Chomsky, 1981] N. Chomsky. *Lectures on Government and Binding*. Foris Publications, Dordrecht, 1981.

[Chomsky, 1986] N. Chomsky. *Barriers*, volume 13 of *Linguistic Inquiry Monograph*. The MIT Press, Cambridge, Massachusetts, 1986.

[Chomsky, 1992] N. Chomsky. A minimalist program for linguistic theory. *MIT Occasional papers in Linguistics*, 1, 1992.

[Cinque, 1993] G. Cinque. A null theory of phrase and compound stress. *Linguistic Inquiry*, 24(2):239–297, 1993.

[Comrie, 1976] B. Comrie. *Aspect: an Introduction to the Study of Verbal Aspect and Related Problems*. Cambridge University Press, Cambridge, 1976.

[Comrie, 1985] B. Comrie. *Tense*. Cambridge University Press, Cambridge, 1985.

[Curry, 1963] H.B. Curry. Some logical aspects of grammatical structure. In *Structure of Language and its mathematical Aspects*, pages 56–68. Americal Mathematical Society, Rhode Island, 1963.

[Deemter, 1991] K. van Deemter. *On the Composition of Meaning*. PhD thesis, University of Amsterdam, 1991.

[Dik, 1978] S.C. Dik. *Functional grammar*. Number 27 in North Holland Linguistics series. North Holland, Amsterdam, 1978. (third printing, 1981, Foris, Dordrecht).

[Dorr, 1993] B.J. Dorr. *Machine Translation: A View from the Lexicon*. MIT Press, Cambridge, Massachusetts, 1993.

[Dowty et al., 1981] D. Dowty, R. Wall, and S. Peters. *Introduction to Montague Semantics*, volume 11 of *Synthese Language Library*. D. Reidel Publishing Company, Dordrecht, 1981.

[Dowty, 1982] D. Dowty. Grammatical relations and Montague Grammar. In P. Jacobson and G.K. Pullum, editors, *The Nature of Syntactic Representation*, pages 79–130. Reidel, Dordrecht, 1982.

[Dreyfus and Dreyfus, 1986] H.L. Dreyfus and S.L. Dreyfus. *Mind over Machine*. Basil Blackwell, Oxford, 1986.

[Earley, 1970] J. Earley. An efficient context-free parsing algorithm. *Communications ACM*, 13(2):94–102, 1970.

[Estival et al., 1990] D. Estival, A. Ballim, G. Russell, and S. Warwick. A syntax and semantics for feature-structure transfer. In *Proceedings of the Third International Conference on Theoretical and Methodological Issues in Machine Translation of Natural Language*, 1990.

[Evers, 1975] A. Evers. *The Transformational Cycle in Dutch and German*. PhD thesis, University of Utrecht, 1975.

[Eynde, 1988] F. van Eynde. The analysis of tense and aspect in Eurotra. In *Proceedings Coling 1988*, pages 699–704, Budapest, 1988.

[Eynde, 1992] F. van Eynde. Towards a dynamic and compositional treatment of temporal expressions. In P. Dekker and M. Stokhof, editors, *Proceedings of the Eighth Amsterdam Colloquium*, pages 153 – 172, Amsterdam, 1992.

[Flickinger *et al.*, 1987] D. Flickinger, J. Nerbonne, I. Sag, and T. Wasow. Toward evaluation of NLP systems. Hewlett Packard Laboratories, Palo Alto, CA, June 1987.

[Fraser, 1970] B. Fraser. Idioms within a transformational grammar. *Foundations of Language*, 6:22–43, 1970.

[Gamut, 1991] L.T.F. Gamut. *Logic, Language and Meaning*, volume II of *Intensional Logic and Logical Grammar*. University of Chicago Press, Chicago / London, 1991.

[Gazdar *et al.*, 1985] G. Gazdar, E. Klein, G. Pullum, and I. Sag. *Generalized Phrase Structure Grammar*. Basil Blackwell, Oxford, 1985.

[Givón, 1978] T. Givón. Universal grammar, lexical structure and translatibility. In F. Guenthner and M. Guenthner-Reutter, editors, *Meaning and Translation*, pages 235–275. Duckworth, London, 1978.

[Godden, 1981] K. Godden. *Montague Grammar and Machine Translation between Thai and English*. PhD thesis, University of Kansas, 1981.

[Graetzer, 1986] G. Graetzer. *Universal Algebra*. Van Nostrand, Princeton, 1986. (Second edition published by: Springer, New York, 1979).

[Groenendijk and Stokhof, 1982] J. Groenendijk and M. Stokhof. Semantic analysis of wh-complements. *Linguistics and Philosophy*, 5:175–233, 1982.

[Groenendijk and Stokhof, 1984] J. Groenendijk and M. Stokhof. *Studies on the Semantics of Questions and the Pragmatics of Answers*. PhD thesis, University of Amsterdam, 1984.

[Groenendijk and Stokhof, 1989] J. Groenendijk and M. Stokhof. Type-shifting rules and the semantics of interrogatives. In G. Chierchia, B. Partee, and R. Turner, editors, *Semantic issues*, volume II of *Properties, Types and Meaning*, pages 21–68. Kluwer, Dordrecht, 1989.

[Groenendijk et al., 1981] J.A.G. Groenendijk, T.M.V. Janssen, and M.B.J. Stokhof, editors. *Formal Methods in the Study of Language. Proceedings of the Third Amsterdam colloquium.* MC-Tracts 135 and 136. Mathematical Centre, Amsterdam, 1981.

[Hendriks, 1987] H. Hendriks. Type change in semantics: the scope of quantification and coordination. In E. Klein and J. van Benthem, editors, *Categories, polymorphism and unification.* Institute for Language, Logic and Information, University of Amsterdam, 1987.

[Hoekstra, 1984] T. Hoekstra. *Transitivity. Grammatical Relations in Government-Binding Theory.* Foris, Dordrecht, 1984.

[Hoogteijling, 1969] J. Hoogteijling, editor. *Taalkunde in Artikelen: een Verzameling Artikelen over het Nederlands.* Wolters-Noordhoff, Groningen, 1969.

[Hopcroft and Ullman, 1979] J.E. Hopcroft and J.D. Ullman. *Introduction to Automata Theory, Languages, and Computation.* Addison-Wesley Publishing Company, Reading, Massachusetts, 1979.

[Hout, 1986] A. van Hout. *Er*-peculiarities in Rosetta: an analysis of Dutch *er* and its translations in English and Spanish. Master's thesis, KUB (University of Tilburg), 1986.

[Huet and Oppen, 1980] G. Huet and D.C. Oppen. Equations and rewrite rules: A survey. In R. Book, editor, *Formal Languages: Perspective and Open Problems.* Academic Press, New York, 1980.

[Hutchins and Somers, 1992] W.J. Hutchins and H.L. Somers. *An Introduction to Machine Translation.* Academic Press, London, 1992.

[Hutchins, 1986] W.J. Hutchins. *Machine Translation: past, present, future.* Ellis Horwood Ltd, Chichester, 1986.

[Hutchins, 1988] W.J. Hutchins. Recent developments in machine translation. In D. Maxwell, K. Schubert, and T. Witkam, editors, *New Directions in Machine Translation,* volume 4 of *Distributed Language Translation,* pages 7–62. Foris, Dordrecht, 1988.

[Huybregts, 1984] M.A.C. Huybregts. The weak inadequacy of context-free phrase structure grammars. In Ger de Haan, Mieke Trommelen, and Wim Zonneveld, editors, *Van Periferie naar Kern,* pages 81–99. Foris, Dordrecht, 1984.

[Isabelle and Macklovitch, 1986] P. Isabelle and E. Macklovitch. Transfer and MT modularity. In *Proceedings Coling 1986,* pages 115–117, Bonn, 1986.

[Isabelle *et al.*, 1988] P. Isabelle, M. Dymetman, and E. Macklovitch. CRITTER: Translation system for agricultural market reports. In *Proceedings of the 13th Conference on Computational Linguistics*, pages 261–266, Budapest, 1988.

[Isabelle, 1987] P. Isabelle. Machine translation at the TAUM group. In M. King, editor, *Machine Translation Today: the state of the art*. Edinburgh University Press, 1987.

[Isabelle, 1989] P. Isabelle. Towards reversible MT systems. In *MT Summit II*, Munich, 1989.

[Jackendoff, 1972] R. S. Jackendoff. *Semantic Interpretation in Generative Grammar*. MIT Press, Cambridge, Mass, 1972.

[Jackendoff, 1977] R. S. Jackendoff. *X-bar Syntax: a Study of Phrase Structure*. Number 2 in Linguistic Inquiry Monographs. MIT Press, Cambridge, Massachusetts, 1977.

[Jaeggli, 1982] O. A. Jaeggli. *Topics in Romance Syntax*, volume 12 of *Studies in Generative Grammar*. Foris, Dordrecht, 1982.

[Jansen, 1992] P.G.M. Jansen. Reversible programming in 4_2. Master's thesis, University of Amsterdam / Institute for Perception Research (IPO), June 1992. IPO Report no. 856.

[Janssen, 1986a] T.M.V. Janssen. *Foundations and Applications of Montague Grammar: part 1, Philosophy, Framework, Computer Science*. PhD thesis, Mathematical Centre, Amsterdam, 1986.

[Janssen, 1986b] T.M.V. Janssen. *Foundations and Applications of Montague Grammar: part 2, Applications to Natural Language*, volume 28 of *CWI tract*. CWI, Amsterdam, 1986.

[Janssen, 1989] T.M.V. Janssen. A mathematical model for the CAT framework of EUROTRA. In *Computerlinguistik und ihre theoretische Grundlagen. Proceedings Symposium Saarbrücken, 1988, Informatik Fachberichte 195*, Berlin, 1989. Springer.

[Johnson, 1981] M. Johnson. A Unified Temporal Theory of Tense and Aspect. In Tedeschi and A. Zaenen, editors, *Tense and Aspect*. Academic Press, New York, 1981.

[Jong and Appelo, 1987] F. de Jong and L. Appelo. Synonymy and translation. In *Proceedings of the 6th Amsterdam Colloquium*, 1987.

[Kaplan and Bresnan, 1982] R.M. Kaplan and J. Bresnan. Lexical-functional grammar: A formal system for grammatical representation. In Joan Bresnan, editor, *The Mental Representation of Grammatical Relations*, pages 173–281. The MIT Press, Cambridge, Massachusetts, 1982.

[Kaplan and Wedekind, 1993] R.M. Kaplan and J. Wedekind. Restriction and Correspondence-based Translation. In *Proceedings EACL*, Utrecht, 1993.

[Kaplan et al., 1989] R.M. Kaplan, K. Netter, J. Wedekind, and A. Zaenen. Translation by structural correspondences. In *Proceedings ACL, European Chapter, Manchester*, pages 272–281, 1989.

[Karttunen, 1983] L. Karttunen. KIMMO - a general morphological processor. In Dalrymple et al., editor, *Texas Linguistic Forum 22*. Linguistic Department, University of Texas, Austin, Texas, 1983.

[Katz, 1973] J. Katz. Compositionality, idiomaticity and lexical substitution. In S. Anderson and Paul Kiparsky, editors, *A Festschrift for Morris Halle*, pages 357–375, New York, 1973. Holt, Rinehart and Winston.

[Kay, 1973] M. Kay. The MIND system. In R. Rustin, editor, *Natural Language Processing*. Algorithmics Press, New York, 1973.

[Kay, 1983] M. Kay. Unification grammar. Technical report, Xerox Palo Alto Research Center, Palo Alto, California, 1983.

[Korst, 1989] B. van der Korst. Functional grammar and machine translation. In J.H. Conolly and S.C. Dik, editors, *Functional Grammar and the Computer*, number 10 in Functional Grammar Series, pages 290–316. Foris, Dordrecht, 1989.

[Koskenniemi, 1983] K. Koskenniemi. Two-level model for morphological analysis. In *Proceedings of the Eight International Joint Conference on Artificial Intelligence, Karlsruhe*, pages 683–685, 1983.

[Koster, 1975] J. Koster. Dutch as an SOV language. *Linguistic Analysis*, 1:111–136, 1975.

[Krauwer and des Tombe, 1984] S. Krauwer and L. des Tombe. Transfer in a multilingual system. In *Proceedings COLING 84*, Stanford, California, 1984.

[Kroch and Joshi, 1985] A. Kroch and A. Joshi. The linguistic relevance of tree adjoining grammars. Technical report, University of Pennsylvania, Philadelphia, 1985.

[Landsbergen *et al.*, 1989] J. Landsbergen, J. Odijk, and A. Schenk. The power of compositional translation. *Literary and Linguistic Computing*, 4(3):191–199, 1989.

[Landsbergen, 1981] J. Landsbergen. Adaptation of Montague Grammar to the requirements of parsing. In J.A.G. Groenendijk, T.M.V. Janssen, and M.B.J. Stokhof, editors, *Formal methods in the Study of Language Part 2*, number 136 in MC Tract, pages 399–420. Mathematical Centre, Amsterdam, 1981. Philips Research Reprint 7573.

[Landsbergen, 1987a] J. Landsbergen. Isomorphic grammars and their use in the Rosetta translation system. In M. King, editor, *Machine Translation Today: the State of the Art*. Edinburgh University Press, 1987.

[Landsbergen, 1987b] J. Landsbergen. Montague Grammar and machine translation. In Pete Whitelock et al., editor, *Linguistic Theory and Computer Applications*. Academic Press, London, 1987.

[Landsbergen, 1989] J. Landsbergen. The Rosetta project. In *Proceedings Machine Translation Summit II*, Munich, 1989.

[Langeveld, 1986] A. Langeveld. *Vertalen wat er staat*. Synthese. De Arbeiderspers, Amsterdam, 1986.

[Leermakers, 1992] R. Leermakers. A recursive ascent Earley parser. *Information Processing Letters*, 41:87, 1992.

[Leermakers, 1993] R. Leermakers. *The Functional Treatment of Parsing*. Kluwer Academic Publishers, Dordrecht, 1993.

[Lewis, 1972] D. Lewis. General semantics. In D. Davidson and G. Harman, editors, *Semantics of Natural Language*. Reidel, Dordrecht, 1972.

[Lindop and Tsujii, 1991] J. Lindop and J. Tsujii. Complex transfer in MT: A survey of examples. CCL/UMIST Report 91/5, Centre for Computational Linguistics, UMIST, Manchester, 1991.

[Lyons, 1968] J. Lyons. *Introduction to Theoretical Linguistics*. Cambridge University Press, Cambridge, 1968.

[MacDonald, 1963] R. MacDonald. General report, 1952 - 1963. In *Occasional Papers on Machine Translation, 30*. Georgetown University Press, Washington D.C., 1963.

[Martin and Tops, 1984] W. Martin and G.A.J. Tops, editors. *Groot Woordenboek Engels-Nederlands*. Van Dale Lexicografie, Utrecht, 1984.

[Martin and Tops, 1986] W. Martin and G.A.J. Tops, editors. *Groot Woordenboek Nederlands-Engels*. Van Dale Lexicografie, Utrecht, 1986.

[McCawley, 1986] J.D. McCawley. Concerning the base component in a transformational grammar. *Foundations of Language*, 4:55–81, 1986.

[Model, 1991] J. Model. *Grammatische Analyse*. Foris, Dordrecht, 1991.

[Montague, 1970] R. Montague. Universal grammar. *Theoria*, 36:373–398, 1970. Reprinted in Thomason (1974),pp. 222-246.

[Montague, 1973] R. Montague. The proper treatment of quantification in ordinary English. In K.J.J. Hintikka, J.M.E. Moravcsik, and P. Suppes, editors, *Approaches to natural language, Synthese Library 49*, pages 221–242. Reidel, Dordrecht, 1973. (Reprinted in Thomason (1974), pp. 247-270).

[Munster, 1985] E. van Munster. The treatment of scope and negation in Rosetta: a Dutch–Spanish view. Master's thesis, University of Utrecht, 1985.

[Munster, 1988] E. van Munster. The treatment of scope and negation in Rosetta. In *Proceedings of the 12th Conference on Computational Linguistics, August 22-27*, pages 442–447, Budapest, 1988.

[Nagao and Tsujii, 1986] M. Nagao and J. Tsujii. The transfer phase of the MU machine translation system. In *Proceedings of Coling 1986*, pages 97–103, Bonn, 1986.

[Nagao et al., 1985] M. Nagao, J. Tsujii, and J. Nakamura. The Japanese government project for machine translation. *Computational Linguistics*, 11(1):91 –111, 1985.

[Nagao, 1984] M. Nagao. A framework of a mechanical translation between Japanese and English by analogy principle. In A. Elithorn and R. Banerji, editors, *Artificial and Human Intelligence*, pages 173–180. North Holland, 1984.

[Nagao, 1989] M. Nagao. *Machine Translation, how far can it go?* Oxford University Press, Oxford, 1989.

[Newman, 1990] P. Newman. Symmetric slot grammar (SSG): A bi-directional design for MT. In *Proceedings of the Third International Conference on Theoretical and Methodological Issues in Machine Translation of Natural Language*, Austin, Texas, 1990.

[Neyt, 1988] A. Neyt. Principes, parameters en parafrases in een vertaalsysteem. *TTT*, 8(3):277–296, 1988.

[Nirenburg and Goodman, 1990] S. Nirenburg and K. Goodman. Treatment of meaning in MT systems. In *Proceedings of the Third International Conference on Theoretical and Methodological Issues in Machine Translation of Natural Language*, Austin, Texas, 1990.

[Nishida and Doshita, 1982] T. Nishida and S. Doshita. An English-Japanese machine translation system based on formal semantics of natural language. In J. Horecky, editor, *COLING 82: Proceedings of the Ninth International Conference on Computational Linguistics*, pages 277 – 282. North Holland, Amsterdam, 1982.

[Noord *et al.*, 1990] G. van Noord, J. Dorrepaal, P. van der Eijk, M. Florenza, and L. des Tombe. The MiMo2 Research System. In *Proceedings of the Third International Conference on Theoretical and Methodological Issues in Machine Translation of Natural Language*, pages 213–233, University of Texas at Austin, 1990.

[Noord, 1991] G. van Noord. Head corner parsing for discontinuous constituency. In *Proceedings of the 29th Annual Meeting of the Association for Computational Linguistics, Berkeley*, University of Texas at Austin, 1991.

[Odijk, 1989] J. Odijk. The organisation of the Rosetta grammars. In *Proceedings of the 4th ACL Conference,European Chapter*, pages 80–86, Manchester, 1989.

[Odijk, 1992] J. Odijk. The Rosetta machine translation project. In A. Nijholt W. ter Stal and H.J. op den Akker, editors, *Proceedings of the Second Twente Workshop on Language Technology: Linguistic Engineering: Tools and Products*, number 92-29 in Memoranda Informatica, pages 87–91, Enschede, 1992. Faculteit Informatica, University of Twente.

[Odijk, 1993] J. Odijk. *Compositionality and Syntactic Generalizations*. PhD thesis, University of Tilburg, The Netherlands, 1993.

[Oversteegen and Verkuyl, 1985] L. Oversteegen and H.J. Verkuyl. De temporele zinsstructuur van het Nederlands: twee tijdsbanden. *GLOT*, 1985.

[Partee and Rooth, 1983] B. Partee and M. Rooth. Generalized conjunction and type ambiguity. In R. Bäuerle, Ch. Schwarze, and A. van Stechow, editors, *Interpretation of Language*, pages 361–384. De Gruyter, Berlin, 1983.

[Partee *et al.*, 1990] B. Partee, A. ter Meulen, and R.E. Wall. *Mathematical Methods in Linguistics*, volume 30 of *Studies in Linguistics and Philosophy*. Kluwer Academic Publishers, Dordrecht/Boston/London, 1990.

[Partee, 1973] B. Partee. Some transformational extensions of Montague Grammar. *Journal of Philosophical Logic*, 2:509–534, 1973. Also appeared in Partee (1976).

[Partee, 1976] B. Partee, editor. *Montague Grammar*. Academic Press, New York, 1976.

[Partee, 1977] B. Partee. Constraining transformational Montague Grammar: A framework and a fragment. In *Conference on Montague Grammar, Philosophy, and Linguistics*, pages 51–102. University of Texas Press, Austin, Texas, 1977.

[Partee, 1979] B. Partee. Montague Grammar and the well-formedness constraint. In Frank Heny and Helmuth S. Schnelle, editors, *Selections from the Third Groningen round table*, number 10 in Syntax and Semantics, pages 275–314. Academic Press, New York, 1979.

[Pereira and Shieber, 1987] F.C.N. Pereira and S.M. Shieber. *Prolog and Natural-Language Analysis*. Number 10 in CSLI Lecture Notes. Center for the Study of Language and Information, 1987.

[Perlmutter, 1978] D. Perlmutter. Impersonal passives and the unaccusative hypothesis. *Proceedings of the Annual Meeting of the Berkely Linguistics Society*, 4:157–189, 1978.

[Pollard and Sag, 1987] C. Pollard and I.A. Sag. *Information-based Syntax and Semantics*. Number 13 in CSLI Lecture Notes. Center for the Study of Language and Information, 1987.

[Pollard, 1990] C. J. Pollard. On head non-movement. Paper presented at the Conference on Discontinuous Constituency, Tilburg, January 1990.

[Pullum, 1986] G. K. Pullum. Footloose and context-free. *Natural Language and Linguistic Theory*, 4(3):409–414, 1986.

[Pullum, 1987] G. K. Pullum. Nobody goes around at LSA meetings offering odds. *Natural Language and Linguistic Theory*, 5(2):303–304, 1987.

[Pullum, 1991] G. K. Pullum. *The Great Eskimo Vocabulary Hoax and Other Irreverent Essays on the Study of Language*. The University of Chicago Press, Chicago/London, 1991.

[Quirk et al., 1972] R. Quirk, S. Greenbaum, G. Leech, and J. Svartvik. *A Grammar of Contemporary English*. Longman, Essex, 1972. (Eleventh Impression, 1985).

[Reichenbach, 1947] H. Reichenbach. *Elements of Symbolic Logic*. University of California Press, Berkeley, 1947.

[Riemsdijk, 1978] H. van Riemsdijk. *A Case Study in Syntactic Markedness*. The Peter de Ridder Press, Lisse, 1978.

[Ross, 1967] J.R. Ross. *Constraints on Variables in Syntax*. PhD thesis, MIT, Cambridge, MA, 1967.

[Rous and Jansen, in prep] J. Rous and P. Jansen. Reversible programming in 4_2. Philips Research Laboratories, in prep.

[Rous, 1991] J. Rous. Computational aspects of M-grammars. In *Proceedings European ACL Conference*, pages 210–215, Berlin, 1991.

[Rupp, 1986] C.J. Rupp. Machine translation between German and English using logically isomorphic grammars. Master's thesis, University of Sussex, August 1986.

[Russel et al., 1986] G.J. Russel, S.G. Pulman, G.D. Ritchie, and A.W. Black. A dictionary and morphological analyser for English. In *Proceedings of COLING 1986*, pages 277–279, 1986.

[Sadler and Thompson, 1991] L. Sadler and H.S. Thompson. Structural non-correspondence in translation. In *Proceedings ACL, European Chapter*, pages 293–298, Berlin, 1991.

[Sadler et al., 1990] L. Sadler, I. Crookston, and D. Arnold. LFG and translation. In *Proceedings of the Third International Conference on Theoretical and Methodological Issues in Machine Translation of Natural Language*, Austin, Texas, 1990.

[Sag, 1991] I. Sag. Linguistic theory and natural language processing. In E. Klein and F. Veltman, editors, *Natural Language and Speech*. Springer-Verlag, Berlin, 1991.

[Sanfilippo et al., 1992] A. Sanfilippo, T. Briscoe, A. Copestake, M.A. Martí, M. Taulé, and A. Alonge. Translation equivalence and lexicalization in the ACQUILEX LKB. In *Proceedings of the Fourth International Conference on Theoretical and Methodological Issues in Machine Translation, TMI-92*, Montréal, Canada, 1992.

[Schenk, 1986] A. Schenk. Idioms in the Rosetta machine translation system. In *Proceedings of the 11th Conference on Computational Linguistics*, Bonn, 1986.

[Schenk, 1989] A. Schenk. The formation of idiomatic structures. In Martin Everaert and Erik-Jan van der Linden, editors, *Proceedings of the First Tilburg Workshop on Idioms*, pages 145–158. ITK proceedings, Tilburg University, 1989.

[Schenk, 1992] A. Schenk. The syntactic behaviour of idioms. In Martin Everaert, Erik-Jan van der Linden, André Schenk, and Rob Schreuder, editors, *Proceedings of IDIOMS*, pages 97–110, Tilburg, 1992. ITK proceedings, Tilburg University.

[Shieber, 1985] S.M. Shieber. Evidence against the context-freeness of natural language. *Linguistics and Philosophy*, 8:333–343, 1985.

[Shieber, 1987] S.M. Shieber. Separating linguistic analyses from linguistic theories. In P. Whitelock, M.M. Wood, H.L. Somers, R. Johnson, and P. Bennet, editors, *Linguistic Theory and Computer Applications*, pages 1–36. Academic Press, London, 1987.

[Slocum, 1984] J. Slocum. *METAL: the LRC machine translation system*. LRC, Austin, Texas, 1984.

[Smit, 1990] H.E. Smit. Van Van Dale-bestanden naar Rosetta-woordenboeken. *TABU*, 20(2), 1990.

[Somers et al., 1990] H.L. Somers, J.-I. Tsujii, and D. Jones. Machine translation without a source text. In *Proceedings of the 13th International Conference on Computational Linguistics (COLING 90)*, Helsinki, 1990.

[Somers, 1990a] H.L. Somers. Current research in machine translation. In *Proceedings of the 3rd International Conference on Methodological Issues in Machine Translation of Natural Language*, pages 1–12, Austin, Texas, 1990.

[Somers, 1990b] H.L. Somers. Current research in machine translation. In *Proceedings of the Third International Conference on Theoretical and Methodological Issues in Machine Translation of Natural Language*, Austin, Texas, 1990.

[Steen and Dijenborgh, 1992] G. van der Steen and B-J. Dijenborgh. Online correction and translation of industrial texts. In *ASLIB, Proceedings of 'Translating and the Computer 14'*, London, 1992. The Association for Information Management.

[Steiner, 1990] E. Steiner. Aspects of functional grammar for machine translation. In *Proceedings of the Third International Conference on Theoretical and Methodological Issues in Machine Translation of Natural Language*, Austin, Texas, 1990.

[Sterkenburg, 1984] P.G.J. Sterkenburg, editor. *Groot Woordenboek Hedendaags Nederlands*. Van Dale Lexicografie, Utrecht, 1984.

[Stowell, 1981] T. Stowell. *Origins of Phrase Structure*. PhD thesis, MIT, 1981.

[Stowell, 1983] T. Stowell. Subjects across categories. *The Linguistic Review*, 2:285–312, 1983.

[Sumita et al., 1990] E. Sumita, H. Ida, and H. Koyama. Translating with examples: a new approach to machine translation. In *Proceedings of the Third International Conference on Theoretical and Methodological Issues in Machine Translation of Natural Language*, pages 203–212, Austin, Texas, 1990.

[Tent, 1990] K. Tent. The application of Montague translations in universal research and typology. *Linguistics and Philosophy*, 13:661–686, 1990.

[Thatcher et al., 1979] J.W. Thatcher, E.G. Wagner, and J.B. Wright. More on advice on structuring compilers and proving them correct. In H.A. Maurer, editor, *Automata, languages and programming*, number 71 in Lecture notes in computer science. Springer, Berlin, 1979.

[Thomason, 1974] B. Thomason. *Formal Philosophy. Selected Papers of Richard Montague*. Yale University Press, New Haven, 1974.

[Thurmair, 1990] G. Thurmair. Complex lexical transfer in METAL. In *Proceedings of the Third International Conference on Theoretical and Methodological Issues in Machine Translation of Natural Language*, pages 91–107, Austin, Texas, 1990.

[Tombe et al., 1985] L. des Tombe, D.J. Arnold, L. Jaspaert, R.L. Johnson, S. Krauwer, M. Rosner, G.B. Varile, and S. Warwick. A preliminary linguistic framework for EUROTRA. In *Proceedings of the Conference on Theoretical and Methodological Issues in Machine Translation of Natural Languages*, pages 1–4, Hamilton, NY, 1985. Colgate University.

[Tombe, 1992] L. des Tombe. Is translation symmetric? *Meta*, XXXVII(4):791–801, 1992.

[Torrego, 1984] E. Torrego. On inversion in Spanish and some of its effects. *Linguistic Inquiry*, 15(1):103–129, 1984.

[Uszkoreit, 1986] H. Uszkoreit. Categorial unification grammars. Report 66, Center for the Study of Language and Information, Stanford, California, 1986.

[Vasconcelles and Leon, 1985] M. Vasconcelles and M. Leon. SPANAM and ENG-SPAN: Machine translation at the Pan American Health Organization. *Computational Linguistics*, 11(1):122 – 137, 1985.

[Vauquois and Boitet, 1985] B. Vauquois and C. Boitet. Automated translation at Grenoble university. *Computational Linguistics*, 11(1):28–36, 1985.

[Vendler, 1967] Z. Vendler. *Linguistics in Philosophy*. Cornell University Press, Ithaca, New York, 1967.

[Verkuyl, 1972] H.J. Verkuyl. *On the Compositional Nature of the Aspects.* Reidel, Dordrecht, 1972.

[Wasow et al., 1983] T. Wasow, I. Sag, and G. Nunberg. Idioms: an interim report. In Shiro Hattori and Kazuko Inoue, editors, *Proceedings of the 13th International Congress of Linguistics*, pages 102–115, Tokyo, 1983. CIPL.

[Williams, 1980] E. Williams. Predication. *Linguistic Inquiry*, 11:203–237, 1980.

[Williams, 1981] E. Williams. Argument structure and morphology. *The Linguistic Review*, 1:81–114, 1981.

[Wirth, 1985] N. Wirth. *Programming in Modula-2.* Springer-Verlag, Berlin, 1985. Third corrected edition.

[Witkam, 1983] A.P.M. Witkam. *Distributed Language Translation: Feasibility Study of a Multilingual Facility for Videotex Information Networks.* BSO, Utrecht, 1983.

[Zajac, 1990] R. Zajac. A relational approach to translation. In *Proceedings of the Third International Conference on Theoretical and Methodological Issues in Machine Translation of Natural Language*, Austin, Texas, 1990.

[Zeevat et al., 1987] H. Zeevat, E. Klein, and J. Calder. An introduction to unification categorial grammar. In N.J. Haddock, E. Klein, and G. Morrill, editors, *Categorial Grammar, Unification Grammar and Parsing*, number 1 in Edinburgh Working Papers in Cognitive Science, pages 195–222. Centre for Cognitive Science, University of Edinburgh, Edinburgh, 1987.

[Zwarts, 1988] J. Zwarts. An analysis of genericity and its translation in Rosetta. Master's thesis, Instituut A.W. de Groot voor Algemene Taalwetenschap, University of Utrecht, April 1988.

Subject and author index[1]

---

[1]This index was generated with TExtract

457